The Two Worlds of Ann Gertrude Wightt

The Two Worlds of Ann Gertrude Wightt

HOW A RUNAWAY NUN BECAME A GRAND LADY OF WASHINGTON, DC, SOCIETY

JOSEPH MANNARD

GEORGETOWN UNIVERSITY PRESS / WASHINGTON, DC

Library of Congress Cataloging-in-Publication Data

Names: Mannard, Joseph, author.
Title: The two worlds of Ann Gertrude Wightt : how a runaway nun became a grand lady of Washington, DC, society / Joseph Mannard.
Description: Washington, DC : Georgetown University Press, [2025] | Includes bibliographical references and index.
Identifiers: LCCN 2024053453 (print) | LCCN 2024053454 (ebook) | ISBN 9781647126223 paperback | ISBN 9781647126216 hardcover | ISBN 9781647126230 ebook
Subjects: LCSH: Wightt, Ann Gertrude, 1791–1867 | Ex-nuns—Washington (D.C.)—Biography | Women—Washington (D.C.)—Biography | LCGFT: Biographies
Classification: LCC F198.W54 M36 2025 (print) | LCC F198.W54 (ebook) | DDC 271/.900753092 $a B—dc23/eng/20250328
LC record available at https://lccn.loc.gov/2024053453
LC ebook record available at https://lccn.loc.gov/2024053454

♾ This paper meets the requirements of ANSI/NISO Z39.48-1992 (Permanence of Paper).

EU GPSR Authorised Representative
LOGOS EUROPE, 9 rue Nicolas Poussin, 17000, LA ROCHELLE, France
E-mail: Contact@logoseurope.eu

26 25 9 8 7 6 5 4 3 2 First printing

Printed in the United States of America

Cover design by Erin Kirk
Interior design by BookComp, Inc.

For Robin

CONTENTS

ILLUSTRATIONS

ACKNOWLEDGMENTS

I first became aware of the life of Ann Gertrude Wightt in the early 1980s while conducting reconnaissance for my dissertation research. I was intrigued by a short paragraph in Eleanore Sullivan's *Georgetown Visitation Since 1799* (privately published in 1975), which referred to a "Sister Gertrude Whyte" who, in 1831, "walked out of the Convent and religious life without saying a word to anyone." Although I had done my master's thesis on the topic of anti-convent sentiment in antebellum America, I had never heard of a "runaway nun" by the name of Sister Gertrude Whyte. I filed away her name for further investigation when I had completed the dissertation.

While working at the Archives of the Archdiocese of Baltimore in 1985, and with the assistance of archivist Sister Felicitas Powers, RSM, I discovered a letter written by Sister Gertrude to Archbishop James Whitfield in which she explained the reason for her flight from the convent. In the years since, I have found more sources and learned that her full name in religion was Sister Ann Gertrude and the correct spelling of her surname is "Wightt." But only when I found myself in need of a paper topic for the Tenth Triennial Conference on the History of Women Religious (2016) did I finally get around to serious investigation of the story of Ann Gertrude Wightt. Because of travel problems, I did not present that paper at the conference, but since that time I have researched Sister Gertrude's life in earnest.

One of the biggest challenges for anyone attempting to write a biography on women's history is locating sufficient sources on the subject to complete the project. I have done my best to find all extant sources by and about Ann Gertrude Wightt. Nevertheless, I turned up only twenty-some documents, dating from 1823 to 1865, penned by Wightt. Of these, the longest is a journal of twenty pages, which she kept in 1840 while raising silkworms. Assuredly there are materials that I failed to track down. While constructing a timeline of Wightt's life, I identified some frustrating gaps in the records. The paucity of sources for a few periods means that this volume cannot be a conventional biography in the sense of chronicling every year of the subject's adult life nor a record of her thoughts about every important event she experienced. For example, one can only guess about Wightt's place of residence from 1833 to 1838 (likely it was the Van Ness Mansion) or during the years of the Civil War (likely the homes of various friends in Union states). Researching the two worlds of Ann Gertrude Wightt was therefore a bit like constructing a jigsaw puzzle, where some sections are fairly complete but others have several pieces missing. Thus in some instances I have inferred from the context or speculated from the known evidence. Some readers may question my conclusions or disagree with my interpretations.

Despite the few sources authored by Ann Gertrude Wightt, I am heartened by the belief that I have found enough primary and secondary sources to closely analyze key parts of her life and guess at reasonable outlines of the rest. I could wish for the exceptional documentary collection that Catherine O'Donnell thoroughly mined in her magisterial study *Elizabeth Seton: American Saint* (2018). But the number of extant documents related to Mother Seton is a rare trove of material, not only among women religious but among nineteenth-century women in general. However, though less than ideal, the limited number of sources written by the subject need not disqualify a biographical project, as the historian Ann Little so aptly demonstrates in her imaginative biography *The Many Captivities of Esther Wheelwright* (2016). In a totally different field, Native American history scholar R. David Edmunds did not let the complete lack of any sources written by his subject prevent him from producing *Tecumseh and the Quest for Indian Leadership* (2000), an incisive study of the Shawnee war chief.

The task of researching the life of Ann Gertrude Wightt has been made easier by funding I was awarded by various institutions. I wish to acknowledge and thank my employer, Indiana University of Pennsylvania, for two research/travel grants—a University Senate Research Committee Small Grant in 2016–17, for travel to Dublin to deliver my first conference paper on Sister Gertrude, and a College of Humanities and Social Sciences Special Projects Funding Grant in 2018–19, for research conducted in the Washington, DC, area, especially at the National Archives at College Park, Maryland. I also am fortunate to have been a recipient of a Mother Theodore Guerin Research Travel Grant from the Cushwa Center for the Study of American Catholicism at the University of Notre Dame. This grant funded a research trip to the New York Historical Society and to the National Archives in summer 2019.

These research and travel grants also allowed me to present some of my findings at six academic meetings: the annual History of Women Religious of Britain and Ireland Conference held at University College Dublin, Ireland, in June 2017; the American Catholic Historical Association's spring meeting at Mount St. Mary's University in Emmitsburg, Maryland, in April 2018; the 11th Triennial Conference on the History of Women Religious at St. Mary's College in Notre Dame, Indiana, in June 2019; the annual meeting of the Pennsylvania Historical Association at Indiana University of Pennsylvania in October 2019; a joint panel for the American Historical Association's 135th annual meeting, and the American Catholic Historical Association's 102nd annual meeting, both held in New Orleans, Louisiana, in January 2022; and the 12th Triennial Conference on the History of Women Religious at the University of Notre Dame in June 2022.

I am grateful to Indiana University of Pennsylvania for granting me sabbatical leave in fall 2023, which allowed me to complete a full draft of the manuscript. Scott Moore, chair of the IUP Department of History, has been supportive throughout my time researching this project, even though it has nothing to do with ancient history. I must also thank my History Department colleagues for their encouragement, in particular Alan Baumler and Wang Xi, who scored perfect attendance at every brown-bag talk where I presented early drafts of some chapters of this work.

While lamenting the lack of any organized collections of papers or writings by Ann Gertrude Wightt, I am still gratified to have uncovered a surprisingly rich array of primary sources about or related to her life in various archives and repositories. These include the Georgetown Visitation Monastery Archives; the Archives of the Archdiocese of Baltimore; the Associated Archives of St. Mary's Seminary and University in Baltimore; the Maryland Province Archives of the Society of Jesus in Georgetown University Manuscripts at the Booth Family Center for Special Collections, Georgetown University; the National Archives in College Park, Maryland; Tudor Place Historic House & Garden in Washington, DC; the New York Historical Society in New York City; and America's Historical Newspapers Collection in the Library of Congress Madison Building in Washington, DC. A subscription to newspapers.com has also allowed me to download numerous contemporary articles of value.

I obtained digital versions of important documents from various online repositories. These include the St. Louis Visitation Monastery Archives; the Brooks-Queen Family Papers hosted by Catholic University of America Archives; the Mason Family Papers hosted by the Virginia Museum of History & Culture; the Dolley Madison Papers digital edition of the University of Virginia Press; and the Peter Family Papers hosted by the Special Collections division at the Fred W. Smith National Library for the Study of George Washington. Also accessed were copies of microfilm records of the Sacra Congregatio de Propaganda Fide and selected correspondence of Archbishops Ambrose Maréchal and James Whitfield with the head of the English College (Rome) found in the Archives of the University of Notre Dame.

The onset of COVID 19–related restrictions prevented planned research trips to the Washinton, DC, area in summers 2020 and 2021. However, I was able to obtain microfilm copies of selected documents in the Augustín de Iturbide Papers that are housed in the Manuscripts Division of the Library of Congress. I wish to thank my university's Inter-Library Loan Service, which saved the cost of a trip to the Library of Congress. I am especially grateful to Theresa McDevitt and Beth Farabaugh of IUP's Stapleton Library for their assistance in obtaining the research materials I needed.

I could not have tracked down so many primary sources by and about Ann Gertrude Wightt without the guidance and assistance of myriad historians, archivists, librarians, and staffs at historical societies, archives, libraries, museums, and other repositories. Special mention goes to Tricia Pyne of the Associated Archives St. Mary's University and Seminary; Sister Madaanne Gell, Susan Nalezyty, Cassandra Berman, and Genevieve Kocienda of Georgetown Visitation Archives; Amanda Gesiorski of St. Louis Visitation Archives; Mary Beth Corrigan of Georgetown University Library; and Grant Quertermous, formerly of Tudor Place Historic House & Garden. Tricia Pyne in particular has been a partner from the start in researching Ann Gertrude Wightt. Church archivists who have lightened my research task include Mary Klein, Sandra Gravina, Richard Grimmett, Anne Kirkwood, and Al Laporte.

I am grateful for the essential assistance provided by the following people on specific areas of research for this project: William Kevin Cawley and Joe Smith at the University of Notre Dame Archives; Lynn Conway and Scott S. Taylor of Georgetown University Library; Matthew Guillen and John McClure of the Virginia Museum of History & Culture; Katherine Hoarn and Dawn Bonner of the George Washington Presidential Library; Wendy Kail, Rob DeHart, and Haley Wilkinson of Tudor Place Historic House & Garden; Eleanor Gillers, Tammy Kiter, and Erin Weinman of the New York Historical Society; David Langbart at the National Archives; David McKenzie of Ford's Theater; Laurie Verge of the Surratt House Museum; and Robert Malesky of the website lincolnconspirators.com (formerly boothiebarn.com).

The following historians responded to specific research questions at various stages of the project: Catherine Allgor, Amy Greenberg, Beth Dowling Taylor, Michael David Cohen, Amy Larrabee Cotz, and Suzanne Krebsbach. Thank you, all.

My special thanks go to the following for their careful reading and feedback on parts of the manuscript at various stages of development: Chris Anderson; Paul Arpaia; Ed Brett, Emmett Curran; Elisabeth Davis; Sister Dolores Liptak; Susan Nalezyty; Catherine O'Donnell; Annie Rose; Sister Sally Witt; Sister Janet Welsh; and Cassie Yacovazzi. C. M. Mayo generously shared a copy of her wonderful novel *The Last Prince of the Mexican Empire* (2009) and offered encouragement throughout the research process. Thanks, too, go to Peter Jerz for preparing the glossary with care and precision.

To my mentors in graduate school—John Belohlavek of the University of South Florida, Tampa, and David Grimsted of the University of Maryland, College Park—I owe much more than I can repay. They provided expert guidance when directing my research and writing and their supportive friendship ever since. From them and my other instructors at USF and UMD I learned the craft of historical research and writing. I am sure they both expected to see a book from their former student long before now. I hope the present volume will make up for the wait.

I owe a special debt to Sister Joanne Gonter, who first welcomed me to Mount De Chantal Monastery in Wheeling, West Virginia, in the fall of 1981, opening its archives for my research. Sister Joanne's personal networking also allowed me to gain access to the archives of Georgetown Visitation Monastery, where she now lives, at a time when access to lay researchers was highly restricted. Through the years Sister Joanne has been constant in her support of my scholarship and her friendship to me and my family.

For their unqualified support over the years, thanks go to my siblings and their spouses, Tom and Kathy Mannard and Patty and Tom Brankin, and their families. I must single out, however, my sister, Mary Margaret Mannard, OP, who entered the Dominican motherhouse in Adrian, Michigan, when I was just five years old. Accompanying my late parents Tom and Bella on visits to see Mary at various parishes in the Midwest helped dispel the mystery of life behind the convent walls. These childhood trips must also have indirectly influenced my later research focused on the history of women religious.

My in-laws, Conrad and Leona Rohrer, hosted me gratis at their home in Silver Spring, Maryland, during many research trips to Baltimore and the DC area. My adult children, Moira, Brigid, Ian, and Kathleen, have joined me in living with Ann Gertrude Wightt for the past ten years. They may be the happiest of all to see this project come to a conclusion. This book is dedicated to my wife, Robin Rohrer, a professor and historian in her own right. Appreciation and love to her and all my family for putting up with me during the process of researching and writing this volume.

I am grateful to the late Al Bertrand, director of Georgetown University Press, for his expertise and good humor in shepherding the manuscript through each stage of the publication process. My thanks also go to the press's publication coordinator Elizabeth Sheridan-Drake, copy editor Ann Baker, and marketing director Francys Reed.

I also thank the following editors and publishers for permission to use parts of articles that first appeared in their journals: Thomas Rzeznik and Leigh Anne McCabe of *American Catholic Studies*; Martina Kado of *Maryland Historical Magazine*; and Father David Endres of *U.S. Catholic Historian* and Libby Vivian Newcumet of Catholic University Press, which publishes the journal. I am grateful to Amy Richert, at *Our Sunday Visitor*, for permission to abridge the glossary related to Catholic religious life that originally appeared in George C. Stewart Jr.'s *Marvels of Charity: History of American Sisters and Nuns* (1994).

ABBREVIATIONS

AAB	Archives of the Archdiocese of Baltimore, held in Associated Archives at St. Mary's Seminary & University, Baltimore
AASUS	Archives of the Associated Sulpicians of the United States, held in Associated Archives at St. Mary's Seminary & University, Baltimore
AHLM	Arlington House, The Robert E. Lee Memorial, Arlington County, VA
AIP	Agustín de Iturbide Papers, 1799–1880, Library of Congress, Washington, DC
AMTP	Anna Maria Brodeau Thornton Papers, Library of Congress, Washington, DC
BQFP	Brooks-Queen Family Papers, Special Collections, Catholic University of America Archives, Washington, DC
GVM	Georgetown Visitation Monastery Archives, Washington, DC
JCP	*The John Carroll Papers*, 3 vols., edited by Thomas O'Brien Hanley, SJ (Notre Dame, IN: University of Notre Dame Press, 1976)
JMTP	Papers of Very Reverend Jean-Marie Tessier, PSS, box 2, folder 21, Archives of the Associated Sulpicians of the United States in the Associated Archives at St. Mary's Seminary & University, Baltimore
LC	Library of Congress, Washington, DC
LRDP	Papers of Very Reverend Louis R. Deluol, PSS, typescript translated by Rev. Alfred Gendreau, box 4, folder 3, Archives of the Associated Sulpicians of the United States in the Associated Archives at St. Mary's Seminary & University, Baltimore

MDCM	Mount de Chantal Monastery Archives, now housed in Georgetown Visitation Monastery Archives, Washington, DC
MPA	Archives of the Maryland Province of the Society of Jesus, GTM 000119, Booth Family Center for Special Collections, Georgetown University, Washington, DC
NYHS	New York Historical Society, New York
PFP	Peter Family Papers, Fred W. Smith National Library for the Study of George Washington, Special Collections, Mount Vernon, VA
PFUNDA	Archives of the Propaganda Fide (Sacred Congregation for the Propagation of the Faith) on microfilm held at University of Notre Dame, South Bend, IN
RFP	Riggs Family Papers, Library of Congress, Washington, DC
RG	Record Group, National Archives and Records Administration, College Park, MD RG 59: Notes from Foreign Legations, Mexico RG 84: Records of Foreign Service Posts of the Department of State, Legation/Embassy in Mexico
SLVA	St. Louis Visitation Archives, St. Louis, MO
TPA	Tudor Place Historic House & Garden Archives, Washington, DC
VMHC	Virginia Museum of History & Culture, Richmond, VA
VNFP	Van Ness–Philip Family Papers, New York Historical Society, New York

Introduction

Enveloped in a Fog of Mystery

Writing in his diary on March 22, 1831, the Reverend Louis Regis Deluol records an unusual, somewhat cryptic, entry: "Sister Gertrude broke her vows as [*sic*] 2:30PM, by leaving the Georgetown Convent." Father Deluol, the superior of the Society of Saint Sulpice and vicar general to James Whitfield, archbishop of Baltimore, continues, "She went to stay in Washington at her cousin's, General Van Ness, who is a Protestant."[1]

The "Sister Gertrude" in question was Sister Ann Gertrude Wightt (1799–1867) of the Order of the Visitation of Holy Mary. While her name is little recalled today even by specialists in American Catholic history, Wightt was an innovative female educator in the 1820s, comparable to her contemporaries Catharine Beecher and Mary Lyon.[2] Prior to her sensational flight from Georgetown Visitation Monastery, Sister Gertrude had lived quietly within its enclosure for more than two decades. After first boarding at the Young Ladies' Academy for seven years, Wightt entered Georgetown Convent in 1814 at age fifteen and professed solemn vows as a member of the Visitation Order three years later. "Sister Getty," as she was soon nicknamed, became an "inspired teacher" in the convent school who was "much loved" by her students and admired by their parents.[3]

By 1825 Sister Gertrude had assumed the position of directress of the academy, placing her in charge of more than fifty boarders and day scholars. During her six-year tenure as headmistress she oversaw major improvements to both the school buildings and the academy's curriculum, which helped Georgetown Visitation Academy earn a national reputation as the educator of the daughters of politicians, judges, physicians, gentleman planters, and military officers. Indeed, Georgetown Academy became the model for more than twenty-five Visitation convent schools that appeared across the country by the end of the century.

The year after her appointment as directress of the academy, Sister Gertrude was also elected assistant superior of the convent. In this office she had responsibility over almost sixty professed nuns and novices. Before turning thirty she appeared on the fast track to becoming the next superior of Georgetown Convent. Then, abruptly and without warning, on that March afternoon in 1831 Sister Gertrude left the Georgetown cloister "irregularly," that is, without permission, never to return.[4]

THE FIRST "RUNAWAY NUN" IN THE UNITED STATES

On one level Sister Gertrude was the precursor to the various real and alleged "escaped nuns" of the 1830s—women like Rebecca Reed, Elizabeth Harrison, Milly McPherson, Olivia Neale, and, most notoriously, Maria Monk. Indeed, Sister Gertrude was the first such "runaway nun" in the history of the United States, a figure that would be a staple of anti-Catholic propaganda until well into the twentieth century.[5] Although attracting momentary national attention, the scandal surrounding Sister Gertrude failed to generate the sustained level of controversy of her better-known successors only a few years later. Nor did her flight, like theirs, generate a spate of anti-Catholic writings or mob action in its wake. Outside the District of Columbia, Sister Gertrude's story was quickly forgotten by the general public.

But Sister Gertrude's actions did threaten to disrupt her religious community by damaging the reputation of Georgetown Convent and Academy. Because she was directress of the academy at the time, her departure publicly embarrassed Georgetown Visitation and potentially imperiled its finances. Worried parents demanded explanations before they would allow their daughters to remain in the school. Moreover, because Sister Gertrude had left religious life without being released from her vows, her case also posed a serious matter for the Catholic hierarchy in the Archdiocese of Baltimore. The archdiocese was the administrative and spiritual head of the estimated three hundred thousand members of the American Catholic minority, composed mostly of Irish and German immigrants residing among a Protestant majority that was overwhelmingly native-born.[6]

Further complicating Sister Gertrude's story is the fact that she was socially well-connected to powerful friends and relatives upon whom to call. On the day of her flight, Wightt found refuge in the mansion of her first cousin Marcia Burnes Van Ness, whose husband, Gen. John Peter Van Ness, was then mayor of the city of Washington, DC. A few days later she moved into the home of

Madame Ana María Iturbide, the former empress of Mexico, who was living in pensioned exile in Georgetown along with her three surviving daughters (former boarders at Visitation Academy). After first abandoning the cloister and then departing the Iturbide household after a couple of years, Wightt spent her remaining thirty-four years living and moving in the world. Except for a time in the late 1840s when she nursed one of the Iturbide daughters during a fatal illness, she resided all of that time in the homes of non-Catholic relatives or friends. During most of the first two decades after leaving the order, she lived in a state of total economic dependency. For much of that time she served as a popular social hostess at the Van Ness Mansion and a frequent dinner guest in capital society. She became a friend and confidant of such Washington luminaries as former First Lady Dolley Madison and the writer and social commentator Margaret Bayard Smith. Such women of the "Revolutionary Generation" mentored Wightt in the art of "parlor politics," or what historian Catherine Allgor identifies as the "unofficial sphere": the ambiguous social space where the public and private spheres overlapped and women might exert not only influence but even power.[7]

While hosting at the Van Ness Mansion, Wightt came to know presidents, cabinet secretaries, congressman, diplomats, and bankers. After living much of her first three decades in an enclosed monastery, in middle age she became an avid foreign and domestic traveler. In the early 1850s, for example, she visited the US legations in both Mexico City and Paris. Upon returning from Europe, Wightt accepted the invitation of Britannia Peter Kennon, her former student at the Visitation Academy, to reside at the Georgetown estate of Tudor Place. A widow, Kennon was the great-granddaughter of Martha Custis Washington and first cousin to Mary Custis Lee, spouse of Robert E. Lee. Although never personally a slave owner, Wightt was born into the Southern gentry and always lived in households that enslaved African American people. Not surprisingly, she sympathized with the Confederacy during the Civil War and remained unreconstructed at the time of her death in 1867.

CAPITAL COMMENTATORS ON ANN GERTRUDE WIGHTT

Given Ann Gertrude Wightt's early contributions as a female educator, her notoriety as a runaway nun, and her later reputation as a "woman of influence" in Washington society, it is surprising how few scholars—historians of American Catholicism, of women, or of the Early Republic—are aware of her existence. Two examples of important works published in the twenty-first century suffice to make this point. Sister Gertrude's story as America's first runaway nun was a likely choice for mention in Louis P. Masur's fascinating chronicle *1831: Year of Eclipse* (2001). Moreover, Cassandra Yacovazzi, in her well-researched monograph *Escaped Nuns: True Womanhood and the Campaign Against Convents in Antebellum America* (2018), certainly would have discussed Sister Gertrude's flight had it been known to her.[8] Moreover, in his otherwise exhaustive pioneering study of anti-Catholic sentiment in the antebellum era, *The Protestant Crusade* (1938), Ray Allen Billington gave no hint of having ever heard of Sister Gertrude.[9]

Overall, a thorough review of scholarly literature from the past century turned up only one journal article and one dissertation in which Sister Gertrude is even mentioned. In a 1964 article on Archbishop Whitfield drawn from his thesis done at Catholic University, Matthew Leo Panczyk cites Sister Gertrude in a footnote but misidentifies her surname as "Wright." This error is noted here not to fault Panczyk's scholarship but to demonstrate how little is known or recorded about Ann Gertrude Wightt, even among church historians. In her 2003 dissertation, which analyzes the spirituality of the members of Georgetown Visitation Convent in the nineteenth century, Marie Pagliarini briefly discusses Wightt's departure from the community, the only other mention. Undoubtedly the case of Sister Gertrude was never intended to be a central focus of either of these works.[10]

If the name Ann Gertrude Wightt remains little remembered today, it was once well known, at least in the nation's capital. Just as her contemporaries speculated about the motivations for Wightt's sudden exit from Georgetown Convent, so too did subsequent generations of Washington chroniclers long remain fascinated and frustrated by the question, Why did Sister Gertrude leave the convent in 1831? The earliest known sketch of Wightt appeared in *Washington, Outside and Inside* (1874), penned just seven years after her death, by the former Civil War correspondent George Alfred Townsend.[11]

Since Townsend's maiden effort, various Washington journalists, memoirists, and local historians from the late nineteenth to the mid-twentieth centuries have offered their take on Wightt's story. These commentators vary greatly, however, in how they treat her life and motivations. The paucity of authoritative sources allows writers free rein to speculate and rely on hearsay to draw conclusions. For instance, the absence of any known portraits or photographs of Wightt means that authors frequently cannot even agree as to her basic physical appearance. On one hand, a few writers do assert that Wightt was blessed with beautiful hair, an attribute that would, of course, have been hidden by her wimple while in her religious habit. Sister Mary Josephine Barber, who was a fifteen-year-old student in the academy in 1831, remembered visiting her former teacher at the home of Madame Iturbide several weeks after the event. "On seeing Sister Gertrude . . . in her worldly attire, smooth, glossy hair and combs, black silk dress, watch and chain, etc.," she recalled, "I burst into tears, and could not speak for sobbing."[12] Townsend confirmed that Wightt "was notable for her splendid black, flowing hair, superb teeth, and great conversational power."[13] On the other hand, there was no consensus on other obvious aspects of Wightt's physical appearance, in particular her height and weight. In 1887 a journalist reported in the *Washington Star* that "very old inhabitants remembered her as tall and willowy."[14] But a 1919 article on the family of John Van Ness, published in the journal of the Columbia Historical Society, reported that "a Van Ness family member remembers Wightt as 'short, stout, and jolly.'"[15] All commentators agree, however, in describing Wightt as an attractive personality whose conversation demonstrated a lively intellect and ready wit. Such gender-stereotyping comments, of course, must be taken with a degree of skepticism. At the same time, these descriptions are found to come from both male and female writers, and from those sympathetic to Wightt as well as those antagonistic to her. This consensus gives more assurance that the reports about her unusual intelligence and attractive personality are accurate.

Speculation over Wightt's motives for her sudden departure also range widely. Everyone, of course, wonders why Sister Gertrude left the convent, and most suggest an answer based on little evidence. "It was never known why she had taken flight," asserts Townsend, "but she became the reverse of a recluse, and was a gay and brilliant woman in society, but she never married."[16] The list comes down to the two most suggested reasons: either love outside the convent or thwarted ambition within it. While the former explanation reflects the romantic assumptions of the era, the press proffered the latter motive more frequently.

In 1886 the noted Gilded Age newspaperman Ben Perley Poore mentioned both motives in the first book of his massive two-volume memoir about nineteenth-century Washington society. "No one ever knew rightly the cause of her departure from the convent," he admits. "Some said it was disappointed ambition at not being appointed the superioress; others that it was a case of love, but she never told and the ladies of the convent were just as reticent."[17] The following year, journalist J. F. Riley published an article for the *Washington Evening Star* subtitled "Runaway Nun from Georgetown" in which he simply paraphrases much of what Poore says about Wightt's case and repeats the same speculations.[18] In 1892 another reporter for the *Star*, John F. Coyle, engaged in some original research and advanced the view that failed ambition had triggered Wightt's action. "On the advent of a new superior another member of the order was appointed in her place," he contends, "and soon after she left the convent while the community was at dinner."[19] In her 1911 memoir, Washington socialite Marian Campbell Gouverneur offered perhaps the best evidence for this same interpretation. Gouverneur recorded meeting Wightt at a Washington dinner party held in late 1852 or early 1853, and subsequently passed along a story heard from a female acquaintance. "Mrs. Charles Worthington, a Catholic friend of mine who was educated at the same convent, gave me the following explanation of her conduct," wrote Gouverneur. "There was an election for Mother Superior, and Miss Wight [*sic*], deeply disappointed that she was not chosen to fill the position, was dissatisfied, and when it became her turn to answer the front-door bell, suddenly determined to leave."[20]

The fullest in-print treatment of Ann Gertrude Wightt's life remains in a chapter in *A Story of Courage: Annals of the Georgetown Convent of the Visitation of the Blessed Virgin Mary, From the Manuscript Records* (1894).[21] The husband-and-wife team of George Parsons Lathrop and Rose Hawthorne Lathrop penned this volume for the centenary of Georgetown Convent.[22] Rose Hawthorne, the youngest child of Nathaniel Hawthorne, and her husband were both writers and poets. They married in 1871 and converted to Catholicism twenty years later. The great advantage of this work is that, as the subtitle indicates, it is based on the manuscript annals of Georgetown Visitation Convent. That is, the Lathrops mined sources to which no previous writers had access. The discussion of "Anna Gertrude 'Whyte,'" however, suffers from their tendency to demonize her and in every instance to attribute the worst, most self-serving motives to her actions, while placing the most charitable interpretation on the actions of others, whether allies or opponents. The Lathrops offer Wightt's story as a cautionary tale—for future novices of Georgetown Visitation and for readers in the outside world—about the sad consequences that result when intellectual pride is placed before spiritual ends and individual ambitions are allowed to override communal concerns.[23]

The only published history of Georgetown Visitation Convent written in the twentieth century is *Georgetown Visitation Since 1799* (1975) by Eleanore C. Sullivan. This work is a documented history of the convent and school, but its one-paragraph treatment of the actions of "Sister Gertrude 'Whyte,'" relies heavily on the negative interpretation presented by the Lathrops.[24] The author of the most recently published account of Wightt's story, a short chapter in a popular history bearing the sensational title *Wicked Georgetown: Scoundrels, Sinners, and Spies* (2013), drew on the chapter in *A Story of Courage* as its source.[25]

Though they differ in many particulars, all commentators agree that Wightt neither offered any kind of public explanation nor recorded the reasons for her unexpected behavior on that early spring afternoon in 1831. For example, Georgetown resident and author Margaret Bayard Smith, who knew Mary Ann Wightt both as a child and a young nun, noted that "she never disclosed her reasons for leaving the convent, and continued to attend the Catholic Church."[26] Writing more than a century later, Washington journalist John Clagett Proctor contended that Wightt "never divulged her reason for changing her mind and leaving the convent, apparently no one but herself ever knew."[27] Ben Perley Poore reported, "It was said she had written a book, exposing the inner life of the convent, to be published after her death, but I never heard of its appearance."[28] Allen C. Clark, an early twentieth-century chronicler of Washington and longtime president of the Columbia Historical Society, best summed up the enigma that surrounds Sister Gertrude's escape. The reasons for her "elopement" from Georgetown Visitation, he argues, remain "enveloped in a fog of mystery." Writes Clark: "She did not give the cause of her change of heart, and no cause of those offered has been verified—that is the mystery."[29]

Commentators at the time and into the twentieth century have speculated as to the motives for Wightt's sudden departure from Georgetown Visitation since she never publicly revealed her reasons for leaving. She did so privately, however, at least three times: the first was in a letter addressed to her convent superior, Mother Madeleine Augustine d'Arregger, written the day of her flight. It has been lost to history. The second was in a letter she wrote to Whitfield that was posted the following day; it rests in the Archives of the Archdiocese of Baltimore, where I stumbled on it almost forty years ago. At the time, I was not fully aware of the document's purpose or import, but was intrigued enough to make a photocopy and store it away for future consideration. I also discovered a third letter of explanation written by Sister Gertrude, dated April 30, 1831, and addressed to Pope Gregory XVI, which offers a somewhat different explanation than the one given in her letter to Whitfield the month before.[30]

QUESTIONS TO ADDRESS

As the first full study of the life of Ann Gertrude Wightt, this biography helps lift some of the fog of mystery that has enshrouded the story of Sister Gertrude since the day of her departure from Georgetown Convent nearly two centuries ago. It also identifies her prior leadership in making the convent's Young Ladies' Academy a nationally known and respected institution. Moreover, it analyzes the impact of her departure on the public image of Georgetown

Convent, its academy, and the American Catholic Church generally in the early 1830s. In so doing, it addresses the following questions: What internal convent problems as well as personal issues may explain her decision to leave religious life? Why did she continue to be, at least initially, a practicing Catholic despite her disenchantment with Catholic religious life? How did the American Catholic hierarchy handle her case in order to minimize its negative repercussions? Why did her "escape" fail to galvanize the nativist press and anti-Catholic mobs as similar real and alleged runaway nuns did later in the decade? Above all, what might the story of Sister Gertrude suggest about both the opportunities and the limitations that Catholic religious life posed for an intellectually gifted, socially prominent, and personally ambitious young woman in America during the Early Republic?

This work also uncovers the second half of Wightt's life, as she made the unlikely journey from the Georgetown cloister to Washington society. Salient questions concerning her "life in the world" include: How did Wightt manage to support herself, since she neither married nor held a wage-earning job? How and why did she gain acceptance into the highest levels of polite society despite the fact that she was a Roman Catholic and the subject of a public scandal? How did she become a notable capital hostess and woman of influence in Washington society, as well as an adept practitioner of parlor politics, with access to presidents, congressmen, diplomats, and businessmen? During the Civil War, why did she sympathize with the Confederacy yet continue to reside in the North? Did she die a Catholic in good standing, and what does the answer reveal about the "two worlds" of Ann Gertrude Wightt?

The life of Ann Gertrude Wightt was both extraordinary and commonplace for a woman of her class and locale. Her life saw unexpected shifts and some surprising turns of fortune. A child of privilege, she faced poverty more than once. Born into a family of the Southern elite, she was orphaned at a young age and raised in an enclosed and circumscribed environment, but as an adult she was known as a brilliant conversationalist and shrewd political observer in capital circles. Leaving the convent as the object of a public scandal, she nonetheless found unqualified acceptance into respectable Washington society. Renouncing the religious life, she yet publicly chose to maintain her vow of chastity until her death. After departing religious life without any material resources, she became a woman of substance and financial independence. A cradle Catholic who was educated in a convent boarding school and consecrated her life as a nun, she was nevertheless buried in an Episcopalian service.

A full examination of the life of Ann Gertrude Wightt, at least as full as the spotty documentation allows, offers a lens to examine the workings of religion, class, and gender in the capital society which she entered after her departure from religious life.[31] In her post-convent years Wightt gained not only acceptance but a measure of prominence such that statesman Daniel Webster would describe her as "a lady well known here and highly regarded in our social circles."[32]

This book recovers the story of a woman whose life is a counterpoint to the course of several prominent nineteenth-century converts from Protestantism—with Elizabeth Seton, Jerusha Barber, Wilhelmina Jones, Cornelia Connelly, and Rose Hawthorne Lathrop being among the best known and most celebrated—who renounced the world and dedicated themselves to lives of prayer and good works as women religious.[33] Wightt followed the opposite path. Understandably, apostates from the faith have attracted far less study by historians of American Catholicism for perhaps the obvious reason that their choices do not make them sympathetic subjects. On a broader level, however, Ann Gertrude Wightt is an important, if overlooked, figure in antebellum American history and culture. Her historical significance is threefold: as an early innovator in female education; as the first and unique case of a runaway nun in US history; and as a Washington socialite practicing parlor politics in the Civil War era. Her life should therefore be of interest not only to scholars of American Catholicism but also historians of education, of women, of anti-Catholicism, and of politics in the Early Republic.

A NOTE ON NAMES

Ann Gertrude Wightt went by different names in different phases of her life. From birth to age eighteen, when she was received into the Visitation Order, Wightt was called by the name given to her at birth: Mary Ann. Upon taking the white veil as a novice of the order in 1817, she received the name "Sister Ann Gertrude." During her time as a member of Georgetown Convent, she went by the shortened and less formal "Sister Gertrude"; colleagues and students sometimes used the even more informal nickname "Sister Getty" or "Sister Jettie." After first leaving the convent in 1831, Wightt continued to refer to herself formally as "Sister Ann Gertrude Wightt." With time, however, she began to sign herself as "Ann Gertrude Wightt" when corresponding with adults and resorted to "Sister Gertrude" only when writing to young and adolescent children. In this volume I use the name "Mary Ann" for the years of her childhood and before her reception into the Visitation Order (1799–1816). I refer to her as "Sister Ann Gertrude," "Sister Gertrude," or "Sister Getty," depending on the situation, for the period when she was a professed member of Georgetown Convent (1817–31) and residing with the Iturbide family (1831–33). During the second half of her life (1833–67), when she lived in the "temporal world," I refer to her as either "Ann Gertrude Wightt" or "Gertrude," except on those occasions where she is corresponding with young people and was known to sign herself "Sister Gertrude."

1

Now Is Your Time to Found in This Country

Born in 1799 and passing away in 1867, Ann Gertrude Wightt's time on earth spanned the first two-thirds of the nineteenth century. In those seven decades the United States matured from a young republic of roughly five million people, whose western boundary was the Mississippi River, to a reconstructing nation approaching forty million. Geographically the country had tripled in size and stretched from the Atlantic to the Pacific, with Alaska purchased the year of Wightt's passing. During the same period, Wightt would have witnessed the Roman Catholic Church grow proportionately, even faster than the rest of the national population, from roughly fifty thousand at the time of her birth to an estimated four million by her death. In the first seven decades of the nineteenth century the locus of American Catholicism also shifted from being primarily native-born English stock residing in rural southern states like Maryland, Kentucky, and Louisiana, to immigrants largely concentrated in northern cities like Boston, Philadelphia, and New York. Along with dioceses, cathedrals, churches, parishes, and schools, among the new institutions that came to identify the Catholic Church in the United States were female convents. Indeed, the nineteenth-century American Church would undergo a "convent revolution" that altered the religious landscape of not only the Catholic Church but that of the United States.[1] From their labors in schools, academies, hospitals, and orphanages, nuns and sisters increasingly became the visible "face of the U.S. Catholic Church" for Catholics and non-Catholics alike.[2]

It is necessary to understand both the changing "Catholic world" in the United States into which Mary Ann Wightt was born at the end of the eighteenth century and the founding of the cloistered world to which she would belong. We turn, therefore, to the decade or so before her birth, when unique conditions of religious freedom ushered in by the American Revolution prepared the way for the establishment of the first convents in the country. These early foundations marked the tentative beginnings of the "convent revolution" that would "take off" in the next century. Indeed, Wightt fortuitously hailed from southern Maryland, the very region that proved to be not only the "cradle of Catholicity" in the American colonies but also the "cradle of the convent revolution" in the new republic.

CREATING A NATIONAL EPISCOPACY

Soon after the end of the War of Independence, Father Ignatius Mathews, a Jesuit priest from Charles County, Maryland, wrote joyously to his sister, Bernadina Mathews, a nun of the Carmelite monastery in Hoogstraeten, Belgium, "Now is your time to found in this country[,] for Peace is declared and Religion is free."[3] Communities of women religious would soon take advantage of the new opportunities the United States offered, though not quite so quickly as Mathews hoped. When that time came, the Carmelites led the way. In the meanwhile, plans for the establishment of a national episcopacy and hierarchy for the American Catholic Church took precedence.

On May 18, 1789, twenty-six priests assembled at Whitemarsh Plantation in Maryland to elect the first bishop of the American Catholic Church. The democratic manner of choosing a prelate itself marked a significant departure from ecclesial norms in Europe. Through the balloting, Father John Carroll emerged as the overwhelming choice. On November 6, 1789, the papal bull *Ex Hac Apostolicae* ratified Carroll's nomination as bishop of the newly organized Diocese of Baltimore. This act, officially establishing a national episcopacy and hierarchy, signaled the dawn of a new era in the institutional life of the American Catholic Church in the same year as the American nation itself embarked on a new form of government under its recently elected president, George Washington. Commentators then and since have often saluted the propitious coincidence of these two events for church and state.[4]

The next summer, just prior to Carroll's formal consecration in Dorsetshire, England, an event occurred that marked the first fruits of Father Mathews's vision. Though attracting far less fanfare from contemporaries and historians than Carroll's elevation, it was in many ways of comparable significance to the history of American Catholicism and that of American women: on July 20, 1790, four Carmelite nuns from Belgium landed in Port Tobacco, a small shipping port in southern Maryland, and there proceeded to found the first convent within the boundaries of the United States.[5]

The introduction of women religious to the United States was linked to two major events—one external, one internal—that transformed the course of American Catholicism in the late eighteenth century. First, the winning of independence from Great Britain granted religious liberty to American Catholics, creating the climate of toleration necessary before any convent foundations could be attempted. Second, taking advantage of the new opportunities inherent in having the freedom to practice their faith, Catholic leaders initiated the policies of rapid organization and institution-building in which convents played an integral and natural role.

On November 10, 1783, barely two months after the signing of the Treaty of Paris that officially recognized the independence of the new republic, John Carroll wrote glowingly to a friend in Rome of the dual blessing of liberty that America's victory had bestowed upon its Catholic citizens. "In these United States," he announced, "our Religious system has undergone a revolution, if possible, more extraordinary, than our political one."[6] In the wake of gaining political independence from Great Britain, Catholic Americans found that they now shared with their fellow countrymen many new religious as well as civil liberties. Thanks to the victory of the fledgling country's military alliance with Catholic France and the service to the patriot cause by prominent Catholics like John Carroll and his cousin Charles Carroll of Carrollton, the atmosphere of suspicion and distrust of "papists" that had existed during the colonial era gave way to a greater spirit of toleration and acceptance on the part of the country's Protestant majority. In his letter Carroll noted that the new nation granted toleration to all manner of Christians and that the states of Pennsylvania, Delaware, Maryland, and Virginia, particularly, had extended "all civil rights" to Catholics. Catholics for their part sought to blend in as dutiful and virtuous citizens of the republic. Six years later bishop-elect Carroll expressed similar hopeful sentiments when reporting to his Roman superiors on their vast potential "to broaden inroads of Catholicism" in the English-speaking New World.[7]

THE EXTENSIVE DIOCESE OF BALTIMORE

The newly created Diocese of Baltimore over which Carroll assumed spiritual and administrative leadership comprised within its original boundaries all the states and territories of the republic; yet Catholics represented in 1790, the year of the first federal census, less than 1 percent of the country's population. The total US population of approximately 4 million people, 700,000 of whom were enslaved, included only about 35,000 Roman Catholics. Carroll's 1785 report to his superiors in Rome "on the condition of religion" in the United States identified the State of Maryland as the population center of American Catholicism. He estimated that some 15,800 of the faithful lived within Maryland's boundaries. Approximately 9,000 of these were white adults and 3,000 were children under twelve years of age. Nearly 3,000 Catholic African Americans lived as bonded laborers on farms belonging to the Society of Jesus and on the tobacco plantations of Catholic gentry in St. Mary's, Charles, and Prince George's Counties. Pennsylvania contained approximately 7,000 followers of Rome, most located in the city of Philadelphia and the state's southeastern counties. Another estimated 1,500 Catholics lived in New York State, while Virginia held another 200 or so. Few other states or territories contained large concentrations of Catholics, although significant pockets existed in areas formerly under French control, such as the region around Detroit.[8]

Ethnically, in the mid-1780s Catholics were predominantly of English descent; geographically they remained centered in the tobacco-growing counties of southern Maryland; socially and economically, the region's planter elite, though less numerically dominant than in the seventeenth century, continued to supply the lay and religious leaders of the entire Catholic community. Most Catholics, however, eked out an existence as yeoman farmers in the Old Line State and its neighbor to the north, Pennsylvania.[9]

The rural nature of eighteenth-century Catholicism in Maryland proved an obstacle to the establishment of an identifiable parish structure. In colonial times, anti-papist restrictions resulted in a dearth of churches, leaving Catholic worship primarily to the private sphere. Due to this shortage of churches and few priests available to service them, as well as the long distances required to travel to attend Mass and receive the sacraments, Catholic worship in the eighteenth century was centered in the home or in private chapels of elite families like the Diggeses and Queenses. In common with their Protestant neighbors, the family unit also served as the chief forum for religious training, with the Catholic mother acting as the primary instructor. In practicing their faith, American Catholics of the eighteenth century followed an English tradition stressing an internal, personal piety rather than the kind of external rituals and devotions that characterized the more baroque Spanish and French varieties of Catholicism and the "devotional Catholicism" of the immigrant American Church of the mid-nineteenth century.[10]

Prior to the War of Independence, periodic legal and political persecution had made Catholics acutely conscious of their minority status within the British colonies. Broad Catholic identification with the patriot cause and noteworthy contributions of individuals like the Carrolls helped soften traditional Protestant fears of papists as political subversives. During the "contagion of liberty" following the end of the Revolutionary War, relations between Catholics and Protestants improved markedly.[11] Religious prejudice, when present, became more muted, causing Catholics to be less conscious of their minority status within the young republic. The American church did not merely acquiesce to the constitution's separation of church and state and freedom of religion; as a minority faith, it enthusiastically embraced both concepts. Spokesmen such as Bishop Carroll publicly endorsed the ideas of religious liberty and pluralism, recognizing that such principles safeguarded the nation in general and Catholicism in particular. For example, writing to the *Gazette of the United States* under the pseudonym "Pacificus," Carroll emphasized his "earnest regard to preserve inviolate forever, in our new empire, the great principle of religious freedom."[12] American Catholics endeavored to retain separate religious beliefs while fully upholding their duties as republican citizens. As a result, during the "republican interlude" of the American Church (1780–1820), Catholics confidently participated in the political, social, and economic affairs of the nation, state, and local community, with little sense of themselves as an oppressed, separate minority experienced by the later "immigrant Church."[13]

THE MARYLAND TRADITION

The demographics of the state of Maryland made it unusual among Catholic communities in the Early Republic. In contrast to most other Catholic enclaves in the country, Maryland contained a relatively large number of native-born English-speaking people, many of whom could trace their origins back to colonial times. Led since the time of George Calvert, founder of the colony, by its native-born landed gentry of largely English stock, the Maryland Catholic community of the Early Republic accommodated itself more easily to mainstream American cultural values than did the predominantly working-class immigrant Catholics in the urban Northeast, a characteristic that church historians such as James Hennesey, Emmett Curran, and Thomas Spalding have dubbed "the Maryland tradition."[14]

The Maryland tradition was itself an American, if Catholic, variation of the older concept of corporatism that dominated British and American society in the eighteenth and early nineteenth centuries. Corporatism, according to the historians Gordon Wood and Paul Gilje, posited a hierarchical society consisting "of a single giant interest" rather than one that accepted the competing interests of a more democratic, egalitarian society. This ideal of corporatism, notes Gilje, "may not have fully reflected reality, but its proponents held that both society and politics were a single body, or corpus. . . . Whether you were rich or poor, whatever your race or gender, all was subsumed to the ideal of the greater interest."[15] Central to this ideal about society having a shared common interest were the notions of paternalism—obligations owed by those in authority above to those being led below—and of deference—obedience owed by those below to their social "betters."

As practiced during the episcopacy of John Carroll (1789–1815), the Maryland tradition was inclusive and marked by openness and social and cultural engagement with the non-Catholic majority. It represented the position of an American Catholic minority that at the turn of the nineteenth century was small in number and largely rural in residence but that was respected by the Protestant majority and well-integrated into the larger American culture. It stood in contrast to the later emerging "immigrant tradition" within the Catholic population which was marked by exclusivity, ghetto-building, and antagonism to the native-born Protestant majority. The Maryland tradition principally reflected the attitudes of a landed gentry that continued to dominate the Catholic population of the state and the District of Columbia politically, socially, and economically until the Civil War. This elite's cultural hegemony was especially evident in the accommodation of Maryland Catholics to the institution of slavery, a stance that took on greater significance in the antebellum era, when the slavery question increasingly polarized north and south.[16]

The writer William W. Warner sees the Maryland tradition as "the first face of American Catholicism" and finds it especially evident in the new Federal City. "As congressman, senators, journalists, government officials, merchants, and distinguished visitors from all over the young republic descended on the nascent capital city," Warner points out, "they did not find an alien 'immigrant church.' . . . Rather, they found well-to-do, educated, and generally tolerant fifth- and sixth-generation American Catholics not very different from themselves."[17]

BUILDING CATHOLIC INSTITUTIONS

Despite the inclusiveness of the Maryland tradition, for Carroll to meet the challenge "to broaden the inroads of Catholicism" successfully, the new bishop recognized that the infant institutional church must be organized and strengthened. In many cases this meant building literally from the ground up. Since Roman Catholics were relatively few in number but widely dispersed throughout the land, and as the state funding accorded to Catholic institutions in many European nations was not allowed in the new republic, Carroll confronted a monumental task. In a letter to Leonardo Cardinal Antonelli in Rome, Carroll listed the major needs facing his fledgling diocese: providing support for priests and churches; constructing chapels; supplying chalices, vestments, and other sacred furnishings; and attending to what he called the "greatest problem of all—building a college for education of Catholic youth."[18]

Carroll was especially interested in founding a seminary in order to ensure an adequate number of homegrown shepherds to tend his scattered flock, but he also saw education as the "main sheet anchor of religion" among the laity. He encouraged the establishment of schools for young men beginning with Georgetown College, founded in the District of Columbia in 1789, and Mount St. Mary's College, founded in Emmitsburg, Maryland, in 1808.[19] Shortages of diocesan finances led Carroll in 1790 to invite priests of the Society of Saint Sulpice, fleeing revolution in their native France, to carry out the actual institution-building and staffing of his education program. The Sulpician fathers opened St. Mary's Seminary in Baltimore in 1791 and St. Mary's College by the end of that decade.

The new bishop also showed a keen interest in schooling for girls. In Europe, the traditional responsibility for female instruction fell to teaching orders like the Ursulines and others. Carroll wanted to attract such teaching communities of women religious to America. In pursuit of this end, Ferdinand Farmer, a priest in Philadelphia, reported to Carroll in June of 1786 that he had contacted Thomas FitzSimons, a leading Catholic merchant and future delegate to the US Constitutional Convention, about building a nunnery in the city or the surrounding countryside. Although nothing concrete came of this early proposal, it foreshadowed what was to become a recurring pattern of involvement by Catholic community leaders—lay and clerical—in attempting to bring women religious to their locales.[20]

The founding of the Carmelite convent in Maryland four years later proved a more successful collaboration of clergy, laity, and religious than the earlier failed efforts in Philadelphia. Three of the four original members of this order's foundation—Mother Bernadina and her two nieces, Ann Teresa Mathews and Susan Mathews—came from the Carmelite monastery in Hoogstraeten, Belgium; the other, Sister Clare Joseph Dickenson, came from the Carmelite convent in Antwerp. While Dickenson was a native of London, England, the Mathews women hailed from a respected old family who had settled in colonial Maryland.[21]

Because Carroll sought to bring nuns to his diocese primarily to serve as educators of young women, he was disappointed that the Carmelites, a non-teaching order of contemplative nuns, had made the pioneering settlement. Although pleased to welcome them for the spiritual contributions they would make to the American Catholic community, he admitted to a friend, "I wish rather for Ursulines," an order specializing in female instruction.[22]

The late appearance of convents in English-speaking America contrasted sharply with the situation in the other New World possessions of its Catholic rivals. Communities of women religious began to appear in both Spanish and French North America within a few decades of initial exploration and settlement. Because the Protestant Reformation of the sixteenth century had abolished monasticism in their country, English Catholics established several religious communities-in-exile across the English Channel in various cities on the Continent. In the seventeenth century, for example, English Carmelite nuns founded three houses in Belgium—Antwerp (1619), Lierre (1648), and Hoogstraeten (1678). British America, dominated by an overwhelming Protestant majority, proved to be less hospitable soil for transplanting "Romish nunneries" than did the lands of the Catholic kings of Spain and of France. In both the Spanish and French New World empires, Roman Catholics constituted the vast majority of the colonial populations and official recognition of Roman Catholicism as the state religion closely linked Church and Crown. Catholics in the British colonies, by contrast, made up a tiny, and sometimes persecuted, sect existing precariously within the de facto, if not always de jure, Protestant society.[23]

Penal laws implemented in colonial Maryland after 1689 forbade Catholics from opening their own schools. Meanwhile, legislation also denied Catholics the right to send their children to Catholic schools in Europe. With the help of Jesuit priests, however, wealthy Catholic colonists, like their co-religionists in the mother countries, shipped their children—girls and boys—abroad for the Catholic education prohibited at home. Young men, among them John Carroll and his cousin Charles Carroll, attended such institutions at the Jesuit college at St. Omer's in French Flanders. Young women enrolled in convent academies in the Low Countries. Several of the passengers in these "educational convoys" eventually entered the seminaries and convents on the Continent.[24]

Female Catholics (at least those belonging to the social elite), therefore, had an option—the convent—not available to their Protestant sisters. Indeed, Protestant women were more likely than Protestant men to recognize that life in a nunnery provided females with many definite benefits—a refuge from marriage and the world, a release from the dangers and debilitations of continuous childbearing, a safeguard against economic deprivation, the social support of true sisterhood, and a shared commitment to ultimate purpose. Beyond its spiritual impulse, a religious calling offered several practical and functional attractions to women who answered it.[25]

The appeal of a convent vocation for Catholic women in eighteenth-century Chesapeake found an outlet on the Continent. More than thirty daughters of southern Maryland took religious vows in Low Country convents from 1721 to 1786. In addition to the three Carmelite monasteries in Belgium, they entered houses of the Benedictines in Ghent, Paris, and Cambrai; of the Sepulchrines in Liege and Pontoise; of the Poor Clares in Rouen and Aire; of the Dominicans in Brussels; and of the Austine Canonesses in Bruges. The surnames of these women reflected many of the leading families in the Maryland Catholic community: Boone, Brooke, Hagan, Neale, Semmes, and Spalding. As noted earlier, three of the women who founded the convent in Port Tobacco came from Charles County by way of Belgium.[26]

CARMEL IN AMERICA

When the four Carmelite nuns debarked at Port Tobacco in July 1790, they arrived in the company of Father Charles Neale, former chaplain of the Antwerp convent. From the sale of land that Neale generously donated, the Carmelites obtained the means to purchase a house and farm of nearly 900 acres near Port Tobacco. This farm, worked by enslaved labor, provided the convent its chief means of support, as the community rule prohibited engaging in teaching or any other form of gainful employment outside their strict enclosure. Numerous clerical and lay benefactors in Europe and America also supplied the nuns with additional funds. Fittingly, the Carmelites occupied their new quarters on October 15, 1790, the feast day of the saint who had reformed the rule of their order, Teresa of Ávila.[27]

The Carmelites composed one of the most ancient and respected orders of the Church, having originated sometime in the early centuries of Christianity. The Port Tobacco community belonged to the Discalced branch of the order, which, according to their adaptations to the monastic Rule of Saint Albert, followed a rigorous life of ascetic denial and pious contemplation. The appellation "discalced" literally means "without shoes," and refers to the fact that such Carmelites wore sandals rather than shoes. In Spain during the Counter-Reformation of the mid-sixteenth century, the great mystic Saint Teresa of Ávila, with the help of Saint John of the Cross, began a movement to restore the observance of the original Discalced rule.[28]

The Port Tobacco monastery reflected the reforms instituted by Saint Teresa, with the nuns sometimes even being referred to as Teresians in her honor. The Carmelites dressed in a distinctive brown habit of coarse material, refrained from eating animal flesh other than fish, and remained silent except during periods of recreation. Nuns wore coarse stockings and slept on straw beds. They meditated twice a day and sang the Divine Office each evening at nine o'clock.[29]

The Carmelites came to the United States chiefly to assist in missionizing the nation. As a contemplative order of cloistered women, however, the Carmelites contributed solely through their prayers for the clergy and laity rather than by an active proselytizing among white Protestants, Native Americans, or enslaved African Americans. Along with praying and meditating, nuns filled their day by copying and binding prayer books, a time-honored tradition of monastic life since the Middle Ages. They also spun and wove their own clothes as well as the clothes of the enslaved who worked their farm.[30]

Though Carroll rejoiced that their example had "aroused many to serious thought on divine things," he continued to wish that the Carmelites would apply themselves to concrete action on human necessities as well. "They would be far more useful," he lamented in a 1792 report to Cardinal Leonardo Antonelli in Rome, "if, according to their rule, and with the background of experience, they undertook the education of girls."[31] The next year Carroll, without the knowledge or consent of the Carmelites, obtained a dispensation from Rome permitting them to teach, "considering the great scarcity of labourers and the defects of education in these States."[32] The nuns, with the support of their spiritual director, Father Charles Neale, nevertheless stood firm in refusing to assume a duty so clearly in violation of their rule and constitutions, dispensation from Rome notwithstanding.

By 1800 the Carmelite monastery was flourishing, with eleven new members and about thirty enslaved people to tend their fields. The latter came to the Port Tobacco community as part of the property in the dowries that candidates provided upon entrance. That same year, Mother Bernadina died, peaceful in the knowledge that she had successfully carried out her mission to transplant religious life for women from Europe to her native land. Carroll then appointed Sister Clare Joseph as Mathews's successor as prioress of the Carmelite monastery.[33]

THE POOR CLARES

Bishop Carroll finally did arrange the establishment of a school for girls in his diocese, but its founders were neither Ursulines nor Carmelites, but rather Poor Clares, another contemplative order originating in Europe. In the summer of 1798 three French nuns settled in Georgetown, Maryland, near the college. The trio—Mother Marie de la Marche, the abbess of the Order of Saint Clare, Sister Celeste le Blond de la Rochefoucault, and Sister Saint Luc—arrived in Georgetown by stagecoach from Baltimore.[34]

Georgetown proved the final destination in America for Mother Marie and her companions after a five-year odyssey that had buffeted them about in Spanish Louisiana and various locales in the United States following their flight from their native land in the fall of 1792. Victims of the anti-religious and anti-aristocratic fever sweeping over revolutionary France, the three Poor Clares, all of noble birth, had fled their motherhouse in Tours disguised in secular clothing, and journeyed to the port of Havre-de-Grace in hopes of booking passage to the New World.[35]

The Poor Clares, like the Discalced Carmelites, normally lived a contemplative existence within the strict monastic enclosure. The order originated in thirteenth-century Italy under the guidance of Francis of Assisi and his early follower, Clare of Assisi, the order's namesake. Each monastery remained autonomous, and its black-veiled sisters followed austere lives of prayer and mortification—fasting and abstaining throughout the year, going barefoot except for when doing outside work, sleeping on straw mattresses, and rising at midnight to chant the Divine Office. The Poor Clares also practiced the strict Franciscan rule of poverty—members could not own property, even in common. In addition to their prayers, the nuns served the Church by making altar breads, by sewing vestments and washing ecclesiastical linens, and by printing holy books. Teaching was not among the normal responsibilities of the Poor Clares in Europe, since that activity interfered with their restrictions about maintaining the sanctity of the cloister. Financial necessity and pressure from Carroll nevertheless compelled them to apply themselves to this task in the United States.[36] Resigned to remaining in the United States for the indefinite future, the Poor Clares looked about for a suitable place to establish a convent. Apparently at the suggestion of Father Louis W. Dubourg, president of Georgetown College, the nuns came to live in Georgetown in the recently created District of Columbia.[37]

Conditions in Georgetown seemed to bode well for the opening of a school for girls. With vocal support from Dubourg and financial assistance from benefactors in Havana, Cuba, the French nuns opened Georgetown Academy for girls in September 1798. Using a loan from the Sulpicians of St. Mary's Seminary, the Poor Clares also purchased a house and property on the corner of Third and Fayette Streets in Georgetown.[38]

THE PIOUS LADIES

In 1799 Father Leonard Neale succeeded Dubourg as head of Georgetown College. Neale was the brother of Charles Neale, the chaplain of the Carmelite convent in Port Tobacco. Leonard Neale brought with him to Georgetown three Irish immigrants he had met in Philadelphia: Miss Alice Lalor, Mrs. Maria Sharpe, and Mrs. Maria McDermott. Father Neale proposed to organize them into a religious community. For the first few months these women resided with the Poor Clares in return for helping them run their school. Neale, however, did not want the trio to join the Poor Clares, and instead planned to form them into a separate community of women religious. To this end he purchased a lot adjoining the grounds of the Poor Clares for his so-called Pious Ladies.[39]

The foundation of the society of Pious Ladies—which eventually evolved into the first Visitation convent in the United States and the one that Ann Gertrude Wightt later entered—resulted from the fortuitous meeting of Father Neale and the three Irish women in Philadelphia in 1798. Emigrating with her family in 1797, the thirty-one-year-old Lalor originally had intended to return to her home in County Kilkenny and establish a convent there. The Georgetown Convent annals show that during her passage to the New World, Lalor became acquainted with Sharpe and McDermott, two widows who shared her desire to pursue a cloistered life. Upon their arrival in the Quaker State, the three women made the acquaintance of Neale, who "begged them to remain in this country." Lalor at first hesitated because of a prior promise to aid the Bishop of Kilkenny in founding a convent in that diocese. Neale, however, convinced Lalor that women religious were needed as much in the United States as on the Emerald Isle.[40]

Lalor and her companions first rented a small house in Philadelphia. There they lived in community without taking formal vows. McDermott's eight-year-old daughter also stayed with them. In order to provide for themselves, the Pious Ladies, as the locals called them, opened a small school for young ladies, the first such Catholic institution in the city. With Maria Sharpe as the principal instructor, the school supplied a modest income by which the women met their most pressing needs. The Pious Ladies also served as volunteer nurses during an epidemic of yellow fever that raged through the City of Brotherly Love that year. While many inhabitants, including the members of Alice Lalor's own family, fled the town to escape the dreaded disease, the Pious Ladies resolutely remained with their patients. One young woman who had joined the little community succumbed to the fever. During the epidemic the three surviving Pious Ladies administered to the sick, comforted the dying, and generally embodied the charitable spirit associated with the original purpose of the Visitation Order, the community with which they would someday formally affiliate.[41]

After less than a year living in the Quaker City, the society of Pious Ladies had made their presence known and respected by its residents. Nevertheless, in 1799 they agreed to move to the newly organized Federal District on the eastern bank of the Potomac River when their spiritual advisor, Father Neale, accepted the presidency of Georgetown College. Although initially placing his little band with the Poor Clares, Neale would not permit the Irish women to join the French community for two reasons. First, the school run by the Poor Clares did not bring in sufficient revenue to support an expanded community. Second, the extreme poverty and rigorous discipline traditionally practiced by the Poor Clares was not the model Neale envisioned for his order.[42]

Convent writings maintain that as a young missionary to Indians in British Guiana more than twenty years before, Neale had experienced "a dream or vision" in which the two saintly founders of the Visitation Order appeared to him: "He saw . . . a long procession of religious headed by St. Jane de Chantal, clad in a costume, which he afterwards recognized as that of the Visitation. St. F[rancis] de Sales was also there who looked most earnestly at the Missionary and said, '*You will erect a House of my Order.*'"[43]

In 1800 Lalor and her companions moved into a small brick house that Neale had purchased. On June 24 of that year, Neale placed the Pious Ladies under the rule of the Visitation Order, although at this time he knew nothing of the order's constitutions or mode of dress. Lalor became the official head of the community, taking the name Mother Teresa.[44] The Visitation Order that the Pious Ladies attempted to emulate had begun in Savoy (now part of France) around 1610 as a daring experiment in active religious life under the direction of Bishop Francis de Sales and Jane Frances de Chantal, a widow of noble birth. After being forced back into the enclosure by church authorities, the Visitandines adopted a sort of via media that combined the prayerful contemplation in the cloister with the education of aristocratic girls from the outside world. Convent life and work followed general monastic routines but without the emphasis on bodily mortification that is found in more austere orders like the Carmelites and the Poor Clares. This mixed kind of religious life appealed especially to women who, for reasons of age, health, or marital status (i.e., widows with children), refrained from entering the more physically demanding contemplative orders.[45]

In 1800, too, Father Neale became Bishop Neale, only the second American to be so consecrated in the Catholic Church. Named as coadjutor to Bishop Carroll in Baltimore, Neale also retained his office as president of Georgetown College. The latter post allowed him to continue to live near his beloved community of Pious Ladies and serve it as their chaplain, confessor, spiritual director, and novice master. The last position made few demands on Neale, since only six postulants entered the community during its first decade. Vocations to the Pious Ladies lagged because priests

FIGURE 1.1. Portrait of Archbishop Leonard Neale, Second Archbishop of Baltimore. Artist unknown, 1817. Courtesy Georgetown Visitation Monastery Archives, Washington, DC.

were reluctant to recommend to prospective candidates "a house of which they feared the dissolution, not yet having either papal or ecclesiastical approval; knowing nothing more of a Rule than the name; the Houses in Europe being unwilling to send them a copy of their Constitutions, as their house was not founded in the regular way, and by professed members of the

Order."[46] The latter point—"not founded in the regular way"—continued to cause uncertainty even after formal affiliation with the Visitation Order was achieved in 1816.

DEPARTURE OF THE POOR CLARES

In the early years of the new century, though the Pious Ladies grew but slowly, the Poor Clares grew not at all. Economic woes continued to plague the French nuns, in part because their main source of income, tuition from Georgetown Academy, had to compete with the school opened by Father Neale's Pious Ladies. Mother Marie de la Marche died on November 20, 1804. Faced with the death of their abbess, a financially struggling school, and no new members after more than a decade in exile, the two surviving Poor Clares resolved to sell their property in America and return to France. Political conditions in their homeland had eased a few years before, thanks to a concordat that Napoleon Bonaparte had concluded with the pope and the Catholic Church. The departure of Sister Celeste and Sister Saint Luc from New York City in July 1806 effectively ended the brief life of both the first convent of Poor Clares and the second community of women religious established in the United States.[47]

Though evanescent, the foundation made by the Poor Clares had lasting significance for its impact on the religious community that remained in Georgetown. In July 1806 the community of Pious Ladies occupied the convent house and grounds that the Poor Clares had sold to Neale prior to their departure for France. They also appropriated the name "Georgetown Academy" for their school for young ladies. Moreover, Father Francis Neale, brother to Leonard and Charles, bought from the Poor Clares their altars, furniture, and library. Most important, this small library contained a French-language copy of the Rule of the Visitation Order. Upon discovery of the contents of this book in 1812, Neale began to organize and direct his Pious Ladies according to the Visitandine discipline.[48] With this find, Bishop Neale could at last fulfill the charge that he believed Bishop de Sales had given to him as a young missionary some three decades before.

The Carmelites, Poor Clares, and Pious Ladies were the first three communities of women religious established in the United States. In 1803 the Ursuline convent in New Orleans became the fourth, when Napoleon sold the Louisiana Territory to representatives of the American government for the bargain price of $15 million. No new convent foundations occurred in the nation from that date, until after the division of the enormous Diocese of Baltimore into five new administrative centers in 1808.[49]

ORGANIZATION OF ARCHDIOCESE OF BALTIMORE

The Diocese of Baltimore as originally created in 1791 contained all thirteen states and western territories within its administrative boundaries. This amorphous situation continued until 1808, when Rome designated Baltimore as a metropolitan archdiocese (led by the first archbishop of the American Church, John Carroll) and carved out four new dioceses—New York, Philadelphia, Boston, and Bardstown, Kentucky—each headed by a new bishop. Archbishop Carroll found that the boundaries of the new Archdiocese of Baltimore, while substantially reducing the area subject to his direct control, still encompassed the state of Maryland, the District of Columbia, and the southern states stretching to the Gulf and the Mississippi. Although lacking formal Vatican recognition of its status as the primary see in the United States, the Archdiocese of Baltimore in fact served as the spiritual and administrative center of American Catholicism—the "American Rome"—throughout the nineteenth century.[50]

Southern Maryland had been the "cradle of Catholicity" in the seventeenth century and continued to be the population center of American Catholicism during the early nineteenth century. However, the episcopates of John Carroll and his immediate successor, Leonard Neale, witnessed the beginnings of a gradual demographic transformation that by the 1820s had shifted the center of the Catholic population from the rural tobacco counties of southern Maryland (St. Mary's, Charles, and Prince George's Counties) to the burgeoning immigrant entrepots of Boston, New York, Philadelphia, and Baltimore. The holding of the American Church's first synod in Baltimore in 1791 both signaled and symbolized this emerging urban orientation.[51]

During the next few years several important changes also occurred within the hierarchy of the archdiocese. Upon the death of Carroll on December 3, 1815, Leonard Neale succeeded him as metropolitan. Neale, however, already aged and in declining health, conducted his two years in the archbishop's chair as a caretaker administration. Ambrose Maréchal, one of the several French Sulpicians who had escaped the anticlericalism of revolutionary France, succeeded Neale upon the latter's death on June 15, 1817.

MARÉCHAL'S 1818 REPORT

After just one year into his episcopate, Maréchal issued a comprehensive report on the state of Catholicism in the nation generally and his archdiocese specifically. He estimated that his see had grown from about ten thousand Catholics just before the revolution to over one hundred thousand at the time of the report. He also recounted that the city of Baltimore contained four Catholic churches in addition to a magnificent Cathedral under construction to serve the approximately ten thousand members of the faithful living in the city. Maréchal further told of the success of his diocese's two seminaries run by the Sulpicians—the major, St. Mary's, in Baltimore city; and the minor, Mount St. Mary's, in Emmitsburg—and the college for young men in Georgetown, staffed by Jesuits.[52]

Maréchal also enthusiastically announced the growth of the three convents of women religious under his supervision. "Assuredly," he wrote, "the sisters and their work are like so many fonts of grace to water abundantly my flock."[53] He optimistically noted the salubrious effect the nuns also had on others: "The Protestants themselves treat them with a certain veneration."

The archbishop went on to describe the three types of religious life available to women in the Church: contemplative, mixed, and active. The Carmelites of Port Tobacco had twenty-three members observing its strict enclosure. "These virgins of St. Teresa live so holily," he wrote enthusiastically, "that I scarcely believe that any other house of this order exists anywhere in the Catholic world in which piety and monastic discipline flourish to the same extent."[54] The nuns of Georgetown Visitation monastery numbered about fifty, a clear indication that they had overcome their early difficulties attracting new candidates. This change in fortunes resulted primarily from the fact that in 1816 Rome had officially recognized the Georgetown community as a branch of the Visitation Order.

Although the Pious Ladies had been living in community since before the turn of the century, they had done so without taking formal religious vows, until 1814. Following the discovery and translation of the French copy of the published Rule and Constitutions of the Visitation Order among the books purchased from the departed Poor Clares, Bishop Neale instituted the monastic discipline of the order upon his Pious Ladies. Soon thereafter he obtained a picture of Saint Jane Frances de Chantal in her Visitandine habit that had been found in a box of religious materials sent to Georgetown College from Europe. Bishop Neale at that point still lacked papal approval to affiliate formally his society of Pious Ladies with the original Visitandine motherhouse

FIGURE 1.2. Ambrose Maréchal, Third Archbishop of Baltimore (1817–28). Courtesy Archives of the Archdiocese of Baltimore, Associated Archives at St. Mary's Seminary & University, Baltimore.

in Annecy, Savoy. The delay in effecting this association had resulted from many problems occurring on both sides of the Atlantic in the first fifteen years of the nineteenth century: the Pious Ladies' ignorance of the Visitation Rule of religious life, the destruction of the Annecy motherhouse during the French Revolution and its later rebuilding, the difficulty communicating with

Visitandine convents in Europe during the period of the Napoleonic Wars, and the captivity of Pope Pius VII by Napoleon.[55]

Upon becoming the archbishop of Baltimore in 1815, Neale petitioned the now-liberated Pius VII for permission to join his Georgetown community with the Visitation Order. Upon receiving an affirmative reply, on December 28, 1816, Neale admitted to solemn vows the community's two surviving founding members—Mother Teresa Lalor and Sister Mary Frances McDermott, the assistant superior—as well as the mistress of novices, Sister Agnes Brent. The chosen date marked the 195th anniversary of the death of the order's founder, Saint Francis de Sales. On the same day, Neale expressed his happiness at fulfilling his dream in a letter to the Annecy motherhouse: "By a happy dispensation of Providence, on the date of the death of Saint Francis de Sales, existence and life were imparted to the first established community of his order in America."[56] The necessity of maintaining a teaching academy forced the Georgetown convent to modify a few of the daily routines normally expected of Visitation monasteries in Europe. For example, teaching sisters would have to exit the convent cloister in order to instruct their pupils in the academy. These changes, though minor, caused some members to worry about their compliance with their order's rule and hence the legitimacy of their religious status.

By 1816 membership in the Georgetown monastery had outpaced membership in the older Port Tobacco convent, in part because the Visitandines lived a "mixed life" that had greater appeal to American females than did the more rigorous rule of the Carmelites. But the Carmelites also strictly adhered to their rule capping membership at twenty women per monastic house. Maréchal reported that whereas the Carmelites had a "sufficiently large income" from their farm and bequests, the Visitandines had fewer resources, forcing them to "live partly on their income [from the school] and partly by the labor of their own hands."[57] The female academy conducted by the Visitandines hardly merited the name. A decade later, however, under the direction of Sister Ann Gertrude Wightt, Georgetown Visitation Academy was educating hundreds of girls—Protestant and Catholic—and had become, along with the Ursuline academies in New Orleans and Boston, the gold standard for all such institutions in the country. Maréchal acknowledged the potential of female education in general and of Georgetown Academy in particular to spread good will toward Catholicism far and wide. "Every year," he wrote glowingly, "there goes forth from this religious home a number of young ladies who diffuse far and wide in the world the lessons of piety taught them in this school."[58]

The third community of women religious listed by Maréchal in his report was the Sisters of Charity of Saint Joseph. Elizabeth Ann Seton founded this congregation in 1809 and headquartered it in Emmitsburg, Maryland. The form of society Seton instituted was unique to the American Catholic community up to that time. Whereas the previous four convents founded in the United States followed some variation on an enclosed life, with the teaching of young females as the sole activity outside the cloister, Mother Seton modeled her congregation on the more active apostolate of Saint Vincent de Paul's Daughters of Charity, a French community founded in the early 1600s to engage in corporal and spiritual acts of mercy. Already by 1818 Seton's community had increased to thirty-two members.[59]

The founding of Seton's Sisters of Charity proved to be a major watershed in the history of American women religious and the history of American Catholic social services. Their active way of life quickly became the model followed by the vast majority of communities subsequently established in the country, so much so that the general public often referred to all manner of women religious as "sisters of charity," whether or not the label was accurate. By abandoning the cloister to engage in teaching, nursing, and orphan care within the larger society, the Sisters of Charity made women religious more visible to the American public, both Catholic and Protestant. In addition, their numerous establishments, particularly in the populous seaports, river towns, and manufacturing centers of the rapidly urbanizing nation, brought Sisters of Charity into contact with a wider number and class of people than did cloistered orders like the Carmelites, the Poor Clares, the Visitandines, and the Ursulines.

In its first two decades of these initial four orders' existence in America (1790–1809), Catholic religious life chiefly welcomed privileged women who both felt called to the habit and whose families had the means to provide a substantial dowry when they entered. Yet the establishment of a nunnery in the United States meant that a religious vocation became a greater possibility for more women than had been true in colonial days. It also meant that American families could remain in better communication with their daughter nuns. As the founding of convents rapidly increased in the next century, the number of orders and congregations became more numerous, their membership more socially egalitarian, their work more diversified and specialized, and religious life in general more adapted to American society and to the needs and interests of the women who entered these orders.

CRADLE OF THE CONVENT REVOLUTION

The foundations of the Carmelites, the Poor Clares, the Visitandines, and the Sisters of Charity in Maryland and the District of Columbia marked the tentative beginning of a historical process I label the "convent revolution" in nineteenth-century America. In the antebellum era, religious sisterhoods both expanded their existing educational works at record rates and introduced numerous new ministries in health and social services. The separate institutions that Catholic women religious constructed in these years paralleled the development of female voluntary societies by which Protestant women took increasingly prominent positions in the "public sphere" as teachers and managers and supporters of philanthropic efforts, traditionally a male preserve.[60]

Although seldom noted by historians of women, the founding of the Carmelites in Port Tobacco in 1790, of the Visitandines in Georgetown in 1799, and of the Sisters of Charity in Emmitsburg in 1809 all belong among the earliest examples in the United States of formal associations of women engaged outside the home for social, charitable, or religious purposes. Indeed, the Carmelite monastery antedated by seven years the formation of what is generally recognized as the first such female organization in the country—the Society for the Relief of Poor Widows with Small Children, founded by Isabella Graham, Elizabeth Seton, and others in New York City in 1797.[61] Then the wife of a wealthy merchant, Seton assumed the charitable obligations of her class in founding the society, the country's earliest known benevolent association directed and controlled by females. The labors of these elite ladies on behalf of less fortunate women in New York City earned them the sobriquet "Protestant Sisters of Charity." Seton's participation in this group thus foreshadowed both her pioneering spirit and the work to which she would eventually dedicate herself as a Catholic woman religious.[62]

Historians typically have not included convents when tracing the origins of female benevolent associations. But what is a convent if not such an institution, although more formal and ancient in origin? At the same time, it must be admitted that convents hardly fit the typical mold for such organizations. The Carmelite convent, for example, proved a significant exception to the general profile in that its members came not from urban middle-class Protestant women of the Northeast, but rural planter-class Catholic women of the Upper South.[63] Likewise, most lay women's societies consisted chiefly of married women whose philanthropic work was supplemental to their primary roles as wives and mothers in the home. Convents, in contrast, contained mostly celibate virgins and a few widows whose whole existence was dedicated to acts of piety and charity. Indeed, widows played a disproportionate role as organizers and leaders of both the earliest female voluntary societies and female religious orders in the Early Republic.[64] Whereas many American women professing Evangelical Protestantism possessed the fervor and means to create a new institution—the voluntary association—to carry out their tasks, Catholic nuns were buoyed by their faith and looked to Church tradition and a medieval institution—the convent—that could be adapted to the new American environment.

Given these obvious differences and others not so obvious, there remains the striking coincidence that Catholic women began to found and join convents in the United States contemporaneously to Protestant women forming and enrolling in their own voluntary societies. Their activities often paralleled each other, sometimes in conscious imitation of, and sometimes in competition to, each other. And both groups were involved in doing something new for members of their gender in the United States. The imitation and influences cut both ways. If, as Bishop Carroll pointed out, convents were "a novelty in this country" at the turn of the eighteenth century, the same could be said of secular female associations. When forming her society, Isabella Graham recognized that for women it "was a new thing in the country."[65] In the succeeding decades, the increasing number of both kinds of female organizations made each less a novelty than had once been true.

As members of the Visitation Order recently founded in the United States, Sister Ann Gertrude Wightt and her sibling, Sister Mary Margaret Wightt, participated in the early stage of the convent revolution in nineteenth-century America. The next chapter examines how these biological sisters came to attend Georgetown Academy and then became sisters of faith who contributed to monastic life at Georgetown Visitation.

2

A Child of the House

Mary Ann Wightt belonged to the initial group of nineteen women in Georgetown Convent that, on January 6, 1817, took the white veil and received the habit as novices of the Order of the Visitation of Holy Mary. At that ceremony the eighteen-year-old also received the name Sister Ann Gertrude. Later that month Sister Gertrude, as she quickly became known, took the black veil, received the black habit, and professed solemn vows as a Visitation nun. By the time of her religious profession, however, Wightt had already spent ten years of her young life residing on the grounds of Georgetown Convent, first as a boarder, then as a member of the Pious Ladies, and finally as a member of the Visitation Order. According to the convent annals, Mary Ann grew up as "a child of the house, almost raised under the eyes of Abp. [Leonard] Neale and Mother Teresa [Lalor]."[1]

In 1799, the same year that the three Pious Ladies under the direction of Leonard Neale established a convent in Georgetown, Mary Ann Wightt was born into a family of the English Catholic gentry in nearby Prince George's County, Maryland. While little is known of Wightt's family background and childhood, it is known that the Wightt family name came from England and can be traced to seventeenth-century Maryland. Many settlers with the surname "Wightt" were members of the Church of England; others were Roman Catholic. There is also evidence of intermarriage between Anglicans and Roman Catholics in the family during the colonial era.[2]

Mary Ann was the firstborn child of Benjamin and Mary Wightt. Susanna, often called Susan, the second child, came along two years later, in 1801. The Benjamin Wightt family is listed in the 1800 census as owning eleven slaves on their farm in Prince George's County, Maryland. Their holdings in real and human property placed the Wightts among the comfortable, if not rich members of the landed gentry of the Old Line State.[3] By kinship Benjamin

Wightt was connected to the wealthier ranks of the planter class. His older brother John had inherited the family plantation "Inclosure" located in the Maryland cession of the Ten Mile Square that made up the original District of Columbia.[4] Their sister, Anne, married David Burnes, whose great wealth resulted from his sale of land to the federal government that was eventually incorporated into the Federal District. Anne and John's daughter, Marcia Burnes, the much older first cousin to Mary Ann and Susan Wightt, was heir to one of the largest fortunes in the Early Republic. In 1802 Marcia married General John Peter Van Ness, a congressman from New York.[5]

That same year, while Mary Ann and Susan were still toddlers, tragedy struck the family when Benjamin Wightt died suddenly from causes that were not recorded. After Benjamin's death, his brother, John, assumed the role of protector to Mary Wightt and her two young daughters. John Wightt passed away only four years later, however.[6] Soon thereafter, their mother placed eight-year-old Mary Ann and six-year-old Susan under the care of Bishop Leonard Neale in Georgetown.[7] In 1807 the Wightt girls enrolled as "pensioners," that is, boarders at the small school of the Georgetown convent of the Pious Ladies. Mary Wightt likely died soon after entrusting her half-orphans to the prelate, as she is not mentioned further in the convent annals.

How did all of the disruptions to their family and home life affect the two Wightt sisters? Convent records offer no comment, but we can speculate. The loss of their father and their uncle and the physical separation from their mother—all in the span of five years—must have left the girls with a precocious awareness of how fleeting and precarious life on earth can be. Their tragic family history likely also drew Mary Ann and Susan closer to and more reliant on one another than most biological sisters experience. Moreover, Georgetown Convent was their home and Bishop Neale and the Pious Ladies their surrogate family. The girls strongly identified with their teachers both in and outside the classroom, a not uncommon dynamic within convent boarding schools that often spurred religious vocations. Doubtless the Pious Ladies served as especially influential role models for the orphaned Wightt girls.[8]

BOARDING AT GEORGETOWN ACADEMY

As pupils in Georgetown Academy over the next seven or eight years, Mary Ann and Susan Wightt lived most of the time within the convent grounds (but outside the cloister), sharing the same plain meals and spare living conditions as the Pious Ladies. During breaks in the school year, however, the Wightt girls did have the opportunity to leave their convent home to visit friends and relatives. Convent records recount one such visit made by the Wightt sisters around 1813. As with many such accounts compiled after the death of an individual nun, the purpose was to offer a moral example, in this case about the formation of Susan's vocation despite her attraction to the secular world. "As she grew up, Susan was attracted to an older girl, a pensioner, who interested her in worldly things," states the convent chronicles. "This caused Archbishop Neale to have a serious talk with her." Her friend told her, "Oh Susan, don't mind that old man. He's trying to make a nun of you."[9]

> That spring and summer, Susan went with her sister [Mary Ann] to visit friends in the country, where both were caught up in a whirl of pleasure. When they returned to school in September, Susan saw one of her classmates clothed as a novice, and a desire to mend her ways, and follow her, was born. The Bishop was delighted when he saw her change of heart. The Sisters were few and there was much work to be done, so he appointed the young girl, then twelve years old to act as sacristan and care for the small chapel.[10]

Like most such anecdotes in convent records, this story was recorded to make a point about the superiority of spiritual values over mere worldly pleasures. At the same time, it also demonstrates that the Wightt girls, despite living within a circumscribed environment for much of the school year, did make occasional forays outside those confines. Since convent sources attest to the fact that both girls were gifted intellectually, it is reasonable to assume that during such sojourns they developed an awareness of the world outside the cloister. Among the homes that they almost certainly visited was that of their first cousin, Marcia Burnes Van Ness, in nearby Washington City. Moreover, the famous capital socialite, diarist, and friend of their cousin, Margaret Bayard Smith, later claimed to have known Sister Gertrude as a child. This acquaintance likely came through their mutual connection to the famous "heiress of Washington City."[11]

Regardless of the trips the Wightt girls managed away from the seclusion of the convent's grounds, the school of the Pious Ladies in which they boarded contained few students and offered classes only in the basics. Indeed, Georgetown Academy during its first two decades featured low enrollments and few facilities, thus generating a barely sufficient income. Indeed, at that time Georgetown Academy was an academy in name only. The school was marked by an undistinguished curriculum and "undisguised poverty." But its small size, though a material drawback, delivered hidden spiritual benefits for the convent. Because there were hardly more students in the school than sisters in the community, each of the nuns became known personally to the boarders and day students, serving as role models to their impressionable charges. Moreover, many of the nuns were either related to or friends with the families of their pupils. In their history, George and Rose Lathrop noted that "the Spartan meagreness of the fare, the early hours of rising and the long walk to and from Mass, in all weathers all conduced to a healthy, vigorous, and spiritualized state of mind and body," for the pupils.[12]

While the school may have been a less than an adequate financial support for the convent in its early years, it nonetheless also functioned as a quasi-novitiate in preparing many of its pupils for religious life. Evidence of this spiritual effect is found in the fact that of the fourteen students enrolled in 1810, eleven later entered Georgetown Convent. In addition to Mary Ann and Susan Wightt, this group included Henrietta Brent (later Sister Mary Agnes), Eliza Matthews (Sister Mary Juliana), Jane Neale (Sister Mary Scholastica), Catherine Manning (Sister Catherine Alphonsa), Mary Ann Boarman (Sister Mary Benedicta), Susan Boarman (Sister Angela), Mary Cummins (Sister Mary Clare Cummings), Louisa Queen (Sister Mary Josephine), and Jenny Neale (Sister Mary Frances). Soon after, the three McNantz sisters—Bernadina (Sister Mary Bernadine), Charlotte (Sister Isadore), and Emilie Marie (Sister Mary Leonard)—enrolled in the school and also felt the call to become spiritual daughters of Francis de Sales and Jane Frances de Chantal.[13]

In 1814, after having boarded in the academy of the Pious Ladies for seven years, fifteen-year-old Mary Ann entered the convent as a postulant. The next year Susan followed her older sister, and both took simple vows in 1815 as members of the Pious Ladies. Upon Georgetown's gaining formal recognition as a Visitation monastery in 1816, Mary Ann received the habit of a Visitation novice on January 6, 1817, taking the name Sister Ann Gertrude. Susan did the same the next week, taking the name Sister Mary Margaret. A fortnight later, Sister Gertrude and Sister Mary Margaret joined seventeen other novices, most of whom had waited many years, to profess solemn vows as nuns of the Visitation Order of Holy Mary.[14]

Affiliation with the Visitation Order in Europe spurred a spike in applicants to Georgetown Convent. No longer did priests fail to recommend the community to candidates who felt called to the religious life. A detailed inventory compiled early in 1819 found forty-nine members then living in Georgetown Visitation monastery. Thirty-five had professed solemn vows: twenty-nine choir sisters, two associate sisters, and four lay sisters. In addition, there were twelve novices and one "out" sister, a member living outside the cloister. There was also one "sister of the Little Habit," that is, a girl who otherwise qualified to be a novice but was not yet old enough to receive it.

It is noteworthy that eight of that group of thirty-five (16 percent) had been married. While seven were widows, Sister Mary Augustine Barber was a special case. Following their conversion to Catholicism, Jerusha and Virgil Barber had been granted a formal separation so the latter could enter the priesthood.[15] Saint Jane de Chantal, the cofounder of the order with Saint Francis de Sales, had herself been a widow of noble rank in seventeenth-century France. The Visitandines therefore welcomed widows, and these women, who were often older and more experienced in the ways of the world, disproportionately found themselves in leadership positions in the convent.[16] Converts were also welcomed into Georgetown Visitation, as shown by the four on the list. As they were frequently better educated than most "cradle Catholics," converts, much like widows, often assumed leadership roles within the convent out of proportion to their actual numbers.[17]

In 1816, the same year its members officially affiliated with the Visitation Order, Georgetown Convent witnessed a surge in vocations. Eleven new members entered, a 50 percent increase in membership in a single year. But this bounty of new candidates proved a mixed blessing. As a result, Georgetown Visitation technically was in violation of its rule, specifically Constitution 1, which limited individual monasteries to no more than thirty-three members.[18] Indeed, Georgetown faced a growing new problem—overcrowding—that added stress to those living in enclosure and led to calls for expansion of the convent building in the next decade.

GEORGETOWN VISITATION AND THE MARYLAND TRADITION

The US Census of 1820 shows almost fifty members residing in Georgetown Visitation Convent, but also lists thirteen enslaved persons living on the convent's premises. The Wightt girls, therefore, had not only been born into a slaveholding family, they also grew up in a slaveholding convent community. Like most Catholics in the Archdiocese of Baltimore, there is no evidence that the Wightt sisters or any other Visitation nun ever questioned the institution of slavery. They certainly did not condemn slavery as an inherently sinful practice, as did Protestant denominations such as the Quakers and some members of evangelical sects like Methodists and Baptists. Reflecting paternalistic assumptions, the Visitandines accepted that slave owners had certain obligations toward their human chattel, just as the enslaved owed certain duties toward their enslavers. Neither as Pious Ladies nor as Visitandines did the Georgetown members demonstrate any guilt for holding fellow human beings in bondage, or even that they thought much about the "peculiar institution."[19]

Most of the monastery's property in human beings came from dowries that novices brought to the convent in lieu of a direct monetary payment. But the convent also sometimes purchased slaves for their own needs and purposes. For example, Mother Teresa Lalor asked Archbishop Maréchal to buy the wife of one of their faithful slaves to keep her from being sold away. But this purchase was not just a matter of compassion; it was also practicality. Lalor planned to hire the woman out and become a source of income to the convent: "She is Wife to our Servant George, who is very much distressed for fear she should be sold away."[20] She further explained, "He has been so faithful a servant to our late Venerable ABishop + continues so to us that we would wish to do every thing in our power for him." As for George's wife, Lalor later admitted, "We do not stand in need of her but if your Revd. thought well of us to buy her, . . . [we would] hire her out." Two weeks later Lalor was pleased to report that "we have purchased George's wife & children & got the necessary papers according to Law."[21]

The story these letters tell begs an important question: How could these women dedicate their lives to prayer and contemplation for the glory of God and at the same time enslave their fellow human beings? As followers of the Salesian tradition in Catholic religious life, the Sisters of the Visitation in America sought to fulfill the commission of their seventeenth-century cofounder Francis de Sales to "Live Jesus." As residents of the slaveholding South, however, members of the Visitation Order carried out that commission within a cultural context of the "Maryland tradition" in American Catholicism. The Visitation Order in America bore the stamp of the corporatist Maryland tradition in its Georgetown origins, in the family backgrounds of the majority of its early members, in the hierarchical relations found among its convent ranks, in the leadership Georgetown exported to new Visitation daughterhouses, and in how it engaged its non-Catholic neighbors through its mission of female education. In particular, a Southern identity and slaveholding culture were integral parts of the Maryland tradition that had developed within the original Georgetown motherhouse in the early 1800s, which was then disseminated as the order expanded during the antebellum years.[22]

Before the Civil War at least 482 women entered the six Visitation convents located in Maryland, Virginia, and the District of Columbia: Georgetown, Baltimore (est. 1837), Frederick (est. 1846), Wheeling (est. 1848), Washington (est. 1850), and Mount de Sales in Catonsville (est. 1852). Cross-checking data that is found in convent vow books against data in federal census schedules for 1850 and 1860 confirm the place of birth for 401

(83 percent) of these women.[23] Of this group of 401, 250 (62 percent) were American-born and 151 (38 percent) were foreign-born, with all but four of the latter born in Europe. Among the 250 native-born Visitandines, the state of Maryland provided 126 women, half of the total. Second to Maryland was the District of Columbia, with 16 percent, followed by Pennsylvania with 14 percent and Virginia with 7 percent. Together these four places supplied 87 percent of the American-born Visitandines residing in these six convents, showing that the order was highly dependent on the states in the immediate vicinity to provide its members. Among immigrant nuns, the overwhelming majority—84 percent—were Irish-born; the next-largest group, from Germany, made up only about 6 percent of the total. Some native-born women were undoubtedly of Irish or German stock, that is, daughters of an immigrant parent or parents. Nevertheless, most American-born Visitation nuns came from the old English-Catholic element of rural Maryland, Pennsylvania, and Virginia that had socially and culturally dominated the Catholic community in colonial America. As church historian Thomas McAvoy first argued three-quarters of a century ago, this relatively small, native-born, English-Catholic group—which later scholars have styled the Maryland tradition—continued to be an important leavening agent within the Catholic minority in antebellum America.[24]

It bears mentioning that in its first two decades the membership of Georgetown Visitation Convent was even more skewed toward native-born women from the Chesapeake region. At least fifty-five women are known to have entered Georgetown by 1820. Of that group, the birthplace of thirty-nine (71 percent) could be identified; of that number, twenty-one (54 percent) hailed from Maryland and seven (18 percent) from the District of Columbia. Taken together, therefore, women who were native to either the Old Line State or the Federal District made up almost three-quarters of the convent membership for these years. Moreover, during that same period, only six (15 percent) of the Georgetown members were of foreign birth, all from Ireland. The demographic shift to a higher percentage of foreign-born nuns in Georgetown only came with the tide of immigrants from Ireland and Germany that began after 1830.[25]

VISITATION CONVENT HIERARCHY

Reflecting its seventeenth-century origins in the rigidly stratified society of Old Regime Europe, the Visitation Order in America also contained four distinct tiers, or ranks: choir, associate, lay, and out. The hierarchy found in

Visitation convents provides a rough gauge of the social origins of its members by their class and level of education. Curiously, this Old World hierarchy transplanted easily into the more democratic New World and appears to have been a key to the order's ability to appeal to women from across the social spectrum, and especially its acceptance in the South.[26] Numerous scholars of the Old South have documented the importance of race, class, and gender hierarchies in maintaining the patriarchal social order of the Old South.[27]

Making up the top rank in the convent—the one to which both Wightt girls belonged—choir sisters "included those employed in the sacred Office of the Choir[,] there to sing the Hours."[28] That is, the chief duties of choir sisters was to read and sing the Divine Office. Because they had to be literate, choir sisters drew their numbers disproportionately from native-born elite and middle-class families, whose daughters had had the greatest opportunities for education. Women who met the educational prerequisites of choir sisters but whose health or constitution was too delicate to perform all the duties of that rank (or a choir sister whose health had declined significantly) became associate sisters. In most other respects there was little significant difference between choir and associate sisters. Members from both ranks filled nearly all the important leadership positions within Visitation convents and academies.[29]

In contrast to choir and associate sisters, lay sisters had as their primary responsibilities the various manual chores associated with housekeeping, thus their alternate name of "domestic" sisters. In a variation on the Mary-Martha dichotomy found in the Gospel story, lay sisters performed the bulk of the muscle labor in the convent, thus freeing the choir and associate nuns to chant the Divine Office during prayer hours and attend to other management duties when not in prayer. As their tasks required the least amount of formal education, domestic sisters came chiefly from foreign-born and lower-class females in antebellum society. These women frequently could not read or write with proficiency, if at all. Lay sisters, as "sisters of the household," further lacked a voice in the government of the convent, and they were not allowed to request admission to the first or second rank. At the same time, the constitutions stipulated that lay sisters "shall in no way be treated differently from the others" as to their temporal needs and spiritual development.[30] Salesian Constitutions set a maximum number of thirty-three members for each monastery, "of whom twenty at least shall be Choir Sisters, and at most nine Associated, and four Lay Sisters," unless granted an episcopal dispensation.[31] Georgetown Monastery frequently had more than fifty women within its walls, but many of its daughter houses established in the antebellum era fell well below the maximum limit, especially in their early years. The economic necessities and sheer amount of work necessary to establish and maintain religious life during the first century of convent-building in America were such that choir sisters often joined in the domestic tasks that were theoretically reserved to lay sisters.

Of course, nothing prohibited a wealthy and genteel young lady from entering in the rank of a lay sister—ideally such selflessness could be an edifying example of humility to the rest of the religious community. In practice, however, this type of sacrifice seldom happened. The Visitation Order, like other sisterhoods, sought to employ the special talents of its members for the benefit of both the convent and the larger Catholic community. It would have been considered wasteful to have a woman with administrative, pedagogical, or leadership talents serve in the convent kitchen or laundry. Of the combined total of 152 lay and out sisters identified here, at least sixty-eight (nearly 45 percent) were illiterate, and the Visitandines did not attempt to educate them once they became members of the order. Examination of vow books shows that, when called upon to renew their vows, those nuns who originally could not sign their names continued to be unable to do so in subsequent years. The exigencies of establishing new Visitation colonies and of conducting elite academies and benevolent schools undoubtedly interfered with any opportunity to provide lay and out sisters with further education, even had that been a stated goal of the order; which it was not.

A fourth classification found among monastic orders like the Visitandines is that of out sisters, also known as "externs." Out sisters provided monasteries with indispensable services but lacked full membership in the sisterhood, living on convent grounds but in separate quarters outside the cloister. Because members of the other ranks—choir, associate, lay—could not leave the enclosure without special permission (except for duties in the academy), they relied on out sisters to handle tasks outside the cloister—answering the door, shopping at the market, accompanying students on walks and outings, and so forth. A convent was supposed to have no more than three out sisters at any given time. Compared with other Visitation nuns, the life of an out sister must have been relatively lonely. An out sister inhabited a sort of earthly limbo, having renounced the profane world but lacking full acceptance into the sacred one. An out sister waited more than two years before taking vows, called an oblation. As less than full members of the convent, out sisters' names were entered in the back of convent vow books, making them more likely to be overlooked by researchers. Moreover, it is likely that the names of out sisters who left convent life before oblation were never recorded in the vow books as members of the Visitation community. Some out sisters eventually gained full membership within the convent, almost always as lay sisters.[32]

The contrasting cases of two early aspirants to Georgetown—Mary Fenwick Neale and Margaret Connor—point to the linkage between a woman's class origins and her rank in a Visitation convent.[33] The former was a fifty-year-old widow, born Mary Fenwick, the daughter of an old Catholic family in St. Mary's County in southern Maryland who had married into the equally pious but even more prominent Neale clan of neighboring Charles County. In 1818 Neale petitioned to follow three of her daughters and a cousin into the Georgetown Convent as a choir sister. She easily gained acceptance for "her property far exceeds the portion of the house," and her good friend and relation Father Benedict J. Fenwick of St. Mary's County could testify to her good character. Already the biological mother of three Georgetown nuns, Neale in 1820 was elected mother superior of the entire community. She died in 1856 at age eighty-seven after nearly four decades with her "second family" in the Georgetown Convent.

Unlike Mary Fenwick Neale, Margaret Connor was a former pupil in Georgetown's benevolent school for girls. After rejecting several of Connor's petitions, Georgetown finally accepted her in 1818 because "from the increase of the community we stand much in need of lay sisters." Conner remained in Georgetown until her death in 1853 at age fifty-five. It bears noting that Connor had applied to become a lay sister but Georgetown did not arbitrarily assign her that rank because of her class affiliation. Convent authorities probably made clear that her appropriate station was as either a lay or an out sister, based upon her qualifications and the community's needs. Working-class females did not automatically serve as domestic sisters; some did gain admittance to the ranks of choir sisters if they had possessed the prerequisite skills.

The membership of the Visitation Order in the six convents sample reflects a strong association between ethnic background and social class. The vast majority of choir and associate sisters (82 percent) were native to the United States. The ranks of lay and out sisters, in contrast, were chiefly filled by women of foreign birth. Seventy-five percent of the sisters in the combined lower ranks were immigrants, most all from Ireland. The Visitation Order may have divided its members into unequal social ranks that reflected class and ethnic differences of the broader society, but those same members were united by a shared vision about the purpose and direction of a communal religious life. This vision required not only obedience and deference to convent authority but also to the mutual bonds of obligation and affection among members joined in spiritual sisterhood, with every sister called to contribute to the communal whole according to her particular talents and abilities. Georgetown Visitation sought to do just that with the Wightt sisters, each of whom demonstrated early signs of intellectual gifts.

"SISTER GETTY"

Recognizing Sister Mary Margaret's aptitude for mathematics from her student days, Georgetown leadership appointed her to revise their accounting procedures. "Because of her elegant hand writing," Mary Margaret "was appointed to care for the books of the monastery, which were in disorder."[34] In 1820, and though just nineteen years of age, Sister Mary Margaret also assumed the duties of mistress of novices. After the mother superior and assistant superior, the mistress of novices is the highest office in a Visitation monastery. The occupant of this position had the important task of the formation of new members. Sister Mary Margaret's appointment came in recognition of her great piety. Constitution 33 of the Visitation Order defines the qualities needed by the mistress of novices required for carrying out her important duties. She "must not only be discreet, gentle, and devout, but even gentleness, discretion, and devotion itself, that she may, with more than a mother's love, bring up her novices step by step to religious perfection, as the future spouses of the Son of God."[35]

Had Georgetown Visitation been longer established, it is unlikely that such a young and inexperienced nun would have been entrusted with such a significant and influential office. It is a sign of the opportunities for rapid advancement that a fledgling institution might offer a young and talented member. Tragically, Sister Mary Margaret's promising life was cut short the following year, when she succumbed to consumption, a common malady among members in the early years of Georgetown.[36] Her death left Sister Gertrude bereft of any surviving members of her immediate family and must have reinforced for her that her home was Georgetown Convent and her family, its members.

As in the case of Sister Mary Margaret, Georgetown Visitation's leadership acknowledged Sister Gertrude's obvious intellectual gifts and executive abilities. Unlike Mary Margaret, Gertrude's talents were not at first afforded a setting to be demonstrated to best effect. But she quickly became recognized as an "inspired teacher" in the school. Her popularity among her students and colleagues soon earned her the affectionate nickname "Sister Getty."[37] During this time (1817–22), teacher training and the academy's curriculum remained so basic that her natural pedagogical gifts lacked the scope to shine through. Fortunately, Sister Getty was still able to connect with her young charges in the academy.

This point is suggested by the earliest written communication we have by Sister Gertrude. It comes as an addendum to a letter penned in 1822 by Sister Jane Scholastica Neale to her young sister, Miss Eliza Neale, of Clement's Bay,

St. Mary's County, Maryland. In her letter Sister Jane warns Eliza that she is surrounded by temptations while living in the world. This admonition echoes an anecdote known from the life of Sister Mary Margaret Wightt. Neale also chides her younger sister for her jealousy and selfishness in complaining that Sister Gertrude had not answered her previous missives. Sister Gertrude, in response, felt impelled to respond directly to the criticism from her young friend. As this is the earliest document known to be written by Wightt, the contents are given in full:

> My Dear Eliza be sure I have not forgotten you tho' I own I have an indifferent memory as you have often heard me say. I feel as much love + interest for you as when you were here + I pray God to bless and protect you, think not hard of my seeming indifference in not answering your letter. I assure it was not for want of intention but of leisure. You well know that all our hours our well filled + it is rare for me that I find time to write to anyone; as *to writing to E. Neale*[,] I *have not nor* has she ever written to me[;] of course you may[.] I would not make the first advance in such an Occasion. I'm glad to hear that your health is better, + hope you will by your prudent care soon entirely recover. Take care also that you advance continually in the path of virtue, give not way to temptations to which you are exposed. Be faithful in following good inspirations, tractably take the advice of your true friends + be constant in the practice of your spiritual exercises. *Think frequently of death which thought will be of great service to you,* it *will show you the emptiness of all sublunary* things + make you set just value on time which if well managed will at the end of your mortal pilgrimage put you in possession of eternal Bliss which is the ardent wish of your Affectionate and loving Sister and Sincere and devoted friend,
>
> Sister Ann Gertrude Wightt
>
> I have you a long letter. My affect[tiona]te love to Caroline + Celestia Combs for whom I have much love and regard, Sr. Agatha sends her love to them also.[38]

This added note is revelatory of some of Sister Gertrude's views when she was a young nun and suggestive of her technique in handling her young charges in the academy. The nun begins by placating Eliza and reassuring her that she meant no offense for the delay in responding to her letter. She expresses her joy at hearing of Eliza's improving health, then uses the reference to physical health to introduce the topic of spiritual health, eventually offering some practical tips on how to avoid temptation in the world.

Again, as in the story about Susan Wightt being temporarily led into temptation by a childhood friend only to be forged into a stronger commitment to a vocation from the experience, we can see from Sister Gertrude's admonishments to her young friend that she had imbibed the Visitandine emphasis on the world as a threat to salvation and the monastery as a haven from those dangers. In closing, she reassures Eliza of her continuing love and devotion, signing herself as "your Affectionate and loving Sister and Sincere and devoted friend." In the postscript she promises a letter and asks to be remembered to the two biological sisters of her colleague Sister Ann Agatha Combs, another native of southern Maryland. Interestingly, she signs herself with the formal "Sister Ann Gertrude Wightt" rather than the informal Sister Getty that the students and sisters called her.[39] Perhaps this is because the note is a reprimand even as it is conciliatory. Eliza Neale must have taken her gentle chastisement in good spirit. The following year it was Sister Gertrude's young friend begging pardon for falling behind in their correspondence. In another letter to her young sister, Sister Jane Scholastica passed along a message from Sister Gertrude that Eliza "need not be uneasy for not having written to her" as "she knows you were not able."[40]

TEACHER TRAINING

While it may have been key to her popularity as a teacher, Sister Gertrude's ability to relate personally to her pupils was less important to their parents than her mastery of the content and technique expected of a proficient instructor. Sister Gertrude further developed and honed her teaching skills as a member of the group of young teaching sisters trained under the tutelage of Father Joseph Clorivière and Sister Mary Augustine Barber, more commonly known as Sister Mary Austin, an anglicization of "Augustine."

Joseph-Pierre Picot de Clorivière was born in 1768 to an aristocratic family in Brittany, France. As a young royalist military officer, Clorivière opposed both the French Revolution and the rise of Napoleon Bonaparte. Forced to leave his homeland after participating in a failed plot to assassinate the French emperor, Clorivière eventually made his way to the United States and entered the Seminary of St. Sulpice in Baltimore. Following ordination in 1812, Father Clorivière's first assignment was St. Mary's Church in Charleston, South Carolina. There the French assistant soon clashed with his Irish pastor, Father Simon Felix Galagher. In addition, Clorivière's authoritarian views and policies conflicted with the more republican sentiments of the parish's lay trustees. In 1819 Father Clorivière welcomed an appointment as spiritual director

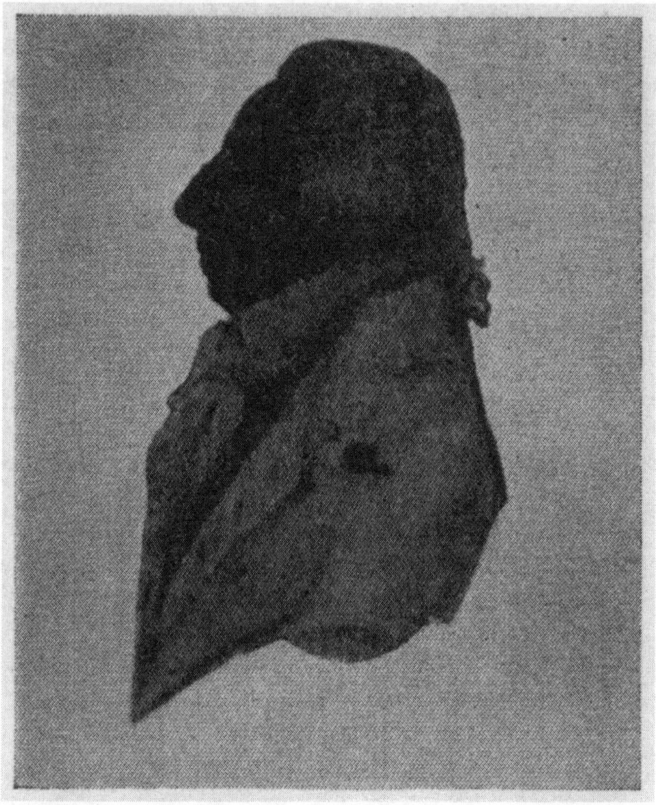

FIGURE 2.1. Silhouette of Joseph-Pierre Picot de Limoelan de Clorivière. Artist unknown, undated. Courtesy Georgetown Visitation Monastery Archives, Washington, DC.

of Georgetown Visitation Convent. For his service in steering the monastery and school through perilous times of the early 1820s, Georgetown Visitation remembers Father Clorivière as its second founder.[41]

Born Jerusha Booth in Newtown, Connecticut, in 1791, Sister Mary Austin had been a young wife and mother of five children. Prior to entering the convent, Jerusha had established and led a successful female seminary, or girls' school, with her husband, Virgil Barber, an Episcopalian priest, in Fairfield, New York. The entire Barber family converted to Catholicism in 1816. The following year, Virgil felt a call to the Catholic priesthood and the couple separated. Jerusha then entered Georgetown Convent in 1817. Three of her young daughters enrolled in its boarding school, and a baby girl lived with her in the convent, while a son attended Georgetown College next door. After her religious profession in 1820, Sister Mary Austin's experience as an educator led to her appointment as mistress of pensioners (boarders).[42] In tandem with Father Clorivière, Barber worked tirelessly to upgrade the academy's curriculum, its instruction facilities, and the training of its teachers.

The impetus for these improvements to the school came in response to declining enrollments in the academy in the early 1820s, brought on locally by competition from non-Catholic female seminaries and nationally by depressed economic conditions ushered in following the financial panic of 1819. Parents withdrew their daughters from the school and by 1820 the academy had only sixteen paying students. Since the school was the main source of income for the sisters, the loss of students threatened the existence of not only the school but also the convent.[43]

In response, Clorivière and Sister Mary Austin in 1822 assembled and published the academy's first prospectus and began erection of a new school building to replace the embarrassingly dilapidated old academy building. The revamped curriculum itemized not only the usual four Rs of reading, writing, arithmetic, and religion, but also English grammar and composition, history, and geography. There was also a nod toward the view of female education as preparation for future domesticity, with the inclusion of "plain and ornamental needlework." Tuition for boarders rose from $137.50 to $150.00 per year, while parents of day students paid $6 per quarter for the junior classes, and $8 for the senior classes. The new academy building was completed by November 1823 and occupied in time for the Christmas observances the next month. The building program and curriculum revisions made the school more attractive to parents seeking a quality education for their daughters. While costly and contributing to the debt of the convent in the lean years of the early 1820s, these changes also helped raise the standards of the academy's curriculum, its physical plant, and its teaching regimen, which together eventually spurred the turnaround in enrollments from sixteen students in 1820 to forty-eight by 1826.[44]

Moreover, to save their convent and school, convent leaders tapped additional streams of revenue. Father Clorivière pledged the proceeds from his military pension and from the sale of his family estates in France. But these funds were tied up in litigation abroad for a few years before becoming available. In the meantime, the convent began to sell some of its real property in the neighborhood. Anticipating the Jesuits' sale of their human property to save Georgetown College in 1838, Mother Agnes Brent and other superiors oversaw the sale of twenty-one enslaved people and the hiring out of others between 1819 and 1822.[45]

FIGURE 2.2. Engraving of Georgetown Convent of the Visitation, ca. 1822. Courtesy Georgetown Visitation Monastery Archives, Washington, DC.

SISTER COUNSELLOR

As Sister Gertrude sharpened and polished her pedagogical skills under the supervision of Father Clorivière and Sister Mary Austin, her executive potential fueled her rapid rise to leadership positions in the convent. In 1823 she gained appointment as one of four counsellors to the mother superior. Counsellor sisters, along with the assistant superior, advised the superior and were also known as the superior's coadjutrixes.[46] According to Constitution 30, the superior "upon her election is, before anything else, to choose four sisters, whom she shall judge most suitable to give her counsel as occasion requires."[47] Furthermore, the superior should "generally confer every fortnight on the affairs, both temporal and spiritual, of the House." Once chosen, the assistant and the four counsellors had to be confirmed by a vote of at least two-thirds of the chapter, or others were to be proposed by the superior.[48] Along with the assistant superior, the counsellors advised the superior in making all major decisions and how best to carry out all policies affecting the community. The superior and her counsellors did so, often without consulting or informing the other sisters.

Only twenty-four years old at her elevation, Sister Gertrude was by far the youngest nun among the group of official advisors to the superior. The assistant superior, Sister Catherine Corish, a forty-seven-year-old widow, was the nearest in age to Wightt. The other members of the council were Sister Teresa Lalor, one of the three original Pious Ladies and Georgetown's first superior, age fifty-eight; Sister Mary de Sales Neale, a widow with three daughters in Georgetown Convent and another former superior, age fifty-five; and Sister Mary Aloysia Neale, the first postulant to join the original Pious Ladies in 1801, age forty-nine.[49] A brilliant representative of the second generation of nuns, Sister Gertrude's appointment suggests convent authorities were grooming her for future leadership positions. Along with the election of Mother Mary Agnes Brent in 1821 (then age twenty-five), and of Mother Mary Juliana Matthews in 1825 (age thirty), the appointment of Sister Gertrude in 1823 at age twenty-four marked the symbolic passing of the torch of leadership of Georgetown Visitation to a new generation.

3

We Cannot Long Subsist as We Are

On October 30, 1823, Mother Agnes Brent disclosed to Archbishop Ambrose Maréchal that a long-brewing financial crisis was threatening to put an end to the struggling Visitation convent in Georgetown. Starting with the Panic of 1819, the convent's debts had mounted to such a point that the convent's spiritual director, Father Joseph de Clorivière had recommended that some of the nuns return to their families. Brent told the prelate that this plan was "not agreeable to me or my Counsellors," among them Sister Gertrude Wightt. The superior expressed to the archbishop that following such a strategy would have dire spiritual and material consequences for the convent's members. For, "being bound by solemn Vows," the nuns "could not go out in this manner." And their families "could sue our Monastery for the dowries they brought and thus sink us deeper in debt."[1] As an alternative strategy, she and her counsellors proposed that the order accept the offer of Father Francis Neale to found a Visitation colony in Port Tobacco, St. Mary's County, Maryland. This plan, she enjoined, would be more in line with the Visitation Rule than Clorivière's proposal.

In this same letter Mother Agnes further pointed out that the number of nuns in the monastery had grown too large to live on its income, especially during the exceptionally hard times they were undergoing. She noted that the current convent membership of forty-six "far exceeds the number 33 mentioned in our constitutions," and "it is our belief that unless we are faithful to our observances . . . the blessings of God will never attend us." Brent also saw the finger of God present in their current misfortunes: "He may have permitted us to come to this to prove how far we are from being real Religious of our Order."

"Our ordinary expenses per ann. are never less than $5500," Brent revealed to Maréchal. But their regular revenue streams did not begin to cover those bills. "Our yearly income from rents [of houses], bonds, notes, and hires of negroes should be $1433.06," but, she lamented, "we do not get a third of it." The academy brought in only "about $1000" because of declining enrollments, while the poor school was "a real expense." Outstanding debts owed on the recently constructed church, groceries, and medical expenses amounted to more than $2,000.

Mother Agnes again used this opportunity to lobby the archbishop, over the objections of the convent's spiritual director, for permission to send a few nuns to observe some Visitation monasteries in England or on the Continent. "Our motive," she revealed, was that after "having seen the observances of our Institute practised we might . . . with some confidence begin to form other houses and thereby lessen the expence of this [house]." "It is quite evident that we cannot long subsist as we are," Brent concluded, "but may God forbid that we should be turned again into a wicked world, which we have so absolutely renounced, we would a thousand times prefer to die together from hunger, than take such a step."

Mother Agnes penned this missive when Georgetown Visitation was just entering the period—fall 1823 to spring 1824—that marked the low ebb of its fortunes. She not only described the immediate financial distress plaguing the monastery, but she also hinted at the main sources of the dissension in the community: overcrowding in the convent, the unclear role of the academy, the influence of a male spiritual director, and uncertainty about how to live as authentic Visitation nuns. Sister Gertrude directly experienced these conflicts, first as a young instructor in the academy and then as a member of the group of the convent's four counsellors. These difficult times shaped her view of convent life and how best to maintain it in the future. By mid-decade the faction to which Sister Gertrude belonged had gained power, leading to her assumption of major leadership positions in both the convent and the academy. Indeed, she emerged as a strong candidate to become the next mother superior.

RISE OF CONVENT FACTIONS

The most important organizational question facing the Pious Ladies who had established Georgetown Convent in the years after 1799 was whether and when they would leave the limbo of an undefined religious life and become a recognized religious order of the Catholic Church that followed an authentic rule and constitution. Notification of Georgetown's official affiliation with the Visitation Order in 1816 at last gave the Pious Ladies that long-desired status. But in answering this one question, the formal recognition as a Visitation house ironically raised a new set of questions just as troubling. Foremost among these was how they were to live authentically according to the rule and constitution of the order when they had no human models to emulate. Anxiety over this question led the entire Georgetown community and many individual nuns to grapple with an ongoing "struggle for legitimacy in the American context," as the religious studies scholar Marie Pagliarini has termed it.[2]

From convent books and other documents in the archives, Pagliarini reconstructed the *horarium* (the normal daily schedule) that was followed in the Georgetown convent:

Horarium
5:00–5:30 a.m.: Rise; Morning exercise (series of prayers and meditations)
5:30–6:30 a.m.: Adoration of the Blessed Sacrament; Morning meditation; Mental prayer
6:30–8:00 a.m.: Prime; Mass; Work
8:00–10:00 a.m.: Terce; Sext; None; Examination of conscience; Work
10:00–11:00 a.m.: Dinner
11:00 a.m.–12:00 p.m.: Recreation
12:00–2:00 p.m.: Obediences given (work assigned for the remainder of the day); Work
2:00–2:30 p.m.: Repose
2:30–3:00 p.m.: Spiritual reading; Prayer
3:00–5:00 p.m.: Vespers; Communal work in Workroom and conversation on spiritual reading
5:00–5:30 p.m.: Compline; Litanies
5:30–6:00 p.m.: Mental prayer; Physical exercise
6:00–8:30 p.m.: Supper; Recreation; Obediences given (work assigned for the following day until noon)
8:30–10:00 p.m.: Matins; Examination of conscience; Lauds; Retire[3]

From the date Georgetown Convent was recognized as a house of the Visitation Order, the academy emerged as a source of tension, if not outright conflict, among the sisters, especially as to how to run the school and still follow the horarium. Recognizing the unique religious and political conditions present in the United States, which differed greatly from those in Catholic countries in Europe, in 1816 Archbishop Leonard Neale had obtained a papal indult from Pius VII that permitted Georgetown to make certain adaptations to the Visitation Rule. For example, lack of state support to Catholic institutions in America required running an academy serving both day scholars and boarders. Only the latter were enrolled in European houses. But how many such changes could be implemented without tainting the authenticity of the Visitation Rule as practiced in Europe?

As a result, many members of Georgetown worried about the legitimacy of their foundation, especially because it lacked any direct guidance by nuns from Europe. Some of Georgetown's nuns, perhaps a majority, yearned for a more "authentic," contemplative religious life that followed the Visitation Rule in accord with Old World practices and with minimal concessions to New World realities.[4] Other nuns, such as Sister Gertrude and Sister Mary Austin, favored further adapting the Visitation Rule to unique American conditions in recognition of how essential the income generated by the academy was to the survival of the convent. Wightt saw the school as a necessary means to achieving the semicontemplative life the Visitandines sought to follow.

Shortly after Pope Pius VII issued the indult recognizing it as a Visitation monastery, Georgetown Convent's leaders began to complain to the archbishop of Baltimore about the rise of factions within the community. Several contested issues divided the community during the next decade and longer. These included the question of clerical authority within the convent; a financial crisis stemming from both declining enrollments in the academy; overcrowding in the convent; and an ambitious but costly building program for the school and convent grounds. Overarching all these issues, moreover, were members' anxieties about their "authenticity" as Visitation nuns. Mother Agnes best summed these communal fears when she told Archbishop Maréchal, "Really almost all know & feel with regret that they are far from being true religious."[5]

Half a century ago the pioneering historian of women religious Mary Ewens documented that concerns about legitimacy in nineteenth-century convents were ubiquitous and hardly unique to members of the Visitation Order. All orders and congregations of women religious in the United States tended to identify European communities as the ideal and worried that American convents were but pale imitations of "real" religious life.[6] In thinking this way, American nuns paralleled a similar sense of inferiority to European models felt by early American artists, musicians, and writers of that time.

Georgetown Visitandines were unique among all other female religious in America with solemn vows, however, in that their foundation was not made by professed members from a European convent. As a result, the members of Georgetown Visitation were especially insecure about the legitimacy of their foundation—even though they had obtained papal approval and recognition from the original Visitation motherhouse in Annecy. Soon after affiliating with the Visitation Order, Georgetown sought to alleviate these uncertainties by attempting to bring over Visitation nuns from England and the Continent to serve as living models of the rules and constitutions, which they could only imperfectly follow from books in translation. Failing that scheme, Georgetown periodically sought to send a few members abroad to observe practices in some Visitation monasteries in Europe. This "struggle for legitimacy" would continue to trouble members of Visitation convents throughout the century.[7]

Over its first fifteen years as a Visitation house, in particular, Georgetown Convent faced layers of issues—administrative, financial, communal, and spiritual—that divided the community. Initial tensions arose over alleged interference in the inner workings of the convent by the spiritual directors who succeeded Archbishop Neale. These problems intensified due to the instability in the office of superior among the successors to Mother Teresa Lalor after she stepped down in 1819. Further stoking dissension were mounting financial problems in the wake of the country's Panic of 1819. Moreover, many of the nuns saw the academy as a sort of necessary evil. The income derived from school tuition was a necessity to the material survival of the community, but the compromises involved in keeping an academy running also made it an "evil" that interfered with a cloistered and truly contemplative life. Underlying all of these internal and external issues was the ongoing struggle for legitimacy within the community.

These internal divisions did not reflect well upon the monastery, and the convent annals and works based on them, like George and Rose Lathrop's *A Story of Courage*, fail to acknowledge the reality of this disunity, let alone try to account for it. As is implied by the title of their volume, the Lathrops were less interested in uncovering a "warts and all" history of the monastery's founding years, than crafting an uplifting "story of courage" that would stress the community as a model of collective sacrifice, selflessness, and harmony. Likewise, Eleanore Sullivan's history makes no mention of the disharmony present in the Georgetown community in the 1820s.[8]

In particular, all three of these works reflect a tendency commonly found in the historiography of communities of women religious, which historian Margaret Thompson identifies as "mythistory." Thompson contends that "the presumed audience for congregational histories [of women religious] were the sisters themselves and those who shared both their piety and their presumptions about religious virtue." She quotes the late historian Barbara Misner to the effect that such works are "characterized chiefly by a desire to edify and inspire."[9]

JOSEPH DE CLORIVIÈRE AS SPIRITUAL DIRECTOR

The private correspondence between the Georgetown superiors and episcopal leadership in Baltimore, however, paints a portrait of tensions, factions, and conflicts during the first decade and a half of Georgetown Visitation. An early example appeared in June 1818, in a letter from Mother Teresa to Archbishop Maréchal, asking for his support in preventing Father Francis Neale, then the convent's confessor, from managing the convent's temporal affairs. Specifically, Lalor pointed to Neale's interference in the dowry of the novice Sister Clare Agnes (Catherine Lancaster).[10] Maréchal recorded that he "tried to obviate some difficulties existing between the community & the Revd. Mr. F. Neale."[11] The following month Lalor reported that Father Neale had left as confessor to the nuns. and she begged the archbishop to appoint a replacement. She commented that things were now calm in the house because, other than the counsellors and herself, the rest of the community "know nothing of the storm that has been the month past."[12] This last comment demonstrates that convent leadership's tendency to act in a paternalistic fashion on behalf of the entire community without informing all the members.

Late that October, Lalor gratefully acknowledged the arrival of the French Sulpician Joseph de Clorivière, to assume the position of spiritual director.[13] Nonetheless, the following June, Sister Mary Frances McDermott, long-time assistant superior and one of the original Pious Ladies, complained to Maréchal about Clorivière's "complete tyranny and oppression" in allowing visitors within the enclosure without the permission of the prelate and contrary to the Visitation Rule.[14] McDermott simply registered the first of a steady stream of complaints from some of the nuns about Father Clorivière. During the French priest's eight-year tenure as Georgetown Visitation's spiritual director, Maréchal periodically received letters from the convent that alleged Clorivière's interference in the temporal governing of the house and his high-handed flouting of the Visitation Rule in the process.

Of course, nuns registering complaints to church authorities about alleged interference by clergymen was hardly new or unique to the Georgetown Visitandines. At the same time, Georgetown was perhaps particularly sensitive to potential violations of their rule, since none of them had ever witnessed its correct practice. The American house of the Visitation was unique in having gained knowledge of their rule only by word and not by deed. That is, they knew of it only from reading the printed page but not from witnessing its actual practice, as in Europe. This uncertainty about the correct practice of the rule translated into increased anxiety among the nuns on how to best carry out its spirit. This uncertainty and anxiety in turn fostered specific disagreements, continuing conflict, and the development of factions among the members. One of the institutional bulwarks in place in Visitation monasteries to minimize conflict within the community was the obedience and deference owed by the nuns to their elected superior. Unfortunately, instability in the office of superior in the early 1820s only served to disrupt conditions in Georgetown Convent.

YEAR OF THE THREE SUPERIORS: DECEMBER 1820 TO DECEMBER 1821

Disagreements over the proper role and responsibilities of the convent's male spiritual director was just one of the issues that revealed division among its members. Contributing to the tensions was the lack of stability at the top. Between December 1820 and December 1821 the office of superior was occupied by three different women. Mother Catherine Rigden (May 27, 1819–December 21, 1820) died after serving only twenty months, and appears to have been incapacitated for much of that time. Mother Mary de Sales Neale (December 28, 1820–December 13, 1821) found the financial problems and factionalism within the community beyond her talents and resigned after only a year.[15] Unlike her two immediate predecessors, Mother Agnes Brent (December 19, 1821–October 7, 1825) did manage to serve a full term and even get reelected, only to be deposed less than five months into her second term. This frequent turnover at the top was due to both misfortune, as in the death of Rigden, and a reflection of the divisions within the ranks of the sisters. Factionalism and finances brought about Neale's resignation and Brent's deposition, and may have contributed to the death of Rigden, and perhaps even led to the paralytic stroke suffered by Clorivière in 1826.

Signs of internal tensions within the community had become more open during the brief tenure of Mother Catherine Rigden, who succeeded Mother Teresa in May 1819. A former resident of Washington, DC, Rigden was a convert to Catholicism and had attended the academy of the Pious Ladies. Prior to entering the convent, she broke an engagement for marriage contracted by her parents. They had in turn objected to her entrance. In 1808, at age twenty-six, she became the sixth member of the Pious Ladies. Rigden served as directress of the academy before her election as superior when she was around thirty-seven years old. She was the second superior of Georgetown Visitation, and the first to be born in the United States.[16]

Sadly for all, Mother Catherine fell seriously ill after only six months into what should have been a three-year term. Her protracted illness was likely a case of consumption, an all-too-frequent disease plaguing the early Visitandines. Whatever the actual diagnosis, the malady prevented her from carrying out the full duties of her office, leaving the community "almost like a body without a head."[17] As a result, Mother Catherine's subordinates assumed most of the actual daily governance of the convent. In mid-March 1820, Sister Eleanor de Sales Miles, the assistant superior, wrote on behalf of Rigden to Maréchal to alert him to a growing spirit of disunity within the community since his most recent visit the previous summer. Sister Eleanor requested that the archbishop come to Georgetown and correct the situation. At the same time, she asked him to keep her letter a secret.[18]

The following month, Sister Mary Magdalen Neale, one of the four counsellors to the ailing superior, lamented the "continuing spirit of party and disunion" in the community. Sister Magdalen repeated Sister Eleanor's petition that Maréchal visit the convent and settle the divisions. As Miles had done, Sister Magdalen begged him to keep her letter secret.[19] In mid-May Sister Eleanor repeated her plea for the archbishop to visit and personally address the dissension. Moreover, she now named Father Clorivière as the source of the discontent: "It seems that our Spiritual Father is the cause of it," for "he has a party of the young sisters that act in every thing as they please."[20] She further alleged that "he makes a boast in saying he has the richest part of the Com[muni]ty at his side, meaning the greatest number, who I may say are Children." (Sister Gertrude Wightt was a member of this group of young nuns being influenced by Father Clorivière.) Sister Eleanor's charges against the group continued in her rather idiosyncratic spelling and grammar: "They act in everything as they please, & say they will obey but one Superior[.] [A]s for our dear and distressed Mothe[r] they find fault with her for every thing shea [*sic*] does and the Father reprimands her for every thing his party disproves of." Miles writes that Clorivière "says he is superior & he can change things & that he is to be obeyed before our Mother Supr, & that he will be respected." She concludes with a description of Clorivière's alleged mistreatment of the ailing Superior: "It is most certain if we continue as we are I think our dear Mother will soon leave us all for he keeps her in continual floods of tears, & it must be most distressing to us all to see her."

It must be noted that Sister Eleanor was not a disinterested party, and her reporting may have even been born of a personal grudge against Clorivière. She admitted that rather than supporting her nomination as assistant superior, the spiritual director had interfered in the election by promoting his own candidate, Sister Gonzaga Jones, which was a clear violation of the Visitation

Rules and Constitutions. Sister Eleanor likely took some satisfaction in relating that three rounds of voting were taken for Sister Gonzaga's candidacy, writing that "there were not near half in her favour," in the knowledge that a candidate "must have two thirds to establish her in that office."[21]

Mother Catherine lingered through the summer and fall, until passing away on December 21. In a special election granted by episcopal dispensation and held three days after Christmas, the members chose Sister Mary de Sales Neale as Catherine's successor. Neale was born into the Fenwick clan, one of the English Catholic families that landed in southern Maryland aboard *The Ark* and *The Dove* in the seventeenth century. She became a member of the even more prestigious Neale family upon marriage to Jeremiah Neale. Sister Mary de Sales entered Georgetown in 1818 "at [the] advanced age" of fifty, some three years after the death of her husband. She joined her three daughters, Caroline (Sister Mary Clementina), Jenny (Sister Mary Frances), and Olivia (Sister Mary Sylvia), all of whom had preceded her into the Visitandines.[22] In the election, Mother de Sales may have been a compromise candidate who appealed broadly to the two dominant factions without alienating either. Her personal humility, her advanced age and long experience in the world (which encouraged deference), her widow status, and her kinship by blood or marriage to several of the members all made Neale a consensus candidate. Even the fact that she had been in the community only three years may have been a plus, as she may not have been there long enough to antagonize or alienate many of its polarized membership.

After only a few weeks into her term, however, Mother de Sales wrote to Maréchal to apologize for her previous lack of submission and obedience. She now believed the disunity in the house was her own fault. Her admission of guilt is rather oblique and unspecific regarding the disobedient behaviors to which she was confessing.[23] Maréchal's reply also did not provide any concrete details. After serving as superior for just shy of a full year, Mother de Sales resigned on December 13. In the face of the poverty and disunity present in the community, she felt overwhelmed by the responsibilities of her office. As the convent annals record in their typical cryptic fashion, "The condition of the House at this time was more than the new Mother could bear, so that after a year . . . she begged to be discharged."[24]

Six days after the resignation of Mother de Sales, Georgetown Visitation, having obtained yet another dispensation from the archbishop, held yet another election for superior. This time the vote announced Sister Agnes Brent as the fourth superior of Georgetown. More ominously, Mother Agnes was the third woman to hold the office in less than a full calendar year.

Like her predecessor, Mother Agnes's kinship ties appeared to have counted heavily in her favor. Brent was the daughter of yet another prominent old English Catholic family from St. Mary's County, the "cradle of Catholicity" in colonial Maryland. She was also the grand-niece of Archbishop Leonard Neale. After attending the academy, she entered the convent of the Pious Ladies in 1812. Along with Teresa Lalor and Frances McDermott, Brent had been one of the first three members to profess solemn vows as Visitation nuns in December 1816. She assumed the office of superior when just twenty-five years of age.[25]

In contrast to the correspondence of convent leaders with the archbishop, the official circular letter of 1822 sent out by Georgetown to sister houses of the Visitation Order sketched a highly positive portrait of Father Clorivière's role as spiritual director. "He has done + still continues to do for us more than it would be possible in the limits of a letter to state," the circular affirms. "He animates, encourages + assists us in every thing; in a word he is a true father + makes our interests his own."[26] It appears that convent leaders wished to publicly portray an image of harmony that contrasted greatly with the private realities inside the convent. Or perhaps Father Clorivière reviewed and "adjusted" the letter before it was sent to Annecy.

When recording the convent annals in the second half of the nineteenth century, Sister Josephine Barber expressed similar lofty sentiments about Clorivière's influence. Indeed, the convent chronicles assert that it was under Clorivière's direction that Georgetown began to follow the forms of a true Visitation house. He did so "by daily translating & explaining a portion of the Rules, Customs & Ceremonial; also in practicing the chant of the Office & Gregorian music & hymns for Benediction, the Office of Holy Week."[27] Moreover, Clorivière translated other documents and informed the community about "what is prescribed for Annual Chapter, the Annual Visit, triennial elections &c, telling them the necessity of changing their Mother Superior every three or six years." The late founder of Georgetown Convent, Archbishop Leonard Neale, "had never spoken on this point[,] having no occasion to do so, as we had not been recognized as Visitation Sisters prior to the indult of Pius VII."

In December 1822, however, Mother Agnes Brent warned Maréchal that Clorivière wanted to employ the convent's out sisters to open a school for the poor in Washington City. Brent also noted that their school, already under-enrolled, was facing competition from non-Catholic female seminaries as well as an academy recently opened in Washington City by the Sisters of Charity. She asked the archbishop to keep the contents of her letter from Clorivière.[28]

THE NADIR: FALL 1823 TO SPRING 1824

Tensions between Mother Agnes and Father Clorivière, along with the factions of their respective supporters, worsened the following year as the financial problems facing the community deepened to crisis. No matter how beneficial, the improvements to the school and grounds by themselves were insufficient to save the school and convent from impending ruin. Indeed, the building program embarked on by Clorivière extended the convent's economic burden long after the country itself had recovered from the depressed conditions that followed the Panic of 1819. The convent's financial situation therefore continued to worsen as the nuns welcomed in the new year of 1823. On January 6, the Feast of the Epiphany, Mother Agnes wrote to Maréchal requesting permission for three nuns to visit a Visitation convent in England to observe the practice of the rule. This request reflected the nuns' concerns not only over their convent's material conditions but also about their spiritual adherence to the Visitation Rule and living an authentic Salesian life.[29]

In March and again in April, Brent followed up her earlier request to Maréchal by telling of Clorivière's unyielding opposition to sending nuns to England or having any European nuns come to Georgetown.[30] By the end of October Brent expressed to Maréchal her distress over the community's deteriorating financial situation and Clorivière's suggestion that the nuns return to their families. She delineated the means of convent income and their debts, and again asked permission to form a new branch of their community.[31] In early November, likely out of desperation, the assistant superior and the counsellors, among them Sister Gertrude, wrote to the archbishop and requested that some nuns be sent to one of their monasteries in Europe to assure the continuance of the Georgetown Convent. Clorivière, in contrast, wanted to send some professed nuns out of enclosure to earn money by teaching. Repeating her previous requests, Brent asked Maréchal to visit them to view the situation for himself.[32]

Immediately upon reception of the request sent by Sister Gertrude and the other counsellors, Maréchal wrote to Joseph-Octave Plessis, Archbishop of Quebec. He told Plessis about the financial crisis affecting Georgetown Convent. Maréchal reported that Archbishop Leonard Neale had established Georgetown Visitation with the understanding that the nuns could support themselves by running a boarding school and doing some sewing. Maréchal noted that the depressed economic conditions in the country, however, had severely reduced the income from these sources. In consequence, Maréchal asked Plessis to accept some Visitandines into his diocese.[33] Two weeks later Plessis replied, proposing to accept six Visitandines in each of two Ursuline convents located in Lower Canada.[34] The following week, Mother Agnes renewed her request to Maréchal to permit three nuns to go to England. Further, she reported that Father Clorivière had convinced the nuns to sell some of their real property over their protestations.[35]

In mid-December 1823 Plessis wrote to Maréchal and repeated his proposal to have Ursuline convents in his archdiocese provide hospitality to the Visitandines.[36] Maréchal replied to Plessis that until recently only the convent leadership—the spiritual director, the superior and her counsellors—had known of the "embarrassed condition of their finances," and, when informed of the dire situation, the rest of the community expressed a desire to die rather be scattered into the world.[37] Maréchal also petitioned Bishop Louis W. DuBourg of New Orleans to take some of the nuns, at least temporarily. In March the Ursuline Convent in the Crescent City pledged to accept "six choir nuns and two lay sisters" to ease Georgetown's burden.[38]

By May, Maréchal had become more optimistic. He told Plessis, "There is no longer any immediate necessity for these holy women to disperse."[39] This welcome change occurred in part because of funding delivered by a kind of deus ex machina in the form of John Baptist Lasala, a wealthy New York merchant. Lasala agreed to pay several years of tuition in advance for his three daughters and his younger sister to be long-term boarders at the academy. In addition, Clorivière pledged to Georgetown funds from his military pension and the proceeds from sale of his ancestral lands in France. Nonetheless, in early November 1824 Maréchal qualified his optimism, noting to Plessis that "I am still afraid that hunger may again force them to have recourse to their Canadian sisters."[40] Ultimately Maréchal's feared result did not come to pass, and the option of relying on an Ursuline safety valve was never exercised. Four years later, however, Sister Gertrude would revive the Ursuline option in a different form in her plan to secure the future of Georgetown Convent, even if not as a Visitation Convent.

DEPOSING A SUPERIOR

The following spring and summer, Georgetown Visitation faced a new threat when the convent became the target of local anti-Catholic sentiment. The entrance and reception of Wilhelmina Jones, the beautiful daughter of the naval hero Commodore Jacob Jones and a recent convert from the Episcopalian Church, triggered crowd protests outside the convent for several nights and hostile stories circulating in the national press much of that summer.[41] On August 15, 1825, Wilhelmina received the habit as a novice of the Visitation

FIGURE 3.1. List of Sisters of Georgetown Community of the Visitation of the Blessed Virgin Mary, 1825. Courtesy Georgetown Visitation Monastery Archives, Washington, DC.

Order and the name Sister Stanislaus. By that same year, if not before, Sister Gertrude had assumed the duties of directress of the academy, or mistress of classes, as the office is called in the List of Sisters for 1825. The opening of the new academy building in late summer of that year helped dispel negative publicity about Georgetown Convent and portended better times ahead.

Sister Gertrude led the sisters in welcoming parents, guardians, and other guests to tour the interior of the new building. Such gestures in savvy public relations worked to restore confidence in the school's future and helped diminish anti-Catholic prejudice at the same time.[42] It was also an early sign that Sister Gertrude took easily to being the gracious host at public gatherings and had a knack for entertaining guests in the process.

Mother Agnes had been reelected as superior the previous May, yet opposition to her governance of the convent surfaced soon thereafter. On September 15, Teresa Lalor, the assistant superior, along with the three counsellors Sister Mary Aloysia Neale, Sister Catherine F. Chantal Corish, and Sister Mary de Sales Neale, wrote to Maréchal for permission to hold a new election for superior. In so doing they were following the final step in the prescribed process for deposing a superior. Constitution 47 specifies that "if the Community ever make such a bad choice of a Superior, that she should deserve to be deposed before the time, the sisters who in conscience shall know that this ought to be done, should inform the Spiritual Father [Clorivière] of it, who should confer about it with the principal officers, and then with all the sisters." Furthermore, the community "should beg the Prelate [Maréchal] of the place to come to the assembly, or depute some person of consideration to be there; and in this third deliberation the deposition would be concluded . . . they then may proceed to the election of a new Superior."[43]

Mother Agnes was deposed as superior only about five months into her second term. Extant sources are frustratingly silent on the reasons behind the action, so we can only speculate as to why the community felt so impelled. Sister Gertrude's signature is no longer to be found among the four counsellors. Perhaps Mother Agnes removed Wightt as one of her counsellors because of the latter's likely sympathy with the Clorivière faction. Also missing was the name of Sister Juliana Matthews, "the assistant and now superior *pro tempore*," following the recent deposition of Mother Agnes, who was on retreat at the time. The counsellors pointed out that being left without a superior, "we feel the want of it, as no temporary Superiors can be so obeyed as a Mother, and all our affairs within and without will be better settled." Significantly, perhaps, the counsellors added, "This is the desire of our Spiritual Father" (i.e., Clorivière).[44]

On October 7, Sister Juliana Matthews, yet another scion of an old Maryland family, replaced Mother Agnes by vote of the members of the community. Father William Matthews, pastor of St. Patrick's Parish in Washington City, received the resignation of the outgoing superior.[45] Ironically, Father Matthews was also uncle to the incoming superior. Three weeks later, Mother Juliana warned Maréchal that the community's well-being seemed threatened by meddling priests who received wrong ideas from the recently deposed superior.

One of those "meddling priests" to whom Mother Juliana referred appears to have been Father Charles Neale, confessor to the Carmelite monastery in Port Tobacco, Maryland.[46] Mother Juliana closed by asking the archbishop to burn the letter after reading it.[47] This request echoes earlier ones made by previous superiors, suggesting the letter's contents would not be viewed favorably by many in the convent.[48] Clearly, the divisions within Georgetown Visitation had not disappeared with the removal of Mother Agnes.

BECOMING ASSISTANT SUPERIOR

The 1825–26 school year saw enrollments in the academy rise, promising a steady income stream to the convent. No sooner did the financial clouds hovering over the convent begin to dissipate than a health issue ushered in a new period of uncertainty. On May 6, 1826, Father Clorivière suffered a paralytic stroke, leaving him unable to speak. Mother Juliana informed Archbishop Maréchal of the debilitating effects on the spiritual director. She hoped that the circumstances of the previous autumn—the deposition of Mother Agnes—had not brought on his attack. Losing the full-time services of their spiritual director threatened to further destabilize the community. Nonetheless, Mother Juliana claimed to have the support of a majority of the members: "It is a consolation to me that the generality of the Community and the principal officers of the House," she reported to the archbishop, "are well affected towards Our Father." She continued, "The Assistant [Sister Gertrude] and Counsellours particularly are very united to us."[49] As when she was a member of the counsellors, Gertrude Wightt, at age twenty-seven, was much the youngest of the group: Sister Teresa, was age sixty-one; Sister Aloysia, fifty-two; Sister Chantal, fifty; Sister Agatha, thirty-five. Mother Juliana was then only thirty years old.

On September 20, 1826, Mother Juliana reported to Maréchal that Clorivière was on his deathbed and shared her concerns about the continuing lack of order and proper tranquility within the convent. She acknowledged that "for some years past there has existed among us a troublesome spirit." Yet, "certain it is (+ all unanimously affirm) that something damages the good order of the house."[50] Because Clorivière was incapable of carrying out his duties as spiritual director, and as "a masterly hand is requisite," Matthews petitioned the archbishop to appoint Father Michael Wheeler, an American Sulpician, as the temporary replacement for the incapacitated priest. Nine days later—almost six months after his stroke—Father Clorivière passed away.

The ascendancy of Mother Juliana and Father Wheeler proved to be good news for Sister Gertrude personally. Both the new superior and the new spiritual director held her in the highest regard. Sometime after her election as superior, Mother Juliana had nominated Sister Gertrude to hold a second key leadership position in the community—assistant superior of the convent. Wightt's appointment to the office of assistant superior required ratification by a vote of at least two-thirds of the community. Mother Juliana's choice of Sister Gertrude to hold both offices of assistant superior and directress of the academy indicates not only the esteem but also the confidence the superior placed in her. Indeed, Mother Juliana thereafter appears to have deferred to Wightt's judgment in all matters related to both the academy and the temporal affairs of the convent.

As assistant superior, Sister Gertrude not only served as subprioress for a community of almost sixty nuns and novices; she also continued to act as one of the chief advisors, along with the four counsellors, to the superior. Wightt remained the youngest member of that leadership group even though as directress of the academy she had the charge of almost fifty boarders and day students. In addition, during the first five years of her tenure, the total number of students more than doubled. As headmistress of the school, Sister Gertrude also acted as the main liaison between the convent community and the outside world. In carrying out her duties, Wightt often had direct contact with the parents and guardians of her students, typically in the convent parlors. As listed in the academy prospectus, one of her tasks as directress was to examine all "letters written or received" by the "young ladies."[51] This responsibility, though time-consuming, would have provided Sister Gertrude with an invaluable font of information about every student and her family members. As assistant superior she also served as the chief contact with government leaders—local and federal—over temporal dealings with the convent.

Holding these offices thus provided Sister Gertrude with a wide range of powers, responsibilities, and contacts in the convent, the school, and the wider community. Her positions also caused her to come into conflict with the three French-speaking Visitandines from the Continent when they arrived in the summer of 1829. The French Sisters came to Georgetown with a mission to bring the convent into conformity with the practices of Visitation monasteries in Europe. Sister Gertrude opposed that mission.

BEFRIENDING THE ITURBIDE FAMILY

In addition to assuming the offices of assistant superior of the convent and the directress of the academy, a third event in the mid-1820s proved momentous for Sister Gertrude. In 1826 Madame Ana Maria Huarte de Iturbide and her family, accompanied by their chaplain, Father José López, arrived in Georgetown after four years of exile from their homeland of Mexico. Madame Iturbide was the widow of the deposed and executed emperor of Mexico, General Agustín de Iturbide. The former empress took an apartment in Georgetown and enrolled her four daughters in Georgetown Visitation Young Ladies' Academy and her youngest son in the Jesuit-run Georgetown College next door. Madame Iturbide frequently stayed with the nuns in Georgetown Convent, where she had "a little cell, a seat in the choir, refectory &c, although she usually took her meals in private or with her daughters." While residing in the cloister, she stayed in a cell [room] and was permitted to wear a version of the Visitation habit. In return, the dowager empress donated to the convent some of "her husband's rich robes & regalia . . . being of costly material wrought in pure gold."[52]

From teaching and supervising the four boarding Iturbide daughters—Sabina, Juana de Dios, Josefa (called Josephine), and Maria de Jesus (called Isis)—Sister Gertrude became especially close to their mother and their confessor. Sister Gertrude's example, and that of the other Visitandines, had a large impact on the Iturbide princesses as well. On October 28, 1828, Juana (sometimes called Johanna) was clothed in the habit and took her vows as a Visitation sister on her deathbed. Juana died at age seventeen and was buried in a vault of the convent cemetery. The convent annalist records the event and adds, "Little more than a year later Sabina entered the novitiate, but remained only a short time."[53] Nevertheless, Sabina and Isis remained friends with Sister Gertrude for the rest of their lives. Moreover, the association of Wightt, Iturbide, and Lopez had major implications for the future of Georgetown Visitation Convent and its Young Ladies' Academy.

4

A Standard of Excellence Equal to Any in the Country

On September 8, 1828, Mother Juliana Matthews wrote to the Visitation Order's monastery in Annecy, informing the motherhouse about what had been happening with the American community since their last communication with Visitation houses in Europe more than six years before. After offering apologies for the lapse in communication, Mother Juliana expressed joy that her convent was now on sound financial footing and made clear that the primary reason for her convent's material turnaround was the growth and success of the Young Ladies' Academy. With 70 boarders and a like number of day students, tuition from the academy provided the principal annual support needed for the nearly 60 members of the convent. Academy tuition also helped fund a benevolent school, where some 150 girls from poor families were educated for free or for a nominal sum. Some of those enrolled in the benevolent school were the daughters of Irish and German immigrants. Surprisingly, the majority of these girls were from Protestant families, thus promising possible conversions as well.[1]

Mother Juliana readily identified the main force behind the positive change in fortunes of Georgetown Visitation: the two priests who had served as the convent's spiritual directors in the previous decade, recently deceased Father Joseph de Clorivière, and his successor, Father Michael Francis Wheeler. According to Matthews, curriculum reforms, land purchases, and building programs begun by Clorivière and expanded by Wheeler had made the Georgetown Young Ladies' Academy, especially its boarding school, the envy of its non-Catholic competitors. "Established as it is today," Mother Juliana boasted, "our boarding school will probably be able to maintain its superiority to all Protestant boarding schools in the United States, and to maintain the esteem and confidence of the various classes of society among the Protestants themselves."[2]

The current consideration is not to question the significant roles played by male clergymen in upgrading Georgetown Visitation Academy. Rather, it seeks to balance the historical record by revealing the equally important leadership of key women religious, in particular Sister Gertrude Wightt. Wightt served as directress of the academy from 1825 to 1831, the crucial years when the school was gaining a national reputation for training young women.

Sister Ann Gertrude Wightt was an important, but overlooked, female educator in the early American republic. She helped transform the school's curriculum and physical plant, established annual ceremonies and traditions, and promoted the school in the press, leading Georgetown Academy to earn a national reputation by the late 1820s. A review of Wightt's tenure as directress demonstrates that she was a visionary female educator worthy of comparison to her far-better-known Protestant contemporaries, Mary Lyon and Catharine Beecher.[3] At the same time, although highly popular among students and parents, the changes enacted under Sister Gertrude were not welcomed by all Georgetown nuns or nearby Catholic clergy. On the one hand, female critics inside the convent feared that Wightt's focus on the school distracted from the contemplative life of an enclosed monastery. On the other hand, male critics outside the convent contended that her ambitious upgrades to the school were financially ruinous to the convent. This opposition to her policies from both within and without is central to assessing and understanding Sister Gertrude's ultimate disillusionment with religious life and her sudden flight from the convent in 1831.

ISSUING THE 1827 PROSPECTUS

Sister Gertrude had first honed her natural talents as an instructor in the early 1820s when she was one of the young teaching sisters under the tutelage of Father Clorivière and Sister Mary Austin. Although everyone in the community recognized her pedagogical gifts, it was Sister Gertrude's executive abilities that led to her early grooming for leadership positions within the convent. As early as 1823 Wightt was appointed as one of the four counsellors to the convent superior and, at only twenty-four years old she was by far the youngest, with all of the others being at least twice her age.[4]

In 1825 Mother Agnes Brent appointed Sister Gertrude as directress of the academy. As headmistress of the school, Wightt worked closely with the mistress of pensioners, her former mentor, Sister Mary Austin, and with the new spiritual director, Father Michael Wheeler. Sometimes in tandem with Wheeler or Barber, and sometimes on her own, Wightt engaged in several initiatives to improve the school. Wightt spearheaded a thorough overhauling of the academy's curriculum and expanded a building program begun earlier in the decade with Father Clorivière. She also oversaw the purchase of additional property in the neighborhood, thereby significantly enlarging the grounds around the convent and school. Moreover, she initiated an unprecedented campaign in the national press that publicized the new buildings of Georgetown Convent, the attractions of its academy, and the accomplishments of its instructors and students.

In 1827, two years after Sister Gertrude had assumed the office of directress and a year after Father Wheeler became the convent's spiritual director, the academy produced a revamped (and more advanced) prospectus. Whereas the first school prospectus completed in 1822 was only one page in length, the 1827 prospectus went on for six.[5] The new curriculum expanded on the "basic subjects" listed in the 1822 curriculum, ascending to a higher level of liberal arts education: algebra; versification and poetic composition; vocal music and guitar; female elocution; logic, ethics, and metaphysics; natural philosophy in various branches; French, Spanish, Italian, and Latin; and popular astronomy at the recently completed Odeum and "with the assistance of the newly invented Geocyclic of Delamarche."[6] The attention to science was consistent with the trend taking hold in the most progressive female schools of the time. Historian Mary Kelley has also demonstrated the importance of writing and elocution classes that trained female students "to stand and speak," showing the importance of these skills for women's later participation in the benevolence, reform, and women's rights movements of the antebellum era.[7]

While Wightt, Barber, and Wheeler seem to have favored stressing the intellectual side of the curriculum, especially the sciences, they also had to bow to parental desires to prepare girls for future domestic roles as wives and mothers in middle- and upper-class homes. The 1827 prospectus announced that, in response to parental wishes that daughters be acquainted with "mantua work, to compose dress in its various forms," "such a course will be provided if required." Moreover, the then-new field of "domestic economy" was given "considered attention in the enlarged system of education."[8] By 1830 the *Georgetown Directory* was assuring parents that such "useful" subjects would not be neglected at the expense of ornamental pursuits: "In the course of studies pursued at the Ladies' Academy, domestic economy is embraced, and made the object of attention at the close of the literary career."[9] These studies included "the various exercises in Pastry and the Culinary Art, Laundry, Pantry, and Dairy Inspection etc. as conducted of the Academy of St. Denis Banlieu de Paris."[10] The French connection was an added attraction. Historian Rebecca Rogers argues that "beginning in the early decades of the century,

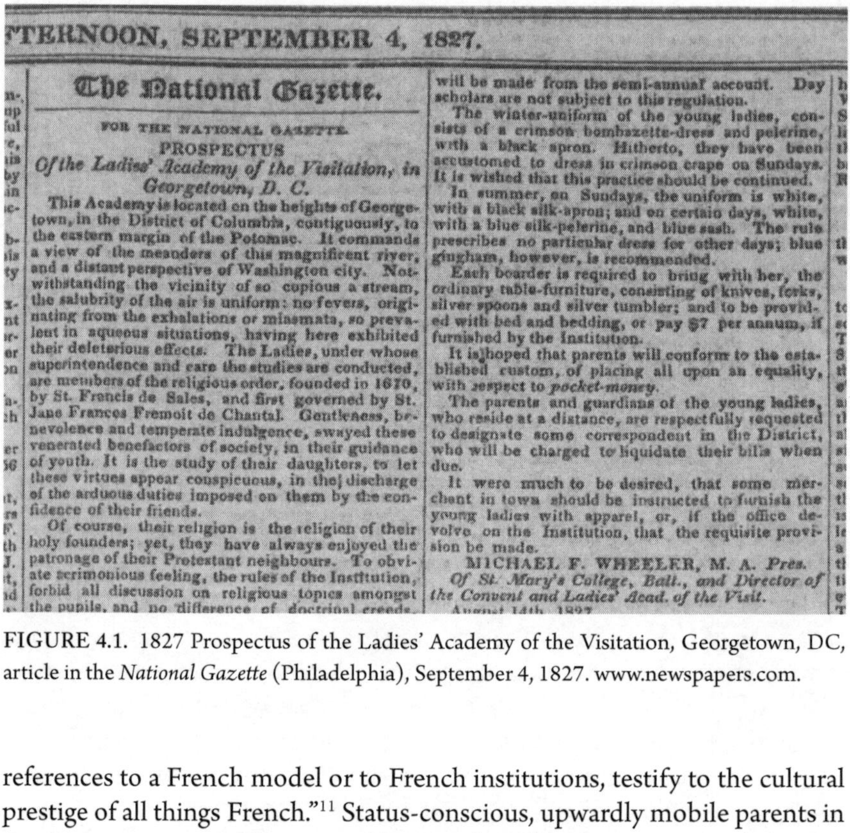

AFTERNOON, SEPTEMBER 4, 1827.

The National Gazette.

FOR THE NATIONAL GAZETTE.

PROSPECTUS

Of the Ladies' Academy of the Visitation, in Georgetown, D. C.

This Academy is located on the heights of Georgetown, in the District of Columbia, contiguously, to the eastern margin of the Potomac. It commands a view of the meanders of this magnificent river, and a distant perspective of Washington city. Notwithstanding the vicinity of so copious a stream, the salubrity of the air is uniform: no fevers, originating from the exhalations or miasmata, so prevalent in aqueous situations, having here exhibited their deleterious effects. The Ladies, under whose superintendence and care the studies are conducted, are members of the religious order, founded in 1610, by St. Francis de Sales, and first governed by St. Jane Frances Fremoit de Chantal. Gentleness, benevolence and temperate indulgence, swayed these venerated benefactors of society, in their guidance of youth. It is the study of their daughters, to let these virtues appear conspicuous, in the discharge of the arduous duties imposed on them by the confidence of their friends.

Of course, their religion is the religion of their holy founders; yet, they have always enjoyed the patronage of their Protestant neighbours. To obviate acrimonious feeling, the rules of the Institution, forbid all discussion on religious topics amongst the pupils, and no difference of doctrinal creeds-

will be made from the semi-annual account. Day scholars are not subject to this regulation.

The winter-uniform of the young ladies, consists of a crimson bombazette-dress and pelerine, with a black apron. Hitherto, they have been accustomed to dress in crimson crape on Sundays. It is wished that this practice should be continued.

In summer, on Sundays, the uniform is white, with a black silk-apron; and on certain days, white, with a blue silk-pelerine, and blue sash. The rule prescribes no particular dress for other days; blue gingham, however, is recommended.

Each boarder is required to bring with her, the ordinary table-furniture, consisting of knives, forks, silver spoons and silver tumbler; and to be provided with bed and bedding, or pay $7 per annum, if furnished by the Institution.

It is hoped that parents will conform to the established custom, of placing all upon an equality, with respect to *pocket-money*.

The parents and guardians of the young ladies, who reside at a distance, are respectfully requested to designate some correspondent in the District, who will be charged to liquidate their bills when due.

It were much to be desired, that some merchant in town should be instructed to furnish the young ladies with apparel, or, if the office devolve on the Institution, that the requisite provision be made.

MICHAEL F. WHEELER, M. A. *Pres.*

Of St. Mary's College, Balt., and Director of the Convent and Ladies' Acad. of the Visit.

FIGURE 4.1. 1827 Prospectus of the Ladies' Academy of the Visitation, Georgetown, DC, article in the *National Gazette* (Philadelphia), September 4, 1827. www.newspapers.com.

references to a French model or to French institutions, testify to the cultural prestige of all things French."[11] Status-conscious, upwardly mobile parents in America were especially susceptible to such Gallic lures.

The 1827 prospectus also announced not just greater systematization in the subjects taught, but also regulations regarding the ages and qualifications of students, and even a corresponding change in uniforms. This new prospectus set age limits for students for the first time: the minimum age for acceptance of new students was seven years, and the maximum age for entry into the senior class was fifteen. Advancement to the senior class now also required satisfactory completion of subjects of "Grammar, Geography, and Arithmetic," as well as composition and history. Despite all these improvements and rigorous requirements, annual tuition for boarders remained at $150.00, while day student tuition rose 25 percent, to $40.00 (paid annually, rather than by the quarter, as previously).[12] This change suggests the academy had a surfeit of day students but desired more "pensioners," or boarders, because those reaped more revenues. The 1827 prospectus, with only minor adjustments, served as the basic model for the next three decades, not only for Georgetown Academy but also directly and indirectly for the ten additional

Visitation academies established in seven different states and in the District of Columbia before the Civil War.[13]

The 1827 prospectus also announced the establishment of what would become a new tradition: the "annual recurrence of the examination and exhibition."[14] Thereafter, this annual public ceremony held in July marked the end of the school year and involved the distribution of "premiums" to worthy students who had demonstrated proficiency in various subjects. The ceremony helped promote the successful work of the academy, not only to the families of its scholars but also to the members of the broader Washington community who attended the festivities.

INCORPORATION OF GEORGETOWN VISITATION

On March 28, 1828, President John Quincy Adams signed into law an act of Congress to "incorporate the Sisters of Charity of Saint Joseph [in Emmitsburg, Maryland] and the Sisters of the Visitation of Georgetown in the District of Columbia."[15] The document lists all of the forty-five professed members of Georgetown Convent—including the two out sisters—by their given names rather than their names in religion. Sister Gertrude is erroneously recorded as "Ann Wright," getting the spelling of her last name wrong. Novices and postulants are not listed, however, as both groups had members not yet vowed to the institution. Under the provisions of the document, the listed women "and their successors" were thereby "made, declared, and constituted a corporation or body politic, in law and in fact, to have continuance forever by the name, style, and title of the Sisters of the Visitation." Section 3 of the charter vested in the corporation "all and singular lands, houses, tenements, rents, legacies, annuities, rights, property, privileges, goods, and chattels, heretofore given, granted, devised, or bequeathed to either of the said . . . Sisters of the Visitation."

Historians have demonstrated how important was the act of incorporation to the growth of female voluntary societies and thus the "origins of women's activism" in the early American republic. "Corporate status," historian Anne Boylan contends, "granted the collective female body a range of legal rights that none of the wives within it could claim individually, including the right to own property, bring legal suits, indenture minor children, invest funds, and control wages."[16] Orders and congregations of Catholic women religious by the 1820s began to apply for corporate charters from Congress and the legislatures of the states where they were established in order to have the same corporate rights that laywomen collectively were gaining for their organizations. "By granting these charters," notes historian Lori Ginzberg, "state legislators created a legally autonomous "person" who was, for all practical purpose, not female."[17] Just as obtaining corporate charters enabled the flourishing of voluntary associations of laywomen in antebellum America, so did the incorporation of female religious orders and congregations help launch the "convent revolution" in the nineteenth century by recognizing their legal status and protecting their financial viability.

Sister Gertrude played a central part in obtaining legal incorporation for the nuns of Georgetown Visitation. In her role as assistant superior of Visitation Convent, Sister Gertrude handled the temporal affairs of the house. The diffident Mother Juliana was "only too glad" to delegate "all the exterior business of the institution"—that is, dealings with the secular world—to her assistant superior.[18] Sister Gertrude developed a network on Capitol Hill to accomplish her political ends. She began with her contacts from southern Maryland and ended on the floor of Congress. That is, she first sent the petition to General William J. Hickey, a Catholic farmer originally from St. Mary's County but also the executive clerk of the US Senate. Hickey passed along the memorial for delivery to Senator John Eaton, a Jacksonian Democrat representing the state of Tennessee. Sister Gertrude tapped her family connections in local and national government as well, to help her religious order achieve corporate status and to promote the school by attracting national dignitaries to its celebrations.

CALLING ON CAPITAL CONNECTIONS

In her dual roles of assistant superior and directress of the academy, Sister Gertrude was the cloistered convent's chief liaison to the outside world. She began to invite prominent national figures to officiate at the school's newly created end-of-year ceremony. In 1828, just two months after he signed the act of incorporation of the Sisters of the Visitation, President Adams presided at the distribution of student prizes at the academy.[19] Avoiding political partisanship, the convent also invited Andrew Jackson, Adams's rival and successor, to conduct the distribution ceremony the following year. Although "Old Hickory" had to decline because of illness, he did visit the convent school on a day when classes were still in session.[20] At the 1830 festivities Commodore John Rodgers, a naval hero of the War of 1812, served as the chief distributor. No doubt, the fact that his daughter Elizabeth was among the students being honored made the task all the more enjoyable for him.[21]

Prior to the Civil War, Presidents John Tyler, James K. Polk, Zachary Taylor, and James Buchanan, among other dignitaries, continued this bipartisan practice in showcasing Georgetown Academy as a premier educator of young women. Sister Gertrude created this enduring tradition during her regime as directress, but one of her important legacies that made the Visitation Young Ladies' Academy a nationally prestigious institution.[22]

It was Sister Gertrude's capital connections that allowed her to book such famous public men for academy events. Her main local contact was her much older first cousin, Marcia Burnes Van Ness, wife of John Peter Van Ness, a former general and congressman and future mayor of Washington City. A loyal Jacksonian, General Van Ness was Sister Gertrude's link to Democrats in the capital. But the nonpartisan Marcia Van Ness was a more popular figure in the capital, as she earned the favor and respect of Jacksonians and anti-Jacksonians alike.[23] Even as Wightt resided in the convent enclosure, therefore, family connections enabled her to reach out to leading public figures.

In 1830 Sister Gertrude drew up a petition to Congress requesting permission to block off further traffic on Lingon Street for the safety of the students in both the academy and the benevolent school.[24] As with the petition for incorporation, she called on the executive clerk of the US Senate, William Hickey. As he had done in 1828, Hickey forwarded the request to John Eaton, who was by then the secretary of war. As Eaton was no longer part of the legislative branch, he forwarded the petition to Senator Elias Kent Kane of Illinois, a fellow Jacksonian, for presentation before Congress. Kane did so in part because he had a daughter enrolled in Georgetown Academy where Sister Gertrude was headmistress.[25] The whole circular process illustrates Sister Gertrude's unique network of personal and political connections, which allowed her to accomplish results in the larger community even as she resided in the circumscribed, enclosed community.

In this instance, however, Sister Gertrude's reliance on national figures faced formidable local opposition from the Corporation of Georgetown and longtime Georgetown mayor John Cox. The mayor feared that property values in the neighborhood would plummet were the street closed to traffic, and Cox's children owned property fronting the street. Cox may have been upset as well because he had already granted informal permission to close off the street.[26]

Anne Boylan argues that for white, Protestant, elite, and middle-class women in the Northeast in the Early Republic, "political access was rooted in their possession of bourgeois feminine respectability—those intertwined class and gender characteristics that ideologically 'conflated femininity and morality' and turned individual women (and some groups of women) into symbols of a social class."[27] That is, these women could sometimes manipulate gender stereotypes to their political advantage. "Using their symbolic status and employing a deferential political style based on personal connections to powerful men," Boylan continues, "some women could claim to speak for all women . . . and wield their collective influence for the benefit of group projects." Nuns in antebellum society offer a somewhat different case, since they appeared to reject the ideal of middle-class domesticity that was expected of respectable women in antebellum society. While Catholic women religious may have renounced a "maternity of the flesh," however, they did practice a "maternity of the spirit": although women religious abjured the forms of domesticity—marriage, motherhood, and home—they nonetheless embraced the functions of domesticity—teaching, nursing, and child care. Wightt, moreover, followed a more personal path when enlisting political support for her plans to improve both the education of elite girls in the academy and provide benefits to the daughters of poor families in the convent's benevolent school.

PUBLICIZING THE YOUNG LADIES' ACADEMY

While Sister Gertrude called on political friends in Washington for assistance, she also used the press to publicize Georgetown Convent and Academy. During Wightt's tenure as directress, favorable stories about Georgetown Academy suddenly began to appear more frequently in the press. Between 1828 and 1830 in particular, there was a noticeable spike in such positive press coverage. While original accounts did appear in some northern periodicals like the *National Gazette* in Philadelphia, stories are more often found in newspapers from cities in the urban Upper South, like Baltimore and Richmond. Reprints of stories might turn up in periodicals published anywhere from the Atlantic seaboard to the Mississippi River.[28] For example, the *Baltimore Republican* printed a description of the 1829 distribution ceremony at Georgetown Academy: "This school . . . is now in the full meridian of success," gushed the reporter, "largely patronized from every section of the Union, and greatly admired by all who are acquainted with it."[29]

In an article titled "Nunnery in the United States," originally published in the *Richmond Family Register* in March 1829 and reprinted in periodicals throughout the country, the writer shared his favorable impressions of a visit to Georgetown Academy and the systemization and discipline he found there. "What strikes the visitor with much pleasure, is the perfect system and order with which everything is done," enthused the observer. "All is perfect clockwork. The young misses who compose the school, are regularly and rigidly trained to do everything on plan and method."[30] In her history of Georgetown Visitation, Eleanore Sullivan assumes that the "system must have been devised by Father Clorivière from his French Army training."[31] Perhaps so, but Clorivière had been dead for three years by the time this article appeared, and the system must have been refined by Sister Gertrude to address the much larger academy enrollments seen at the school by the end of the decade.

The Richmond *Enquirer* showcased the letter of a Washington resident who had recently witnessed "an interesting spectacle" of the visit of students to the White House of President Andrew Jackson. The writer describes a scene marked by "beautiful pageantry" involving students from the "Female Catholic Seminary of Georgetown, usually called the Nunnery." "The young ladies tastefully and uniformly dressed formed in line and, with their matrons heading the column and bringing up the rear, marched to the President's House." Accompanied by "their matrons" [out sisters], the girls "made him a return of respect [for a previous visit to the academy by Jackson]. . . . The uniform was snow white, blue cape, bonnets trimmed with blue ribbon, each lady carried a parasol."[32]

The Georgetown Directory for1830 carries a two-page description of the monastery and academy. Under the heading "The Convent of the Visitation," the article is quintessential local boosterism in its glowing description of the new dormitory building recently added to the academy. "The reputation of the Ladies' Academy having brought it more inmates than could be conveniently accommodated," enthuses the author. "Mr. Wheeler also enlarged the institution by adding a compact building to the one erected by Mr. Cloriviere. . . . By this means," the article continues, "the Academy is now provided with all the conveniences and arrangements to be met with the best regulated establishments of this kind, at home or abroad; and may lodge with ease 150 pupils."[33] Anticipating later accounts by church historians that focus solely on clergymen, the directory singles out the male spiritual directors for personal credit but fails to acknowledge any of the individual or collective members of the female staff or instructors. The nuns—Sister Gertrude, Sister Mary Austin, Sister Stanislaus—remain anonymous and their essential contributions were simply taken for granted.

To be fair, it must be said that the lack of public acknowledgment of individual women religious is not just the fault of early church scholars, but is a sort of self-inflicted wound. Historian Patricia Byrne calls attention to the concept of "singularity" and how it worked to prevent recognition of the individual nun rather than the community. "Despite the sisters' intimate involvement in the most convulsive events of the century in American history," she writes, "they showed an extraordinary reserve in discussing them afterwards. . . . Their reticence was likely inspired by a desire to avoid 'singularity'—a considerable transgression of convent manners."[34] This reluctance to call undue attention to self has also frustrated modern scholars seeking to bring to light the past experiences and contributions of communities of women religious.

A letter to the editor in the *Baltimore Gazette and Daily Advertiser* gives an impression of the 1830 distribution ceremony at Georgetown Academy: "The young ladies were examined in Geography, History, Mythology, Astronomy, and elementary Chemistry; in French, Spanish, and Vocal and Instrumental Music; and exhibited a proficiency in their several studies, which confirmed our previous opinions of the general excellence of the Academy," reports the attendee.[35] "The examinations were chiefly conducted by the Father Mr. Wheeler, formerly of St. Mary's College, whose character as a polished gentleman and accomplished scholar, is well established in this city." The observer describes the distribution of premiums following the examinations, in which students were recognized for individual achievements:

> The examinations were followed by a distribution of premiums, the annual festival of the Academy. On this occasion the whole school appeared in Academic uniform, of white dresses with sky-blue capes, etc. . . . The whole exhibition was truly captivating, being diversified at intervals by performances on the harp and piano, and by duets, trios, etc. which were executed by the children in splendid style. . . . But the closing scene of all was exquisitely delightful—and far, very far, beyond my power of description. Two young ladies, one from the senior and one from the junior circle, elegantly attired, were crowned with splendid wreaths, the testimony of superior merit; and as the queens of the day, were each attended with maids of honor decorated in like manner—this ceremony was followed by a full and appropriate chorus from their companions, chaunted in brilliant style and with glowing enthusiasm, whilst the sparkling eyes and throbbing breasts of the audience told how enchanting was the effect and how fervent were the reciprocal feelings.

On such formal public celebrations of the school, Sister Gertrude and the instructors in the academy were conspicuous among the dignitaries present. The observer at the 1830 ceremony reports, "We found the young ladies seated in the form of a hollow square, within which were the Directresses of the Academy, several Rev. gentlemen from the town, and the gallant veteran Commodore Rodgers who officiated as prize distributor."[36] In opening the annual distribution ceremony to the public, Sister Gertrude may have been influenced by the example of the monastery's next-door neighbor. Beginning in 1817, Georgetown College had also conducted an end-of-year distribution to promote the school and anchor its status in the larger community.[37] Established under Sister Gertrude's regime as headmistress, the annual public distribution ceremony was another legacy she left to Georgetown Academy.

Press coverage of Georgetown Academy of this type and scale cannot be found during the years prior to or immediately following Wightt's time as directress. The increased newspaper attention suggests that Sister Gertrude may have been feeding stories to the press or encouraging friends outside the convent to do so, or both. The timing of this media blitz also coincided with Father Wheeler's leave of absence in Europe—September 1828 to August 1829. It is reasonable to surmise, therefore, that Sister Gertrude largely orchestrated the publicity campaign that coincided with Wheeler's absence and which continued after his return.[38] Besides such circumstantial evidence, there is additional concrete evidence of at least one occasion of Sister Gertrude working to advance her personal agenda for the convent and the school without the knowledge or approval of Wheeler.

ATTEMPTING TO CHANGE THE ORDER

For most all the changes introduced during her tenure as directress of the academy and assistant superior of the convent, Sister Gertrude found in Father Wheeler a strong partner. Wheeler had an impressive academic mind with an expertise in mathematics and physics. Sadly, his formidable intellect was matched to a frail constitution. In the fall of 1828 the priest planned a voyage to the south of France to restore his poor health. At the request of the Georgetown Visitation leaders, Archbishop James Whitfield appointed Father López to be Wheeler's temporary replacement as the convent's spiritual director.

While on the Continent, Wheeler planned to visit Rome and some Visitation monasteries. He wished to solicit a few of their members to return with him to observe how well the Georgetown monastery was fulfilling the Salesian Rule.[39] In doing so, Wheeler hoped to ease long-term tensions over adherence to an authentic Visitation religious life that had plagued members of Georgetown Convent since its affiliation with Annecy in 1816. For example, only one year before, the community had contacted their good friend Father Samuel Eccleston on his return from France. Addressing him as "Uncle Sam" and signing themselves as his "unworthy daughters and cordial nieces," the nuns invited the priest to return soon and tell them all about the French Visitandines.[40] Their letter suggests that many in the community continued to worry about living in accord with practices governing the French Visitation convents.

Wheeler embarked from New York City for Le Havre, France, on October 1. A month later, with the backing of Madame Iturbide and Father López, Sister Gertrude proposed to the sister counsellors a bold plan to change the rule of Georgetown Convent from the Visitation Order to that of the Ursuline Order.[41] Wightt called for this change on the grounds that the Ursuline Rule was more flexible and better adapted to American conditions. She also favored the switch because the Ursulines took a vow of dedication to female education (in addition to the three vows of charity, chastity, and poverty taken by the Visitandines). Sister Gertrude's brainchild arrived stillborn, however, when the Visitation sisters overwhelmingly voted down the plan. "The proposal was so positively + unanimously rejected by the Com'ty that the plan was dropped," recorded the Georgetown annalist, "+ our dear Visitation survived the storm which threatened its destruction."[42] This would not be the last time Wightt's policies were repudiated by opponents inside and outside the convent.

Sister Gertrude and her Mexican allies had sought to act while Wheeler was away, planning to present him with a fait accompli when he returned with his European Visitandines in tow. The plan itself was a not unreasonable solution to a long-standing problem the convent faced: how to adapt religious life most effectively to the American setting with the least risk to both the members' spiritual mission and material sustenance. The stealthy manner by which Wightt tried to effect the plan, however, is the least defensible part of her actions. Going behind the back of Wheeler also does not reflect well on her personal character. But it does suggest her level of desperation to blunt the impact of Wheeler's return to Georgetown with French Visitation nuns.

If the ends sought by Sister Gertrude may be justified, the means she followed cannot. It is unclear, however, what roles were played by her two chief allies in the project, Madame Iturbide and Father López. The Georgetown annalist questions the motives of Sister Gertrude: "Madame Iturbidie [*sic*] + her Chaplain agreed to the plan and wished it carried into effect before Fr. Wheeler's return + the arrival of the French Sisters he would bring, + to whose coming Sr. W. was opposed." But, at the same time, the annalist attributes only the best intentions to Wightt's two confederates: "The intentions of Mdme. Iturbidie no doubt were good, hoping thereby to render service to religion."[43] Likewise, the Lathrops use almost identical language to absolve the well-intentioned empress and priest, implying they were misled by the ambitious, prideful nun. "Father Lopez and Madam Yturbide both strongly favored the change proposed; believing, no doubt, that it would really advance the cause of religion," they averred.[44] From the scant evidence, however, it is difficult to know whether Iturbide and López fell under the influence of Sister

FIGURE 4.2. Portrait of Madame Ana Maria Huarte de Iturbide, Empress of Mexico. Attributed to Claude Baptist Tailleur, 1862. Courtesy Georgetown Visitation Monastery Archives, Washington, DC.

Gertrude, or vice versa. López was, after all, the acting spiritual director of the convent, and Iturbide, as a former empress, was imperious by nature. At the same time, Sister Gertrude gave no indication of deferring to either of her partners in the scheme. Perhaps, all three simply found a common cause but with differing personal motives.

The lack of documentation surrounding Wightt's "attempt to change the order" is striking. If not for a chapter titled "The Attempt to Change the Order" recorded in the Georgetown annals in 1866, as well as a like-named chapter in the Lathrops' *A Story of Courage*, there is remarkably little evidence that the event ever took place. The surprising lacunae in primary sources raises the question of whether convent leaders at the time sought to avoid mentioning the painful incident in the hope of thereby erasing it from the communal memory. In her surviving correspondence from the time with both Whitfield and Wheeler, Mother Juliana never mentions Sister Gertrude's proposal or the reaction to it (though the superior does complain to the prelate about the comparatively minor matter of the timing of the annual visitation by López, the acting spiritual director to the convent).[45]

Perhaps the proposal took on a more sinister tone only in the wake of Wightt's departure some two years later. After all, Georgetown Convent did have a previous history of flirting with the notion of becoming an Ursuline house. Dating back to the early days of the Pious Ladies, Bishop Neale had considered the idea, only to ultimately reject it. Moreover, during the financially depressed conditions of the early 1820s, Archbishop Maréchal had solicited Ursuline convents in Quebec and New Orleans to accept some of Georgetown Convent's nuns, if only temporarily, until better times returned. Entertaining a solution to their woes that somehow included a role for the Ursulines was not without precedent for Georgetown Convent.

That said, an intriguing item does appear in one of the letters Wheeler wrote to Mother Juliana while he was in Rome. In the letter he expresses joy at learning that Sister Gertrude's health had returned after what appeared to be a long illness. He also tells the superior, "Be very careful of her. She ought to be dear to the community."[46] This remark not only demonstrates Wheeler's special regard for Sister Gertrude but also suggests that he remained ignorant of her machinations of the previous autumn. One wonders, too, whether Sister Gertrude's illness may have been psychosomatic, resulting from the stress and disappointment at the community's decisive rejection of her plan to change the order.

While visiting Rome, Wheeler pleaded the case of the American Visitandines before the Holy Father. On May 10, 1829, Pope Pius VIII issued a second indult that affirmed the status of Georgetown nuns in light of the adaptations allowed to their monastery. "These changes neither do nor shall prevent them from being considered nuns of the Visitation," ruled the Holy Father, "or from enjoying the same rights and privileges bestowed on the other nuns of the Visitation, who follow St. Frances de Sales as their founder and leader."[47] This document both confirmed and extended the 1816 indult of Pius VII, which permitted Georgetown Visitation to make certain adaptations of the Salesian Rule to the American context. At the same time, Wheeler confided to the Pontiff his intentions "to obtain some Sisters of the Visitation to accompany me to the convent of Georgetown, one particularly to be a *future superioress* and another the *mistress of the noviciate.*"[48]

Although Wheeler and Wightt were close allies in the running of the academy, they found themselves at odds over the question of importing French

Sisters to Georgetown Convent. Sister Gertrude may or may not have shared her views with Wheeler before he sailed for Europe. She also likely knew of Wheeler's plan to return with European Visitandines well before he revealed his intentions to the Pope. That is perhaps why she moved forward with her plan to switch the monastery to the Ursuline Rule so soon after Wheeler departed for the Continent.

THE "FRENCH SISTERS"

Father Wheeler returned to Georgetown in August 1829, having been away for about eleven months. He brought with him not only the papal indult but also three Francophone nuns from three different Visitation monasteries in Europe. The trio comprised Sister Madeleine Augustine d'Arregger from the house in Fribourg, Switzerland; Sister Mary Agatha Langlois, from Le Mans, France; and Sister Marie Regis Mordant, from Valence, France. Wheeler described them as "so much desired and so dearly obtained."[49] They had come to observe the Georgetown convent and to report on its observance of the order's holy rule. Soon after their arrival, Sister Mary Agatha was appointed mistress of novices for Georgetown. In that office she earned the sobriquet "the Living Rule." Langlois's immediate elevation shows that Europe remained the model of authentic religious life for most of Georgetown Convent's members. "It is easy to see that far removed from Annecy, our holy Source," Sister Madeleine commented, "our Sisters of Georgetown could not well be formed according to our practice and customs. Hence they profited of this providential circumstance to make an appeal to the Visitandines of Europe."[50]

In reporting to her superiors in Europe, Sister Madeleine nonetheless favorably reviewed the conduct of the Georgetown nuns. Her comments also reveal much about the ideal attitude and behavior expected of Visitandines: "It would be impossible to convey to you an idea of the impression made on us by the sight of their meek and humble Mother [Juliana]. She is all humility and simplicity. . . . We did not expect to find so great a resemblance between our American sisters and ourselves. . . . Their docility, their zeal for the exact observance makes them willing to do anything in order to become true Visitandines."[51]

The presence of the French Sisters at Georgetown Visitation Convent served to alleviate but not eliminate anxieties about the "struggle for legitimacy in the American context." For example, Sister Mary Paulina Millard belonged to the first class of Visitation novices formed by Sister Mary Agatha.

Years later, as a member of the original band of sisters sent from Georgetown to found Baltimore Visitation Monastery in 1837 and later as superior of that convent, Millard never forgot the lessons she had learned from the Living Rule. According to the annalist of Baltimore Visitation, Mother Paulina sought to adhere to the rule as practiced in Annecy, even as accommodations to conditions in America had to be made:

> From its earliest days, this Community has been one of fervent piety, great exactitude to our holy Rules, and fidelity to all that was practicable. . . . Our dear Mother [Paulina] now gave a particular attention to every iota specified in our holy writings, watched to see if the practice corresponded with the written Rule, and compared one with the other until everything was "a la Annecy." Customs, Answers, Rubrics, etc., were read and re-read, studied and explained. . . . Indeed it became a saying with us, "The Book says this, the book says that; what does the Book say?" etc., and unless we could promptly prove our words from the Book itself, it was useless almost to pronounce them. . . . "The Rule, the Rule," was often heard amongst us in our recreations, Assemblies and the like, and it may amuse a little to give some verses of a song written by a Sister who was brought over [from the school] in vacation and made to begin an exact observance of what she called the "Tertianship." A waggish Sister [Mary Xavier Queen] wrote the following.
>
> School being over, and the pupils all gone,
> I'm rous'd from my bed the first crack of morn,
> Because, says our Mother, now there's no school
> *I wish you to live* according to Rule.
> The mornings long prayer, I scarcely do feel
> But to keep wide awake is *tres difficile,*
> And if I nod the *least bit* or lean on the stool,
> *There's a tip up behind* with a- "follow your Rule."
> Up late at night like the rest of my rank,
> Screw'd in the corner, so lean and so lank,
> I twist and I turn to keep myself cool,
> *Or I would not be* able to "follow the Rule."
> From morning to night I scarce speak a word,
> And walk on *tiptoes* for fear I'd be heard—
> Oh! don't I pay for living in school?
> *I'm sure to die Martyr* from keeping the Rule!

On the feast of St. Ann, I asked for a time
On the Piano forte in the forefront of noon:
The answer was "'No,' it's a feast of the Rule
Which you can observe now there's no school."
I then got a June bug—tied it to a string,
Was amusing myself with hearing it sing—
When out came a Sister and looked at me cool,—
Says I, "It's squirrels and dogs not *'bugs'* in the Rule."
Up went a row and Mother comes out,
Says she: "What's all this noise and hurrah about?
Sister Xavier, remember you're not in the school,
If amusement you want, go study your Rule.
Take the string off that bug, and throw it away,
Then go to the Choir your prayers there to say;
You're so out of *gear* from living at school,
That I almost despair of your learning the Rule."[52]

If this witty Visitation Sister in Baltimore could be satirical about "learning the rule" in the 1850s, such was not the case for her predecessors in Georgetown in the 1820s. Upon their arrival, the three French Sisters found that "the system of education required in an almost Protestant country often interferes with the *time* for their religious duties."[53] Although the nuns decried the situation as far less than ideal, they also recognized the need for Georgetown to accommodate the demands of tuition-paying families or risk forfeiting the opportunity for their charges to imbibe the virtues of a convent education. The French Sisters only reluctantly accepted that in such a non-Catholic land would compromises in the religious regimen be accepted. Otherwise, "parents would send their children to schools having a more extended course of study, thereby the young hearts would lose the lessons of piety here rec[eive]d."

The ascendance of the French Sisters within the convent continued the following year. In either May or September 1830, Mother Juliana resigned as superior in deference to the election of Sister Madeleine Augustine d'Arregger.[54] The elevation of Mother Madeleine struck a blow to the efforts of not only Sister Gertrude but also Father Wheeler. In what some of the nuns saw as election interference, the spiritual director had made clear that his candidate was Sister Agatha Langlois. In bringing the French Sisters to Georgetown, Wheeler hoped to heal some old wounds within the community. He may have succeeded, but in the process he also opened some new ones.[55]

1831: YEAR OF ECLIPSE

As the year 1831 dawned and launched a new decade, the American people, some with anticipation, some with trepidation, awaited a solar eclipse that was predicted to appear early in the year. Arriving on February 12, the eclipse failed to live up to expectations, much to the disappointment of many and to the relief of others.[56] Conversely, in that same year, as tensions simmered within its religious community, the public image of Georgetown Visitation Convent and Academy continued to rise. The convent basked in the favorable publicity surrounding the "miraculous cures" of two members of Georgetown Visitation—Sister Mary Appolonia Digges and Mrs. Ann Mattingly, the latter a postulant on trial—that had occurred through the intercession of a German priest, Prince Alexander Hohenlohe. Whitfield saw the cures as the workings of Providence for the benefit of both the patients and the Catholic Church: "I think Almighty God had in view particularly in the cure of St. Appolonia not only to relieve her but to convert souls to the Catholic faith," he wrote to Father Stephen Dubuisson. Whitfield immediately commissioned the priest to publicize the cures to the benefit the Church, saying, "We must cooperate on our part, in publishing it, if, after thorough examination it be deemed a miracle."[57] Their stories soon appeared in the pamphlet *Narrative of Two Wonderful Cures Wrought in the Monastery of the Visitation at Georgetown.*[58]

With the coming of the new year, prospects for Georgetown Convent and Academy had never appeared brighter, at least to outsiders. On the surface, too, the community appeared more united in its adherence to the letter and spirit of the founders of the order—Saint Francis de Sales and Saint Jane de Chantal. Neither had enrollments in both the academy and the benevolent school ever been so high, nor their reputations more secure. Mother Madeleine reported that "at the Academy a full course was pursued, including the common and higher English branches, modern languages, Latin vocal and instrumental music. There were 100 pupils in the Academy + 150 in the free school. The Com[muni]ty with novices numbered 57."[59] That is, none of the nuns or clergy, nor the students or parents, nor the Catholic or non-Catholic neighbors foresaw the looming cloud of events that was about to cast a long shadow over the convent, the academy, and the Church.

OPPOSITION TO SISTER GERTRUDE'S AGENDA

On March 22, 1831, less than two years after Father Wheeler returned from Europe, Archbishop Whitfield dismissed him as spiritual director of the convent. The reason for Whitfield's dissatisfaction with Wheeler stemmed as much from financial problems as any spiritual failures on Wheeler's part.[60] Father Louis Deluol traced the problems to the alleged spendthrift ways of the spiritual director of the convent working in tandem with, and perhaps under the influence of, the directress of the academy. In caustic comments that reflected his own sentiments and those of Whitfield, Deluol not only condemns Wheeler but also unintentionally reveals that Sister Gertrude was at least an equal partner to Wheeler in the planning and running of the academy: "Considering the ideas of M. Wheeler and Sister Gertrude," Deluol laments, "it would make it unbelievable that they would limit themselves to necessary expenses. . . . The expenses would exceed the income by $1500 per year."

What were the "ideas of M. Wheeler and Sister Gertrude" that Deluol contended went beyond "necessary expenses"? A key example is found in correspondence between the superior and the archbishop and between the spiritual director and the convent leaders, respectively, at the end of January 1829. The month before, Mother Juliana experienced sticker shock when she saw the construction bill of $1,618.50¼ for the new observatory atop St. Michael's Hall in the academy. In her letter to Whitfield, Mother Juliana reminds the prelate that he had previously labeled the project "a useless expence."[61] It must be acknowledged that such a steep price tag (the equivalent of over $55,000 today) was beyond the budget of most female schools of the time. Georgetown College, by contrast, would not add an observatory to its campus until more than a decade later.[62] According to the superior, the observatory was "only desired by the two head teachers of the school—Sister Gertrude and Sister Mary Austin."[63] Sister Gertrude, as directress of the academy, and Sister Mary Austin, as mistress of pensioners, saw the observatory as a valuable upgrade to the school's science offerings, with science being a major focus of the most progressive female schools in the Early Republic.[64] People less directly involved in the academy, including Mother Juliana and Archbishop Whitfield, viewed the observatory as "a useless expense."

In response to a now-lost letter from Mother Juliana, Sister Gertrude, and the four counsellors, dated December 12, Wheeler, writing from Rome at the end of January 1829, attempts to reassure the superior, her assistant, and her counsellors not to panic over the fact that the convent was facing the highest debt in its history as the result of the many improvements to the physical amenities at the school. Wheeler promises to pay for the expensive new observatory himself, without specifying where he plans to obtain the funds to do so.[65]

The priest reminds the worried convent leaders that, in contrast to earlier in the decade, enrollment in the academy was now overflowing and its reputation was secure. "Had you, at the time of your financial difficulties of 1824, an academy reputable and deservedly reputed?" he asks rhetorically, "was it then thought a recommendation to a young lady, to have been educated at the academy of the Visitation?"[66] He avers that such positive results could not have been achieved without spending, which he sees as a sound investment in the prosperity of the school and hence the survival of the convent. "No greater humiliation," he admits, "could befall me than the frustrations of my designs for your prosperity and permanent establishment." Rather prophetically (predicting his own dismissal by Whitfield only two years later), Wheeler confesses, "It would be of course a pain to me were I withdrawn from your direction by the archbishop before the completion of my projects for your happiness and advancement spiritual and temporal."

In consequence, in the letter the priest specifically asks the convent's leaders to refrain from sharing their financial situation with the rest of the community. Wheeler makes sure that this point is not missed by writing at the top of the letter: "Read this letter by yourselves and keep its contents secret." Halfway through the missive Wheeler warns, "I would not even let the abp. [archbishop] be apprised of your financial state—no good could result from it," and predicts that only "trouble and confusion would ensue; public confidence would gradually evaporate; you would be looked upon as the dupes of another Don Quixote, your poor father would hang down his head in shame."

Following this brief detour into self-pity, Wheeler directly addresses the immediate issue of paying the bill for the construction of the observatory: "As to the observatory on St. Michael's hall, . . . The apparatus was engaged before the archbishop spoke the word you sent [perhaps "a useless expence"] I shall have to pay for it. If I cannot be assisted in America then I shall have to strain every nerve to do it here." In closing, just in case the nuns missed the message the first two times, Wheeler repeats his request to keep the finances of the convent *entre nous*. "I shall look upon it as a great offence if your alarms spread beyond the council and dear Father Lopez."

The policies that Father Wheeler and Sister Gertrude pursued together in the late 1820s must be understood in the context of the dire financial situation Georgetown Visitation had faced earlier in the decade. In the wake of the Panic of 1819, the academy had suffered a precipitous drop in enrollments that failed to recover until mid-decade. The financial crisis nearly forced closure of the convent and dispersal of its members either to Ursuline convents in Canada or back to their families.[67]

Wheeler's and Gertrude's desire to improve the teaching, curriculum, and physical plant of the academy drew upon several factors. Primary was the practical reality that the convent's main source of income was the tuition received from the academy. In following the "improvement" approach, the pair took a page from the book of Father Clorivière. Early in the decade Clorivière engaged in deficit-spending to upgrade the school plant, racking up high debt in the process. He later paid down this debt by donating close to $10,000 of his own funds, tapping into his military pension and the sale of ancestral lands in France. Unfortunately, Father Wheeler and Sister Gertrude lacked such personal assets to tap.

During the hard times of the early 1820s, Sister Gertrude had been among the young sisters trained in pedagogy by Father Clorivière and Sister Mary Austin. Among the lessons she took from this experience, a view she shared with Wheeler, was that improving the academy's buildings, curriculum, and instruction methods was key to ensuring the convent's long-term survival. Her focus on the academy was not simply a matter of practicality on her part. The language of the 1827 prospectus signed by Father Wheeler suggests that he and Sister Gertrude also shared a genuine philosophical commitment to raising the standards of female education generally, as well as those of Georgetown Academy in particular.[68] Finally, it cannot be denied that, as directress of the academy, Sister Gertrude pursued goals that, if achieved, might raise her to greater public acclaim, especially from graduates and their families, given the conspicuous nature of her agency in the projects. Such behavior was not consistent with the self-effacement expected of a Visitation nun. Nonetheless, to attribute her actions solely, or even primarily to intellectual pride and personal ambition—as do Sister Josephine Barber in the annals and as the Lathrops do in their history of Georgetown Convent—is to give the least generous, most self-serving interpretation to Sister Gertrude's motives while ignoring the more general concerns she legitimately sought to address.[69]

As previously noted, concerns over the role of the academy had long existed among the nuns in Georgetown Convent. Many members worried about the legitimacy of their foundation, especially its lack of any direct guidance by European nuns. On the one hand, perhaps a majority of the community yearned for a more "authentic" contemplative life of following the Visitation Rule in accord with Old World practices and allowing minimal concessions to New World realities.[70] For these nuns, the academy was at best a necessary evil and a compromise that distracted from the contemplative life of prayer they desired. On the other hand, some of the nuns, chiefly Sister Gertrude and Sister Mary Austin, and perhaps Sister Stanislaus as well, favored the adaptations of the Visitation Rule to unique American conditions. The latter group recognized how essential was the income generated by the academy to the survival of the convent. Sister Gertrude in particular saw the school as both an end in itself and a necessary means to achieving the semi-monastic life that Georgetown Convent promised its members.[71]

Even Gertrude's sternest critics, the Lathrops, grudgingly credit her for her pivotal role in upgrading the academy: "When in the course of time a more extensive plan, a higher range of studies, was undertaken at the Academy," they write, Sister Gertrude "was chosen to carry it out, by reason of her natural and cultivated qualifications for this especial work. . . . All the energies of her powerful mind were bent to the task of raising the Academy to the highest standards of the time."[72] In making their assessment, the Lathrops no doubt draw upon the testimony of the convent annalist, Sister Mary Josephine Barber, who wrote that Gertrude used "her utmost efforts to raise the Academy to a standard of excellence equal to any in the country."[73]

Such praise for Sister Gertrude's talents, coupled with criticism of her motives, marks out some of the boundaries of Catholic religious life within which she was allowed to work but not cross. While serving as headmistress of the school and subprioress of the convent, she found plenty of latitude for applying her intellectual expertise and for drawing on her social contacts in the service of the community. Any hint of personal ambition in her designs, whether real or imagined, however, smacked of "singularity." It must be discouraged, even chastised, as contrary to the Salesian spirit.

The Lathrops attribute Wightt's fall from grace to "a few grains of poisoning pride that had carelessly let fall into the well of knowledge from which she was at liberty to draw freely."[74] While they admit that "the highest reaches of intellectual splendor may be perfectly accordant with spiritual faithfulness or humility"; they nevertheless warn that "even a little mere pride of learning may be destructive of true spiritual equilibrium." They blame Sister Gertrude's opposition to changes introduced by the French Sisters on her "wounded vanity" and "ambitions thwarted." Certainly, Wightt's feelings were hurt. But the Lathrops seek no answer to Wightt's actions other than personal failing. The story of Sister Gertrude highlights much about both the opportunities and the limitations that Catholic religious life in the early American republic might offer to an intellectually gifted, socially prominent, and personally ambitious young woman.

Moreover, although possessed of extraordinary executive abilities, which led to her appointment as a sister counsellor, directress of the academy, and assistant superior of the convent, all while still in her twenties, Sister Gertrude's glaring shortcoming as a leader was her inability, or unwillingness, to build a community consensus for her desired projects and goals. This failure is evident not only in her abortive attempt to change the order in the fall of 1828, but also in the policies she enacted as directress of the academy. Despite their intrinsic value and many positive results, Wightt's educational plans ultimately proved neither compatible with the type of religious life desired by most in the Georgetown community nor financially responsible in the eyes of her clerical and religious superiors.

Wightt shared some similarities with another brilliant visionary of the Early Republic, Alexander Hamilton. As secretary of the treasury, Hamilton's forward-looking financial policies were controversial and polarizing to many voters. Establishing a bank of the United States appeared to him a "necessary and proper" power of Congress, but to his opponents it appeared as both an unsound and unconstitutional undertaking. Likewise, Sister Gertrude saw her agenda for the academy as necessary and proper to the convent, while to others it appeared as a wasteful objective, one in violation of their rule and constitutions. In the end, Wightt either lacked the political acumen or disdained the political cajoling necessary to convince both the convent members and church leaders to sustain her ambitious and expensive educational vision for Georgetown Visitation. This failure, along with her opposition to policies enacted under the French Sisters, ultimately led to her disaffection from her religious community and likely contributed to her decision to flee the convent.

5

Sister Gertrude Eloped from the Convent

Father Stephen Dubuisson, SJ, a former president of Georgetown College, recorded in his journal the only known description of the Chapter proceedings convened in Georgetown Visitation Monastery on Saturday evening, March 19, 1831. Although Dubuisson had not attended the meeting, his entry drew upon the account sent to him by an unnamed member of the convent who had been present. The members gathered to discuss the governance of the community. Archbishop Whitfield and four priests were also present. The seriousness of the event is demonstrated by Dubuisson's mention of the fact that an estimated "40 nuns spoke, some of them very eloquently—(an affecting scene). All with tears—declaring their ardent desire of observances and Sr. Magd. Aug. for their Mother." On the morning of Tuesday, March 22, before he returned to Baltimore and "after the most mature deliberation," the archbishop "removed the . . . Director (Rev. Michael F. Wheeler) and appointed the Rev. Willm. Matthews." At about 2:30 that same afternoon, "Sr. Gertrude eloped from the convent."[1]

Later that day Sister Gertrude wrote two letters to her religious superiors—one to Mother Madeleine and one to Archbishop Whitfield—revealing the reasons for her abrupt exit. The letter addressed to the convent superior has been lost, but the letter to the prelate was preserved, and it provides a valuable window into Sister Gertrude's state of mind in the hours following her departure.[2]

LETTER TO ARCHBISHOP WHITFIELD, MARCH 22, 1831

Wightt's letter to Whitfield constitutes the closest equivalent to a "smoking gun" document about her case. At the very least her letter provides Wightt's personal perspective on the event and is therefore important on a number of levels. First, the letter contains the only extant statement composed immediately after the event explaining why she left religious life. She began the communication on the day of her flight and completed it the next day. The missive thus permits a unique and revealing insight into her thoughts within the first twenty-four hours following her actions. Second, it is a private communication. Her thoughts therefore are neither crafted after long reflection nor filtered through the haze of memory, nor motivated by a desire to court public opinion. The document thus may be accepted as an authentic and accurate rendering of her state of mind at that moment, although not necessarily an objective picture of the state of affairs at Georgetown Visitation Convent before she left.

Wightt opens with a salutation to Whitfield as "My Lord + Dear Father," and appears to adopt an informal, friendly tone by acknowledging that the archbishop "will no doubt be greatly surprised" to receive mail from her postmarked from Washington rather than Georgetown. In the very next sentence, however, Wightt launches into the reasons that led her to steal away from Georgetown Convent. Indeed, the letter reads like a legal brief in which she relates her disillusionment with Catholic monastic life in general and itemizes her charges against the current superior, Mother Madeleine, and other unnamed members of Georgetown Visitation Convent. She raises all these issues in a somewhat breathless manner that mixes undeniable hints of paranoia with several reasonable and possibly legitimate complaints about interference by the superior into how she ran the academy.

In no apparent particular order of importance, Wightt identifies four distinct but related reasons that influenced her decision to leave. She claims she had been the victim of mistreatment and espionage within the convent. She holds that "*religious persecution* had [been] raised nearly to its height against me [and] that I was to be placed under a new band of spies."

Wightt also mentions recent difficulties she encountered in directing Georgetown Academy:

- "that I was to have the responsibility of the Academy on me without authority to act"
- "that many changes were to take place there [the academy], which would cause discontent to the scholars and of course to their parents"
- "that I was to be questioned [by parents] at the parlours to know why these changes were made"
- "that for religion's sake I would be forced to tell falsehoods"

Moreover, and almost as a seeming afterthought, Wightt alludes to a perception "that I was too popular out to be so within." Presumably Wightt meant

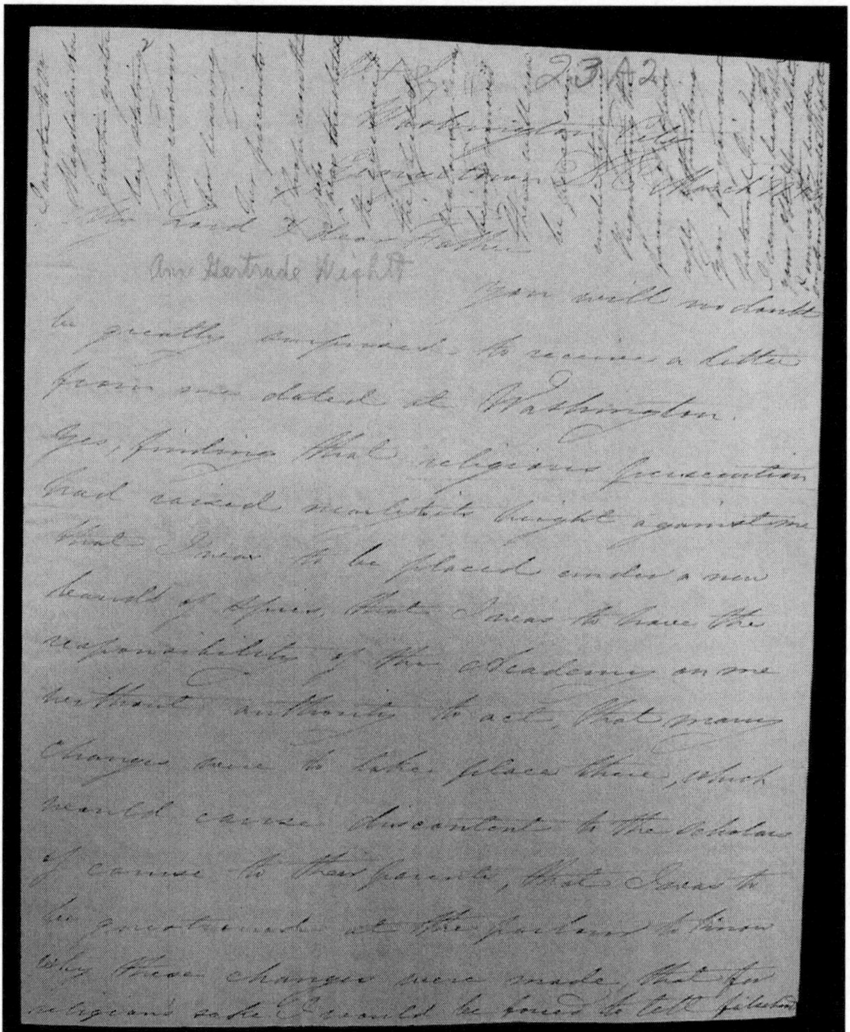

Ann Gertrude Wightt

You will no doubt be greatly surprised to receive a letter from me dated at Washington.

Yes, finding that religious persecution had caused [illegible] that I was to be placed under a new [illegible] that I was to have the responsibility of the Academy on me without authority to act, that many changes were to take place there, which would cause discontent to the scholars of course to their parents, that I was to be questioned [illegible] why these changes were made, that for religion's sake I would be forced to tell falsehood

FIGURE 5.1. Letter from Sister Ann Gertrude Wightt to Archbishop James Whitfield, dated March 22, 1831. Courtesy Archives of the Archdiocese of Baltimore, Associated Archives at St. Mary's Seminary & University, Baltimore.

some members of Georgetown Convent believed that her relationship with the parents of students was too close, too worldly, for a cloistered nun.

Wightt also acknowledges her personal and administrative differences with the current convent superior, Mother Madeleine, contending "that it was utterly out of my power to offer satisfaction to the actual Foreign Superioress."

Only halfway through her letter does Wightt identify her primary reason for leaving Georgetown Convent, while also recapping her general grievances. She makes clear that her ultimate concern was a desire to save her soul. Rightly or wrongly, she felt that her salvation was endangered by having to obey policies instituted at Georgetown with the arrival of the three French nuns—Mother Madeleine, Sister Agatha, and Sister Marie Regis—some nineteen months before. In summing up, Wightt gets more specific in mentioning who had been "persecuting" and "spying" on her, causing her to act for her own salvation. "Never could I ever have saved my soul amidst such broils + under such despotism," she contends. "The espionage and suspicion with their consequences which particularly since the French Sisters came are kept up," she asserts, and "renders the convent a *perfect Inquisition.*"

Wightt also reflects on her soured view of Catholic religious life brought on by her unhappy experience during the tenure of Mother Madeleine and the French Sisters: "This I unhesitatingly declare, that as long as I profess my intellect I never will again enter an enclosed convent." She concludes, "I now have unfavourable opinions of them all." In her next line Wightt anticipates a standard trope repeated in later anti-convent exposés authored by alleged "escaped" nuns: of the innocent young woman whose illusions are dashed after learning too late the inquisitorial realities of cloistered life. "Were convents as I fancied they were," she writes, "certainly they would be the happiest places on earth but I was egregiously deceived."

Once resolved to leaving her longtime home and faith family at Georgetown Convent, Wightt sought refuge in the home of her kinswoman Marcia Van Ness in nearby Washington City. "I took my determination to leave them + seek my tranquillity in the bosom of cousin Mrs. Van Ness's family," she writes, "and accordingly, yesterday at about two o'clock I bid a final adieu to those walls in which I had suffered more than tongue can tell."[3]

Although fully expecting condemnation for her actions from the clergy and the faithful, Wightt nonetheless holds fast to her decision, taking a stand, like Martin Luther three centuries before, on personal conscience: "You and all the clergy together with the mass of Catholics will blame, nay, reprobate my conduct," she defiantly tells Whitfield, "but could you know my exact case, philanthropy would call forth your kind indulgence and show you that for me the step [was] unavoidable." "The whole world may raise against [me]," she acknowledges," but I am fully satisfied in my conscience that I have taken the only step left to free me from the insurmountable difficulties that were in my way to the tranquillity and salvation of my soul. I place my whole confidence in God my father, he alone knows all."

Just prior to closing, Wightt informs Whitfield of her letter to Mother Madeleine, using the opportunity to fling a final dart at her victorious rival. "I wrote to Madeleine Augustine yesterday, stating my reasons for leaving her precincts," she explains, "+ I hope now I who was the obstacle, the eyesore + the object of jealousy + envy being removed there will now be peace and understanding even under *tyranny.*"

After reciting a scathing indictment of the Catholic convent system, Wightt rather surprisingly closes the letter as a faithful Catholic. She thanks Archbishop Whitfield for his "most paternal kindness," signing herself his "ob[edien]t and humble s[er]v[an]t and unworthy daughter. Sister Ann Gertrude Wightt." By using her religious name, Wightt indicates that, even though she had flouted enclosure, she still considers herself both a Catholic and a nun, bound by her vows of poverty, chastity, and obedience. She will now seek her salvation not in the cloister, but in the world, as a still faithful yet admittedly imperfect member of the Church.

Wightt's letter presents her frank, if highly selective, interpretation of the events that led up to her flight. What she does address is often done in an elliptical and unspecific manner, and must be decoded within the context of what is known of the divisive conditions within Georgetown Convent in the preceding years. Nor is Wightt forthcoming in all respects. Her statement, therefore, is important as much for what it does not say as for what it does. On the one hand, Wightt identifies most all her problems as resulting from the disruption to the convent routine following the ascension of the three French-speaking nuns into positions of authority. On the other hand, she makes no reference to Whitfield's dismissal of Father Michael Wheeler as spiritual director of the convent as a catalyst for her sudden departure.

Nor does her letter mention the fact that prior to the French Sisters coming to Georgetown in August 1829, Wightt's preemptive but unsuccessful attempt to change Georgetown convent from a house of the Visitation Order to one of the Ursuline Order. Wightt saw the Rule of Saint Angela as better fitted to the unique American conditions than that of Saint Francis de Sales. The Ursulines, for example, take a fourth vow "to employ themselves in the instruction of young girls." Wightt thereby sought to preserve a religious life closer to that which had prevailed in Georgetown during its first three decades. Gertrude and her sister had grown up in that convent community acting as their surrogate family, and Mary Margaret was buried in the convent crypt. For Wightt, the arrival of French Sisters threatened radical alterations to the letter and spirit of the Georgetown community under which she had been raised and lived for nearly a quarter century. Seen in this light, Sister Gertrude's plan to change the order may be understood as her desperate attempt to hold on to, or restore, a version of Georgetown Convent closer to that of the Pious Ladies or at least that of the early years as Sisters of the Visitation. The majority of the Georgetown nuns did not agree, however, and voted down her proposal.

According to Wightt, the changes to the convent and the academy put into place by Mother Madeleine and the French Sisters had shattered her illusions and opened her eyes to the "true" nature of convent life. Indeed, her short time under the alleged "tyranny" of the French women had convinced her that convent life in general was corrupt, despotic, and unredeemable. "I now have unfavorable opinions of them all," she concludes, "and although I have left my convent for good reasons, I believe it is as good if not better than any in Europe."

The tensions between Wightt and d'Arregger in part stemmed from a clash of personalities. Both women had strong egos that did not accommodate easily to alternate points of view. Still, the core of the conflict between the foreign-born superior and her native-born assistant reflected the clash between European and American notions of authority, obedience, and religious life in general. On one side stood the directress of the academy who had grown up literally as a "child of the house." She favored the American adaptations to the Visitation Rule that had formally governed Georgetown since affirmation by papal indult in 1816 and reaffirmation by a second indult in 1829. Failing that, Sister Gertrude opted for affiliating Georgetown with the Ursuline Order. On the other side stood the new superior, who had come to Georgetown with a mission to make its convent and school hew more closely to the Visitation Rule as understood and practiced in European monasteries. Working out the boundaries between the two views remained a matter where reasonable people might disagree. On March 22, 1831, however, Sister Gertrude was no longer in a mood to be reasonable.

The specific question that sparked the strife between Wightt and d'Arregger focused on the former's role as directress of the academy. Sister Gertrude herself phrased it this way: "I was to have the responsibility of the Academy on me without the authority to act." Unfortunately, Mother Madeleine has not left us her interpretation of their quarrel, at least not one that has been discovered. Wightt had enjoyed a close personal relationship with Mother Juliana, the previous superior. Mother Juliana had recognized a clear demarcation between the respective roles of superior of the convent and directress of the academy and had refrained from any direct interference with Wightt as headmistress. Wightt's relationship with Mother Madeleine, however, was neither as cordial nor as personal as the one she had with Mother Juliana. Wightt not only opposed the changes in the academy initiated by d'Arregger but also convinced herself she could not implement them without violating her conscience.

The elopement of Sister Ann Gertrude Wightt marked the first recorded case in the United States of a woman religious under solemn vows violating enclosure without permission. Wightt's previously overlooked letter to Whitfield tells her side of the story, something that previously has been only a matter of speculation.[4] Her testimony confirms that key to her discontent were the new policies instituted in Georgetown Convent by the French Sisters, especially the unwelcome interference in the running of the academy by the "Foreign superioress." Valuable as it is, Wightt's missive in places remains problematic and incomplete. Her omissions sometimes conceal as much as her actual testimony reveals about what caused her disaffection and decision to leave. Her account must therefore be cross-referenced with other known primary sources—the diaries of Fathers Louis Deluol and Jean Marie Tessier, the correspondence of Archbishop Whitfield with the Propaganda Fide in Rome, extant letters by Visitation nuns, and contemporary newspaper articles, as well as the annals of Georgetown Convent. Only through such a comparison can we more fully dispel the mists surrounding her otherwise unexplained behavior on that March afternoon in 1831.

FATHER DELUOL'S DIARY

Evidence from the diaries of Father Deluol and Father Tessier, two French-born Sulpician priests, makes clear that it was Archbishop Whitfield's termination of Father Wheeler on the morning of March 22 that triggered Wightt's hasty exit later that day.[5] Since 1826 Wheeler had been a close ally of Wightt, especially in her efforts to revise the curriculum and upgrade the facilities of Georgetown Academy, and even in the face of the resulting debt that led to his sacking. Wightt recognized Whitfield's firing of Wheeler for what it was: the prelate's vote of no confidence in her ambitious plans for the academy. These included such items as an astronomical observatory. Things Whitfield judged as frivolous and unwise expenditures, Wightt saw as sound investments in the future of the school. For Wightt the academy was not only an end in itself; it was also the means to ensuring the long-term financial viability of Georgetown Convent. She remembered the financial crisis of the early 1820s, when the monastery was on the verge of disbanding because enrollments in the academy, its main source of revenue, had plummeted.

If Wightt's letter to Whitfield on March 22 offers the best window into her *motivations* for leaving the convent, the diary of Father Deluol provides

FIGURE 5.2. Reverend Louis R. Deluol. Courtesy Archives of the Associated Sulpicians of the United States, Associated Archives at St. Mary's Seminary & University, Baltimore.

the best available source to understanding the *timing* of her sudden departure and her actions in the weeks immediately following it. The Deluol diary is especially valuable for its insights into how the Catholic hierarchy in Baltimore, and Whitfield in particular, handled the scandal within the archdiocese, which threatened to go national and tarnish the reputation of the American Catholic Church. However, it must be noted that Deluol remained entirely unsympathetic to Sister Gertrude and his diary entries must be viewed with the same caution as that applied when assessing Wightt's letter.

The immediate chain of events that triggered Wightt's flight from Georgetown Visitation began on March 9, when Whitfield convened a "long meeting" with the clerical leadership of the archdiocese "about the affairs of the Visitandine Convent in Georgetown."[6] Those present included not only Michael

FIGURE 5.3. James Whitfield, Fourth Archbishop of Baltimore (1825–18). Courtesy Archives of the Archdiocese of Baltimore, Associated Archives at St. Mary's Seminary & University, Baltimore.

Wheeler, the convent's spiritual director, but also his fellow Sulpicians Jean-Marie Tessier, James Joubert, and Jean-Baptiste Damphoux, and Deluol.[7] Nine days after the conference with his advisors, Whitfield traveled to Georgetown for what appeared to be a regular visit to the convent, but was in reality a fact-finding trip to investigate its finances.[8] On Saturday evening of March 19, the archbishop met in chapter with the entire convent membership for a discussion of convent's finances and other matters of governance. On Tuesday morning he departed Georgetown by coach and arrived back to Baltimore by 4:30 in the afternoon.[9]

Before leaving Georgetown, Whitfield wrote to Wheeler, informing him of his removal as "Spiritual Father of the Georgetown Convent" and his replacement with Father William Matthews, the long-time pastor of St. Patrick's Church in Washington City. By coincidence, and as noted in Deluol's diary, that same afternoon Sister Gertrude "broke her vows . . . by leaving the Georgetown Convent without permission."[10] Or was it a coincidence? The significance of the timing of these two events has never been noted by any investigator into the Wightt case. Yet it seems significant that Sister Gertrude's spontaneous flight followed only hours after the dismissal of Wheeler, her main clerical ally in promoting the academy.

Deluol's entry from the next day reveals that Whitfield's dissatisfaction with Wheeler stemmed primarily from financial rather than spiritual matters. According to Deluol, Whitfield showed him "many documents" received at the chapter of the convent "proving that the administration of M. Wheeler had been a disaster both in the Spiritual and Temporal domains."[11] Deluol contrasts the alleged financial excesses under Wheeler with the solvency in which his predecessor, Joseph de Clorivière, had left the school and convent. At the time of Clorivière's death five years earlier, Georgetown Visitation had "capital of $15,000 and an annual income of $1400 without debts." Clorivière had calculated that the latter sum, when supplemented by tuition from at least thirty boarders per year, would provide the sisters with an "honorable living." Even though the current number of boarding students had reached thirty-six and growing, however, "the Chapter showed the Archbishop a document proving that even if the present number of boarders continued . . . they would not make ends meet."

Whatever future financial problems Deluol had forecasted for Georgetown Visitation Convent, both the convent members and the archbishop soon faced a far more immediate crisis in public relations stemming from the unauthorized flight of Sister Gertrude.

THE CURIOUS INCIDENT OF THE NUN IN THE AFTERNOON

On April 2, 1831, the *Episcopal Recorder*, a religious weekly published in Philadelphia, printed the extract of a letter from one of its readers residing in the District of Columbia. It reports an unusual event that had recently transpired near the nation's capital: "There has been no little excitement in this community within a few days past, and especially among the Romanists," writes the anonymous correspondent, "arising from the recent *elopement* of a principal Nun, (*Sister Gertrude,*) from the Nunnery in Georgetown."[12]

By her action, Sister Gertrude was the precursor to several alleged "escaped nuns" of the 1830s—women like Rebecca Reed, Milly McPherson, Olivia Neale, and, most notoriously, Maria Monk. Indeed, Sister Gertrude was the first such "runaway nun" in American history, a figure that would serve as a well-worn trope of anti-Catholic propaganda well into the twentieth century.[13] Although of great local concern—for the nuns of Georgetown Visitation Monastery, for the academy students and their parents, and for the American Catholic hierarchy—the scandal surrounding Sister Gertrude failed to reach the sustained level of national controversy generated by her more infamous successors only a few years later. Nor did her flight, unlike that of later alleged escaped nuns, inspire a spate of anti-convent writings and mob actions or calls for legislative inspection of "priests' prisons for women."[14] All this begs the question: Why did Wightt's case garner relatively little lasting attention, when some of the women who later mimicked her actions became national figures and best-selling authors? Reaction in the press to Sister Gertrude's flight, or the relative lack of reaction, might be termed the "curious incident of the nun in the afternoon."

Readers of Arthur Conan Doyle will recognize that phrase as a nod to "the curious incident of the dog in the night," a line of dialogue found in the Sherlock Holmes short story "The Adventure of Silver Blaze." In this classic tale, the famous detective deduced that the central clue in the case was the failure of a watchdog to bark. Similarly, "the curious incident" about the purported escape of Sister Gertrude was the failure of the emerging anti-Catholic media to bark louder and with more effect.[15] Wightt's relatively rapid banishment to general obscurity is all the more puzzling in light of the notoriety gained by the alleged runaway nuns that followed her, most especially Rebecca Reed in Boston and Maria Monk in New York City.[16] While nativist ministers, editors, and publishers in those cities tirelessly, and profitably, promoted the tales of those supposed escaped nuns, the case of Sister Gertrude found no such champions in the Archdiocese of Baltimore in 1831.

Indeed, the public's response after learning of Wightt's story may be most significant for what did not happen—the scandal resulted in relatively little lasting damage to the public image of the American Catholic Church in general and the reputation of Georgetown Convent and Academy in particular. Although Wightt was the first runaway nun in America, the reason her story is not better known stems from her own intentions and behavior in the wake of the event, from the proactive efforts at damage control by

Archbishop Whitfield and his allies, and from the corresponding inability on the part of the sectarian and anti-Catholic press in America to exploit the scandal effectively.[17]

Despite the claims made by the author of the letter to the editor printed in the *Episcopal Recorder*, that Wightt's "elopement" had produced "no little excitement" in the District of Columbia, the curious point is how relatively little excitement it did cause, both locally or nationally. For example, no newspaper in the town of Georgetown or that of nearby Washington City carried any notice of Wightt's departure from the convent in the days following the incident. Moreover, Wightt herself clearly had no wish to go public. Rather, she was content to keep her quarrel within the Catholic family, so to speak, remaining a loyal member of the Church, although one disenchanted with life in the cloister. She later petitioned Whitfield to remove her ruling of excommunication (for leaving the convent enclosure without permission) and to dispense her from the requirement to live within the convent but not from her solemn vows of poverty, chastity, and obedience. Whitfield eventually wrote to Rome in support of her petition. Perhaps the Catholic hierarchy used its influence to lobby the local secular press not to publicize an event so potentially damaging to the Church.[18] No contemporary evidence confirms this claim, however. Moreover, the local population, with the exception of the academy's students and their parents, seemed little aware of Sister Gertrude's departure. Indeed, the first press accounts discussing Wightt appeared not in the local media but in the *Episcopal Recorder*, a low church evangelical journal published in Philadelphia.

It was not until April 2, a full eleven days after Wightt took flight, that the *Episcopal Recorder* published the first press report of the incident in an excerpt from a letter to the editor in an article titled "Papal Education." The sectarian paper printed the letter extract to warn its non-Catholic readers against patronizing Catholic schools, and in particular from sending their daughters to convent boarding schools like Georgetown Visitation Academy. The clergyman editor decried "the heedlessness in which Protestant, and in some cases pious families, commit the education of their children, to papists."[19] He singled out Georgetown Academy for "the iniquitous influences of the whole system of education, there carried on," and he admonished parents if "they value the immortal interests of their children, to rescue them from the pestilence and ruin, involved in a nunnery education."

Much as a contemporary news story on the internet may go viral in a matter of hours no matter its factual accuracy, once this first belated report of Wightt's getaway was published, it spread rapidly, at least by the standards of the early nineteenth century. From early April to mid-May, full and partial

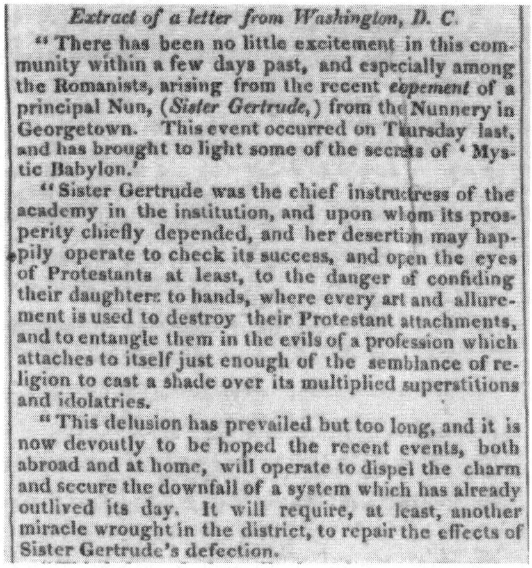

Extract of a letter from Washington, D. C.

"There has been no little excitement in this community within a few days past, and especially among the Romanists, arising from the recent *elopement* of a principal Nun, (*Sister Gertrude*,) from the Nunnery in Georgetown. This event occurred on Thursday last, and has brought to light some of the secrets of 'Mystic Babylon.'

"Sister Gertrude was the chief instructress of the academy in the institution, and upon whom its prosperity chiefly depended, and her desertion may happily operate to check its success, and open the eyes of Protestants at least, to the danger of confiding their daughters to hands, where every art and allurement is used to destroy their Protestant attachments, and to entangle them in the evils of a profession which attaches to itself just enough of the semblance of religion to cast a shade over its multiplied superstitions and idolatries.

"This delusion has prevailed but too long, and it is now devoutly to be hoped the recent events, both abroad and at home, will operate to dispel the charm and secure the downfall of a system which has already outlived its day. It will require, at least, another miracle wrought in the district, to repair the effects of Sister Gertrude's defection.

FIGURE 5.4. Article in *Episcopal Recorder,* April 2, 1831. https://archive.org/details/pub_episcopal-recorder?sort=title.

reprints of this same extract appeared in dozens of newspapers from Maine to Georgia and as far west as Ohio. Further, as with internet stories, the extract generated various related threads that newspaper and journal editors used to fill space, entice readers, and promote special causes. Various periodicals demonstrated less interest in establishing the truth about Wightt's actions than in shaping the narrative in the way most likely to appeal to the interests of their readers or to advance a journalistic agenda.

At least fifty-three newspapers and periodicals from the time reprinted the original report about Sister Gertrude in part or in whole.[20] Forty-four of those represented the secular press, plus six from the Protestant religious press and three from ideologically partisan periodicals, or what might be called the quasi-religious press. The sectarian press group of nine includes the aforementioned *Episcopal Recorder* (in Philadelphia), plus two Congregationalist organs, the *Boston Recorder* and the *Connecticut Observer* (in Hartford); two Baptist periodicals, the *Christian Watchman* (Boston) and the *Christian Secretary* (Hartford); and the *New York Evangelist,* a Presbyterian weekly. There were also two overtly anti-Masonic periodicals published in Providence, Rhode Island: the daily *Rhode Island American* and the *Microcosm and Weekly American.* One abolitionist organ, *The Liberator,* was then publishing in only the fourth month of what would be a successful thirty-five-year struggle to end chattel slavery in the United States.

THE SECULAR PRESS

Four days after the first report of Wightt's flight appeared in the *Episcopal Recorder*, an edited reprint of the letter was published in a secular Boston newspaper, the *Columbian Centinel*.[21] The next day the story found its way into another Massachusetts paper, the *Newburyport Herald*. In both cases the story appeared under the provocative title "Elopement of a Nun."[22] This change in title marked a shift in emphasis from that of the *Episcopal Recorder*, which offered the unhappy tale of Wightt as a way to condemn female convent schools and warn Protestant parents against patronizing them. The editor of the *Columbian Centinel*, however, chose "Elopement of a Nun," making a thinly veiled reference to a different point. While the word *elopement* in its general sense means "to slip away secretly," the title evoked the more popular meaning "to run away secretly to marry," often in defiance of parental authority. By juxtaposing *elopement* and *nun* in the same heading, the *Centinel* probably hoped to sensationalize Wightt's flight and titillate its readers with a hint of forbidden sex. Dozens of newspapers reprinted the letter under this more suggestive headline. Such language also played on public suspicions that the convent, despite Catholic assurances to the contrary, was in fact a den of secrecy that hid its sex and sedition.

If "Elopement of a Nun" proved the most popular heading for the story's reprints, the *Philadelphia Gazette* offered a different, perhaps more playful title: "I Won't Be a Nun!"[23] This title hearkens to a popular tune of the time. Ironically, the song's origins come from Catholic Ireland. The opening stanza and the chorus read:

> What a pity that such a pretty girl as I
> Should be sent to a nunnery to pine away and die!
> So I won't be a nun, I cannot be a nun!
> I'm so fond of pleasure that I cannot be a nun.

The tune's well-known lyrics portray the walls of the cloister not as a device to hide sexual debauchery, as later charged by Maria Monk and many of her imitators, than its opposite: a vehicle for safeguarding a nun's life as an unfulfilled and wasted existence, with women being condemned to unnatural confinement, austerity, and self-abnegation. In a later stanza the song laments how the convent denies a woman such worldly delights as shopping, "men flattering," and "fashionable clothes," as well as "music and dancing and chatting with beaux."[24]

The more ideological partisan press also sought to exploit Wightt's story for their particular issues. For example, the *Rhode Island American* reprinted the full text of "Elopement of a Nun" and linked it to the cause of anti-Masonry. An accompanying article identifies parallels between the suspicious secrecy of the Catholic convent and that of the Masonic lodge. The author compares the purported apostasy of Sister Gertrude from her religious vows with the apostasy of a renegade Mason like William Morgan from his oath of secrecy. Anti-Mason periodicals like the *Rhode Island Ameri*can and the *Microcosm and Weekly American* used the extract to attack all secret societies as having no place in an open, democratic republic.[25]

THE SECTARIAN PRESS

While the secular press tended to reflect the notion of the convent as an unnatural retreat from the joys of marriage and motherhood and the nun as an object of curiosity at best and pity at worst, the religious press more often followed the original lead of the *Episcopal Recorder.* Sectarian organs stressed the themes of convents as schools of subversion and of nuns as papal agents carrying out Vatican designs to undermine the American republic by corrupting its Protestant daughters. The *Boston Recorder,* a Congregational journal, referred to Wightt in an article titled "Catholic Schemes Exposed!!" The editor cites the case as among the "many facts [that] have lately transpired, which have in some degree, opened the eyes of the community to see the real design . . . of so many Roman Catholic Seminaries in our midst."[26] Specifically, the paper warns its readers against the "Ursuline community at Mount Benedict" in Charlestown. It narrates the story of an anonymous young girl "about 14 or 15 years of age" who had recently enrolled at the Ursuline academy. After only a week boarding at this institution, the intolerable conditions she endured there, "like Sister Gertrude, caused her to elope." The editor asks his readers, "What can one say of this institution, but that . . . it is one of those thousand snares set in this country, to entrap the rising generation." He concludes, "Let Protestants then beware; for, by sending their children to them, they *may* do a deed, over which coming generations will have cause to weep tears of blood!" This article found troubling parallels between the alleged torturous experiences of a nun in the convent with that of a pupil in a convent academy.

It is perhaps more than coincidental that in January 1832, Rebecca Reed followed Sister Gertrude's example by eloping from the Ursuline Convent after only four months as a postulant. Reed, a convert from the Episcopalian Church, had entered the Mount Benedict Convent the previous September. Some two and a half years later, in July 1834, a temporarily deranged nun, Sister Mary John (Elizabeth) Harrison fled from the same institution before returning voluntarily upon regaining her senses. Harrison's escape, nonetheless, helped spur the inspection of the convent premises by a group of town selectmen. Frustrated when legal means failed to produce evidence of Catholic foul play, a mob of nativist workmen who blamed Irish immigrants for reducing their wages and job opportunities burned the convent to the ground on August 10, 1834. The following year, Rebecca Reed published the first convent narrative in American history, *Six Months in a Convent*, purportedly an authentic account of her time as a postulant in the Ursuline community at Mount Benedict. This work sold so well that it paved the way for publication the following year of the even more popular *Awful Disclosures . . . of the Hotel Dieu Nunnery at Montreal* by Maria Monk, the best-selling book in the country until publication of *Uncle Tom's Cabin* by Harriet Beecher Stowe in 1852.[27] The notion that Wightt not only preceded Rebecca Reed as an escaped nun but may actually have influenced Reed has not been previously suggested in the scholarly literature.

THE CATHOLIC PRESS

In the wake of Archbishop Whitfield's advocacy to Rome on behalf of Sister Gertrude's petition for release from excommunication, the nascent Catholic media joined the fray, seeking to squelch rumors about her that were circulating nationally in the sectarian and secular press. One of the only three American Catholic newspapers then in circulation, the *Catholic Press* published by the diocese in Hartford, Connecticut, sought to correct the public record, control the press narrative, and defend the Church and its convent system from further public scandal.[28] To achieve this end, the paper's editor penned an article titled "Miss Ann Wightt (alias) Sister Gertrude" to "our brother Editors of the liberal cast" across the country. The *Catholic Press* offered a corrective counternarrative by addressing his colleagues: "*Messrs. Editors,*— Relying upon your liberality, I would ask the insertion of the enclosed article from the *Hartford Catholic Press*, being a correction of the unfair paragraph generally published entitled 'Elopement of a Nun.'"[29]

The Hartford paper attempted to combat rumors about Wightt by citing several facts that had come to light in the months following her flight from

Georgetown. Rather than an apostate from popery, as had been frequently reported, the paper announced that Wightt "still holds as sacred the Catholic faith, has acknowledged her error, been absolved from the ecclesiastical censure to which her precipitous step subjected her." The excommunication having been removed, she was again "admitted to holy communion." Although no longer living in the cloister, the editor notes, she "adheres still to her vows under the Archbishop of Baltimore" and "still signs her name Sister Gertrude." Finally, the article made clear that Sister Gertrude was contrite "and weeps sincerely in secret for the scandal she has caused."[30] In its particulars, this piece is essentially correct. The full facts would have been known to few beyond the principals involved. It therefore seems likely that Whitfield, or one of his lieutenants, leaked information about Wightt to the editor of the *Catholic Press*.

The *Catholic Press* ardently committed itself to setting the record straight and to defending all things Roman Catholic from those who might try to use the story of Sister Gertrude to discredit the Church more generally. Nevertheless, there is scant evidence that the diocese's campaign to address the scandal and answer the falsehoods swirling around it had much effect on shaping public opinion in either direction. By the time the newspaper entered the fray in mid-June, the wave of reprints of the letter from the *Episcopal Recorder* had already ebbed. There is no record of any newspaper reprinting the story from the *Recorder* in any form after mid-May. Moreover, only one newspaper, the *Georgian,* published in Savannah, is known to have acknowledged the letter of the *Catholic Press,* printing its contents without further comment.[31]

THE ANTI-CATHOLIC PRESS

At the same time, the lack of follow-up by either the secular or the religious press, both locally and nationally, on the original report on Wightt is noteworthy. The reasons relate as much to where and when the event occurred as to the personalities involved. Above all, there is the fact that the Archdiocese of Baltimore, which at the time comprised the faithful residing in the District of Columbia and most of the state of Maryland, was unique in the Early Republic. This region had a strong Catholic presence that began in colonial days, with a large native-born Catholic population of English descent that was well integrated into American life and culture. In contrast, both Boston, where Rebecca Reed became infamous, and New York City, where Harper & Brothers published Maria Monk's *Awful Disclosures,* had been bastions of anti-Catholic sentiment during the colonial era. By the mid-1830s the rising tide of Irish immigrants in both cities galvanized a strong nativist backlash marked by some of the most notorious anti-Catholic incidents of the time. A mob torched the Ursuline Convent in Charlestown, just outside Boston, in the wake of an anti-Catholic sermon delivered by the Reverend Lyman Beecher, which was later published as part of his *A Plea for the West* (1835). In New York City, Samuel F. B. Morse published his best-selling *Foreign Conspiracy against the Liberties of the United States* (1835), which sounded the claxon as to a papal plot to use immigrants to destroy republican institutions in America.[32]

Earlier in the decade, however, the Archdiocese of Baltimore proved far less fertile ground for anti-Catholic agitation. This situation prevailed despite the efforts of the Reverend George Bourne, editor of *The Protestant,* who founded the journal in 1830 as the first overtly anti-popery publication in the country. In a fiery editorial that foreshadowed the militant rhetoric by which William Lloyd Garrison would soon condemn Southern slaveholders in *The Liberator,* Bourne challenged the Catholic media and clergy in the Archdiocese of Baltimore: "We ourselves are enjoined to 'be quiet and let the Marylanders alone!' We will not be silent," he wrote defiantly. "Their own Press dare not expose their iniquities; *ours shall.* Their own preachers are not at liberty to call things by their right names; we will."[33] True to his word, Bourne soon engaged in a journalistic duel with Father Charles Pise, editor of *The Metropolitan,* the official organ of the Archdiocese of Baltimore and the first Catholic monthly magazine in the country.[34] Despite his bold manifesto, however, Bourne proved unsuccessful in his goal to establish an anti-popery beachhead in the archdiocese. At the end of August 1830, Whitfield reported to Rome that *The Protestant* had failed to gain an audience "in Baltimore, where our religion is so much respected that not one of the many public papers tho' edited by Protestants, would consent to publish the prospectus."[35] Whitfield concludes, almost gleefully, that Bourne "complains that Baltimore is lost to them being completely under the sway of popery." Such was the chilly climate for anti-popery activities in the Archdiocese of Baltimore seven months later when Wightt abandoned Georgetown Convent.

It is worth noting that had Wightt walked out four years later, her case would have certainly attracted much greater local and national attention from the growing anti-Catholic media. The anti-popery crusade first gained a toehold in the Archdiocese of Baltimore in 1835 when a group of clergymen formed the nonsectarian Protestant Association in the city of Baltimore. In January, the Reverend Robert J. Breckinridge and Reverend Andrew B. Cross, two Old School Presbyterians and founding members of the group, began publishing the *Baltimore Literary and Religious Magazine* as the mouthpiece for the Protestant Association. The editors' agitation of anti-popery action in general and of the convent question in particular prepared the ground for a riot in 1839 against the Carmelite Convent in Baltimore following the flight of Sister Isabella (Olivia) Neale, a mentally ill nun from that institution. In the 1850s Cross revived this same theme and led a grassroots petition campaign calling for Maryland lawmakers to inspect all convents in the state. In 1856 the Know-Nothing majority in the state legislature appointed a "convent committee" to look into the question of whether young women in convents were being held against their will by profligate priests.[36]

Sister Ann Gertrude Wightt may have been the first runaway nun in America, but her public notoriety proved fleeting. The local media never reported on her departure, and the national media, content to reprint a single account (albeit under different titles), never chose to follow up on her story. Wightt did not fit the profile later established by her better-known successors in antebellum America. Unlike Elizabeth Harrison and Olivia Neale, Wightt's flight never triggered an anti-convent riot. Unlike Rebecca Reed and Maria Monk, Wightt never publicly renounced Catholicism. Also, unlike Reed and Monk, among others, Wightt never attempted to pen an exposé of life in a convent. Rather than seek to capitalize financially or otherwise on her temporary notoriety, Wightt preferred to withdraw into the bosom of her Catholic friends from Mexico, the Iturbide family. Accepted as a quasi-member of the family, Wightt resided at their apartment in Georgetown for two years following her brief stint in the public eye. She earned her keep by acting as a kind of governess to the daughters, a role she had already filled as their instructor at Visitation Academy. Nonetheless, the aftermath of her unexpected departure did create an immediate crisis for her former convent and academy and a long-term problem for both the Archdiocese of Baltimore and the Propaganda Fide of Rome.

6

She Is in a Dangerous Frame of Mind

On June 6, 1831, Archbishop Whitfield wrote to the Propaganda Fide to report the unhappy news of a "runaway nun" in his archdiocese. Whitfield identifies the main issues and personalities behind the event, which had occurred some two and a half months earlier. The archbishop explains to Rome that one "from amongst the sisters of the Convent of Georgetown, named Gertrude (formerly Wyght) [*sic*], abandoned her home, the mother superior and other sisters none the wiser." He continues, "After she had made her way through the girls school adjoining the convent" dressed in the borrowed clothes of students, she hired a hack to take her to "the home of Mr. Van Ness, where she was kindly received by his wife."[1] The home in question was the elegant Van Ness Mansion owned by General John Peter Van Ness, mayor of Washington City, and his wife, heiress Marcia Burnes Van Ness, first cousin to Sister Gertrude. What concerned the archbishop about the nun's kinfolk was less their political and social prominence than their Protestant affiliation. Whitfield feared how that connection might complicate any attempt to contain the public scandal surrounding the wayward nun.

Because she was headmistress of the academy at the time of her departure, Wightt's actions had the potential not only to embarrass Georgetown Visitation Convent but also to threaten its finances, as bewildered parents demanded an explanation for her conduct. Moreover, because Wightt had left the cloister without permission and without being dispensed from her vows, she was automatically excommunicated and barred from communion with the Church faithful. Her case thus posed a vexing problem for both her personal salvation and in public relations for the American Catholic hierarchy. Adding to the archbishop's difficulties was the fact that Wightt was well-connected socially and, according to Whitfield, her influential relatives were no friends of Rome.

FIGURE 6.1. Marcia Burnes Van Ness. Wikimedia Commons.

What were the actions taken by the American Catholic church leaders, male and female, clergy and lay, in attempting to control the damage from the scandal associated with America's first runaway nun? Catholic leaders moved to address concerns about 1) the peace and well-being of the sixty members of Georgetown Convent; 2) the reputation and finances of Georgetown Academy in the minds of its one hundred students and their parents; 3) the spiritual and mental state of Sister Gertrude herself; and 4) the public image of the

Catholic Church just as a new wave of anti-Catholicism was about to break. It also reveals how Sister Gertrude did not sit by passively during the process, but sought to influence events by some unorthodox moves of her own.

Whitfield and several of his allies among the clergy, the women religious, and the laity labored in a variety of ways to prevent the scandal from becoming a public relations disaster for the Catholic Church in general and for Georgetown Visitation Convent in particular. Most demonstrated a genuine concern for Wightt's spiritual and mental health. At the same time, extant documents reveal they were motivated primarily by a desire to contain the damage to the Church from the scandal. They endeavored throughout to handle her case solely as an internal Church matter to avoid the harmful publicity that occurred later around other reputed escaped nuns. In particular, in their personal correspondence and other writings Whitfield and his vicar general, Father Louis Deluol, testify to their initial worries that the unpredictable nun might pen a hostile account of her life in the cloister, which could fuel growing anti-Catholic sentiment in the country. She might therefore damage the institutional Church and delay or even prevent altogether the nascent convent revolution in the United States from entering its "takeoff" period.

CONCERN FOR GEORGETOWN CONVENT AND ACADEMY

Wightt's sternest nineteenth-century critics realized that her departure had a devastating impact on her Visitation community. According to Sister Josephine Barber, primary chronicler of Georgetown Convent, "After Supper, while the Community was assembled at recreation hour, one the French Sisters, Sr. M. Agatha, entered, pale as death, & raising her hands exclaimed: 'My God, Sisters! Sr. W. is out she is gone!'" The nuns reacted with "sobs & tears. . . . Some went to the choir to prostrate before the B[lesse]d Sacrament & seek for solace at the foot of the Tabernacle. All wept & prayed for the loved & lost one."[2]

The Lathrops' account echoes and elaborates on Barber's account:

> The news was received with sobs and tears . . . it may seem strange that the sisters should so deeply take to heart this willful secession of one of their number. But it meant, to them, the peril of her soul; because of her violating promises to God, the most sacred and profound, which involved her whole existence here and still more hereafter. . . . All wept and prayed for her whom they had so loved and now had lost!—who perhaps had lost herself; and some went to the

choir, where they prostrated themselves before the Blessed Sacrament, petitioning for pity and mercy towards her.[3]

Contemporaneous testimony from others support such later accounts. A little over two weeks after the incident, Sister Ann Agatha Combs reflected on how the tragic case of Sister Gertrude served as a lesson for all Visitandines: "Oh how much do we prize & esteem our holy vocation, particularly, since the sad downfall of unfortunate Sister Gertrude. How necessary it is for us to be humble + submissive to our Superiors."[4] Despite having a history of opposition to Sister Gertrude's policies regarding the academy, Sister Ann Agatha was also saddened by Sister Gertrude's departure and her remarks suggest that she saw Gertrude as too proud and not sufficiently submissive to convent authorities, an interpretation later shared by the Lathrops.

While the nuns lamented the loss of their monastery's subprioress, the students were equally dismayed to learn of the loss of their school's headmistress. Early in June, Josephine Barber, then attending the academy, and another student called on Sister Gertrude, who was now living with the Iturbide family in Georgetown. Youngest daughter of Sister Mary Austin, the fifteen-year-old Josephine had known Sister Gertrude since infancy. The sight of Sister Gertrude in secular dress rather than a religious habit greatly upset the impressionable teenage girl. Barber immediately pleaded, "Sister, won't you go back to the convent?" "'No indeed,' she replied, with a peculiar shake of the head which all who knew her remember."[5] Despite her emotional reaction, Barber managed to converse with Wightt for about twenty minutes, answering the latter's questions about the Ursuline Convent in Charlestown, Massachusetts, where Barber's eldest sister was a member. Coincidentally, three years later a mob of Protestant workmen torched this very institution in the wake of the rumored escapes of Rebecca Reed and Sister Mary John Harrison, perhaps the most infamous anti-Catholic incident in US history.[6]

Despite reeling from the immediate shock of Sister Gertrude's unexpected departure, the nuns in the convent and the students in the academy appear to have suffered surprisingly few lasting negative effects. About three weeks after the event, Whitfield and Father John Joseph Chance visited Georgetown Convent. They returned to Baltimore and noted their pleasure at finding that the situation in the monastery and at the school had calmed down. In a letter to Deluol, Chance reports that he found "at the convent, things are going rather smoothly."[7] Deluol then records in his own diary: "The Convent and the Academy are quiet. 4 or 5 of the nuns, who care for Sister Gertrude, are somewhat disturbed, but there is no bad spirit among them."[8] He also notes that the archbishop "is rather happy about his trip to Georgetown."[9]

The testimony of Ann Mattingly, then a Georgetown postulant struggling to discern her own religious vocation, confirms that rumors about Sister Gertrude's actions circulated even among those closed off from the outside world. On April 16, writing to Father Dubuisson, Mattingly comments on the plight of Sister Gertrude: "People have another subject for conversation, at present, & painful it is to hear the scandalous reports that are rumoured, of unfortunate Sister Gertrude. She is still at Mrs. Iturbide's, and is impenitent as ever."[10] Mattingly then reflects on the irony of Sister Gertrude's actions in light of her own aspiration to a religious calling: "Oh that it were in my power to embrace what she has renounced!" she implores, "but, I am not without hope . . . I may still be called." She writes that from her vantage point things had settled down in the convent and the academy and also that she believed that the students had responded positively to the regime of Mother Madeleine, a view directly at odds with Sister Gertrude's perspective. "I have also been to the Academy," Mattingly observes, and "I have there found all in harmony and peace. The children are delighted with dear Sister Madeleine Augustine."

Perhaps in response to Wightt's charges against Mother Madeleine, the fifty or so professed members of the monastery held an election for superior on May 13. This date was several months before a new election might have been expected to occur under normal circumstances and was scheduled to affirm the community's support for their leader. The result was "a nearly unanimous vote" of confidence for Mother Madeleine. Upon hearing the news, Deluol triumphantly reports in his diary, "The whole Convent is at peace and the Academy prosperous."[11] Further easing the transition, Sister Stanislaus Jones was named the new directress of the academy. "Sister Stanny," as she was known to the sisters and students, was a multitalented and much-loved instructor in music and languages. Replacing "Sister Getty" with "Sister Stanny" must have reassured many students and parents about the stability of the academy's operations.[12]

Near the end of the disrupted school term, Sister Mary Cecilia Brooks, an opponent of Sister Gertrude, seconded these assessments in a letter to the archbishop. She assures Whitfield that, despite the Sister Gertrude affair, the academy had retained the support of the families of their students. "We are still honoured with [the] confidence of the parents + Guardians of our Young Ladies, + indeed, God seems to watch over us with redoubled kindness."[13] She notes that one "Mr. Lasala," a wealthy New York merchant and father of three boarders, "has just written to his eldest daughter, stating that the clouds which recently overcast our institution, are now dispersed, and that the beam of splendor appears with more refulgency than ever." During the financial crisis of the early 1820s, John Baptist Lasala had stepped in providentially to save the convent and academy. Now, in 1831, when the convent and academy faced a different kind of crisis, Lasala once more donated his considerable financial and social capital to help restore confidence in Georgetown Visitation.[14]

In anticipation of the upcoming school term in August, Father William Matthews, Father Wheeler's replacement as spiritual director of the convent, issued a new, but little altered, academy prospectus. Appearing on the front page of such major newspapers as the *National Gazette* from Philadelphia, this document demonstrated continuance of the best practices in teaching and curriculum that patrons of the school had come to expect.[15] Over that spring and summer, continuity in practices despite change in leadership personnel served to reassure most parents and their daughters that Georgetown Visitation Convent and Academy would carry on just as effectively as before.

CONCERN FOR SISTER GERTRUDE

Just as the nuns in the convent and students in the school worried about Sister Gertrude's salvation, so too did some members among the clergy and laity outside the cloister. For example, on the very evening of her flight, two Jesuits from nearby Georgetown College visited Sister Gertrude at the Van Ness residence. The meeting quickly reached a stalemate, however. The clergymen urged the wayward nun to repent her actions and return to her home in the cloister. The nun refused to comply but did ask for the priests' blessings. The priests refrained from giving them because in their eyes the nun remained impenitent. The Jesuits departed with neither side giving way.[16]

Although personally condemnatory of Wightt's conduct, Father Deluol's diary entries in the weeks following her flight testify to the distress felt by her friends over her mental and spiritual welfare. These worries are especially evident in Deluol's reports of Madame Iturbide's persistent pleas to Father Chance to visit the distraught nun. Over the previous five years, as both an academy parent and occasional resident in the convent, the widow Iturbide had come to know Wightt well. Deluol records Iturbide's genuine alarm at Wightt's altered mental state and Iturbide's repeated calls to him for help.

Only four days after Sister Gertrude's flight, Iturbide wrote to Chance, informing him that Wightt had moved into the family's apartments in Georgetown. The former empress of Mexico begged the priest to visit soon, "as he is the only one who can save Sister Gertrude."[17] It is not clear why Iturbide targeted the Sulpician priest as key to Sister Gertrude's salvation. Chance was a native of Baltimore, son of refugees from Saint-Domingue, and an instructor at St. Mary's Seminary, but he was not known to be a close acquaintance of Wightt. Nor is the meaning of Iturbide's cryptic comment exactly clear. Did she want to "save" Wightt's soul, her life, or both? What does seem likely is that, in the days immediately following her departure from the convent, Wightt was suffering from depression, perhaps even a nervous breakdown, as the full implications of her impulsive and irrevocable action dawned upon her.

After three days with no reply, Iturbide sent a second note to Chance, again "begging him to go to Georgetown, for Sister Gertrude," and on March 31 she followed with a third message "urging him to go."[18] About two weeks after receiving the first note, Chance complied with Iturbide's desperate requests. On April 7 he accompanied Whitfield on the latter's monthly visit to Georgetown. From the extant records it is not clear why Chance delayed, nor why Madame Iturbide felt he was the only one who could save Sister Gertrude. The priest's lack of haste suggests he did not share Iturbide's alarm. After meeting with the wayward nun, Chance pessimistically told Deluol that he found "little hope for Sister Gertrude."[19] Again, his comment is cryptic: Did the priest hold out little hope for Wightt's mind, her body, her soul, or all three? Whatever he meant, Chance clearly thought her condition was not good. Throughout the crisis Chance's actions or, more accurately, his inaction suggest a rather surprising indifference to the nun's fate, especially once he had satisfied himself that her flight had no lasting harm to either the convent or its academy.

Much as Madame Iturbide tried to get help for Sister Gertrude, so too did Georgetown's former spiritual director, Michael Wheeler. The day after her flight, Wheeler met with Deluol, his Sulpician superior, and "complained that the Archbishop was rather harsh toward him, in that whole affair."[20] In his diary Deluol reveals that, while financial debt incurred by "unnecessary" improvements for the academy was primary in Whitfield's "harsh" treatment of Wheeler, a contributing factor may have been rumors of a "special friendship" between Wheeler and Wightt.[21] On March 25, agitated by reports of Sister Gertrude's precarious mental health, Wheeler asked Deluol for permission to visit her. Deluol refused on the grounds that such a meeting would feed idle talk of a sexual relationship between the priest and the nun. "I told Him No," wrote Deluol, "then I told him about the unfortunate rumors which had been circulating in Baltimore and Washington about him and Sister Gertrude, for a year."[22] There is no evidence that such rumors had any basis in fact, but Deluol recognized that perception often trumps reality. Despite the warning from his superior, Deluol notes that Wheeler "seems to have hinted that he would go to see her, if she wishes it." But Wightt later wrote Wheeler asking him *not* to come visit her, as "it would not be wise . . . considering the rumors about him" and lest he suffer consequences to his reputation.[23]

CONCERN FOR THE CHURCH

In his diary entry dated March 22, 1831, Father Deluol recorded not only the news of Sister Gertrude's flight but also that she sought refuge "in Washington at her cousin's, General Van Ness, who is a Protestant."[24] Deluol's identification of the religion of John Peter Van Ness was not just a passing reference; it reflected the fear Deluol shared with the archbishop and other Catholic clergy—that a hostile element of the press might exploit her case to advance budding anti-Catholic nativism, or what the historian Ray Billington would later label "the Protestant Crusade."[25]

Two days after her flight, Wheeler informed Deluol that he had received a letter from Wightt. The contents of this missive greatly worried the Sulpician superior, who found it "far from orthodox . . . in which she complained of despotism, spying, etc., in convents."[26] Wightt's letter to Wheeler is now lost, but it appears to have repeated charges found in Wightt's letter to Whitfield as well as contents of the now-lost letter to Mother Madeleine.[27] Deluol describes both of these letters as "written in the style of a Luther."[28]

What, specifically, did Deluol mean by "written in the style of a Luther"? At one level Sister Gertrude's behavior demonstrated that, like Martin Luther's famous stand at the Diet of Worms of 1521, she was pitting her personal conscience and her own understanding of the Word of God against her obedience to the authority of Rome.[29] On another level Deluol appears much more concerned about Wightt's reference to her own "persecution" and to the convent as a "perfect inquisition." Such charges echo denunciations of monastic life made by Luther and other writers of the Protestant Reformation and by Enlightenment-influenced renegade clerics like the Italian bishop Scipio de Ricci and the apostate Spanish priest Blanco White. English translations of the works of both of these authors had been published and widely distributed in Britain during the parliamentary debate over the Catholic Emancipation Bill of 1829 and gained an audience in the United States as well.[30]

PASTORAL LETTERS OF THE FIRST PROVINCIAL COUNCIL

That same year, the nation's Catholic bishops met in Baltimore to convene the First Provincial Council of the American Catholic Church, with Archbishop Whitfield presiding. The gathering of prelates called attention to works they considered dangerous in its decrees and, in particular, the pastoral letters addressed to the clergy and to the faithful, respectively. Decrying the growing "attacks on the faith," the bishops in their letter to the laity asserted: "Amongst the various misfortunes to which we have been exposed, one of the greatest is misrepresentation of the tenets, the principles, and the practices of our Church."[31] They continued by saying, "The public press, the very bench of public justice, have been all influenced by extraordinary efforts directed against us; so that . . . we are exhibited as what we are not, and charged with maintaining what we detest." Besides condemning the disturbing rise of anti-Catholic sentiment in the sectarian press, the council also promoted support for the infant Catholic press, if only on the grounds of self-defense. "If you look around and see how many such [periodicals] are maintained . . . by our separated brethren," the shepherds encouraged their flock, "it will indeed be a matter of reproach should we not uphold a few of our own." The concerns of the prelates were not unjustified. The following year, *The Protestant,* the first overtly anti-Catholic weekly newspaper in the United States, began publishing in New York City under the editorship of the Reverend George Bourne.[32]

In their letter aimed at the nation's clergy, the bishops lamented how scandals associated with the clergy (and, by extension, members of religious orders, including nuns) damaged the Church's reputation in the eyes of both its enemies and the faithful. "In other days and in other nations the crimes of the clergy have caused the degradation of the Church, the contempt of the institutions of religion, sanctioned the vices of the laity, been the sources of schism, and the origin of heresy," the prelates admitted. "Let us rather call upon you to aid us in guarding our infant churches against such dreadful calamities for the time to come."[33] Whitfield and Deluol feared that the scandal surrounding Sister Gertrude had the potential for just such a deleterious impact on the American Catholic Church.

When viewed in light of the contemporary developments in the Church and in the culture, Deluol's comparison of Sister Gertrude to Martin Luther suggests that his concern was less for her spiritual and mental well-being than for the potential damage she might inflict on the Church. Just as Brother Martin became a heretical monk, Sister Gertrude might become an apostate nun with a tale to tell. In the many entries in his diary about Sister Gertrude, Deluol demonstrates little to no sympathy for the state of her mind and soul, remaining ever wary of her unknown intentions and unpredictable behavior. When describing a recent dinner he attended at the archbishop's residence, for example, Deluol could barely contain his glee upon seeing a "Protestant newspaper in which Sister Gertrude was bad-mouthed."[34] What Deluol identifies as a "Protestant newspaper" was in fact an issue of the *Episcopal Recorder,* the sectarian weekly published in Philadelphia that gave the first press coverage to Sister Gertrude's flight. As previously noted, this newspaper had less "bad-mouthed" Sister Gertrude than used her escape as an occasion to warn of the dangers of educating Protestant daughters in Catholic academies. As other reprints of her story began to pop up in the national press, Deluol saw that, rather than bad-mouth Sister Gertrude, anti-Catholic propagandists hoped to use her as a weapon to bad-mouth the Catholic Church.[35]

Most worrisome of those hostile periodicals was Bourne's *The Protestant.* The Presbyterian editor immediately recognized the potential of Wightt's unique story to advance the nascent anti-popery cause that he had been nurturing for more than a year. His paper reprinted the original article as it appeared in the *Episcopal Recorder* but under the more sensational title "Escape of a Nun." Bourne prophetically identified Wightt's departure as "probably, the first instance in the U. States, of female liberation from the snares of the Jesuits." He confidently predicted, "that sister Gertrude will explain the dread secrets of the unholy prison house of girls in which she has so long been immured."[36]

Only a few years later, such language and imagery would become familiar tropes in a booming anti-Catholic literature industry. Thanks to publication of anti-convent exposés like Rebecca Reed's *Six Months in a Convent* and the even more notorious and popular Maria Monk's *Awful Disclosures,* the sale of anti-Catholic works became a thriving business. Marketing of such "prejudice for profit" was meant to alert thousands of American readers to the alleged iniquities to be found within such "priests' prisons for women."[37]

In 1831, however, such horror stories had yet to be written in America, let alone purchased and read. Indeed, Bourne had previously bewailed his difficulties trying to promote the anti-popery gospel within the boundaries of the Archdiocese of Baltimore, the self-described "American Rome." Bourne hoped the Sister Gertrude scandal would allow him to establish a beachhead in that stronghold of popery in America.[38]

The outcome for which Bourne fervently wished is one that the Catholic hierarchy in Baltimore honestly feared. Two days after the escaped nun article appeared in *The Protestant,* Deluol records in his diary that "Sister Gertrude does not want to return to her convent (where they don't want her, anyway), nor does she wish to join any other Community. She wants to keep her vow of chastity, but wishes to be dispensed of the other two." He then adds, ominously, "She is in a dangerous frame of mind."[39] The most generous meaning of the phrase "a dangerous frame of mind" is that Deluol honestly worried for Sister Gertrude's mental health. But a more likely reading is that it revealed the priest's deep suspicion that this wayward nun may endanger the Church and its convent system.

Deluol and Whitfield in Baltimore, along with the Sisters of the Visitation in Georgetown, reflected on Sister Gertrude's dangerous frame of mind

PRINTED WEEKLY AT TWO DOLLARS PER ANNUM, BY ROBERT NESBIT,

VOL. II. NEW YORK, SEPTEMBER 24, 1831.

THE PROTESTANT.

REV. GEORGE BOURNE, EDITOR.

"THE DEVIL IS COME TO YOU."

We have just received the prospectus of the Convent and Monastery at George Town, and also of the Monastery at Baltimore—and a few sentences which we quote in their own words, will aid Protestants, to form a correct estimate of those "cages of unclean and hateful birds."

GEORGE TOWN CONVENT. "The Ladies will be vigilant in requiring an exact compliance with every rule of the Institution.—— *Protestant young ladies attend at the church hours, and are expected to observe the general regulations of exterior worship.* ——— *Young ladies, when visited, are always attended by a sister.* ——— *Letters written or received by them* ARE EXAMINED, *by the Directress, previously to their delivery.*" ——— No child is received before the conclusion of her seventh year, and young ladies above fifteen must not expect to be received.

The cost is five dollars entrance. Board, &c. *one hundred and fifty dollars;* Ink, quills, &c., *four.* Use of apparatus, &c. *ten* dollars. Each language, except English, *twenty* dollars. Drawing and Painting in water colors, twenty dollars; and in oil colors, *twenty* dollars. The Harp, *eighty* dollars; Piano, *forty-eight* dollars; Guitar, *forty-eight* dollars—Vocal Music, *forty* dollars—and Dancing—what they please. So that including the French language, and excluding the Harp and Guitar—the female youth at George Town must pay only, *three hundred and twelve* dollars per annum, besides pocket money, and the crimson merinos, and azure silk dresses, and azure bonnet and other paraphernalia, for the privilege of becoming a Jesuit Nun, and an idolatrous devotee of the "Queen of Heaven!" All this is gravely signed by WILLIAM MATTHEWS, the Jesuit Director of that Convent of Sisters.

Notwithstanding the late elopement of *Sister Gertrude* from this den of iniquity; the National Gazatte states—"that all which is undertaken and promised in the Prospectus, is ably and faithfully performed. The institution has always had a number of inmates and pupils of other religious denominations, and the pledges given with respect to them have never been violated." Would any person believe it possible that in direct contradiction to multiplied facts, that Protestant girls have been transformed into genuine Papist idolaters and seducers, through the artifices of those Franciscans and Jesuits, the conductor of a Journal in Philadelphia would have the Papistical effrontery, thus to falsify, and blind the public to the horrors and beastliness of female Convents.

GEORGE TOWN COLLEGE. From the Prospectus we quote the following statements. "The Students are always under the eye of the prefect, even in their ordinary walks and recreations. *The exercises of religious worship are Catholic, but members of every other religious denomination are received, of whom it is required, that they respectfully assist at the public duties of religion with their companions.* All letters are to be addressed to the President."

MARY'S COLLEGE BALTIMORE. Attached to the advertisement of this Jesuit Monastery; there is a fulsome eulogy of the erudition, discipline, &c. of that institution, from one of the Baltimore Papers. This is intolerably shameless. Some years ago the Professors and Tutors of that juvenile prison, were the laughing stock, even of sciolists, for their ignorance. The discipline is neither more nor less than a system inveterately pursued to make the boys Papists and Jesuits—and competent judges affirm, that any approximation to academic scholarship, has never been exemplified by a single pupil, who has passed through that "house of bondage."

SPRING-HILL, MOBILE. At this Monastery, eight ecclesiastical, and fifty lay students are employed in learning "the mystery of iniquity."

Babylonish Temples. A large Masshouse is speedily to be erected at Mobile. At Pensacola an idolatrous house is now finishing. A Masshouse is to be constructed at Collins' Cross Roads, South Carolina.

ADVERSARIES. Six Jesuit Massmen are now roaming, and two others are daily expected to commence their "going about, seeking whom they may devour," in Alabama and Fiorida.

POPISH HIERARCHY IN THE U. S. John England has issued a proclamation to the people of America, dated 29th of August, 1831—from which we extract the following summary of Popery; in the most authentic form demonstrating, that the Dragon has set up the BEAST in this Republic, and given him

FIGURE 6.2. Article in *The Protestant,* September 24, 1831. Courtesy New York Historical Society.

not only out of concern for her personal sanity and salvation, but also for her story's potential to tar the public image of the Church. By the nineteenth century, tales of escaped nuns already had a long history in Europe and Sister Gertrude had the potential to become the first such protagonist in the United States. Seeking to prevent such an unwelcome outcome, Whitfield sought authorization from Rome to handle the case.

WIGHTT'S LETTER TO ROME, APRIL 30, 1831

Wightt's actions appear to confirm her dangerous frame of mind. On April 30, 1831, she took the unprecedented step, at least for an American nun, of petitioning Pope Gregory XVI, care of the Propaganda Fide in Rome, to be absolved of her excommunication for leaving the convent's enclosure and be dispensed from her solemn vows, save the vow of chastity. The milder, deferential tone of this letter was a far cry from her letter to Whitfield of March 22, the one Deluol referred to as "written in the style of a Luther." In her letter of April 30, addressed to "His Holiness," Wightt admits her error in the way she left the convent, but also reiterates that she had no desire or intention to return to the cloister, either in Georgetown Visitation or any other convent.[40]

The letter opens by addressing Pope Gregory as "Most Holy Father." She then systematically relates the reasons for her entering religious life, for her disenchantment with it, and for her departure from it. The contrast with the almost stream of consciousness style found in her March 22 letter to Whitfield suggests that her agitation had been replaced with equanimity. Throughout the entire April missive Wightt refers to herself in the third person. She begins the narrative by mentioning her birth in Prince George's County, Maryland, in 1799 and her education beginning at age eight in the Academy of the Convent of the Pious Ladies.

She identifies three reasons for her attraction to religious life. First, "she adopted the idea that salvation in the world was impracticable," a belief she attributes to "the limited manner in which she was educated and without having the least experience [in the world]." Second, she admits to "attachments to some of her teachers" during her time as a student. Nuns serving as role models for their pupils was a common source of religious vocations. Third, Wightt blames "an overrated opinion of the invariable *tranquillity,* and happiness of the religious state" that motivated her "to take the veil at the early age of fifteen."

Wightt details the specific ways that she remained innocent of the true nature of religious life, in particular the role of vows and her knowledge of the rules of convent life. She claims to have "made her profession [in 1817] without knowing exactly the nature of vows and without paying attention even to the form in which she + the other religious took." She claims to have been ignorant of the "full implications of her vows because of the lack of necessary books to understand them." As she notes, once Georgetown became a Visitation convent in 1816, subsequent correspondence "from European convents made clear that Georgetown lacked some key books about religious life and did not follow some of those they did have." Ultimately, Sister Gertrude argues that she had "followed vows without knowing the rules, imagining them to be simple when they were complicated." Here she does not appear to mean the canonical differences between simple and solemn vows, but her own ignorance of the Visitation Rule as applied in European monasteries.

Sister Gertrude directly addresses the reasons for her disillusionment with religious life and admits to having hesitated to renew her vows when it became obvious that she and the members could not practice the rules. This refusal appears to have begun sometime after the French Sisters came to Georgetown in August 1829. Soon thereafter, Sister Mary Agatha, one of the newcomers, was named mistress of novices. The next year, Mother Juliana resigned as superior, in favor of Sister Madeleine Augustine, one of the French Sisters. That is, after living as a professed member of Georgetown Visitation Convent since 1817, under a Visitation Rule adapted to an American setting and approved and reapproved by papal indults, Sister Gertrude now felt forced to follow European standards of the rule which involved many changes that she opposed. Indeed, she came to believe that conforming to these changes would violate her conscience and hence jeopardize her salvation. Only after confiding her doubts about renewing her vows to her confessor (Father Wheeler or Father López) did she reluctantly agree to do so.

Sister Gertrude provides a list of reasons why the tranquility of convent life turned out not to be what she had expected, citing "the strange manner in which the Convent had been established." Here she means the foundation of the convent of the Pious Ladies. It came into existence without any of its founders being professed members of an established order, it continued for seventeen years without any formal rule, and it only established one after affiliating with the Order of the Visitation in 1816. Wightt also disparages "the injudicious choice of members." By that she seems to be pointing to the fact that so many of the Pious Ladies and early Visitandines were blood relations, not only of the convent's male founder, Archbishop Leonard Neale, but also of each other. In consequence, factions emerged that divided the community in the early 1820s. Wightt further laments what she labels "the egregious mismanagement of funds from the commissioners." This complaint appears to refer to the financial crisis that plagued the convent in the early 1820s, long after the rest of the country had recovered from the effects of the Panic of 1819. Finally, the experience of barely surviving the financial crisis had driven home to Sister Gertrude "the absolute necessity of keeping an Academy for support of the Community." At the same time, Wightt admits the paradox surrounding the academy "(which of itself is contrary to the rules) but which stern necessity compelled, and which was often subject of discussion etc. were all so many causes of concern, and failed not to disturb the tranquillity of the Convent." This conundrum, of Georgetown Convent maintaining both a contemplative life and an academy, Wightt had tried to solve with her abortive attempt to change Georgetown from the Visitandine Rule to that of the Ursulines.

According to this letter, Wightt based her decision to leave the convent on a constellation of related reasons. She admits to "finding it impossible to preserve tranquillity of mind + conscience amidst the disturbances so frequently arising" within the monastery, perhaps an allusion to either the factions within the community during the early 1820s or, more likely, to her recent personal and administrative disagreements with Mother Madeleine. Wightt confesses to finding herself a minority voice on the question of the best strategy to secure the long-term existence of the community, admitting "she could not agree with the generality in sentiments on some points which she deemed essential for the prosperity of the house." (Here she might have listed the community conflicts over the proper of role of the academy, her failed attempt to change the convent to the Ursuline Rule, and her plan to construct an observatory.) She also cites that in "her responsible offices arose matters submitted to her judgements or on which she was obliged to to [*sic*] think." On this matter, Wightt refers to her sense that Mother Madeleine sought to undermine her authority both as assistant superior and as directress of the academy. In closing, and for the sake of her own peace of mind and the "tranquillity" of the community, she made "a determination to seek for peace out of the convent and accordingly left it." Repeating sentiments she had shared when pleading her case in her letter of March 22 to Whitfield, Wightt fell back on the defense that she acted "thinking that she did right and believing that for her tranquillity there was no other recourse." She also repeats the claim made to Whitfield, that she had left not solely out of self-interest but also for the common good. Again, referring to herself in the third person, she claims, "In this momentous step she lost not sight of the welfare of her Community and was persuaded that her leaving would be conducive to its peace."

Wightt then reiterates the two requests she had already made of Whitfield in her March 22 letter: absolution from excommunication for breaking enclosure and permission to practice her vows but not live in Georgetown Convent or any other convent. Wightt then summarizes the contents of Whitfield's response to her letter. The date of his reply is not given and the letter itself appears to be lost. She writes that the archbishop had previously explained that he could not then grant her appeal but would ask the pope for permission to release her from excommunication and dispense her from residing in enclosure. In the interim Whitfield had given Wightt permission to reside with a Catholic family rather than in the convent and had added other restrictions that she does not specify.

Wightt concludes the letter to the Holy Father with an admission of personal fault, acknowledging breaking enclosure. But she also petitions to receive four things: absolution from excommunication; dispensation from obligations of religious life, especially living in a convent; permission to live instead with a pious Catholic family; and permission to continue to practice the vow of chastity. Again, this list repeats many of the sentiments first expressed in her letter to Whitfield immediately following her departure from the convent. Wightt asserts that she cannot return to convent life of any kind because "she knows her interior," presumably a reference to her mind, or conscience, or soul. Almost as an afterthought, she mentions "the bad state of her health." It seems likely that this is a reference to her mental as well as her physical condition, as evidenced by Madame Iturbide's many pleas to Father Chance to visit Sister Gertrude out of concern for the former nun's well-being. It is worthy of note that in her letter to the pope, as in her letter to Whitfield sent the day after her flight, Sister Gertrude often invoked the word "tranquillity" as a contrast to her own troubled condition.[41] According to the church father Saint Augustine of Hippo in his work *City of God* the personal experience of peace is "the tranquility of order" produced by the regular practice of virtues. This tranquility prepares the "restless" soul disordered by original sin for the goal of salvation by controlling its restlessness. The writings of Saint Augustine of Hippo, and other patristic writings were among the books that Sister Gertrude had in her personal library.[42]

About two weeks later, on May 16, the archbishop met with the repentant nun who, as in her letter to the pope, had grown more compliant and less defiant than on the day of her flight. That same day Deluol entered in his diary that the archbishop had "absolved Sister Gertrude" from "a violation *clausurae, et apostasia a suo ordine* [a violation of the enclosure, and apostasy from their course], on condition she agreed to submit in everything to the decision of the Holy See."[43] Sister Gertrude signs her assent, "with Fr. [Joseph] López and Mrs. Iturbide signing as witnesses." She had achieved a conditional absolution pending either confirmation from Rome or permission to allow Whitfield to handle the case on his own.

WHITFIELD'S LETTER TO ROME, JUNE 6, 1831

On June 6, 1831, Archbishop Whitfield wrote to the Propaganda Fide requesting it grant either a dispensation for Sister Gertrude or permission that he "be given the requisite faculties" to settle the case himself, according to his conscience. Examination of the contents of the letter, translated from the Latin, provides a good window on the dual concerns that motivated him in the case.[44] The archbishop first calls attention to a "matter which while certainly sad, must be communicated," then describes the details of Wightt's flight and her taking refuge in the home of her cousin. Whitfield reveals his larger fears about how Wightt's flight was being exploited by opponents of the Catholic Church and how the local clergy were acting to blunt its effects. Clear are Whitfield's fears that, had Wightt remained in the home of her non-Catholic cousin, the results would harm both her personal commitment to the Catholic Church and the Church itself. According to Whitfield, Marcia Burnes Van Ness was strongly anti-Catholic and "so she tried in all ways possible to undermine her own kin's faith" by means of "private conversations and heretical books." Moreover, he reports that Van Ness had initiated a rumor campaign, picked up in the secular press, that Wightt "would renounce her Catholic faith and make public the wicked and defective ways of the convent." This remark alludes to the letter to the editor in the *Episcopal Recorder* written by a reader in Washington City that appeared in the anti-Catholic article "Papal Education," published on April 2 and subsequently reprinted in many other newspapers that spring. The effect of this bad press meant that "the abundant flock of protestants was eagerly gulping down this poisonous breeze." Because that original submission to the newspaper contained some "inside" details about Sister Gertrude and Georgetown Convent, Whitfield suspected Van Ness of breaking the story of Sister Gertrude's flight, either by writing the letter herself or by leaking the story to a correspondent, who sent it to the sectarian organ in Philadelphia.[45] Whitfield's suspicion that Van Ness was the source for the letter may be valid. For one, she was a member of the Episcopal Church and would have been privy to Sister Gertrude's complaints. But it also may be more a reflection of the archbishop's own fears of this woman of wealth and influence in Washington City.

As Sister Gertrude's departure from the convent was by now known to the public, Whitfield notes that several priests had visited her at the Van Ness home in a fruitless attempt to have her return to the convent "and to expose the devil's crafts and temptations that she had been deceived and entangled by." The archbishop comments on the incendiary letter sent by Wightt the

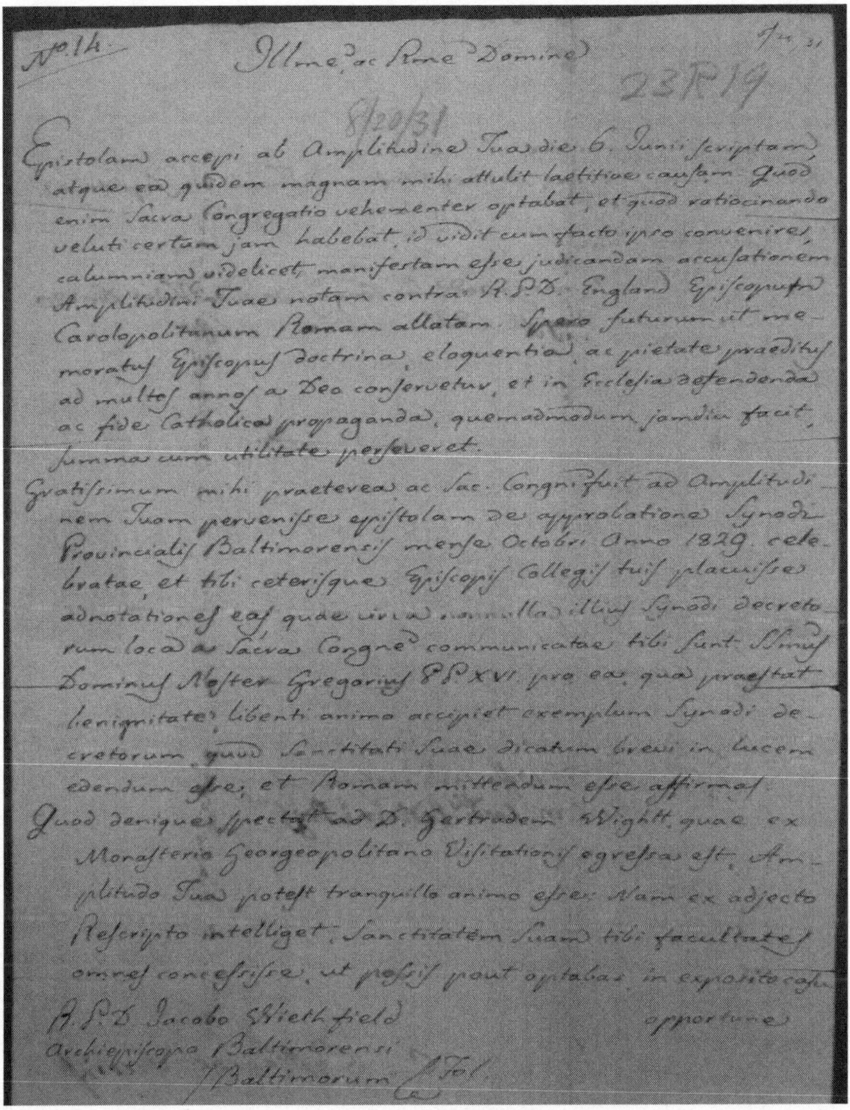

No. 14 Illme. ac Rme. Domine

23R19

8/20/31

Epistolam accepi ab Amplitudine Tua die 6. Junii scriptam atque ea quidem magnam mihi attulit laetitiae causam. Quod enim Sacra Congregatio vehementer optabat, et quod ratiocinando veluti certum jam habebat, id vidit cum facto ipso convenire, calumniam videlicet manifestam esse judicandam accusationem Amplitudini Tuae notam contra R.P.D. England Episcopum Carolopolitanum Romam allatam. Spero futurum ut memoratus Episcopus doctrina, eloquentia, ac pietate praeditus ad multos annos a Deo conservetur, et in Ecclesia defendenda ac fide Catholica propaganda, quemadmodum jamdiu facit, summa cum utilitate perseveret.

Gratissimum mihi praeterea ac Sac. Congni fuit ad Amplitudinem Tuam pervenisse epistolam de approbatione Synodi Provincialis Baltimorensis mense Octobri Anno 1829. celebratae, et tibi ceterisque Episcopis Collegis tuis placuisse adnotationes eas quae circa nonnulla illius Synodi decretorum loca a Sacra Congne communicatae tibi sunt. Ssmus Dominus Noster Gregorius PP. XVI. pro ea, qua praestat benignitate, libenti animo accipiet exemplum Synodi decretorum, quod Sanctitati Suae dicatum brevi in lucem edendum esse, et Romam mittendum esse affirmas.

Quod denique spectat ad D. Gertrudem Wightt, quae ex Monasterio Georgeopolitano Visitationis egressa est, Amplitudo Tua potest tranquillo animo esse. Nam ex adjecto Rescripto intelliget, Sanctitatem Suam tibi facultates omnes concessisse, ut possis prout optabas in exposito casu opportune

R.P.D. Jacobo Whitfield
Archiepiscopo Baltimorensi
Baltimorum

FIGURE 6.3. Letter from Cardinal Pedicini of Propaganda Fide to Archbishop James Whitfield, August 20, 1831. Courtesy Archives of the Archdiocese of Baltimore, Associated Archives at St. Mary's Seminary & University, Baltimore.

day after her flight, written "in almost this manner," but where she asked for his help. He claims that Wightt "begged this one thing" in particular: "that she not be forced to spend her life in a religious house," asserting that "she would not be able to attend to the salvation of her own soul in a house of this kind." As to the questions of her vows, "she will keep her vow of chastity, she swears to God, for as long as she lives." Furthermore, he affirms that she promises to maintain her vow of poverty "while she lives off of the resources of friends" and swears to be "obedient to the admonitions of her confessor."[46]

Whitfield also expresses evident relief that Wightt had left the "heretical home" of Van Ness and, in answer to prayers, currently resides with the pious Madame Iturbide and her family in Georgetown. The archbishop reveals that he traveled to Georgetown and with help of "pious and learned men" evaluated Wightt "with regard to her penitence for her misdeed and her intention of obedience to the monitions and rules of her superiors."[47] Whitfield contends that Wightt "promised and declared in writing that she would obey the orders of the . . . Bishop" and "be submissive in all things that I might deem necessary to prescribe."[48] Whitfield therefore "placed her under the direction" of the devout Iturbide "so that she would not give herself over to public attention but instead remain piously at home, and be free from holy and religious obligations." Rome replied only two months later, granting Whitfield "power to dispense with [it], as in conscience he shall deem proper" to decide at his discretion.[49] The rapid response suggests the Propaganda Fide understood that this historic case required immediate attention and quick resolution.

DISPENSATION GRANTED, NOVEMBER 22, 1831

After receiving authorization from Rome to decide the case, Whitfield took another four months before issuing his formal ruling, which was spelled out in a letter to Wightt dated November 22. It is not clear why the archbishop delayed so long in announcing his official decision, since his letter to Rome in June had supported Wightt's petition for the same results. Perhaps Whitfield was waiting to see how Wightt behaved in the world before he rendered final judgment in her case. If so, he substituted the normal probationary period of a postulant in the convent for a probationary period of a nun in the world. Whitfield's prudence may also have drawn upon recognition that the case would set a precedent regarding any future nun in the United States who sought release from enclosure or vows taken. Moreover, once his fear about Sister Gertrude's harmful intentions had not materialized in the

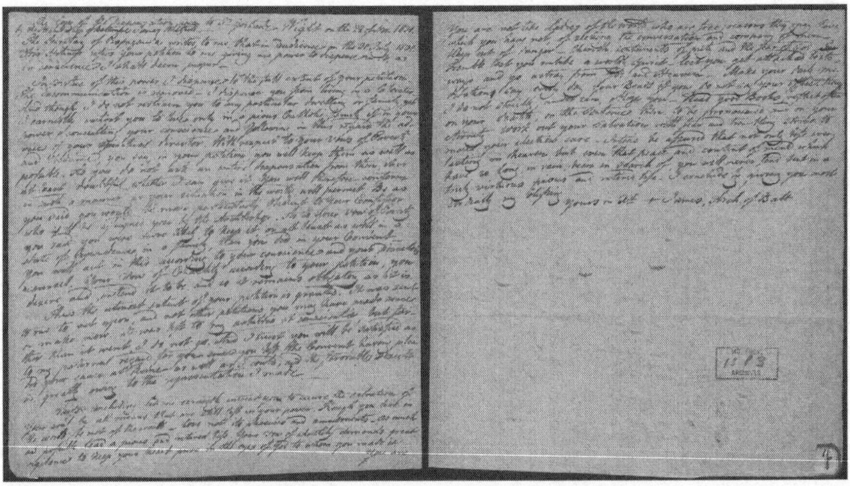

FIGURE 6.4. Copy of the dispensation by Archbishop James Whitfield for Ann Gertrude Wightt, dated November 22, 1831. Courtesy Archives of the Maryland Province of the Society of Jesus, box 103, folder 4, Booth Family Center for Special Collections, Georgetown University Library, Washington, DC.

months following her flight, the archbishop may have determined that there was no longer any need to rush.

In the document granting the formal dispensation, Whitfield addresses the petition to the Propaganda Fide, in which Wightt requested a dispensation from living in the cloister and removal of excommunication for having left the convent without permission. Whitfield formally lifted the ruling of excommunication and dispensed Wightt from the regulation of living in the convent cloister, but he also bound her to keeping her religious vows, particularly the vow of chastity. Wightt had not petitioned to be dispensed from her vows of poverty and obedience. With regard to them, Whitfield stipulates that she "conform in such manner" as her "situation in the world will permit." Neither had she asked to be dispensed from the vow of chastity, "and so it remains *obligatory* as it is."[50]

Having granted the substance of her petition of April 30, the archbishop proceeds to offer Wightt pastoral advice and counsel on how to gain salvation outside the cloister. He warns her to guard against the temptation of living in the world and enjoins her to live "a pious and retired life" by not "seeking the conversation and company of men." Instead, he recommends daily meditation and recitation of the rosary and calls on her to read good books and to "rethink often on your death."[51] Ending eight months of canonical limbo, the judgment reinstated Wightt as a practicing Catholic—bound by her religious vows, but freed from having to live within the convent enclosure. Gertrude Wightt was now positioned to live in the secular world, though admonished not to be of that world.

SCANDAL AND WASHINGTON SOCIETY

Two weeks prior to receiving notification of Whitfield's formal dispensation, Wightt's transition from Georgetown nun to Washington socialite was already set in motion. Margaret Bayard Smith, a veteran participant in capital society of the Early Republic, was among the women who would launch Gertrude Wightt on her journey from the parlors of Georgetown Convent to the parlor politics of Washington City. On November 7, 1831, Smith wrote to her sister Jane Bayard Kirkpatrick about her near neighbor in Georgetown: "Madame Iturbide, the former Empress of Mexico, is close to us. We could, were we so inclined, almost shake hands from our back windows."[52] Smith mentions that "Sister Gertrude, the nun, who last spring escaped from the convent at George Town, is an inmate of her family, in fact, an adopted daughter and has the whole charge of her three daughters." Smith claimed acquaintance with Wightt, but also that she had, years before, once offered to aid Wightt to leave the cloister if she so wished. "Sister Gertrude I knew well in her childhood, saw her now and then through the convent grate," Smith contends, "and on one occasion when accidently alone with her, offered if she wished to leave it, to communicate her desire to her relatives" (Marcia Burnes Van Ness). Instead, Sister Gertrude had then told her that "she was confined more by her own inclination, than by her vows, or the walls that surrounded her." Intrigued by the presence of her new neighbor, Smith wrote, "I shall try to renew our acquaintance."

That a pillar of the Washington establishment such as Margaret Bayard Smith would announce her intention to call upon Wightt is significant. It demonstrates that the scandal surrounding Sister Gertrude had not tarnished her personal reputation in the eyes of one of the key social arbiters in the nation's capital. This seemingly small gesture underscores the difference between the scandal involving Sister Gertrude versus that of her more notorious contemporary, Margaret O'Neale Timberlake Eaton, who was popularly, if incorrectly, called "Peggy" Eaton.[53] Rumors of sexual improprieties prior to the death at sea of her first husband, John B. Timberlake, made Eaton socially suspect. Her subsequent marriage to John Eaton only nine months later, on January 1, 1829, made the young second wife of the secretary of war persona

FIGURE 6.5. Margaret Bayard Smith. Wikimedia Commons.

non grata in the home of any "respectable" political wife in the Federal District. Smith labeled Eaton "a lady whose reputation, her previous connection with him [John Eaton] both before and after her husband's death, has totally destroyed." The fact that Margaret was also of common origins, "the daughter of O'Neal [*sic*] who kept a large tavern and boarding house," did not help her cause among the elite. Smith added that because of questions about her class and morality, "she has never been admitted to society."[54]

In contrast to her public shunning of Eaton, Smith appeared eager to welcome the wayward nun into polite society. Smith dismissed Wightt's "elopement" from the convent as an understandable action and no more than an internal affair of the Catholic Church. In this case, the nun's behavior left no stigma, no indelible mark of social shame, thus making the surrounding "scandal" a totally different event in nature and magnitude from that involving Margaret Eaton. However temporarily embarrassing to herself, her convent and school, and her church, Wightt's unscheduled flight from Georgetown Visitation did not cause her to lose the title "lady." Nor, in her post-convent years, would it prevent her from being received into the highest circles of capital society. Author William W. Warner might have been referring specifically to Ann Gertrude Wightt when he wrote that some Catholics in antebellum Washington "moved easily in high circles, from the White House and cabinet departments to the city's . . . drawing room salons."[55] Wightt's sojourn in that world was a testament to an unrelenting desire to pave her own path.

7

Miss Wightt of Washington

On April 26, 1833, Father Deluol made a final entry into his diary concerning Sister Ann Gertrude Wightt. He wrote, "M[ister] Chance went to see Sister Gertrude, who seems about to leave the Iturbides."[1] Soon after, Wightt did move out of the Iturbide household, following two years as an unofficial member of the family. The reasons behind her departure remain unclear; at the time, she remained a close friend of Madame Iturbide and her grown children. Indeed, in November 1832, when the Iturbide family moved from Georgetown to Philadelphia, Wightt relocated with them. But she returned to the District of Columbia some six months later.[2]

The timing of her return to the Washington area suggests it was in response to the likely invitation of her relative John Peter Van Ness. Marcia Van Ness had died the previous September, perhaps a victim of the first wave of cholera to hit America's shores.[3] Congress marked the passing of Mrs. Van Ness by adjourning for her funeral, the first woman so honored in the United States. But the death of Marcia left her sixty-three-year-old widower without someone to assume the duties of social hostess in the Van Ness home, one of the most distinguished residences in a city not yet known for distinguished residences.[4] Ann Gertrude Wightt came to fill this role for more than a decade. In those years she became an increasingly well-known and respected figure in capital society. This temporal world proved a far different environment than the more spiritual world in which she had dwelled for most of her first thirty-four years. Nevertheless, at the same time, the experiences of her previous life had in some ways prepared her to adapt to her new conditions with surprising rapidity and success. For the first two decades of her post-convent life, perhaps her central concern was securing some degree of personal financial independence.

A STATE OF DEPENDENCE

Similar to Elizabeth Bennett, the fictional heroine of Jane Austen's novel of manners, *Pride and Prejudice* (1813), Mary Ann Wightt was born into the gentry class but as a young woman faced an uncertain financial future from her lack of any personal fortune or prospect of inheritance. While her social status as the daughter of a gentleman was never in dispute, Wightt's economic security came into question in her early childhood and plagued her for most of her adult life, as both a Georgetown nun and a Washington socialite. In addition to the many other challenges Wightt faced in her sixty-eight years on earth, a precarious dependence on extended family, friends, and fellow religious haunted her for much of her existence. This financial dependence helps explain the choices that were made for her as a child and the choices she made as an adult. Gertrude Wightt chose not to depend on the kindness of strangers. Rather, throughout her childhood and much of her adulthood she relied on members of her extended family, members of her religious community, and personal friends. Only when she reached her early fifties did Gertrude gain a measure of financial independence, which she was able to maintain for her remaining years.

Archbishop Whitfield had acknowledged Wightt's dependent situation when dispensing her from living in the convent but not from her vows of poverty, obedience, and chastity. He had bound Wightt to her vow of poverty "while she lives off of the resources of friends" and specified that she remain "obedient to the admonitions of her confessor."[5] At the same time, Whitfield recognized that maintaining vows of poverty and obedience outside the convent would pose unique problems and counseled Wightt to "conform in such manner" as her "situation in the world will permit."[6]

From the time she left the convent until her death thirty-six years later, Wightt never owned her own home. Rather, she always resided in the homes of others, either as a relative or a guest, though always contributing to the family economy. For example, between April 1831 and November 1832 she resided as a quasi-member of the Iturbide family at their apartment in Georgetown. Their nearby neighbor Margaret Bayard Smith called Wightt "an adopted daughter" who "has the whole charge of her [Iturbide's] three daughters."[7] That is, although an intimate friend of the Iturbide family, Wightt was not a charity case of the former empress. She earned her keep by acting as a kind of governess, or maiden aunt, to girls who were her former students.[8]

HOSTESS OF THE VAN NESS MANSION

In the early decades of the century, Washington City was unheralded in terms of its infrastructure and architecture, with muddy streets and few dwellings of note. Among those few, however, were the Octagon House designed by William Thornton and the Blair House designed by Benjamin Latrobe.[9] In 1816 Latrobe completed a mansion for the Van Nesses, calling it the "best house I ever designed."[10] The Van Ness Mansion was then arguably the finest home in the city. The only private dwelling in the city at the time that could compete with it in "scale and grandeur" was the Octagon House owned by John Tayloe.[11] Washington society by the 1840s saw an increasing number of congressmen abandoning the boardinghouse "bachelor" existence and "congressional mess" so common earlier in the century. Instead, more of the members, when serving in the nation's capital, brought their wives and children with them and rented houses or apartments to accommodate the family.[12]

In taking on the domestic management of the Van Ness household, Wightt fulfilled a somewhat ambiguous role, a kind of hybrid: neither an employee nor a blood member of the family. In any case, presiding over the prestigious Van Ness home left Wightt far better off materially than her stay in the Iturbide apartments in Georgetown could have provided. As social hostess she ran a large household that included the immediate family members as well as a number of enslaved servants. According to the 1840 Census, the sixty-eight-year-old general supported a household of ten people: four adult white males, two adult white females (one of whom was Wightt), two enslaved males (one adult), and two enslaved adult females.[13] Wightt's previous duties as assistant superior of the convent, where she had authority over more than fifty nuns, and as directress of the academy, where she had charge of some one hundred students, well prepared her to effectively supervise the operations of the Van Ness house.

It should be noted, however, that by leaving the Iturbide family, a Roman Catholic household, and moving into the Van Ness Mansion, an Episcopalian household, Wightt was no longer complying with one of the strong recommendations that Whitfield had made when dispensing her from living in the cloister: "I do not restrain you to any particular dwelling or family," Whitfield had enjoined her two years earlier, "yet I earnestly exhort you to live only in a pious Catholic *family* if in your power, consulting your conscience and following in this regard the advice of your spiritual director."[14] In living with the Van Ness family Wightt was not technically violating a specific condition of the dispensation but her choice might be construed as violating the spirit, if not

FIGURE 7.1. Van Ness Mansion. Wikimedia Commons.

the letter, of that document. She was no longer living with a "pious Catholic family," as Whitfield had encouraged her to do "if in her power." Indeed, she had moved into the home of the very Protestant relative whom Whitfield had suspected of harboring anti-Catholic sentiments.

Nevertheless, Wightt may have rationalized her decision by the fact that she would be providing a necessary social service to the elderly widower General Van Ness, a relative by marriage if not by blood. Such a choice was consistent with the two culturally accepted roles for a spinster found in antebellum popular literature: "maiden aunt" and "sister of charity." According to historian Lee Virginia Schiller-Chambers, both models represented "selfless women who cared first for their parents, then for other relatives, and finally for the poor, sick, orphaned, or sinful of their communities."[15] Such acts of benevolence toward others were also consistent with a nun's practice of "maternity of the spirit." That is, while a nun may have renounced some forms of domesticity—marriage, motherhood, family, private home—she was expected to fulfill the functions of domesticity in practicing a kind of spiritual maternity by teaching children, nursing patients, and caring for orphans.[16]

Wightt was still bound by her religious vow of chastity. But, in her post-convent years she gradually discarded her vows of poverty and obedience without suffering any visible pangs of guilt. In her surviving writings, Wightt never discusses why she was especially adamant about retaining her vow of chastity. She was known as an attractive person who enjoyed the company of men as much as that of women.[17] Although it is not possible to know for certain, Wightt's personal history suggests that she may have been asexual. Certainly she demonstrated no interest in marriage, even when she was without material means, and a husband could have been a way out of her poverty. At the same time, after leaving the convent Wightt developed strong personal relationships with at least three men: General Van Ness, his nephew Colonel Eugene Van Ness, and Judge John Young Mason. In each case, however, she was equally close to the wives of these men.

Ann Gertrude Wightt belonged to the first identifiable group of women in the United States who consciously chose not to marry. Schiller-Chambers argues that the early nineteenth century produced the first generation of women who remained single by choice rather than because of adverse circumstances or financial conditions. She contends that their decision reflected independent judgment and a desire to pursue greater personal freedom, autonomy, and self-development.[18] Wightt, therefore, may have shared the view of her much-younger contemporary Louisa May Alcott, that "liberty is a better husband than love."[19] That is, she rejected marriage perhaps to maintain a relative degree of personal independence even though she remained economically dependent on family and friends.

More recently the historian Marie Molloy has shifted the spotlight from elite and middle-class women of the Northeast to single slaveholding women of the Old South. Molloy finds that the "cult of single blessedness" played out differently in that region. "Singleness," Molloy argues, "gradually became accepted as an alternative model for unmarried women, albeit within a conservative social ethos that continued to try to dictate what their behavior should be as single women."[20] "Single women did their best to replicate the role of their married sisters in the commitment they showed to the southern family." By conforming to this standard of female behavior, however, elite single white women in the South might gain greater personal autonomy. In the plantation mansions of southern Maryland, in the parlors of Georgetown, in the dining rooms of Washington City, and at the warm springs spas of western Viriginia, Gertrude Wightt learned how to traverse the cultural minefield of antebellum Southern society as a single woman.

At the same time, some of Wightt's former companions in Georgetown Visitation Convent saw her post-convent behavior in a negative light. They worried that by embracing the outside world—acting as social hostess in a non-Catholic home—Wightt was imperiling her eternal soul. Sister Mary Austin Barber, once her foremost female ally in the plans to improve Georgetown Visitation Academy, and Sister Agnes Brent, her one-time but deposed superior, greatly feared for the eternal salvation of the former directress. Writing to her daughter, Sister Josephine Barber, who had grown up in Georgetown Convent and was now a member of the Visitation Order, Sister Mary Austin expressed her alarm at Wightt's choice to live "entirely according to the world" after leaving Georgetown, and she called for prayer for her "conversion":

> Sr. Benny [Agnes Brent] as well as myself will be very glad if you will join us in praying our B[lessed] Lady to obtain the conversion of poor Sr. Gertrude. There is no human probability of it, but all things are easy to God. It is said she lives entirely according to the world. She may appear cheerful, but I know it is impossible for her to be happy whilst living so contrary to her obligations. Conscience is too faithful a monitor to suffer her to repose in so miserable a state. Do pray for her; she is truly to be pitied: the more so, as she *appears* not to see her danger.[21]

Sister Mary Austin's charge that "poor Sr. Gertrude," who now lived "entirely according to the world," is as revelatory about the author as it is about the subject. Barber had first lived in the world as a Protestant, a wife, and a mother. After conversion to Catholicism and separation from her husband, she became convinced that her own salvation required abandoning the world and entering a monastery. Sister Mary Austin must have thought her friend deluded in thinking she could gain salvation by abandoning the monastery and reentering the world. Barber's call for prayers to effect Sister Gertrude's "conversion" is an interesting choice of words to use in describing a remedy to Wightt's current situation. Recall Marie Pagliarini's scholarly insights into Visitation spirituality, which understood Wightt's behavior—continuing to live outside the convent—as endangering her soul.

If Visitation nuns prayed for the spiritual conversion of their former colleague, Wightt appears to have materially thrived in her new environment with no sense of guilt. While entertaining dinner guests of the Van Ness family, she met an array of politicians, judges, and diplomats and was on fairly intimate terms with some of their wives and children. As the mistress of the house, moreover, Wightt ingratiated herself with the members of the Van Ness family. A commonplace example is found in a letter from the British diplomat William Gore Ouseley, husband of John Peter Van Ness's niece, Marcia Van

Ness. After several pages lamenting the cost of living in Paris as compared to his previous posting in Brazil, Ouseley's closing paragraph shifts gears to family matters. He notes that his wife "wrote some days ago to Miss Wightt, and I daresay told her all the news. Both she and the Baby are very well, and the Mama sends her love to you and yours."[22] This excerpt is only telling because of its utter banality. Wightt had employed the same kind of charm and appeal to win over members of the extended Van Ness family that had made her popular with the parents and students of the academy.

One of the eminent guests to the Van Ness home whom Wightt came to know well was Dolley Madison. The former First Lady dined at the Van Ness Mansion in March 1838.[23] The following year, Madison made her earliest known reference to Wightt. In a letter to Cornelia Van Ness, she asked "to present me affectionately to Miss Wight [*sic*] and your excellent Uncle."[24] One of Madison's early biographers, Allen C. Clark, describes Wightt's role in the Van Ness Mansion thusly: "In the concluding years of the Van Ness reign of hospitality, Miss Ann Gertrude Wightt was the hostess. She had personal beauty and conversational talent; she was a welcomed guest in high society; she was an intimate of America's beloved, Dolly Madison."[25] Clark seems to have formed his view from an interview with one of Wightt's much-younger contemporaries, Kate Kearney Henry, who was still alive when he published his life of Dolley Madison in 1914. Clark quotes Henry on her impression of Wightt: "She was [a] most charming person in her manners and conversation, and was sought as an honored guest on all distinguished occasions."[26]

A LITERARY WOMAN

After living in a circumscribed existence for most of her first thirty-two years, one may wonder how Gertrude Wightt seemed so effortlessly to adapt to the temporal world. After all, she had been orphaned in early childhood, attended a boarding school offering only the most basic curriculum, and entered an enclosed convent that discouraged the reading of secular literature. Recall, however, that as a young nun Wightt received a more finished education by the standards of the time as a participant in the teacher-training program conducted by Father Joseph Clorivière and Sister Mary Austin Barber. Above all, the reason may be found in Wightt's natural intellect and interests—which included literature of all types.[27]

One indicator of the latter may be found in the six books that remained in her possession following her exit from Georgetown Convent. Four of the books are French editions (English versions of the titles given here): *Discourses of Saint Bernard to His Sister the Nun* (1820); *Chosen Letters of the Fathers, Vols. 1 and 2* (1824); *The Office of the Blessed Virgin, following the Reforms of the S. Councils of Trent and of Pope Urban VIII; Provides for the Use of the Religious of the Visitation of Saint Mary, Revised, Corrected, and Expanded* (1824). Two are in Spanish: Juan Gabriel De Contreras's *Eucharistic Awakening and Sweet Invitation* (1815); and *Elementary Logic Lessons: Arranged with a Simple and Easy Method* (1826).[28] As might be expected, all but one of these volumes are spiritual in content, with *The Office of the Blessed Virgin* being the most important. Reading the Daily Office was still expected of Wightt even while living outside the convent and the collection demonstrates her command of at least two foreign languages.

One nonreligious book in her personal library, *Elementary Logic Lessons*, may be suggestive of one of the courses in which Wightt instructed her academy students. Another of her books in English is Samuel Parkes's *The Chemical Catechism, with Notes, Illustrations, and Experiments* (1821).[29] This work was a popular text of the time that went through many editions; its popularity derived in part from the author's ability to impart scientific knowledge in a question-answer format pleasing to young readers. It also reinforced children's belief in God by offering arguments for divine design in nature. For example, Parkes describes the process of plant respiration using the following verse:

> Thus while the vegetable tribes inhale
> The limpid water from the parent vale,
> Their vegetating organs decompose
> To blend it with the carbon of the soil,
> And form bitumen, resin, wax, or oil;
> The free'd caloric bursts the expanding mass,
> And swells the nascent oxygen to gas;
> Which, from its inmost cells, each leaflet pours
> In viral currents through its myriad pores.[30]

Parkes reportedly compiled the book as a series of lessons for his own daughter. If so, it is understandable why Wightt might have assigned it as a text to her pupils or used it as a guide for her own teaching of the subject.

Moreover, the parents and guardians of her charges found Sister Getty to be a most charming headmistress. When directress of the academy, Wightt was the main liaison between the convent and the world outside the cloister, with the exception of the out sisters who did the shopping for the community and accompanied students on walks around the neighborhood and on visits to the White House and similar educational jaunts. Unlike the out sisters, Wightt lived within the convent enclosure but interacted directly with students in the classroom and with their parents in the convent parlors. Moreover, as directress of the Academy she hosted the annual premium distributions at the end of the school year every summer. On these occasions she had first honed the "conversational talent" that Clark notes made her a "welcome guest in high society." Her command of languages, with French being essential and Spanish a further plus, would have added luster to her reputation as a brilliant hostess in capital society.

The contents of Wightt's library salvaged from the convent, then, suggests an intellect with a broad general knowledge as well as specific focus on spiritual concerns. In this regard, perhaps the most intriguing find in her library is a book that she would certainly not have in her possession while a nun, even though it was published at the time: Mme. La Baronne de Staël's *Corinne, ou L'Italie* (1807).[31] One cannot help but think that Wightt may have identified with both the heroine and the author of the novel, Madame de Staël, the former Anne-Louise Germaine Necker. De Staël was a noted French-Swiss literary woman and brilliant conversationalist. It is a measure of the change in Wightt after leaving the enclosed convent environment that she owned a copy of this novel. No volume penned by that author would been approved reading material for a member of Georgetown Visitation Convent. It is intriguing to wonder whether Wightt linked the book's main character with her own personality and struggles. Corinne, the protagonist, is a woman of genius who chafes at the limits society imposes on her. The parallels with Wightt's personal frustration of her plans for the convent and academy seem evident. Although, in her case, the limits would have been imposed by her religious community rather than secular society.

THE POLITICS OF CALLING AND VISITING

Books, especially books of poetry and fiction, proved a way for Wightt to connect with her new female acquaintances in capital society. Wightt enjoyed borrowing and lending books with friends, a practice that both broadened her reading experience beyond the approved literature of a nun and deepened bonds of attachment with family and friends. In 1842, for example, Dolley Madison returned to Wightt a copy of Robert Tyler's *Ahasuerus*, an epic poem written by the poet son of John Tyler, president of the United States. In an accompanying note, Madison writes, "I return this book my dear Miss Wightt which you were so good to loan me—the perusal of which enchained my attention and as it deserved—my admiration. The following lines among many others manifest feelings and principles all must approve."[32]

> Sure God's bright smile is on this sunny earth,
> And all his gifts and mercies showered on man;
> For all may drink of pleasure's fragrant cup,
> Who walk apart in an unblemish'd life,
> From Fashion's follies or the rage of vice.

Madison's catalog of social calls for the month of November 1841 lists receiving calls from Ann Gertrude Wightt and Matilda Van Ness on November 27 and again on November 29. Madison also records having returned these calls.[33] Social appointments of this type, or "visiting," had become a ritualized part of upper- and middle-class social life by the antebellum period. From her study of advice literature from the colonial period through the Civil War era, historian C. Dallett Hemphill contends that in the Early Republic, "visiting was important because it served the crucial (but inadmissible) function of defining one's acquaintances by class. Visiting was a ritual performed with social equals, and one's visiting circle constituted a social set constituted by class."[34] There were two types of visits: friendly and ceremonious. Friendly visits involved "intimate acquaintances," so these were informal as to time and purpose. Ceremonious visits "were highly ritualized, so that the message they conveyed would be clear to all." Should the person called upon not be at home, the visitor would leave a calling card. Visits were expected to be returned in person or by calling card. Ceremonious visits went by the name "morning visits," although they were paid in the afternoon. According to etiquette writers of the day, "morning meant any time after noon and before dinner . . . often required no more than fifteen minutes."[35] Hence for Wightt, it was a sign of her acceptance into capital society that someone as august in reputation as the beloved Madison would not only receive her call but return it.

Like Wightt, Sarah Childress Polk, wife of James K. Polk, saw Madison as both a friend and kind of mentor. Madison's younger protégés likely knew each other, since they moved in similar circles. According to Sarah Polk's biographer, Amy Greenberg, "few obligations for the wife of a Washington politician were more time consuming than that of 'calling' on other women."[36] Rules of etiquette required that when someone visited and left a calling card at her residence, a woman had three options: 1) ignore it; 2) return the visit and leave one's own card; or 3) make a personal visit. "In Washington, D.C.," Greenberg argues, "calling was a political act" for both sexes.

FIGURE 7.2. Calling card of Ann Gertrude Wightt. Courtesy Tudor Place Historic House & Garden Archives, Washington, DC.

Making social calls in the capital, therefore, was a part of the process of parlor politics, which has been described and defined by historian Catherine Allgor. In Washington City "such transactions took place in women's spaces, such as parlor and dining rooms, during social activities usually considered private, such as *calling, visiting, and dining*."[37] Allgor points out that a "home setting shifts the focus from the official males to the unofficial women, which allows the official players to maneuver and negotiate."

That is, although women in early Washington were barred from participating in the "official sphere" of procedural government, making policy decisions and crafting legislation on the floor of Congress, they nonetheless engaged in politics through the "unofficial sphere," behind the scenes in the capital parlors, drawing rooms, and dining rooms. The unofficial sphere was the gray zone that existed between the official public sphere of business and politics reserved for men and the domestic sphere of home and family culturally assigned to women. Political women like Wightt learned to navigate the unofficial sphere to seek patronage positions for friends and family members and ask favors for themselves. As Allgor asserts, "Smoke-filled rooms and a lady's parlor are both political spaces."[38]

Wightt, for instance, also called on her friendship with Madison to obtain a note of introduction for a planned trip with some friends to Mount Vernon. As Wightt explains, "Although I have been there several times within the last ten years, I do [not?] feel sufficiently well acquainted to introduce them." She suggests, "You can say 'Miss Wightt of Washington & party &c &c.'" To reciprocate, Wightt pledges "some evening during this or coming week, I promise myself the pleasure of taking tea with you." She signs herself, "Yours most affectionately, Ann G. Wightt."[39]

Wightt's friendship with Madison from the late 1830s to the late 1840s provided her with another role model, along with Marcia Burnes Van Ness

FIGURE 7.3. Dolley Madison and niece Anna Payne. Wikimedia Commons.

and Margaret Bayard Smith, from the Revolutionary War generation. From each of these figures Wightt learned something of how a woman might successfully navigate the partisan waters of the capital. Madison was the common link between Wightt and the John Young Mason family of Virginia. In a long career of public service Mason also served as the private attorney for Madison in her later years. Indeed, Mason and his wife, Mary Fort Mason, were personal friends of Madison. On occasion they even extended personal loans to the former First Lady who was in a constant state of debt in her later years due to the actions of her dissolute son.[40]

Wightt probably made the acquaintance of the Mason family through their mutual friendship with Madison. For example, when writing to Mary Ann Fort Mason while on a trip to Philadelphia in 1846, Wightt asked to be remembered to "dear Mrs. Madison + Annie Payne. Love to them + Mary Cutts."[41] Along with the Iturbide family of Philadelphia, the Van Ness family of Washington City, and the Peter family of Georgetown, the Mason family of Southampton County, Virginia, were those closest to Gertrude in her post-convent years.

Another way that Wightt forged closer bonds with members of both the Van Ness family and other elite Southern families like the Masons was by summering at the sulfur spring spas nestled in the mountains of western Virginia, most famously the resort at Fauquier Springs. These Virginia springs were sites where the "ladies and gentlemen" of the planter class were "on display," thereby establishing and maintaining who belonged among the Southern elite. An article published in the *Richmond Enquirer* in 1847 relates "Scenes at the Fauquier Springs Virginia." The reporter describes a medieval "tournament" held on September 1, a pageant that might have been lifted straight out of the pages of a Sir Walter Scott novel. The event was followed the next evening by a "fancy ball" at which the guests donned costumes. "One of the most attractive and interesting groups of the evening, was composed of three young people just entering the world of fashion, representing Father Ambrose and sisters Cecilia and Gertrude. . . . Sister Gertrude was in plain white muslin, and strikingly resembled a certain beautiful Nun of Georgetown."[42] The reporter's allusion to "a certain beautiful nun" is clearly to "Sister Gertrude" Wightt. The fact that the author assumed that no further identification was needed suggests that Wightt was by then a well-known habitué of the Virginia watering holes of the planter class.

CULTIVATING SILKWORMS AND CAPITAL FRIENDSHIPS

In addition to cultivating close friendships by hosting prestigious dinner parties at the Van Ness Mansion and reinforcing such ties each summer at Virginia spas, Wightt deepened bonds of affection with certain prominent Washington families by participating in the antebellum sericulture movement of raising silkworms for production of raw silk. The practice of sericulture goes back to ancient China. In antebellum America, however, sericulture became a quite popular way to try to supplement the family income across, class, party, and region. Enthusiasts established formal organizations, such as the American Silk Society in Baltimore and the United States Silk Society in Washington City, to spread the gospel of sericulture to new disciples. Agricultural journals promoted sericulture, and specialized periodicals like the *Silk Culturist* offered how-to advice on the care and feeding of silkworms for the novice enthusiast. In 1840 the United States totaled over 60,000 pounds of silk cocoon production. A mere two years later the country produced more than four times that amount. By 1844 the total rose to almost 400,000 pounds. Soon thereafter, however, a series of cold winters and a fungal blight in 1844 burst the mulberry tree bubble and domestic silk production plummeted. The year 1850 saw not quite 11,000 pounds. Americans, writes historian Ben Marsh, "simply turned to imports of superior grade from China and Italy."[43]

During the boom years of the first half of the 1840s, the mid-Atlantic region of Washington DC, Delaware, Maryland, New Jersey, New York, Pennsylvania, and Virginia consistently produced more silk cocoons than any other region except New England. Whereas men were usually behind the promotion of the raising of silkworms, it was usually women who engaged in the actual labor such as "the concentrated leaf picking, worm feeding, cocoon sorting, baking, intricate reeling, and home twisting and dyeing."[44]

The longest extant piece of Wightt's writing happens to be the twenty-page journal she kept in the summer of 1840 chronicling the ups and downs of raising, feeding, and caring for silkworms. The journal records her meticulous, often tedious daily observations about how weather and temperature fluctuations affect the "little creatures."[45] But her observations reveal occasional insights into her personality and brief glimpses into her inner self. The entries kept during the spring and summer of 1840 are also revelatory about her personal character. They show Wightt's self-discipline, attention to detail, and willingness to be self-critical when it was merited. All are qualities she would have imbibed from her years in Georgetown Convent and recall the public airing of personal failings in a "chapter of faults." Whereas this procedure of the Visitation Order involved admitting personal shortcomings before the community, the journal entries contained confessions to self.[46] Although no longer living in the convent cloister, Wightt nonetheless retained the spirit of self-reflection and self-criticism absorbed during those years.

The entry for May 29, 1840, reads, "Upon sending to the ice house for my silk worm eggs found they had all hatched out and died."[47] Wightt not only confessed her "sins," but consulted secular "scripture" on how to reform. "Much chagrined, and at first somewhat discouraged at finding there was no security even in an ice house, but upon consulting the Silk journal, found

FIGURE 7.4. John Peter Van Ness. Wikimedia Commons.

I had erred in placing them there, too late, the 1st of April, instead of the 1st of February as this work advises." Upon recognizing the error of her ways, she resolved to make changes with the help of others: "I determined to repair my loss as early as possible," she remarks, and "spoke to Mr. Van Ness who kindly offered to go before breakfast on Monday . . . to purchase some eggs for me."

Investing in the silkworm craze received the enthusiastic support from the mansion patriarch, General Van Ness. Wightt acknowledges the help she received from him, whom she often refers to as "the General," as well as from her friends and neighbors engaged in sericulture. For instance, in the entry for June 20 she reveals, "My mind is somewhat relieved, as I find the General is determined I shall have food sufficient. I only fear it will be expensive."[48] Two days later she records, "The genl. Got up by sunrise to get leaves + sent out for a cart load."[49] On June 26, Wightt notes the day was "raining but not very cool. Thermometer at 70. Had a fire to dry the leaves. The General stayed nearly all day at the cocooning + assisted us greatly in feeding etc. He takes great interest in getting food + thereby greatly relieves my mind."[50]

Despite some initial failures, Wightt remains undiscouraged and resolved to get it right the next time. She not only learned from her own mistakes but questioned the experts when her experience conflicted with their advice. "This must be a lesson to me," she reasons. "Never, never again will I attempt it without having a sufficiency of food." She also challenges the "silk press," as it was called. "The books say one acre to 100,000 silk worms, I say two. I am astonished that writers on the Subject say so little about the quantity these little creatures consume." The willingness to trust her own judgment when it clashed with accepted authority is a constant in Wightt's personality and character. Her skepticism of the advice of the so-called experts in the silk press proved to be borne out over time. The silk journals had ballyhooed the silk movement sometimes out of sincere optimism, sometimes out of self-interest, often out of a combination of the two. "Pro silk propaganda," notes a scholar of the movement, was prone to "omissions, exaggerations, false claims, and inflated 'scientific' data."[51] From her own experience, Wightt began to see this was the case, but she still believed in the overall project.

She kept at the laborious tasks all that summer of 1840 with but indifferent success. "I continued coming out until 30th Aug. I left them in the cocooning until 6th September when I perceived some of the eggs had changed color as if they were about hatching[,] eventually on the 8th some came out although I had two days before removed them to the cellar."[52] Rather than be discouraged or resigned to the futility of the project, she sought lessons that could be applied for future success. "Next year I must remove them day by day as they hatch."[53]

Ultimately sericulture for the Van Ness Mansion and most Americans proved to be a financial failure. For Wightt, however, raising silkworms turned out to be a social success that allowed her to deepen her personal relationships with prominent neighbors. For example, her entry for June 19 demonstrates how the raising of silkworms could be a bonding experience with old friends and a way to cultivate new ones: "In the evening went to Mr. [John Young] Mason's cocooning," she recorded. "At six O'clock found Mrs. [Mary Fort]

Mason's had fed for the night. Determined to follow her example, instead of adding to my old plan of feeding them at 9 or 10. Mrs. M worm[s] is in all stages + all doing well."[54] The following evening Wightt hosted other elite families that shared her new passion for silkworm raising: "Mr. + Mrs. A. Tayloe" and other friends "made me a visit. Seemed pleased with our arrangements, said they would call again when the worms grow larger."[55] The Tayloe family resided in the Octagon, the only home in the early capital that rivaled the Van Ness Mansion.

HOSTING A SENATORIAL DINNER PARTY

We are fortunate to have an account of one of the dinner parties hosted by Gertrude Wightt. In February 1846 Alexander Gardiner was among those in attendance at a senatorial dinner, one of the last to be held at the Van Ness Mansion. Gardiner describes the evening to his sister, Julia Gardiner Tyler, the young second wife of President John Tyler.

Although General Van Ness was an ardent Jacksonian Democrat, the group of eight US senators in attendance showed a political balance of Whigs and Democrats. The Democrats included William Allen of Ohio; Lewis Cass of Michigan; William H. Haywood Jr. of North Carolina; and Levi Woodbury of New Hampshire. The four Whigs comprised William L. Dayton of New Jersey; George Evans of Maine; Henry Johnson of Louisiana; and Jacob W. Miller of New Jersey.

This bipartisan guest list was typical of the way Dolley Madison as First Lady hosted dinner parties and drawing room soirees at the White House. Although James Madison was the one of the founders of the Democratic-Republican party, his wife had never let political differences enter into the decision as to who was invited to the events she planned. For this she was loved by members of both parties, permitting her to use her role as First Lady to foster national unity during one of the most divided administrations in the country's history. Benefiting from mentoring she had received from the likes of the first generation of political wives like Dolley Madison, Margaret Bayard Smith, and Marcia Burnes Van Ness, Wightt began to learn and practice the art of parlor politics. These experiences of conducting political dinner parties at the Van Ness Mansion in turn made "Miss Wightt of Washington" a well-known capital hostess in the 1840s. Her command of languages, knowledge of literature, brilliant conversation, and attractive appearance also made her much in demand as a dinner guest. In consequence, in the 1840s Ann Gertrude Wightt became acquainted with past and future presidents John Tyler,

James K. Polk, Millard Fillmore, Franklin Pierce, and James Buchanan. The sole exception was Zachary Taylor, who died suddenly after serving little more than a year and whose wife famously eschewed capital society and refused to entertain in the White House during her husband's tenure.[56]

DIVIDING THE VAN NESS ESTATE

On May 7, 1846, less than a month after this political dinner party, General Van Ness passed away in his seventy-seventh year. Van Ness died perhaps the richest man in the Federal District, but he also died intestate, leaving his heirs in a state of legal limbo regarding who would inherit what.[57] Not being a blood relative, Wightt had no legal claim on any part of the estate. In the eyes of most of the Van Ness heirs, to whom she had grown close, however, her years of service to the patriarch and the family gave her a moral claim to some sort of compensation.

Britannia Peter Kennon, with whom Wightt later resided at her estate of Tudor Place in Georgetown, offered a more ominous take on the whole situation. Kennon, apparently based on a confidence from Wightt, claimed that General Van Ness, when he invited Wightt to live at the Van Ness Mansion, had promised to provide for her in his will. But "at his death no will was found and it was generally supposed that [Cornelius] his brother (of whom little was thought) had destroyed it so that the estate would go to his [own] children."[58] Kennon further points out that "the General had acquired his fortune through his wife, Marcia . . . she being a relative of Miss Wightt's."

Whether Cornelius Van Ness was quite the villain Kennon portrayed him to be, Wightt did protect her interest by hiring Judge John Young Mason as her attorney. Initially Cornelius Van Ness, the only surviving brother of the deceased, agreed to pay Wightt an annuity of $600.00, or the equivalent purchasing power today of about $23,000. For the first year this annuity was paid in installments of $100.00 every two months.[59] The annuity was intended to tide her over the next year, but she had no guarantee that it would continue nor did she have any assurance as to how long she might continue to live in the Van Ness Mansion, which soon went up for sale.

More than a year after the death of General Van Ness, legal negotiations over the division of his estate were resolved, when each of his surviving relatives contributed a portion of their share to Wightt. His real property was valued at $120,000 and divided three ways, among his surviving heirs. Besides his brother, Cornelius, these included a sister, Mrs. Gertrude Hoffman, and the adult children of his deceased brother, William Van Ness (Charles,

Eugene, Edward, and Matilda). Under the agreement, Cornelius received land (improved and unimproved) valued at $40,000; Gertrude Hoffman received the same; and the William Van Ness offspring split the remaining $40,000 in property.[60]

Cornelius Van Ness describes the settlement made on Wightt in a letter drafted for the perusal of her attorney, John Mason. "The heirs of my brother, J. P. Van Ness, having agreed, as you are aware, to make a donation to Miss Wight [*sic*] of unimproved lots in the city [Washington] of the value of $15,000, at the corporation assessment."[61] Cornelius informs Mason "that the lots, have been duly selected, and a list of them delivered to R[ichard] Smith Esq., who will soon be empowered to make a legal and proper convergence of them." Cornelius had contributed $5,000 in property from his $40,000 share. Likewise, his sister, Gertrude, matched that amount. The Van Ness offspring pledged $3,000, and the remaining $2,000 came from a later division of the funds of all the parties.

It is worth remembering that the Van Ness heirs were under no legal obligation to see that Wightt received any part of the estate. The general had left no will and Wightt had no blood connection to him or any of his side of the family. But Wightt's bond with his nephews and niece was especially close and remained so in the future. In their hearts, if not by law, Wightt had become a full member of the family. The heirs, with the possible exception of Cornelius, recognized a moral obligation to her, at least for longtime service rendered to the deceased.

Having thus settled on Wightt what he considered a more than sufficient sum, Cornelius wished to terminate the $600 annuity that Wightt had received the first year. "The suggestion in your letter to me," he told Mason, "and which has been repeated by Miss Wight [*sic*] that the annuity first agreed upon of $600 per annum, should be continued for another year, in addition to the *real* estate of $15,000, has been under consideration by those of the heirs."[62] Cornelius contends that heirs declined to continue the annuity as of July 1, that is, just two weeks hence. "They consider the donation of real estate in fee to the amount of $15,000 to be a most liberal one," Cornelius argues, "and have no doubt that Miss Wight will be able immediately to realize sufficient ready money upon it to answer all her purposes, and without any sacrifice of property." Despite Cornelius's claim that July 1, 1847, marked the date of the final payment, the account book of his lawyer, Richard Smith, records a payment of $150.00 made to Wightt on October 5, 1847. It reads: "To Miss Wightt for Gov. Van Ness' obligation to her for annuity."[63]

It is not clear as to when Wightt moved out of the Van Ness home, but it may have been as early as 1847, after the family settled on her the lots of unimproved land. According to Britannia Kennon, Wightt failed to realize anywhere near the $15,000 valuation of the lots due to "having to sell them, as she needed the money."[64] Even with these funds, therefore, Wightt remained in a dependent position, lacking a regular income or a permanent residence. Perhaps the cash that she did realize allowed her to stay with Van Ness relatives in New York or Baltimore without making herself a burden. Her own uncertain personal circumstances, plus new financial and health crises affecting the Iturbide family, led Wightt to return to her old friends still residing in Philadelphia. She likely stayed with the family during 1848 and much of 1849, helping Madame Iturbide pursue a financial matter and nursing Isis Iturbide during her mortal illness.[65]

MEETING WITH PRESIDENT POLK

Six weeks after the death of General Van Ness, the United States declared war on its fellow republic to the south, Mexico. These two events—one personal, one public—brought Gertrude Wightt back within the orbit of the Iturbide family. Because of the death of Van Ness, Wightt was left without a residence or a means of support. Because of the hostilities with the United States, the government of Mexico ceased monthly payments of the annual pension awarded to the descendants of the deceased Emperor of Mexico, Agustín de Iturbide, so the Iturbide family, too, was left without its chief means of support.

On the afternoon of February 17, 1848, Wightt accompanied Madame Iturbide to meet with President James K. Polk in the parlor of the White House. Only two weeks earlier representatives from both nations had signed the Treaty of Guadalupe-Hildalgo, ending the Mexican-American War. But the treaty had yet to be ratified by Congress. Under its terms, Mexico ceded more than half its territory to the United States in return for a payment of $15 million. Madame Iturbide asked Polk to intercede on her behalf and pressure the Mexican government to resume payments of her pension, which had been suspended since the onset of hostilities two years before. "Her object," wrote Polk in his diary, "was to have it reserved and paid out of the military contribution levied by our forces in Mexico."[66] The president suggested that Madame Iturbide take up the matter with his secretary of state, James Buchanan. Polk found Iturbide "to be an interesting person," but confided, "I don't see how I can grant her request." When they met the next day, Iturbide asked Buchanan for "*written permission* for herself and family to return to Mexico."[67] Polk "reluctantly" decided that "it would, under existing circumstances, be inexpedient to grant her permission."

During the audience with Polk, Iturbide had not spoken English—although there is written evidence that she was fluent in the language—and instead relied on Wightt as her interpreter. Polk recognized Wightt and described her as "Miss White, the niece of the late Mr. General Van Ness of this city."[68] The fact that Polk misspelled her name and misidentified her kinship to John Peter Van Ness suggests that Wightt was only a social acquaintance of the president. It seems likely, therefore, that Wightt had used her friendship with John Young Mason to arrange the meeting between the US president and the former empress of Mexico. Mason not only served Polk as attorney general and secretary of the navy, but was a longtime personal friend of the president. The two had been classmates at the University of North Carolina.[69]

BEQUEST FROM ISIS ITURBIDE

Having failed in their mission in the capital, Iturbide and Wightt returned to Philadelphia, where they faced a different crisis, not related to family finances but to health. Isis Iturbide was bedridden with what proved a mortal illness. Wightt stayed by her side to nurse her former student on her deathbed. Dr. Samuel Jackson, a leading physician and a professor at the University of Pennsylvania, treated Isis, and Wightt tended to the patient's daily needs over the next year or more. On July 5, 1849, Isis prepared for her imminent death by composing her will. She left to her mother all lands "as my portion from the grant made by the Mexican government."[70] She divided up among five people the amount of $70,000, which she estimated was her share from the pension previously settled on her family. The largest bequests went to three of her siblings, Salvador, Sabina, and Angelo [Angel], but she also remembered "Miss Wightt" and "Dr. Jackson" with substantial sums as well. "As I am not able to specify the amount of my portion of the sum due from the Mexican government to my Father's heirs," the will stipulates, "I will state it at seventy thousand dollars. Should it be less, the Legacies herein named, must diminish in proportion." Having outlined the conditions, Isis itemizes her bequests: "To my sister Sabina I leave eighteen thousand dollars. To my brother Salvador, nineteen thousand dollars. To my Brother Angelo eighteen thousand dollars. To Miss Wightt ten thousand dollars. To Dr. Jackson my kind Friend and physician, five thousand dollars." In the section of the will distributing her personal property, Isis awards Wightt her "garnet ring" and "writing desk." The former was easily transferred from her finger to that of Wightt, and the latter could be sent to Wightt when she returned to the District of Columbia.

Collecting the cash bequests proved far more problematic for the recipients. Following the end of the war, the Mexican government had not renewed making payments to the Iturbide family. Indeed, between the debts that were added and the territory that was ceded as a result of its military defeat, Mexico was unlikely to renew any pension payments in the near future. How then would Wightt collect the bequest made to her in Isis's will? She and Madame Iturbide had been unsuccessful in their attempt to solicit the aid of the US government to pressure the government of Mexico to resume payments to the family. Wightt nonetheless had gained valuable firsthand experience in how the process worked and learned the lesson well. She therefore wrote directly to the new secretary of state, John Clayton, for assistance from the State Department in collecting her bequest from the Mexican government. This correspondence would lead her to an eventful journey to Vera Cruz and Mexico City.

8

A Lady Well Known Here and Highly Regarded

On May 1, 1851, Secretary of State Daniel Webster composed a lengthy "private and confidential" letter to General Mariano Arista, president of Mexico. For several pages Webster discusses the current negotiations over the proposed Treaty of Tehuantepec, which had exposed potentially irreconcilable tensions between the two North American republics. In closing, Webster shifts the tone to a more personal and harmonious subject: "I was quite pleased with the manner in which you complied with the request of Miss Wightt," said the Whig statesman, "a lady well known here and highly regarded in our social circles."[1] In his reply sent one month later, President Arista addresses the serious matters threatening renewed war between the two sovereign states but then, just as Webster had done, ends his correspondence by referring to a small matter on which the two men could find consensus: "I have sufficient interest in favor of Miss Wightt," Arista assures Webster, "and will hereafter, pursuant to your wish, do every thing I possibly can for her."[2] Why did these major leaders of two antagonistic powers mutually pledge assistance to Ann Gertrude Wightt?

Wightt's visit to Mexico proved to be a key event of her post-convent years, yet the trip's origins were based in personal relationships she had established while headmistress of the Visitation Young Ladies' Academy. Specifically, she successfully enlisted individuals in the US State Department to help her collect the monetary bequest made by Princess Isis Iturbide, her former student. Isis died in Philadelphia on July 10, 1849, at age thirty-two, with Wightt tending at her deathbed. Wightt then turned to her political connections in Washington to aid her in pressing the government of Mexico to make good on the $10,000 claim from Isis, estimated to be worth almost $420,000 today.[3] Invested wisely, this amount could provide Wightt with a degree of financial independence for the first time in her life.

FIGURE 8.1. Daniel Webster. Wikimedia Commons.

The funds for these bequests were contingent upon the government of Mexico making the payments on a $1 million pension awarded in the early 1820s to Agustín de Iturbide, Isis's father, for services rendered during Mexico's War for Independence from Spain. In the mercurial politics of that country, Emperor Iturbide lost his throne in 1823 and his life the following year. This change in fortune forced his family into peripatetic exile, first in New Orleans and then Baltimore before arriving in Georgetown in 1826. In the ensuing decades Mexico paid installments to the family only sporadically and ceased payments altogether in 1847 because of war with the United States. It seemed unlikely that Wightt would ever see any of the bequest from her grateful former student.

ENLISTING THE US STATE DEPARTMENT, 1849–50

To recover this legacy, Wightt called upon political connections she had made while serving as social hostess of the Van Ness Mansion. The recently concluded Mexican-American War (1846–48), during which the Democratic administration of James K. Polk had annexed half of the territory of its neighbor to the south, had soured relations between the two republics. Wightt must have been pleased to be dealing with a State Department under the Whig administration of Zachary Taylor. Her first step was to write in late December 1849 to Secretary of State John M. Clayton, seeking his assistance in supporting her claim. By contacting the State Department, Wightt followed her established pattern of proactively seeking help from those in power. Even when residing in the cloister, Wightt had reached out to several leading public figures, including Secretary of War John Eaton and Senator Elias Kane of Illinois, to present her petition to Congress. Moreover, Wightt expedited a decision on her excommunication by writing to Pope Gregory XVI. Taking her case directly to Rome, much less the pope, was a most unusual and possibly unprecedented step for an American nun in the nineteenth century, demonstrating Wightt's agency and resourcefulness.[4]

In her correspondence Wightt explains to Clayton the historical basis of her financial claim. "After General Yturbide, father of said [Maria de] Jesus de Yturbide, declared the Independence of Mexico," she writes, "Congress to show the gratitude of the nation to him (their Liberator as they called him) voted him a Million of dollars."[5] "This debt has always been recognized by the Mexican Government," Wightt assures him, but over the decades the Iturbide family had received few payments. As Wightt points out, this is "From want of funds, but little of it has been paid and that in very small installments."

Demonstrating her understanding of the diplomatic process, Wightt requests "a special favor" of Clayton, to "bring this affair to a speedy and successful issue." Specifically, she asks him to direct the US minister to Mexico, Robert Perkins Letcher, to "induce the Mexican Government to make a

FIGURE 8.2. John M. Clayton. Wikimedia Commons.

prompt exertion to pay this debt to the Yturbide family (who have resided in this Country more than twenty years) [and she] would be greatly obliged and benefited, as would Dr. Samuel Jackson of Philadelphia, another citizen of the United States." It is noteworthy that in her original letter, Wightt petitioned on behalf of not only herself and Dr. Jackson, "another citizen of the United States," but first and foremost for the "Yturbide family," who, while not US citizens, "have resided in this Country more than twenty years." Three days later, on Christmas Eve, Clayton grants the "special favor" Wightt had requested. He responds by instructing Letcher, a former governor of Kentucky, that he "should be glad if, by your personal good offices, you could be instrumental in realizing the legacy for that lady."[6]

Wightt's request was unusual, possibly unique, for two reasons. First, it was out of the norm for an American woman to register a financial claim against a foreign government. Most claims were brought by males, whether American shippers whose vessels and cargoes had been seized in foreign waters or traders and businessmen whose goods had been confiscated on the borderlands. Second, it was even more unlikely that a woman would personally travel to Mexico City—a dangerous journey—to press her claim. Indeed, the manner and language Letcher uses to recommend her petition to the Mexican government points to the peculiar nature of Wightt's claim.

US RECOMMENDATION TO MEXICO, SEPTEMBER 10, 1850

After presenting his credentials in the Mexican capital, Letcher pleaded for "the very interesting case of an American lady, Miss Anne [*sic*] Wight [*sic*]."[7] Referring to himself in the third person, Letcher asserted that "he would not apply to it the *cold* term of a *claim*—Such a word cannot be appropriately employed in such a case." Instead, Letcher resorted to high-flown, sentimental language, even by diplomatic standards. "It is a case, which at once appeals to the justice, to the sympathies, to the gratitude of every man, woman and child in the Republic of Mexico," Letcher declared unabashedly. He averred that the case "presents the fairest opportunity imaginable for the exercise of the noblest feelings implanted in the human bosom, and at the same time calls aloud upon a nation for the interposition of its generosity." The Kentucky Whig argued that Wightt's case "assumes therefore, loftier ground, than a mere claim . . . [and] stands upon its own intrinsic merits, above all argument. *It speaks for itself.*"

Despite his contention that the case spoke for itself, Letcher recounted the historical background for the claim, and employed language meant to appeal to romantic gender stereotypes shared by people of both nations.

> Miss I Yturbide, with her mother, brothers, and sisters, were all banished . . . from their own country. . . . In their new home, they found many kind friends, but none so constant, so untiring, so self sacrificing as Miss Wight [*sic*]. She gave up everything, for years devoting all her time and her little means to the use of the exiled family. . . . [Isis] lay

FIGURE 8.3. Robert P. Letcher. Wikimedia Commons.

> ill for years, Miss Wight was her friend her comforter and her nurse, and as fondly attached to her as a sister could be. . . . Upon her dying bed, [Isis]. . . wishing to reward her faithful friend . . . appealed to her own country to pay Miss Wight, a part of the money, which had been generously promised her by her Government.

Having faithfully narrated the origins and justification for the claim, Letcher moves next to the material evidence. As "Exhibit A" in the hypothetical case of *Ann Gertrude Wightt v. the Government of Mexico*, Letcher submitted "a copy of the last will and testament" of Isis Iturbide. Once again referring to himself in the third person, Letcher closes by assuring that "should it be the pleasure of the Mexican Government, to comply with the last request of Miss I Iturbide, he will take the greatest pleasure in the world in communicating the glad tidings, not only to Miss Wight [*sic*], but to his Government."[8] Six weeks later Letcher reported the "glad tidings" to Daniel Webster, Clayton's successor as secretary of state. The "Claim of Miss Anne [*sic*] Wightt of Washington City (ten thousand dollars) has been allowed by the Mexican government," he announced, adding that the legacy "will be paid in installments, one thousand dollars every two months."[9] Again, it is worth noting that neither in his letter to the Mexican government nor in his letter to Webster did Letcher mention either of Wightt's additional requests, to assist Dr. Jackson and the Iturbide family in collecting their respective claims against the Mexican government.[10] Nor is it clear how the other claims got lost in the bureaucratic shuffle.

WIGHTT'S LETTER TO DANIEL WEBSTER, JUNE 3, 1851

To ensure that Mexico comply with this agreement, Wightt in spring 1851 took passage on a ship to Vera Cruz. Angel Iturbide, a member of the Mexican legation in Washington, probably accompanied her on the voyage, acting as both a protector of Wightt and an envoy for his family's own claim. From Vera Cruz they traveled by stagecoach the 250 hazardous miles to the capital.[11] Soon after arriving in Mexico City, Wightt sent a most revealing letter to Daniel Webster that once more demonstrates her grasp of the art of parlor politics by asking on behalf of others before herself.

Wightt begins by thanking Webster for soliciting the assistance of President Arista of Mexico in collecting the additional payments on her bequest. "I feel under many obligations to you for the kind mention you made of me in your letter [May 1, 1851] to Genl. Arista & trust it will produce some effect."[12] She then appears self-effacing by asking that priority be given to the case of a "Mr. L[ouis] S. Hargous of this City [Vera Cruz], for his Claim was upwards of a million & he got but half." Wightt asks Webster, "Can you not see that he gets it?"[13] Should that have proved impossible, the resourceful Wightt offers another approach: "Would it not be quite legal," she suggests, "for you to [retain?] it [the funds paid] for the benefit of other American Claimants whose claims have been allowed by the Mexican government & who have not been paid merely because there is little or no money in their Treasury." Although the Mexican government had recognized the validity of her own claim and promised to pay the $10,000 seven months prior, Wightt states that "I have received but $1,000 of it & that was in March last [1851]." She queries, "Could you not retain $9,000 of the $10,000 for me?" She concludes this section of the letter by dropping the name of Mexico's minister to the United States, noting he was a supporter of her petition: "Mr. [Luis de la] Rosa is my Friend, knows the merits of my claim & probably would not oppose its payment in the [end?]. I suggest, [this?], is if *you* wish it & can lawfully *do* it. Of course I leave it to your discretion.

Having pleaded her own case and that of Louis Hargous in the first half of the correspondence, Wightt then abruptly shifts gears. She launches into an informed, if jingoistic discussion of the political and diplomatic wranglings over controversial provisions of the proposed Treaty of Tehuantepec. Mexican leaders and the public saw the provision that gave the right of passage to American citizens crossing the Isthmus of Tehuantepec as a humiliating coda to the loss of more than half their country in the Treaty of Guadalupe Hildalgo only three years before.[14] Wightt's discussion of "the Tehuantepec question" began with a review of the political situation, revealing a subtle grasp of the processes of the Mexican government. She notes that the current extraordinary session of the Mexican Congress would not take up the treaty, which she deemed fortunate, considering the level of opposition to it. She hopes, nevertheless, for action during the regular session, "with Genl. Arista's influence & Gov. Letcher's exertions & popularity it will . . . be carried." She then laments that ill health had forced Letcher to return temporarily to the United States.

In praising Letcher, Wightt also reveals her distrust of Great Britain and her sophisticated understanding of the issues surrounding the negotiations. "Had the Governor been here," she writes, "I do not believe that Congress would have annulled Garay's grant, that was done mainly by British influence."[15] She adds, "To be sure it does not materially affect the Tehuantepec Treaty, but it was done with a view to give it a deadly blow, for the English cannot bear the idea of the Americans having anything like a foothold in Mexico." She continues with her assessment of why the British diplomatic service is effective: "They wish to predominate every where, & I trust we will allow them no such primature. . . . To accomplish their purposes here, their Charge or Minister is always endowed with discretionary powers & I need hardly tell you he uses these to the utmost extent." However wary of "perfidious Albion," Wightt yet gives grudging praise to "John Bull," thereby offering insight into her own case. "One thing however I do admire in the English," she acknowledges, is that "they take special care of the interests of their subjects here & everywhere." Because of this, she contends, the English "are no where more feared & do meet [*sic*] out justice."[16] Wightt appears to admire the policies of Lord Palmerston, at the time the British foreign secretary, whom historian David Brown calls "the gunpowder minister."[17] It is worth recalling that Wightt did have direct connections to British diplomats in Latin America through her friendship with Marcia Van Ness, and Marcia's husband, British diplomat William Gore Ouseley, who had already served in Argentina and Brazil.[18]

Wightt expresses her fear that, because much of the Whig Party had opposed the recent war with Mexico, the British legation would be inclined to think the Millard Fillmore administration timid and try to take advantage of perceived American weakness. To gain the respect of the English, Wightt counsels an aggressive showing of the American flag by using a tactic later termed "gunboat diplomacy." Specifically, she advocates that Minister Letcher return "to Vera Cruz in a Man of War well-armed. . . . Such demonstrations, on their people would produce a wonderful effect," she contends, "& would teach them that although we Whigs disliked the war & yet we are determined to be treated with consistency & respect." Lest she appear to have overstepped with her bellicose suggestions, Wightt in the next sentence assumes a more deferential tone though still justifying her proposal: "Do not for a moment suppose I have any idea of dictating to one so highly gifted [as] yourself," she contends, "but taking an interest in your Treaty, I could not help writing a few of my impressions."[19]

In late spring 1852 Wightt returned to the United States with a larger bank account and an enhanced reputation in capital circles. Some months later she attended a dinner party with US congressmen and foreign diplomats hosted by Secretary of State Edward Everett. Daniel Webster had died on October 24, 1852. Everett served as his successor in the interim, from November 6 until March 5, 1853, when the Democrats took control of the State Department. In her memoir Marian Campbell Gouverneur recalled sitting across from Wightt at Everett's dinner party, which must have occurred sometime between those dates.[20]

Many years later Gouverneur recorded her unfavorable impression of the former Georgetown nun turned Washington socialite. Borrowing a line from Shakespeare's *Othello,* she mused, "Miss Wight [*sic*] was more devoted to 'the pride, pomp and circumstance' of the world than many who had not led such deeply religious lives."[21] Gouverneur recounts that her dinner escort, Mr. Philip Griffith, a member of British Legation, quietly shared an anti-Catholic comment with her: "We have an escaped nun here; are we to have an *auto da fe*?" Gouverneur responded that "autos da fe were solely a courtly amusement." Clearly, not everyone in capital circles succumbed to the charms of Ann Gertrude Wightt.

CHANGING RELATIONS WITH THE ITURBIDE FAMILY

If the US State Department and the Mexican Government thought well of Gertrude Wightt in the wake of her trip to Mexico, surviving documents show the Iturbide family members came away with mixed feelings about their longtime friend. Wightt likely had journeyed to Mexico in the company of Angel Iturbide, son of the former empress and a member of the Mexican Legation in Washington, DC. Certainly he was in Mexico City for much of the time that Wightt was there in 1851 and 1852. Judging from correspondence between Angel and his eldest sister, Sabina, they at first hoped that Wightt and Jackson would give up the bequests Isis had bestowed on her nurse and her physician. The Iturbides saw both claims as slices taken from the family pie that the Mexican government had promised them a quarter century before yet from which they had received but few crumbs. A year after the death of Isis, Sabina confides to Angel, questioning Wightt's motives in pursuing her claim: "I wrote to Miss Wightt about our dear Isis' will. She is I think very much disappointed + says in answer to my letter that although she does not care for money, she hopes for Mama's sake (because people will speak against her) that she will not set aside Isis' will."[22] Less than convinced by Wightt's protestations of her lack of pecuniary interest, Sabina reveals her skepticism and frustration with her former instructor: "I cannot tell you all the nonsense she says besides, because it would take me too long, + it would be of no use."

Ater first hoping that Wightt would renounce the bequest, by the following year (July 1851) Sabina had partly changed her mind on the matter. She now wished that having successfully obtained the help of the State Department to pursue her own claim, Wightt might also lobby Secretary of State Webster and US minister Letcher on behalf of the Iturbide family's much larger pension claim.[23] Angel even met with Minister Letcher to solicit assistance for his family similar to that provided to Wightt.[24] In the end, however, while the Mexican government agreed to award Wightt the unpaid $9,000 on her claim, to Jackson it awarded only $2,500 (half of the actual bequest) and it gave another $10,000 to the Mexican official Javier Echevarria (apparently his attorney fee for seeking the claim). This left only $28,500 to be divided evenly among Madame Iturbide and her seven surviving children.[25] This settlement, going to eight members of the Iturbide family, amounted to only slightly more than half the $55,000 that Isis had bequeathed to four of her siblings in her will. Moreover, when all the payments of the agreement are totaled, the sum is $20,000 short of the $70,000 that Isis Iturbide had estimated as her share of the $1,000,000 family pension. Recall that Isis qualified the amount of each bequest subject to the amount of her actual share: "Should it be less [than $70,000]," she stipulated, "the Legacies herein named, must diminish in proportion."[26] In the final tabulation, therefore, only Wightt received the full bequest as set forth in the will.

Once it became clear to all that the terms of the financial settlement favored Wightt alone, Sabina's letters to Angel took on a different tone. She told of Madame Iturbide's bitterness toward Wightt for gaining her full share and of the empress's frustration with Letcher for his inability to secure more for her family. "We have no right to take that which belongs to others nor will they give it up," an ambivalent but resigned Sabina laments to her brother. "But God knows I wish they would all consent. I think it would be far better (+ I wish it) for Miss W[ightt] to get the whole of her share, + I wish the Dr. [Jackson] would get his too." She goes on to say that not everyone in the family felt so generous, however. "Mama + Josephine [Iturbide daughter] do not think we have to be thankful to Mr. Letcher + Mama refuses to write to him." Unlike her mother and sister, Sabina was grateful to Wightt and Letcher and promised to "write to Miss Wightt as soon as I can secure time to give her."[27] At the same time, Sabina acknowledges feeling ambivalent about the settlement and Wightt's intentions: "God knows that I wish Miss W. + the Dr. would reconsider the whole of this bequest but we cannot take that which belongs to an other [*sic*]." Nonetheless, in a second letter written the same day, Sabina shows herself to be more emotionally torn about what to think about Wightt's actions: "I hope Miss [W] will not refuse to do what Mama proposes because if so, it will at once show that she was not sincere in what she said about giving up her share."[28]

By the time Wightt returned to the United States in the spring of 1852, Sabina had become more suspicious of her former teacher's intentions. "I saw Miss W. on her return from Mexico but she did not say a word of business to me." She also upbraids her brother for being too trusting of Wightt: "I cannot understand why you left it to her to inform us . . . [as] Mama + she are no longer friends. Mama and Josephine still refuse their share to Miss W."[29] Indeed, Sabina even asserts that Wightt "told the Dr. that she was determined to get her $9,000, + his $2,500 although she knew that Mama, + Josephine do not consent."

Two days later Madame Iturbide wrote to Letcher and made known her displeasure with how the claim had been settled. Rather than blaming Letcher, however, the former empress thanked him for his efforts on behalf of her family and focused her resentment on Wightt alone: "Through my Sons I know the interest you have taken regarding our family affairs for which my daughter and myself feel extremely obliged to you," she explains to Letcher.[30] "My opposition to Miss Wightt's receiving for the present the whole of the $9,000 left to her by my daughter, may have cooled said interest; however, I wish you to know that only my being without means (as Miss Wightt well knows) has prevented my compliance." The Mexican empress assures the American minister, "All I wish is, that an equal division may be made."

Three days after her mother expressed her displeasure over Wightt's settlement, Sabina wrote to Angel: "I hear that Miss Wightt has written to a friend . . . that she has already received from the Govt $8,000 + will continue to get $1,000 per month till the whole is paid to her."[31] That July, the Iturbide Petition was sent to the US government, itemizing each family member's claim.[32] Nonetheless, the following October Sabina pondered the result in a letter to Angel: "Miss Wightt has her $9,000 it is most strange that we do not receive our share."[33]

As a native-born American national, Gertrude Wightt was able to enlist help from the US State Department to lobby on behalf of her personal claim. As resident aliens, the Iturbide family lacked both the right and the ability to do the same. Instead, they sought to ride Wightt's diplomatic coattails in their ongoing attempts to get the government of Mexico to pay up. In contrast to the perpetually frustrated Iturbide family, Wightt collected her entire bequest from Mexico, which she immediately parlayed into successful investments in businesses, stocks, and bonds, establishing her as a woman of substance as well as "influence" in capital society. Wightt thus completed her transition from Georgetown nun to Washington socialite in antebellum America, confirming the description offered by Daniel Webster: "a lady well known here and highly regarded in our social circles."

Later in the decade, and despite the strains in their personal relationship, the exiled Iturbide family again sought to tap into Wightt's growing reputation as a capital power broker. Sabina and Angel worked through Wightt to gain "access" to Washington diplomats, politicians, and bankers to help collect more of the $1 million pension promised them three decades earlier.[34] For example, in 1859 the American wife of Angel wrote to her older sister, Maria Devereux, saying, "We agree with you in thinking that Miss Wightt has influence, and therefore hope she will exert it in our favour."[35] The correspondence of the Iturbide family members in that year documents that Wightt did "exert" her "influence" on their behalf, if to no avail.

TRAVELING WITH THE MASON FAMILY

Following her withdrawal from Georgetown Convent, Wightt established, or in some cases reestablished, close ties with a number of important persons and families in Washington society. In doing so she either consciously or unconsciously sought a substitute for the community she had renounced. Indeed, her new ties, and the relationships they represented, followed the pattern she had established as directress of the academy, where she had acted as the main go-between for the nuns in the convent, the scholars in the academy, and their parents in the outside community. In her post-convent years Wightt replicated this pattern in the intimate relationships she established, in particular with the four families in capital society with whom she had the strongest ties: the Iturbides, the Van Nesses, the Masons, and the Peter/Kennons. Two of these were the families of former students at Georgetown and another had six daughters in that same age group.

John Young Mason belonged to the first generation of professional politicians in Washington. Mason's political career followed a steady rather than meteoric climb up the rungs of the respective ladders of state and national politics. After having attended the University of North Carolina, Mason read law at Litchfield Law School. In the 1820s Mason served in the Virginia state legislature, first in the House of Delegates and then in the Senate. In the 1830s he served three terms in the US House of Representatives. Mason was back in private practice, providing legal services to Dolley Madison, when he first made the acquaintance of Ann Gertrude Wightt through the efforts of the former First Lady. A loyal states-rights Democrat, Mason was rewarded by lame-duck president Martin Van Buren in 1841 with an appointment to the federal district court of Eastern Virginia. Over the next two decades Mason served four presidential administrations as either a cabinet officer or a diplomat: secretary of the navy (1844–45) for fellow Virginian John Tyler, attorney general (1845–46) and secretary of the navy (1846–49) under former college classmate James K. Polk, minister to France under Franklin Pierce (1854–57), and the same post for James Buchanan (1857–59).[36]

President Pierce appointed Mason as minister to France on January 22, 1854. In May of that year Pierce granted permission for Wightt to accompany the Mason family on the voyage to France to join him.[37] The Mason entourage arrived in Paris in the midst of the Crimean War. The previous October, France, Great Britain, Turkey, and Sardinia-Piedmont had declared war on Russia. Wightt remained with the Mason family in France through the summer and into the fall, meaning she was present when Mason gained notoriety as one of the three US ministers—along with Pierre Soule, minister to Spain, and James Buchanan, minister to England—who met in Ostend, Belgium, from October 9 to 11 and issued the infamous Ostend Manifesto. Their foray into high-handed diplomacy came in the wake of Soule's failed attempt the year before to purchase Cuba from Spain in order to add more slave territory to the Union. In the manifesto, Soule, Buchanan, and Mason called for the United States to seize Cuba if Spain refused to sell, on the pretext of preventing a slave revolt on the island similar to what happened in Haiti half a century earlier. When news of the meeting in Ostend leaked out, the Northern press and newly organized Republican Party denounced it as a plot hatched by Southern politicians (Soule and Mason) and Northern "doughface" allies in the Democratic Party (Buchanan) to advance the "Slave Power Conspiracy."[38]

CORRESPONDING WITH THE MASON FAMILY

In the 1840s and 1850s Wightt corresponded with various members of the Mason family. Unfortunately, only nine letters from these years have been found. However small, this sample provides a window on the nature of her relationship with the members of the Masons and suggests how and why Wightt was able to navigate the waters of elite Washington society with such success. Five of the letters are addressed to the family patriarch, John Young Mason, whom Wightt always calls "Judge." Three letters were sent to the eldest of the six Mason daughters, twenty-five-year-old Elizabeth, called "Bettie." The remaining letter, also the earliest dated of the group, was sent to Mary Ann (Fort) Mason, the family matriarch. Hardly exhaustive, the collection vastly undercounts the number of letters likely sent to Mary Ann. Taken as a whole, however, Wightt's correspondence with the Mason family testifies to her adroitness at moving back and forth between the business and political activities of the public sphere occupied by Judge Mason and the personal and social events of the domestic sphere, the cultural arena dominated by women. For example, on the one hand, Wightt's letters to the female members of the Mason clan demonstrate her skill at moving in the social whirl and conversing on topics expected of a Southern lady. Her letters to Mary Ann and to Bettie contain little about national or world affairs except when public events intersect with the private sphere—such as state dinners and balls, where women served as both hostesses and guests, and where they might exert "unofficial" influence. On the other hand, Wightt's correspondence with Judge Mason provides extensive commentary on political affairs in America and in Europe. She mixes her views on these public matters with her concern for Mason's health when he was laid low by a serious illness. Wightt once again adheres to the roles of the unmarried woman as the maiden aunt or sister of charity.

One other practice that Wightt frequently employs in her personal letters is crosshatching. That is, when writing to friends, Wightt might take a sheet of stationery already written on, turn it at a ninety-degree angle, and continue writing over the same page. She picked up this habit, which uses space on the sheet of paper economically and thereby saves on the cost of stationery, from her time in the convent, where it was commonly used by the nuns. Such thrift may have been needed during dire times in the convent, but Wightt's continued use of the measure thirty years later suggests that she found some old habits hard to break even when they proved no longer necessary. While crosshatching may have been a penny saver, the method must have made for difficult reading for her correspondents, as it surely does for later researchers.

CORRESPONDING WITH THE MASON WOMEN

Wightt's single letter to Mary Fort Mason focuses entirely on family affairs and related private concerns. Wightt expresses her relief that Mason's health was improving after an illness that may have been a stomach disorder. She also must have considered her relationship with the family close enough to offer unsolicited advice on his exercise and diet regimen: "Pray do not let him walk at all during the summer," she pleads, as "the sun is entirely too powerful + the effects would probably bring on a bilious fever. Until he is perfectly reestablished, I hope he will abstain from vegetables + fruit and even after that, be careful."[39]

Wightt also tells Mary Ann of meeting Fanny, the Masons' fifteen-year-old daughter, in Philadelphia and going shopping with her. "She told me you said she could get a dress & a black silk cape, so I went with her to purchase them a few days since," writes Wightt. "I hope you will like them. She is a sweet child + wins all hearts." This letter suggests that in her post-convent years, Wightt forged social relationships with parents and their children that followed the pattern established when she led Georgetown Academy. In a sense Wightt was recapitulating the behavior that made her a popular and successful headmistress: she knew how to connect with both parents and children at their respective levels.

There is also a generational difference in Wightt's relationship with both the adults and the children. Whereas Wightt always signed her letters to Mr. and Mrs. Mason in the same way as "Ann G. Wightt," in her letters to Bettie she usually signs herself "Sr. Gertrude." In 1855 Bettie was twenty-five years old and was scheduled to wed Roscoe Briggs Heath, a lawyer of Petersburg, Virginia, that summer in Paris. Nonetheless, the origins of her close relationship with Wightt went back to a time when she was only ten. All six Mason girls remembered Wightt fondly as "Sister Getty" or "Sister Jettie."[40] This difference in signatures suggests that in her interactions with the Mason family Wightt saw herself as replicating her role as academy headmistress in the outside world. For example, in a different letter to Bettie, written some months after her return from Paris, Wightt admits to being "disappointed" in having to learn of the recent illness of John Mason from Secretary of State William Marcy, a mutual friend, rather than from Mary Ann or Bettie. Her tone can best be described as a mild reprimand to the entire family: "I did flatter myself that after the crisis had passed, some one of the family would remember that I was one who always took the deepest interest in the Judge, his family &c. . . . However I will try not to think of that past, but only rejoice that your dear Father is so much better & in a fair way of perfect recovery."[41]

In a follow-up letter two days later, Wightt expresses her continued disappointment at the lack of contact: "Another packet, the *Pacific* [is] in, and no letter from any of you! I do not think it is over & above kind in you & Mollie, dear Bettie. Could the dear Judge have written he would have sent me a few lines I am sure."[42] Wightt strikes the tone of a caring headmistress writing to a beloved student to express disappointment in her behavior in the hope of correcting it.

Both letters also take up domestic concerns. Wightt relates her happiness that Judge Mason was recovering and passes along unsolicited recommendations to keep him on the mend. She then moves on to relate the recent marriages, relocations, and other social goings-on about mutual friends and families known to the Masons.[43] Wightt is not above relating the latest gossip to the Mason girls. "I neglected to mention to you that Willie Jessup is spending the winter here with his Father," she relates.[44] "From what I hear of him, I fear he is not as yet a paragon of regularity etc." At the same time, she admits, "he is handsome & seems to be quite a beau at the parties. With ladies I believe he manages to keep himself sober." In contrast to his brother's shortcomings, she writes, "Charlie Jessup is doing remarkably well at the Point. He was careless, until he heard that several young men were looking out for the vacancy that he was to create. Then, he took to good behaviour and hard study & it is thought he will ultimately acquit himself creditably."

Wightt's letters to Bettie are dominated by similar news of family, mutual friends, and other personal matters. On the occasions when Wightt mentions public figures, she does so in terms of personalities rather than issues. "I see from the papers you are having a mild winter, that the roses & other flowers are blooming the Palace gardens," she notes, then asks, "How do you like the appearance of the Emperor [Napoleon III] & Empress [Eugenie]?"[45] She adds, "I wish I could give you more news of your family in this part of the world, but no doubt they write frequently to you."

Writing to Bettie from Baltimore the following March, Wightt is joyful at the news that Judge Mason continued to recover from his illness. "I am really charmed at what you tell me & trust by this time he is able to resume the duties of his office."[46] At the same time, Wightt cannot restrain herself from warning that he not resume his duties as minister too quickly, even as she lobbies to raise his pay. "But dear Bettie he must be cautious and not work much or hard. I hope he received my letter about the increase of salary &c."

Following the obligatory discussion of Mason's health, Wightt mildly reprimands Bettie regarding her treatment of a mutual acquaintance. "I am sorry you seem to dislike Mrs. Piatt . . . so much," Wightt writes. "She seemed to be a very inoffensive person & [Mr.] Piatt I always liked for his admiration

& fondness of the Judge, his obliging disposition & good common sense." Wightt goes on to qualify her view of the lady in question: "Mrs. P seemed to have some opinion of herself, but that is so very common a thing now a days, that it ought to come no surprise, nor even comment. I am sure she has good qualities enough to counterbalance that defect. She seemed to me to have a very good heart & kind feelings as far as I could judge." Wightt then reverts to full headmistress mode, instructing a favorite pupil on the obligations that come with the privileges of her class: "At all events your position, that is your Father's, being above hers, you could afford to be kind + forbearing without compromising your dignity. Magnanimity is a beautiful virtue." Having doled out a loving admonition, Wightt is then conciliatory, saying, "Of course, dear, I shall never mention the thing to any one. You know I am no great talker, but I speak freely to you on the subject as you have done to me."

In the same letter Wightt also discusses newspaper accounts of social events in Paris and Europe. "I see from the papers, that you were all at the great dinner of 22 ult.," she notes. "Do tell me in your next, what dresses each of you wore, + how you looked, + who you sat by etc. Tell me every thing. It must have been a brilliant affair judging from the accounts in papers." This passage suggests that far from suffering ill effects from the worldliness of her social life in the years after she left the convent, Wightt was interested in the activities and accoutrements of the Mason women. She comments how "rumours of the Czar's death, caused great excitement a few days since. I do not yet believe it but were it so, would greatly deplore it," and continues by sharing her admiration for the Russian autocrat: "He is worth all the rest of the crowned Heads put together, in my opinion and would a great, an irreparable loss at this crisis particularly.

Following this uncharacteristic political aside in her letters to the Mason women, Wightt fills in Bettie and, by extension, the Mason family, on tragic news from Baltimore about Ellen Key, wife of Barton Key, son of Francis Scott Key. "I enclose you a notice of your dear Ellen Key's death, only see how sudden!" Wightt reports. "She died yesterday in her confinement, with her fifth child. . . . Poor Barton! Do you not pity him?" Wightt alleviates the sad news of death from Baltimore with happy tidings of a recent birth in the same city. "I am here on a visit to my friends Col. Van Ness's family & to stand for my little namesake, Ann Gertrude Wightt Van Ness, a beautiful little lady, two months old. I have become quite attached to her already." She mentions her plans to return to the capital later that month for the wedding of Florence Greenhouse to a Lieutenant Moore of the US Army.

Matters of business and politics enter only at the very end of this letter to Bettie and are really messages to be relayed to Bettie's father. Wightt asks

Bettie to "tell your father Mr. McAllister has been made Circuit Judge of California & goes out immediately to assume the duties of his office." Hall McAllister, a leading lawyer, politician, and judge from Savannah, had headed to San Francisco in 1850 to exploit opportunities deriving from the recent gold rush but continued to be involved in Georgia state politics. McAllister was well known to both Judge Mason and Gertrude Wightt.[47]

Wightt closes with a request to receive more letters, trying to instill guilt in both father and daughters to be more regular in their correspondence. "I hope the Judge will write to me when he can. Indeed I feel sure that he will." If Wightt was so sure, one may wonder why she felt the need to remind him. To one of Mason's daughters, she is even more insistent: "I suppose Mollie knows she owes me a letter or two." She ends by asking Bettie to "write soon," then signing herself "Sr. Gertrude."

CORRESPONDING WITH JUDGE MASON

Wightt's correspondence with Judge Mason in the 1850s strikes a very different note, both in tone and content, from her letters to the women of the family. Evident throughout her letters to Mason are Wightt's interest and understanding of political matters. Upon hearing of Mason's selection as a delegate from Virginia to the 1852 Democratic National Convention in Baltimore, she asks, "Tell me also who is to be nominated for the Presidency & Vice Presidency if you can."[48] Wightt also asks that he and his wife either join her in that city or pick her up in Washington on their way back to Richmond. "I am sure that after the Convention, you will have business with your political friends here, or at all events will wish to see them. I do not wish you to put yourself to the trouble of coming to Washington only for me, but I should rejoice if blessings or pleasure or both, bring you here at the time I need to go." Wightt, an unmarried woman who would not be expected to travel alone and would still need to watch her finances after just returning from Mexico, is supplicating his assistance.

Wightt also mentions the recent death of a common friend, a Doctor Greenwell of Washington City. In fulfillment of the sister of charity role expected of antebellum spinsters, she adds, "In consequence, although I have offered + offered my services to assist, I have not seen him since my return from Mexico." Wightt explains that she could not be present at the doctor's death because she had sat up "all night with Mrs. Jameson, who was + still is ill. I have stold away from her for a few minutes to write you these hurried lines."

Wightt's letters to Mason also provide examples of her practice of parlor politics in the unofficial sphere, that ambiguous place where women could

FIGURE 8.4. John Young Mason. Wikimedia Commons.

nevertheless exert both influence and power. For instance, while staying with the Masons in Paris in the summer and fall of 1854, Wightt lobbied the judge over an appointment to his law firm in Richmond for Bedingfield Queen, the son of her kinsman. Although not personally acquainted with the young man, Wightt could testify to the uprightness of his family. "The Queens are old acquaintances of mine, good people & *miserably* poor, since Mr. Queen lost his office," she writes.[49] "They tell me Bedingfield is very steady & capable. His appearance is prepossessing, this is all I can strictly answer for, as I have no intimate acquaintance with him, still I believe him to be what his parents represent him." Wightt asks, "If you can *conveniently* do any thing *for him* you will add another to the thousand obligations under which I am already for so much of your delicate, kindness on all occasions." Wightt's reference to "the thousand obligations" she owed to Mason and his "delicate kindness on all occasions" appears to be more than just the usual rhetoric in such circumstances, suggesting that this style of framing her requests may have been common practice between them.

Following her return from France in autumn 1854, Wightt maintained a vigorous correspondence with Judge Mason on a variety of topics related to politics and personal finances, very different subject matter from that found in her letters to his daughter Bettie during the same time period. In a letter to Mason in March 1855, Wightt first rejoices at his return to good health. But, following the usual pleasantries, she launches into a critique of the inadequate salary afforded the US minister to France: "The pittance you had before, was a disgrace to our Government," she railed. "You see dear Judge they did not make the salary of the Minister of France equal to that of London."[50] Wightt had lobbied members of the senate to raise the pay for Mason to the level of the US minister to the Court of St. James, telling them "that Paris was as expensive a place as London." Wightt shows signs of regret: "I tried hard for it, but the Senators told me they were afraid that any attempt to change the Bill, would jeopardize the whole. So we had to submit, in vain." At last, even she admitted the cause was hopeless under present conditions. "I saw myself towards the last, that it would not do to risk the whole, by attempting to change any part of the Bill."

This passage demonstrates Wightt's sophisticated knowledge of the salaries of the diplomatic service and of the political logrolling involved in getting a bill through the US Senate. Indeed, the document reveals Wightt's hard work on behalf of Mason's financial interests by lobbying members of the Senate, however unsuccessfully, on this occasion. Such behavior hearkens to her petition to Congress while still a nun, with the help of a cabinet officer and a US senator, as well as when she later offered advice to the US secretary of state regarding an impending foreign treaty. Such acts do not accord to accepted cultural norms for a nun or for a laywoman in antebellum society. As a nun and a laywoman, however, Wightt could sometimes exploit aspects of gender stereotypes by advocating selflessly on behalf of others.

As she did in a letter to Bettie Mason written that same day, Wightt mentions the recent deaths of both a family friend and an international leader: "I have told Bettie of poor Ellen Key's sudden death yesterday," she relates to the judge." She comments on rumors of the passing of Czar Nicholas I. "Even now, I do not believe it. The dear, good great Czar to die at this crisis, as if to oblige his enemies, the Allies! I cannot, I will not, believe it until I have more solid data." She confesses her admiration for the Romanov autocrat, lamenting, "Should it prove to be true, I really would grieve over it, more than if all the other crowned Heads had died . . . for in my opinion, he is worth the whole of them put together." Her defense of Nicholas I by implication blames the Allies for the war and is a prayer for Russian victory: "He did not make the War. I had hoped that he would live to fight it out or dictate his own terms of Peace." Comparison between how Wightt discusses the same event—the Czar's death—with Judge Mason and his daughter Bettie, respectively, offers an example into how comfortable Wightt felt when moving between the public sphere of politics and business and the private sphere of home and family.

Just as she avidly kept abreast of world events, Wightt was no less current on developing trends in national politics. Specifically, she notes the surprising rise of the anti-immigrant, anti-Catholic American Party, better known as the Know Nothing Party. "The 'Know Nothings' are walking over the course here + all accede that they are to give us our next President." She offers her own assessment of their appeal by saying, "I go with them in their opposition to Foreign influence + preponderance of any particular denomination whether Catholic or Protestant." Wightt's comment of "opposition to Foreign influence" is especially telling when read in light of the alleged "tyranny" she claimed to have suffered in Georgetown Visitation Convent under the regime of the "foreign superioress," Mother Madeleine, and the other French Sisters. Her comment suggests that the psychic wounds leading to her departure from the convent a quarter of a century before had never fully healed.[51] By this date Wightt was living at Tudor Place, the Georgetown estate of Britannia Peter Kennon, another of her former students. She had also begun attending Episcopal services with members of the Peter/Kennon family, though she exhibited no particular animosity toward the Catholic Church.

In another letter to Judge Mason two months later, Wightt begins as usual with inquiries into his recovering health. "I feel truly grateful to divine Providence for sparing you, and returning you once more to your family friends + country."[52] She quickly ties her concern for his health to his duties as minister to France. "Your trip to Nice will no doubt perfectly reestablish your health. Still dear Judge, I beg you will not resume your duties too soon. . . . Take all the rest + comfort you require. Your health is of the first importance. I do not know of any very urgent necessity for you to make exertions just now, there is nothing I believe of very great importance pending between the two Countries." She then shifts to recent developments in Crimea. "Indeed, I fancy France is so taken up with the war against Russia, that she can attend to little else. Is it not so? Sebastopol not yet taken! Nor will it be. I should be grieved it were, I am sure."

Wightt ultimately was proven wrong about the fate of Sevastopol, but she was not alone among Americans in siding with Russia in its struggle against the alliance of Britain, France, and Turkey. Southerners in particular tended to be anti-British and pro-Russian in the struggle. This sentiment perhaps had more to do with anger with British abolitionism and British opposition to Southern expansion into the Caribbean than any great sympathy with the Russian Empire. Wightt, however, genuinely admired Czar Nicholas I. As with her support for the royalist émigré Father Clorivière and her friendship with the ex-empress Madame Iturbide, Wightt sometimes revealed an affinity for authoritarian leaders and methods so long as they were not directed against her, as in the case of Mother Madeleine.[53]

In her letter to Mason, Wightt goes on to offer her unsolicited views on what she deems England's unprofitable alliance with Napoleon III: "Poor England, I begin to pity her. She does indeed seem to have fallen from her high estate. What a stupid Alliance for her! I am curious to know the end of this War. Is it not likely that all Europe will be involved in it? I cannot see how it can keep out." She considers Napoleon a weak sister involving his ally in his ill-fated ventures, asking "Will Louis Napoleon go to the Crimea or not? The papers differ on the subject. Were I in England's place, I would not let him. She may not however be able to prevent him. He seems to do pretty much as he pleases. I wonder how long his reign will last." Wightt here rather shrewdly sizes up the fate of the French emperor.

After expressing to Mason her views on the foreign policy of Russia, France, and England, she fills him in on the latest developments in Virginia and national politics. "I left Washington about a fortnight since to join my friend, Mrs. Hargous, who has just arrived from Mexico + who is not very well." Suzanne Jeanette Gallagher Hargous and her husband, Louis, the American consul in Vera Cruz, had come to know Wightt when the latter landed in that port on her way to press her claim against the government in Mexico City.

Writing from the Hargous home in Trenton, New Jersey, Wightt informs Judge Mason, "We are going to Frankfort [KY] on a visit to Gov. and Mrs. Letcher, + then to the Mammoth Cave." Wightt's relationship with the former Kentucky governor and his wife stemmed from Letcher's time as US minister to Mexico, when he had argued successfully for her $10,000 claim. The lasting friendships Wightt made while in Mexico provide telling examples of how she ingratiated herself with those who could also help pursue her personal financial interests.

Wightt also updates Mason on the latest personnel changes in the bureaucratic leadership within the State Department. Ambrose Dudley Mann of Virginia, the country's first assistant secretary of state, resigned and was succeeded by William Hunter of Rhode Island, chief clerk in the State Department.

"At present, William Hunter is performing the duties, + I would not wonder were he to remain permanently," she tells Mason, "particularly as I see from the papers, that Mr. [Robert Smith] Chew [of Virginia] has taken Hunter's post." Both of Wightt's judgments about the promotions of these civil servants turned out to be correct and provide examples of how Mason benefited from her political information and advice.

On the upcoming governor's election in Virginia, Wightt reports that Democratic Party candidate Henry Wise "was very sanguine of his success, expects to get 20,000 majority." Senator James Murray Mason and Senator R. M. T. Hunter "have been stumping some parts of the state for him + have made some of the finest speeches ever spoken," Wightt editorializes. She was especially effusive about Hunter's speech delivered "at Pittsburg, Va., [which] was I think, one of the very best productions I ever read. It contained so much learning, research, solid sense + convincing argument." Despite Henry Wise's confidence in victory, Wightt predicted, "'The Know Nothings' continue pretty strong + will give Mr. Wise a close race, if they do not defeat him." As for the national situation, Wightt held, "I am of opinion that there will be no change in the Cabinet during this Administration."[54] As it turned out, Wightt's instincts were wrong on the gubernatorial race in the Cavalier State. Henry Wise handily defeated his Know Nothing opponent.

Commenting on US Senate activities, Wightt compares the superior merits of the two solons from the Old Dominion with those from some prominent free states. "Virginia in the Senate is always better represented than any other states," she asserts biasedly but unequivocally. "Compare the New York Senators, [William] Seward + [Hamilton] Fish with Mason + Hunter." She further measures the two Virginian lawmakers against their Massachusetts counterparts, Charles Sumner and Henry Wilson, "two fanatics + one of them, a shoe maker." She immediately denies, however, "that I despise honorable traders, but at the same time do not think them calculated to expound views seriously." Wightt's freely expressed opinions demonstrate that her political views were becoming increasingly sectional and that her social views remained essentially elitist.

Mason showed respect for Wightt's knowledge and understanding of domestic politics, especially the behind-the-scenes activities. Stationed an ocean away in Paris, Mason especially valued her updates on developments in the "unofficial sphere" of Washington City. It is difficult to know for sure how consciously he agreed with her views or followed her advice on international affairs. But the fact that Mason maintained a long-term correspondence with Wightt during his years as a diplomat does suggest that he valued the information and perspective she provided. Indeed, during the 1850s Wightt served Mason as a kind of informal advisor, and she worked to advance his career on more than one occasion.

Only a month after the presidential election of 1856, for example, Wightt lobbied president-elect James Buchanan on behalf of Mason's reappointment as minister to France. In her letter to Mason written a month after the election, Wightt includes the text of Buchanan's written reply to her request to reappoint Mason, dated December 11.[55] Their correspondence underscores the degree to which the nation's highest elected official took seriously Wightt's political acumen. Buchanan explains that, as much as he respected Judge Mason as a public servant and liked him as a friend, he could not at that time guarantee his reappointment to Paris. "This places me in a most painful dilemma," admitted the president-elect. "I am as much attached to Judge Mason Mason [*sic*] + his family, as to any person in the world." Buchanan also temporized, citing reasons why he could not grant Wightt's request at the present time. First, from personal conversations with him, Buchanan understood Mason had "limited his stay to the term of Genl. Pierce's Administration." Second, there was the patronage system, whereby diplomatic posts were among the plums to be doled out to key supporters. During the recent election, "Old Buck" explains, "Those who have directed time + money + personal exertions in the conflict . . . expect there will be a general change in the Foreign Ministers after they shall have been four years abroad." Buchanan quotes another American foreign minister to the effect that "many meritorious Democrats who have borne the heat + burden of the day at home, will deem themselves justly entitled to the places of such of their brethren abroad." Finally, there was the matter of public opinion, which favored rotation of diplomats after four years of an administration. "That such is the opinion of the country, there can be no doubt," averred the president-elect.

After reviewing the restrictions on his choices, Buchanan concludes, "Now, you perceive 'the fix' I am in!" On the one hand, the president-elect contends, "I cannot at present promise that he [Mason] shall permanently remain in Paris." On the other hand, Buchanan does promise that Mason "shall not be recalled without due notice or at an unpleasant season of the year." He concludes by affirming his more than filial devotion to his Virginia colleague. "His health + his wishes shall be regarded as far as in my power," wrote Buchanan, "I shall endeavor to do more for Judge Mason than I would for my brother."[56] Buchanan signs himself, "From your Friend."

When breaking the news to Mason of Buchanan's noncommittal response, Wightt attempts to soften the blow by finding a silver lining in the fact that she obtained a written rather than just an oral statement from the Pennsylvanian. "Now, my dear Judge if I had gone to Wheatland [Buchanan's estate in Lancaster, Pennsylvania], I could not have got any thing more explicit than the above from Mr. Buchanan. The fact is, I thought something written, would be more satisfactory and tangible." Wightt also attempts to reassure Mason of Buchanan's continued esteem for him as both a public servant and loyal party member: "It is evident that he has the greatest regard for you + is determined to do all in his power to further your wishes, but as he says, he is in 'a fix.'" Wightt further notes that the president-elect is besieged by office seekers. "I hear that Wheatland [his estate] has become another Mecca and that Mr. Buchanan not infrequently says, to his intimate friends, 'I can now readily imagine the course of General [William Henry] Harrison's death.'"[57]

Wightt confesses to disappointment at her failure to secure a promise for Mason's reappointment, but attributes it not to any failing on his part but rather "the fix" in which Buchanan found himself by trying to satisfy his loyal supporters. "I am rather disappointed, as I wish you to be gratified in *your every desire*, yet at the same time, I see Mr. B's dilemma." Wightt then expresses the upside to Mason's potential return: "If you wished to come home, I would be charmed to see you + all the family back." This last comment, however, would hardly assuage the wound of being recalled.

In closing, Wightt shrewdly observes how serving abroad, however honorable to his country and valuable to his party, has hurt Mason's opportunity to advance his own career, even perhaps appointment to another position in the cabinet. "I have some time feared your protracted absence, justifiably as it is voluntary, would mean some of your friends [forget] you. Indeed, I have sometimes fancied if you were home you might again come into the Cabinet." Wightt reveals her awareness of the political reality that public service to one's country can sometimes mean sacrificing personal ambition and civic virtue many times requires putting aside self-interest when it conflicts with the common good.

Wightt adds a postscript in which she apologizes for failing to secure his reappointment to Paris but remains ready and willing to work on his behalf in the future. "P. S. If I can do any thing else for you dear Judge, you know you have, but to say what it is. I am sorry I have succeeded so badly this time, but you know it is not my fault." While Wightt may have come up short this time, Mason's reliance on her suggests she had succeeded in the past and would continue to do so in the future. In the end, we know that Mason remained minister to France until his death in 1859. Whether he retained his post because of or in spite of Wightt's efforts is not clear from the fragmentary evidence known. What is clear, though, is Wightt's dedication to advancing the career of her friend and thereby enhancing her own reputation for "influence" in capital society.

9

Aunt Wightt of Tudor Place

In spring 1856, Augusta Blanche Berard, a young resident of Virginia, visited the District of Columbia in the company of her friend Markie Williams, niece of Mary Custis Lee and Robert E. Lee, of Arlington, Virginia. In a letter to her mother and sisters, Berard describes an unexpected encounter with Gertrude Wightt at the Tudor Place estate in Georgetown. Williams and Berard had called at Tudor Place, the former's birthplace, and Berard thought it "a grand house although not so imposing as Arlington."[1] On this day, however, its owner, Britannia Kennon, was not home. Instead, Gertrude Wightt welcomed them and escorted them around the grounds. Together they "walked to the greenhouse—looked into Mt. Vernon mirrors and saw other interesting furniture, admired the beautiful view & flocks of black birds in the trees, and then departed." This first meeting left Berard with a changed opinion of the woman she had previous heard of only as "the escaped Nun." Berard found Wightt to be a "very accomplished and agreeable person + extremely kind." Indeed, the two women were so taken with each other they agreed to meet again the following week. "Miss Wight [*sic*] kindly saying she would call on Saturday . . . & go with us to the Presidents."

As promised, Wightt accompanied Berard to the White House the next Saturday, to call upon President Franklin Pierce. As Berard recorded in a letter to her parents, on this occasion Wightt demonstrated her access even to the highest seat of power in the country. When the party arrived at the White House before midday, "Miss W[ightt] sent up her card. We feared greatly, it being in the morning that he [the president] might be engaged." Pierce, however, personally welcomed them only minutes later, and the women "had a most satisfactory agreeable interview" with him. Whereas Berard spoke with the president "about Congress and the debate I had heard," Wightt and Pierce "spoke of matters of local interest which were discussed in the House."

Following these discussions about political matters, Pierce ushered them on a personal tour of the White House. Beginning with the East Room, whose carpet was woven in Scotland especially for that room, he led his guests sequentially "to the Blue the Green the Crimson and the Dining Rooms." Berard found the wallpaper "beautiful especially the Green & Gold of the Green Room—carpets and furniture to match." The outside "of the House & grounds" she thought also "beautiful—circular portico of pillars and balustrade so entwined with honeysuckle that when in leaf and bloom you see nothing but the foliage & flowers."

Upon taking their leave, the two women visited the Capitol Building, where they "saw those beautiful frescoes." They continued to the State Department Building and government greenhouses containing plants from China and Japan. Upon arriving at the US Patent Office, Berard declared herself too tired to explore its contents. Although only half the age of her fifty-seven-year-old companion, an exhausted Berard bid goodbye to the indefatigable "Miss Wightt" and returned to Arlington with Mrs. Robert E. Lee.

RESIDING AT TUDOR PLACE

In late 1854, soon after returning from her visit with the Mason family in Paris, Wightt moved into Tudor Place, the Georgetown home of the widow Britannia Wellington Peter Kennon. As she had done with the Iturbide family, Wightt once again returned to a relationship first established when she was directress of the Georgetown Visitation Young Ladies' Academy. Britannia Peter was the great-granddaughter of Martha Washington; she had attended the school in the years when Wightt served as its headmistress. Like many of her classmates, the teen-aged Britannia formed a close bond with Sister Getty. Britannia later told her grandchildren that Wightt "always said that she loved me better than anyone in the world."[2]

In December 1842, Britannia, age twenty-six, married Commodore Beverley Kennon, some twenty years her senior. Kennon was a career officer in the US Navy and a widower with two teenage sons. The couple welcomed their only child, daughter Martha Custis Kennon, to Tudor Place the following October. On February 28, 1844, Commodore Kennon was among the six people, including two Cabinet members, killed in the disastrous explosion of the new deck gun, "the Peacemaker," during a public demonstration on the USS *Princeton* on the Potomac River south of Alexandria, Virginia.[3]

From the scant evidence it is not clear whether Wightt had maintained ties with Britannia after both left Georgetown Visitation or they reconnected

FIGURE 9.1. Britannia Wellington Peter Kennon. Courtesy Tudor Place Historic House & Garden Archives, Washington, DC.

some years later. Whatever the case, upon the death of her mother, Martha Parke Custis Peter, on July 13, 1854, Britannia inherited the estate and soon thereafter invited Wightt to come and live with her and her daughter.[4] By early November, if not before, Wightt had taken up residence there. Anna Maria Thornton, wife of Dr. William Thornton and a frequent visitor to Tudor Place, records in her diary that she and a friend "went to see Mrs. Kennon." Britannia was not home, but they found "Miss Whyte [*sic*] there."[5] Some sixteen years senior to her host, Wightt acted the role of elder sister to Britannia, filling the emotional gap left by the death of her husband as well as the recent passing

FIGURE 9.2. Tudor Place, ca. 1858. Courtesy Tudor Place Historic House & Garden Archives, Washington, DC.

of her mother and her deceased older sisters, America and Columbia. Just eleven years old when Gertrude came to live with the family, Britannia's only child, Martha, nicknamed "Markie," called her "Aunt Wightt."[6]

In some ways the move to Tudor Place might be understood as another step in Wightt's lifelong quest to reconstitute a lost family. In early childhood, the death of their father, followed soon thereafter by the death of their uncle, had left Mary Ann and Susan as "half" orphans. Once their mother placed the girls under the protection of Bishop Leonard Neale, the Pious Ladies of Georgetown Convent became not only their instructors but their surrogate family. This bond was formalized when Mary Ann and Susan took simple vows as members of the Pious Ladies. The bond was reinforced by their solemn vows taken when Georgetown Convent gained recognition as house of the Visitation Order. Georgetown Monastery remained the permanent home for Sister Mary Margaret following her early death. For Sister Ann Gertrude it remained so until the regime of the French Sisters disrupted the convent home and family she had come to know. When Wightt first left Georgetown Convent, she sought refuge in the home of her closest living relative, Marcia Burnes Van Ness. Within days, however, Wightt relocated to the Georgetown apartment of Madame Iturbide. She remained as an adopted member of the Iturbide family for two years. She left the Iturbides soon after the family's move to Philadelphia and the death of Marcia Van Ness the same year. She then took over the hostess duties at the Van Ness Mansion. In this capacity Wightt supervised the household of the widower General Van Ness, his many nieces and nephews, and the mansion's enslaved laborers, becoming a beloved member of the Van Ness family in spirit if not by blood. After the death of the patriarch and the sale of the mansion, Wightt temporarily returned to the Philadelphia residence of the Iturbide family to nurse the fatally ill daughter, Isis. Following Isis's death, in the early 1850s Wightt forged deep social bonds with the Mason family of Virginia by way of Washington City. After traveling with the Mason women to join their husband and father in Paris in 1854, Wightt accepted the invitation of the widow Britannia Peter Kennon to live at Tudor Place with her and her daughter. Her move to Tudor Place also linked Wightt to other members of the Peter family and Britannia's extended family in Arlington, Virginia—the Custis, Lee, and Williams families. Tudor Place, with some breaks due to the Civil War, marked the final destination in her quest to reestablish a "family."

ATTENDANCE AT THE EPISCOPAL CHURCH

Unlike the Iturbide daughters, Britannia Kennon was not a Roman Catholic, so Wightt's time residing at Tudor Place further loosened her ties to the Church of Rome and bound her closer to the Episcopal Church. Sources about her religious activities before the 1850s are scarce, but Wightt's faith journey probably started during her time residing at the Van Ness Mansion. John Peter and Marcia Burnes Van Ness had been founding members of St. John's Episcopal Church, which was designed by Benjamin Latrobe and completed in 1816. General Van Ness served as an original trustee and vestryman, and he owned a pew in this famous "church of presidents," a capital landmark.[7] Part of Wightt's unofficial duties as hostess at the Van Ness home likely included attending Sunday worship along with the rest of the family. Her attendance at Episcopal services may therefore have begun more as a matter of politeness and good manners rather than from any deep attraction to Episcopalian doctrine on the one hand, or any conscious rejection of Roman Catholic doctrine on the other.

Soon after moving into Tudor Place, Wightt stood as godmother for Ann Gertrude Van Ness, the sixth child of Colonel Eugene and Julia Van Ness. Like his uncle, General Van Ness, Colonel Van Ness and his family were Episcopalians.[8] When the colonel was reassigned from Washington City to Baltimore, his family began attending Emmanuel Episcopal Church in that city.[9] In antebellum America, no Episcopal priest or bishop would have permitted Wightt to serve as godparent at a baptism without assurance of her bona fides as a member of the denomination. Likewise, no Catholic priest or bishop would have permitted Wightt to serve as godparent at an Episcopalian christening and remain a Catholic in good standing.[10] This would have been especially true of both denominations in the mid-1850s. At that time, anti-Catholic nativism had reached its zenith in response to unprecedented numbers of Catholic immigrants from Ireland and the southern German states plus the rise of the Know Nothing Party in the American political landscape.

Like the Van Ness family, Britannia Kennon also belonged to the Episcopalian denomination. But the Tudor Place household mainly worshipped at Christ Episcopal Church, established in 1818. Indeed, the Peter family members were among the most prominent pewholders at Christ Church, the oldest continually operating Episcopal house of worship in Georgetown. The church was the site of Britannia's marriage in 1842. Local historian Mary Mitchell asserts that "most southern families, if they belonged to any church, were members of Christ Episcopal Church." Furthermore, Christ Church "had a slave gallery and a well-run Sunday school."[11] In contrast to the high church services held at St. John's Church, Christ Church in Georgetown was decidedly evangelical and part of the anti–Oxford Movement.[12] It is unlikely, therefore, that Wightt was primarily attracted to the Episcopal service either because of its similarities to Roman Catholicism—that is, at St. John's Church—or because its worship was so different from what she had known in Catholicism—at Christ Church. Rather, her attendance at both congregations derived from a mix of personal convenience, good manners, and respect for the religious preference of her current host.

Evidence suggests that during the 1850s the Peter/Kennon family sometimes attended St. John's Episcopal Church, Georgetown, whose building was designed by William Thornton and was completed around 1804. After debts closed the building in 1831, it reopened for services in 1838. Markie Williams, niece of Britannia Kennon, was born at Tudor Place and later frequently visited. During one visit to her aunt and cousin at Tudor Place in 1858, Markie Williams records in her diary attending St. John's Episcopal with the family, including Gertrude Wightt, on her birthday: "I went to dear old St. John's in the morning with Aunt Brit, Markie, Kate Upshur & Miss Wight [*sic*]."[13] Markie also attended Easter services there the following Sunday. "I attended old St. John's with Kate, Aunt Brit, Miss Wight [*sic*]" along with members of her extended family.[14]

The nature of her known encounters with the Episcopal Church suggest that Wightt had no sudden conversion experience of a "road to Damascus" variety.[15] Rather, she followed a more gradual and uneven process over the course of two decades that culminated in her burial with an Episcopal funeral service. From 1833 to 1855 Wightt appears to have gradually drifted away from the Roman Catholic Church and toward the Episcopal Church. As noted earlier, she probably began attending St. John's Church with the Van Ness family as early as the 1830s. At the same time, there is no definitive documentation that she was ever formally received into the Episcopal faith.[16] The relevant evidence is only circumstantial and based on her behavior. During her last visit to friends and family in Baltimore mere weeks before her death, for example, she attended services at both Emmanuel Episcopal Church with Anna Van Ness Loney and an unidentified Catholic Church with the sister of one of the nuns of Baltimore Visitation Monastery.[17] Indeed, during the 1850s and 1860s, Wightt followed a kind of eclectic Christianity that saddened her former Visitation companions and was bound to dissatisfy true believers in both faith traditions.

While living at Tudor Place, Wightt not only worshipped at various Episcopalian churches; she also changed her summer leisure destinations. When residing at the Van Ness Mansion in the 1830s and 1840s, she often escaped the summer heat of Washington City by joining the family in taking the waters at Fauquier Springs and perhaps at other resorts in the mountains of western Virginia. She did so as well with Britannia in 1856. Markie Williams reports in her journal entry being "at Tudor, where I witnessed the departure of dear Aunt Brit Bev & Miss Wight [*sic*] for the Springs" on the early Saturday morning of August 9.[18] During her time at Tudor Place, however, Wightt also began to summer with Britannia Kennon and other friends in the White Mountains of New Hampshire. Indeed, Kennon and her daughter scheduled a trip to the White Mountains in 1861 that they eventually canceled because of the outbreak of the war. The change in venue must have appealed to Wightt's love of travel, seeing new places, and making new friends.[19]

LEAVING TUDOR PLACE, FALL 1858

According to Britannia Kennon, after Wightt returned from France in late 1854, she "came to Tudor where she remained with me" until after the marriage of Markie Kennon in 1867.[20] But Kennon's claim of the date is not technically accurate concerning Tudor Place. Because of mounting debts, Kennon leased Tudor Place in the summer of 1858 to Virginia lawyer William Armistead Pendleton, his wife, Mary Ann, and their three young children. Kennon hoped to raise some income while her daughter was away at boarding school in Philadelphia. She took rooms in the home of a widow, Mrs. Abbott on P Street in Georgetown. Renting out Tudor Place turned out to be a decision Kennon would come to regret.[21]

One of Kennon's circle of friends, Elizabeth Lindsay Lomax, kept a diary in the late antebellum years in which she recorded many engagements at her friend's Georgetown estate. The entry for May 7, 1857, notes, "Mrs. Kennon wishes us to dine with her again at Tudor Place Next Tuesday evening. I love to go there. Tudor Place is delightfully situated on the Heights of Georgetown with a beautiful view of the Potomac and hills of Virginia."[22] The next year, however, Lomax received a dinner invitation from the new occupants of Tudor Place. The Pendletons "called this afternoon to invite Anne and myself to dine with them at Tudor Place on New Year's Eve," she records. "They seem to be enjoying that lovely home, but I believe our dear friend Mrs. Kennon rather regrets renting it."[23] One of those regrets, for Kennon, was her physical separation from Gertrude Wightt.

ASSISTANCE TO THE ITURBIDES IN WASHINGTON

While still residing at Tudor Place, Wightt again began assisting the Iturbide family in their efforts to recover the pension promised by the government of Mexico. At the time of her return from Mexico in 1852, Wightt's relationship with Madame Iturbide and her daughter Josephine was completely estranged. Nevertheless, her friendship with Sabina and Angel Iturbide had been repaired. For Sabina and Angel, the willingness to reconcile with "Miss Wightt," as they called her in their correspondence, may have been equal parts convenience, necessity, and affection. They clearly saw Wightt as a potential ally in their continuing efforts to recover the family's full legacy from the Mexican government.

In 1854, the same year Wightt moved into Tudor Place, Angel Iturbide had been named secretary of the Mexican legation in the US capital. The following year he married Alice Forrest Green, a nineteen-year-old belle renowned for her beauty. Gertrude Wightt was likely a guest at the wedding, which took place at Rosedale, the bride's family estate located in the Northwest section of the District of Columbia. Green had grown up in the picturesque home built by her maternal grandfather, Revolutionary War hero and congressman General Uriah Forrest. Moreover, her great-grandfather George Plater III had served as the sixth governor of Maryland. By any definition of the term "American elite," therefore, Alice Green's family qualified for membership. Yet,

FIGURE 9.3. Alice Green Iturbide and Angel Iturbide. Wikimedia Commons.

sadly for the newlyweds, none of the groom's family attended the ceremony. The imperious Madame Iturbide would not accept the daughter of a mere purser in the US Navy as a suitable match for her royal son. "I regret to tell you," Sabina wrote to Angel in June 1855, "that Mama remains unchanged in her purpose not to see your wife."[24]

In contrast to Madame Iturbide's willingness to cut off old friends like Gertrude Wightt and shun new family members like Alice Green, Sabina sought to maintain good relations with both women. In the same letter Sabina tells her brother, "I saw Miss Wightt the day you left here. She and Miss _____ had been to several of the Hotels to look for you."[25] Nine months later Sabina wrote Angel, "Should you see Miss Wightt give her my love + tell her to expect a letter from me very soon."[26]

By 1859, as the impending crisis over slavery's expansion widened the sectional divide and foreshadowed civil war, Angel and Alice, with the help of their friend Gertrude Wightt continued to try to find ways to enlist US officials in pressing the family's financial claims against Mexico. During this tumultuous year, the correspondence between Alice and her older sister Maria Green Devereux is particularly revealing about the role the women believed Wightt could play on their behalf. To collect both the cash payments and land rights in California granted as part of her husband's pension, Madame Iturbide had sought guidance from the law firm of E.W.F. Sloan of San Francisco. The Green sisters, in contrast, had followed the example of their friend Gertrude Wightt by seeking the assistance of the US State Department. Specifically, Wightt provided access to Secretary of State Lewis Cass and Robert Milligan McLane, US minister to Mexico, through the Democratic administration of Wightt's friend James Buchanan.[27] The Greens frequently strategized on how "Miss Wightt" might intercede with these dignitaries on behalf of the Iturbides' claim. For example, on April 18, Alice wrote to Maria, "Let me, however, conclude by saying, that, unless Mr. Cass instruct Mr. McLane to act with great zeal, the thing had better not be launched at all." She then adds, "Might you not speak to Miss Wightt on the subject, what do you think? Act according to your judgment."[28]

Maria's reply to Alice demonstrates not only that Wightt provided them the needed access to key members of the US State Department but also that she tutored them on the most effective way to present their case. "I saw Miss Wightt," Maria informs Alice. "She considers it obligatory to know the exact amount of the sum, the origin + date of the claim before it can be placed even in an informal manner before our government as before Mr. Cass can instruct he must be fully informed."[29] Maria adds that Wightt "is so practical + so successful in what she undertakes that she must understand what she advises," and notes further, "The claim in California cannot be valid in the present order of things, but Miss Wightt assures me it is a very sufficient basis for a petition to our Congress, which would be a better method of appealing to our government than(?) thru the Courts of Law." That is, Wightt advised against pursuing the avenue followed by Madame Iturbide. Moreover, Maria informs Alice that "Miss Wightt says she has been expecting [Angel] Yturbide to write her + seemed surprised he had not." Maria concludes that "perhaps a request from *himself* would be of better [sense?] than thru us?"

Even as Wightt worked closely with the Greens, they realized that their friend's assistance had to remain hidden from "Philadelphia." This word was code for the members of the Iturbide family residing in that city and refers not only to Madame Iturbide, for whom Wightt was persona non grata, but also to Sabina Iturbide, who still corresponded with Wightt. Speaking for her husband and herself, Alice writes, "We agree with you in thinking that Miss Wightt has influence, and therefore hope she will exert it in our favour." But "she must [not?] even hint the thing to Phil[adelphia]. Because under the present circumstances it would [not?] be providential."[30] Days later Alice repeats her worries of the possible consequences should Madame Iturbide learn about Wightt's labors on their behalf: "I hope, my dear Sister, that Miss Wightt has not communicated to Philadelphia even the slightest hint upon which I have written to you," she warns Maria. "Such a proceeding on her part might, under the present circumstances, do a great deal of harm to [Angel] Iturbide, and could not possibly benefit any one else."[31]

To aid Angel, Wightt lined up major American diplomats, such as "the gruff old Secretary" Lewis Cass and US minister Robert McLane. Wightt also enlisted the leading Washington banker George Washington Riggs, locally known as "the President's banker," through whose financial institution any payments from Mexico would have to be transferred. Maria, nevertheless, finds reason to criticize their friend's "worldly" behavior: "Miss Wightt has gone to the White Mountains," Devereux notes. "I fancy she sees or hears little of the Philadelphia family," Maria reports, "having communicated but seldom even with Sabina over the past winter."[32] Maria admits to conflicted feelings about the former nun, who "seems to me to have [become] so thoroughly worldly, or perhaps I see so little of her I do not understand her rightly; but I certainly think her very influential." Of course, any reservations she might have had about Wightt's worldly lifestyle did not prevent Maria from using Wightt's contacts to advance the financial interests of Angel and Alice Iturbide. "I saw Mr. [George Washington] Riggs on y[ou]r request, he was very polite, even kind, he does not think that at present any interference would be of avail," Maria informs Alice. The banker thought it best to wait to write to him until after Minister McLane arrived in Mexico City as "he does not see how he can suggest anything at the present time."[33]

By October, if not earlier, Alice had joined her husband in Mexico City to help him press the family claim. Alice agreed with her sister about Wightt's value to their cause. "As you say that Miss Wightt has much influence," she suggests, "you had better speak to her again."[34] At the same time, Alice again implores Maria to remind Wightt that she must not "communicate one word on the subject to Philadelphia." Alice assures Maria, "I believe that you could not have chosen a better agent than Mr. Riggs." Rather more cynical about the men on whom they placed their hopes, two weeks later Maria responds, "I have seen Mr. Riggs, who has promised to speak to Mr. McLane himself; unfortunately I have no faith in public men and less in rich ones."[35]

The following month, Angel wrote to his mother from Mexico City: "What we want is a strong recommendation from the U.S. Gov. which may serve not only for the present, but for the future, if nothing can be done now."[36] Perhaps as a sign of his growing desperation to achieve a settlement, Angel called on his most refined diplomatic language to play a risky gambit, one that his wife and her sister had long warned against. "*Should you think it advisable,*" he suggests to the imperious former empress, "you may consult Miss Wightt and ask her to go with you to Mr. Cass, impressing upon her, however, the necessity of *not communicating* a *word on the subject to any body whatever*, as it might in the present state of the country, do us much harm without a possibility of benefiting others." Recognizing that the mention of Wightt might cause his mother to forget her family's best interests out of personal spite, Angel sought to soften the blow to her pride by affirming his faith in her judgment. "Still in regard to seeing Miss Wightt as to every thing else," he confirms, "you must act according to your own discretion, in which I have great confidence."

Writing from Mexico City in early December, Alice thanks Maria for her continuing efforts working with Wightt in Washington and remarks that Angel "is perfectly aware that the U.S. Government cannot interfere in our behalf, + he never for a moment has wished them to do so, for he has too much patriotism for that."[37] Instead of interference by the US Government, what Angel actually desires, Alice explains, is "a mere recommendation such as Miss Wightt obtained when she recovered the legacy which his sister Isis had left her." This statement shows that for Alice and Maria, Wightt was valuable for the access she provided to important government and finance connections in the capital, whereas for Angel she offered a model to follow in hopes of obtaining a recommendation from the government to support their family claim in Mexico. As Alice notes, "Such a recommendation may be useful now or it may be useful hereafter; it will be altogether voluntary and graceful act on the part of the U.S. government, which must be taken advantage here according to circumstances."

It is not clear that even the strongest "recommendation" from the US government would have enabled the Iturbide family to collect the cash and land once promised by the government of Mexico. What is clear is that Angel and Alice Iturbide sought to follow the template Gertrude Wightt had used to collect her own legacy, and they turned to her in pursuit of their goal. As late as May 1861 Alice Iturbide and Maria Devereux were still contemplating how to enlist the new Republican secretary of state, William S. Seward of New York, and the newly appointed minister to Mexico, Thomas Corwin of Ohio, respectively.[38]

By the 1860s, governmental crises in both the United States and Mexico eliminated any chances for the Iturbides' negotiations to succeed, however. During the secession winter of 1860–61, the seven states of the Deep South had left the Union before the new Republican administration of Abraham Lincoln had taken office in March 1861. Armed conflict began the following April with the firing on Fort Sumter. Likewise, later that year Mexico, under President Benito Juárez, faced invasion by the troops of Emperor Napoleon III, who was seeking to collect debts owed to France. By 1864 the French installed the Austrian archduke Maximillian I as head of a puppet regime in Mexico City. And Angel and Alice Iturbide had given up custody of their only child, Agustín, to Emperor Maximillian and Empress Carlotta to be heir to their ill-fated Mexican Empire.[39]

ENDURING THE CIVIL WAR

At the moment Confederate forces fired upon on Fort Sumter in April 12, 1861, Britannia and Markie Kennon found themselves caught behind Confederate lines while visiting their friend Elizabeth Lomax in Staunton, Virginia. After a tortuous journey from Norfolk to Baltimore across Chesapeake Bay, under a flag of truce, Britannia left Markie at Lynwood, near Ellicott Springs, Maryland, the family estate of her brother, George Washington Peter. Britannia at last reoccupied Tudor Place on New Year's Day 1862.[40] Later that year, Britannia confirmed Elizabeth Lomax's suspicion that the experiment in leasing the mansion had not gone well: "Mrs. Kennon of Tudor Place had tea with me this afternoon," Lomax writes. And "She advised me strongly to hold on to my own house and not be induced to rent it."[41] To avoid federal seizure of Tudor Place for uses as a military hospital, Kennon turned the building into a boardinghouse for Union officers and physicians. As a Confederate sympathizer, she banned all discussion of the war from the dining table and got on well with her clients.[42]

Wightt, of course, had ceased to live at Tudor Place after Britannia rented the property in summer 1858. She possibly did not return to the estate until after the end of the war. Plotting Wightt's location during the war years is uncertain, however, because there are few reports on her whereabouts. It is likely that she rotated living with different friends and family members during that time. Although her sympathies rested with the Confederate cause, for logistical and safety reasons she probably stayed at locations in Union-friendly states. Among the households with whom she may have stayed were branches of the Van Ness family in New York and Baltimore and of the Peter family in Georgetown and Ellicott City, Maryland. If she did venture farther south, it was likely as the guest of the Mason family in their home in Richmond or on their plantation, "Fortsville," in Southampton County, Virginia. After the death of Judge Mason in 1859, Wightt remained close to his widow and adult children.

On one hand it is unfortunate that there are few known sources about Wightt's whereabouts and activities during the Civil War years. On the other, what is more certain is that she fully supported the Confederacy in its attempt to secure independence and self-determination. Based on her family and convent history as a beneficiary of chattel slavery, her growing identification with sectional political interests in the 1850s, and her personal links to the family at Tudor Place, it is understandable, if not especially admirable, that she supported Confederate efforts to create a slaveholders' republic.

During the Civil War many Union supporters viewed Washington City as a "hotbed of secession," making little distinction between permanent and temporary residents.[43] According to local historian Mary Mitchell, "When hostilities broke out in '61, Mrs. [Britannia] Kennon, with her ties to the Lee family, was undoubtedly the leading Georgetown woman who sympathized with the South."[44] William Norwood, pastor of Christ Church, "was a wealthy slaveholder from North Carolina."[45] Norwood refused to obey his bishop's order to pray for Lincoln and resigned from his pulpit on October 6, 1861. His actions left Christ Church without a permanent pastor until the Reverend H. A. Bonte assumed the post on January 8, 1864.[46]

If she supported the Confederacy in her heart, Wightt, like many local citizens, sometimes found herself torn between new political loyalties and old personal ties. On the one hand, she came into the orbit of the family of Robert E. Lee through her friendship with Britannia Kennon. Kennon was first cousin to Mary Custis Lee, granddaughter of Martha Custis Washington, George Washington's wife. The Lee family called Kennon "Cousin Brit," or simply used the pet name "Brittie." The Peter/Kennon family knew Mary Lee's husband as "Cousin Robert" long before he became the great Confederate hero.[47] On the other hand, Wightt also had long and deep bonds with the family of Colonel Eugene and Julia Van Ness in Baltimore, as she was godmother to their youngest daughter and her namesake. A career officer in the US Army, Colonel Van Ness had previously served in the Seminole Wars and the Mexican-American War. Although an enslaver, Van Ness remained loyal to the Union after Fort Sumter. He held the position of deputy paymaster for the US Army until his death in Baltimore on May 28, 1862.[48] In her will, made only months after Lee's surrender at Appomattox, Wightt left substantial bequests in stock and bonds not only to her goddaughter, but also to the three other children of her "dear Friends," the Van Nesses.[49]

If Wightt was torn between her friends and relatives on both sides in the war, there is no doubt that she favored a Confederate victory. One genealogical source from the early twentieth century even contends that upon the outbreak of hostilities, Wightt "went at once to Richmond and offered her services as nurse for the sick and wounded."[50] This same source, however, went on to claim that Wightt died before she could "perform this heroic and holy charity." Except for the exaggerated report of her death, part of this story may be true. Such behavior was entirely consistent with Wightt's previous actions on behalf of family and friends. And the Mason family did have a residence in the Confederate capital, where Wightt might have stayed. However, no primary documentation or additional secondary sources corroborate this claim. It does seem that if Wightt had indeed volunteered her services, then Britannia Kennon, herself an ardent supporter of the Confederacy, or some member of the Peter or Mason clans would have acknowledged such admirable commitment to the Confederate war effort.

What is known is that the war hit especially hard and personally for the owner of Tudor Place, and by extension her friend Gertrude Wightt. On June 9, 1863, Colonel William Orton Williams and Lieutenant Walter Gibson Peter—nephew and first cousin of Kennon, respectively—were hanged as spies after being captured by Union soldiers near Franklin, Tennessee.[51] The two Confederates had attempted to pass themselves off as Union officers assigned to inspect a US fort. They dressed in Federal uniforms, held false papers, and gave false names. General James Garfield, later US president, gave the order to arrest the two men. They were then tried, sentenced, and executed by a military tribunal only six hours after being taken prisoner. *Harper's Weekly*, the most widely read magazine of the era, printed a sketch of the executions on the front page of the July 4, 1863, issue. The manner of these deaths both angered and saddened the residents of Tudor Place. Moreover, that very day Vicksburg surrendered to General Ulysses S. Grant, and the day before General George Meade had repulsed Robert E. Lee at the Battle of Gettysburg.

The formal surrender of Lee's Army of Northern Virginia to Grant's Army of the Potomac at Appomattox Court House on April 9, 1865, did nothing to diminish Wightt's loyalty to the Confederacy. Indeed, like many Southern white women, Wightt was an early advocate of what historians would later call the "Lost Cause" interpretation of the Civil War. Her defiant attitude is evident in her last will and testament, composed only three months after the "stillness at Appomattox."

LETTER TO BRITANNIA KENNON, JULY 13, 1865

In July 1865 Wightt was visiting Rochester, New York, in order to nurse Louisa S. Childs, a sick widow friend. The recent demise of the Confederacy coupled with the near-death experience of Childs seems to have caused Wightt to ponder her own mortality. Anticipating her own passing, the sixty-six-year-old composed her last will and testament before returning to live with Britannia and Markie Kennon at Tudor Place in Georgetown.

The day after the witnessing of the will, Wightt wrote to Kennon, not only to explain its contents but also to describe the arrangements she desired for her funeral. She named her friend her "residual legatee" and, in the division of her property, admitted to having "done the best I could for you."[52] Referring to Kennon as her "ever precious child," Wightt requested that she arrange "a decent but not extravagant funeral" costing between $200 and $300. She added, somewhat philosophically, "After all, what is done for the body, matters little." She then offered a standard Christian view of death and salvation: "The great point is for the Soul to be at rest with its dear Saviour." Such a statement Wightt might have uttered while a member of Georgetown Convent. She also testified to "a firm faith in the efficacy of his merits + death, & an abiding trust in his mercy." The language of this letter to Kennon suggests that Wightt near the end of her life remained an orthodox, if nonsectarian, Christian.

To keep the ceremony simple and inexpensive yet tasteful, Wightt asked for a tombstone with "the same inscription as on the plate of . . . [her] coffin." She left it up to Kennon to pick a "sentence of Scripture, a verse of a Hymn," or whatever the latter felt appropriate. Her laissez-faire attitude toward the language of the inscription suggests that Wightt found the choice to be more pro forma than reflective of the deep piety she had displayed as a young nun. Her funeral instructions carry little of the religious fervor found in her extant correspondence from her time in the convent, or those of her fellow sisters. Wightt also demonstrated indifference to the appearance of her body when laid out. She left it up to her former student to "dress me as you like in my coffin." She did not want her friends to become "fatigued" from observing mourning rituals and keeping vigils at her grave, admonishing Kennon, "You are not to lose your rest on my account."

DEATH IN RICHMOND

After composing her will, Wightt lived another two years. Yet, despite all of her preparation for death, it arrived unexpectedly. At the time, Wightt was on the next to last leg of one of her long sojourns visiting relatives and close friends. She had planned to touch base with members of three of the four families to whom she had been closest since leaving the convent in 1831: the Peter/Kennon family in Georgetown, the Baltimore branch of the Van Ness family, and the Mason family in Virginia. Only the Iturbide family in Philadelphia was not on the itinerary.

Before embarking on what turned out to be her last round of visits, "Aunt Wightt" first attended the wedding of her "niece" Markie Kennon to Armistead Peter at Tudor Place on April 21, 1867.[53] Then, in early fall, she set off on a journey scheduled to take her to Baltimore, Richmond, and Fortsville, the Virginia plantation home of the widow Mary Ann Fort Mason. While in Baltimore she first stayed two weeks at the residence of "Ellen," the biological sister of one of the nuns in Baltimore Visitation Monastery whose surname is not given.[54] She then spent a few days with Anna Van Ness Loney, daughter of Julia Van Ness and the late Colonel Eugene Van Ness. In Richmond, she visited Mary Ann Mason Anderson and her husband, Colonel Archer Anderson, formerly of the CSA and then of the Tredegar Iron Works.[55] Soon after arriving at the Anderson home, Wightt came down with a case of pneumonia and remained there for weeks of convalescence. On November 19, 1867, just as she was recovering from the illness and arranging to head to Fortsville, Wightt suffered an apoplectic stroke. She collapsed in her bedroom and expired after only fifteen minutes. Britannia Kennon had the body of her friend brought back to Tudor Place for the funeral. Two days after her death, Ann Gertrude Wightt was buried in the Peter/Kennon family plot in Oak Hill Cemetery, Georgetown.[56] That same day, the *New York Evening Post* carried the notice of her passing.[57]

PROVISIONS OF WIGHTT'S WILL

The provisions of her will revealed that Wightt had accumulated substantial capital and had invested it in a number of businesses, stocks, bonds, and land. At the same time, because many of her investments in stocks and land were located in former slave states, it is unclear how much she or her heirs would have realized from their sale in the wake of the destruction wrought in the former Confederacy. The will also shows that she was owed a total of $22,000 by three important men, all of whom originally hailed from the South: Hall McAllister, Isaac Edward Holmes, and Colonel Edmund H. Taylor.[58] These names demonstrate that Wightt had established connections with leading figures in not only politics and diplomacy but also law and finance. Presumably, based on the sums she was owed, Wightt invested substantial funds in faraway places through these prominent men.

Matthew Hall McCallister, a noted lawyer and judge, owed Wightt $8,000. Born in Savannah, Georgia, in 1826, McCallister was lured to San Francisco by the California gold rush in 1849. There he struck a mother lode, not in the goldfields but in the courtrooms of the state. The *New York Times* reported in his 1888 obituary, "He is said to have made more money out of his profession than any lawyer in America, his annual income being from $75,000 to $100,000."[59]

Isaac Edward Holmes of Charleston, South Carolina, owed Wightt $6,000. Holmes was also a lawyer and former US congressman who headed to San Francisco after his sixth term in the House ended in 1851. Holmes shuttled back and forth between San Francisco and Charleston over the next decade, then returned to the Palmetto State in 1861 after the passing of the Ordinance of Secession, which he opposed. He served as a commissioner in the failed peace negotiations with the federal government.

Colonel Edmund H. Taylor of Kentucky owed Wightt $8,000.[60] Born in 1830 in Kentucky, Taylor, at the time of Wightt's death, was a banker in Frankfort. But only two years later, Taylor invested in his first whiskey distillery. Because of innovations he brought to the industry, Taylor earned the sobriquet, "father of the modern bourbon industry."[61]

Moreover, in her will Wightt owned itemized stocks and bonds worth $12,200, as well as considerable land holdings whose values are not specified. Her diversified portfolio included $3,000 in city bonds for St. Louis, Missouri, yielding 6 percent annually. Her stock investments comprised $4,200 in Western Union and eight shares of Russian extension Telegraph Stock (value not stated). The will also listed $5,000 in Virginia and Tennessee state stocks. One could hope, for the sake of her heirs, that the stocks of former Confederate states held their value after the war. Even had she lost these stock investments, Wightt retained a one-quarter ownership in a sawmill, plus coal and iron lands on the Cumberland River in Kentucky. In addition, she owned land lots near St. Paul, Minnesota.

The first person listed to receive a bequest is her cousin, "Dr. William Queen of Charles County, Maryland." Queen had graduated from Georgetown College and studied for the Catholic priesthood before family responsibilities required that he give up his calling to heal souls for one to heal bodies. Although already in his early seventies during the Civil War, Queen was reputed to be the leading Confederate agent in southern Maryland, a prime tobacco-growing, slaveholding region since colonial days. The 1860 US Census, for example, lists Queen as owning nineteen slaves. Queen met with John Wilkes Booth to plot the kidnapping of Abraham Lincoln. The plan was to hold the president, ironically, in the old Van Ness Mansion, where Wightt had once hosted dinner parties. Queen died on March 1, 1866, so he never inherited the $3,000 in city bonds for St. Louis that Wightt left to him. There is no evidence that Wightt knew of Queen's plot against Lincoln. But neither is it clear that she would have disapproved of her cousin's conspiring with John Wilkes Booth.[62]

In addition to the distributions of real property and cash, the will's codicil lists personal items like "trinkets, books, [and apparel]" that Wightt gave to friends and relatives. When dividing her personal property, Wightt made some bequests that combined the political with the personal. To her friend Mary Custis Lee she left a pearl cross given to her by one of Lee's relatives.

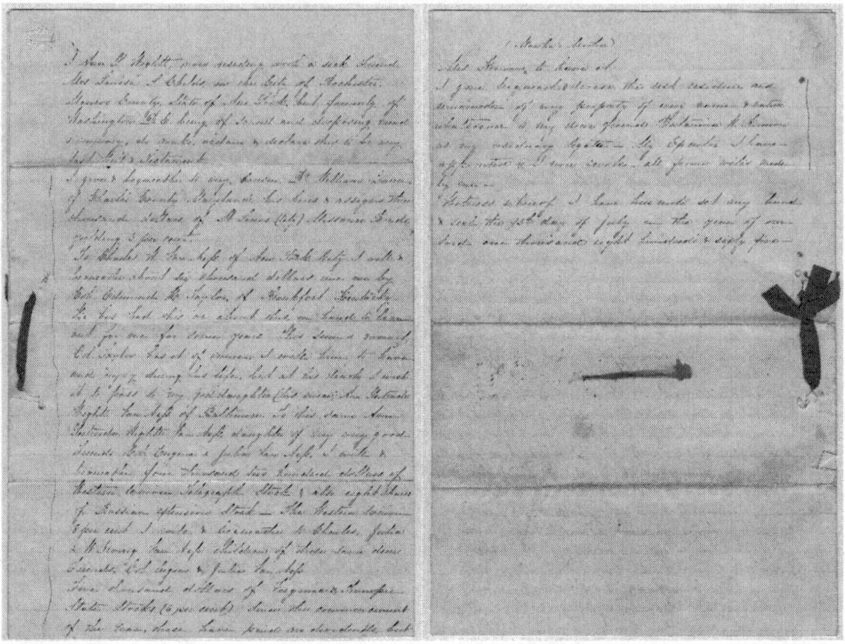

FIGURE 9.4. Last Will and Testament of Ann Gertrude Wightt, July 12, 1865. Courtesy Mount Vernon Ladies' Association, Mount Vernon, Virginia.

"It is a very small token of my *regard* . . . for Mrs. Lee & admiration for her husband Gen. R. E. Lee," it states. This bequest was immediately followed by one for "Mrs. Jefferson Davis for the same reasons I leave my diamond cross set in enamel." Wightt's personal link to Varina Davis is less clear. They may have become acquainted in the 1850s, when Jefferson Davis served as secretary of war in the Pierce administration and then as a US senator from the state of Mississippi.

Wightt's will reveals that she owned $12,200 invested in various stocks and businesses. As noted earlier, she was also owed another $22,000 from McAllister, Holmes, and Taylor. Her list of bequests in property and cash begins with a blood relative, followed by relatives by marriage, and then close friends. The bequest of $3,000 in stock to William Queen came first. Members of the Van Ness family received the next group of bequests: $6,000 from debts owed to Charles Van Ness of New York, an adult nephew of the late General John Peter Van Ness; at least $4,200 in telegraph stocks to Ann Gertrude Wightt Van Ness, her godchild; and $5,000 in Virginia and Tennessee state stocks to be divided among three other children (Charles, Julia, and

Washington Irving) of the late Colonel Eugene Van Ness and his widow Julia Van Ness of Baltimore.

Of the remaining $14,000 in cash owed to her, Wightt stated that Britannia Kennon should receive at least $4,000. Kennon's daughter, Markie, should receive $1,000, as would her four nieces—Martha C. ("Markie") and Columbia ("Lum") Williams and Mary and Ellen Peter—plus Kennon's two great nieces—Kate and Gertrude Upshur. The remaining $2,000 was to be equally split between W. Carroll and John Mercer, the minor sons of Wightt's "dear friends" Thomas and Violetta Mercer of Washington, DC. In addition to awarding cash to the sons of her physician, Wightt also gave property, in the form of a fourth ownership of a sawmill on the Cumberland River, to Louis and Sidney S. Henop. These boys were the sons of her "excellent & dear friends" S. L. and Jullia Henop of New York, her lawyer and the sole executor of her will. Wightt's final bequest of property went to Richard Bowder, child of her "dear good friends" Solomon and Fannie Shepperd of Burlington, New Jersey.

Wightt bequeathed the bulk of the cash of her known fortune ($18,200) to the children of friends and family. In this way she was once again playing the role of the beloved maiden aunt who, in the caring and doing for others found a viable substitute for never herself having a family of procreation. Moreover, she found herself once again in the position similar to her time as directress of the academy, benefiting the children while maintaining good relations with their parents.

Together her accumulation of personal and real property demonstrate that Wightt died a woman of substance by the standards of the capital circles in which she moved during the second half of her life. Along with being financially independent, she was socially respected and politically influential. In the eyes of the world, Ann Gertrude Wightt had lived a life of material success.

Her erstwhile companions in Georgetown Monastery, however, might beg to differ. In the eyes of her former sisters in the Visitation Order, Wightt's life since that fateful day in March 1831 had been on a downward spiral. This descent led her, if never to renounce the values of a cloistered Catholic world, then to drift away from them. No matter, the results were the same: by embracing the values of the outside world, Sister Gertrude endangered her soul in the next world. Nothing brings home this conflict more clearly than Wightt's final meeting with members of the Visitation Monastery in Baltimore only weeks before her death.

Epilogue

Did Miss Wightt Die a Catholic?

Less than a month before he dispensed Sister Gertrude from living in the Visitation cloister, Archbishop James Whitfield sent a quick note to Father Francis Dzierzynski, superior of the Maryland Mission of the Society of Jesus, to ask his advice. "Were I to let her live in a Catholic Family, what religious exercizes [*sic*] should she perform, what restraints should be laid upon her," the prelate wondered.[1] He clarified for the Jesuit, "For certainly by what she petitioned she did not wish to live a secular life as Ladies in the world live." However accurate Whitfield's assessment of Sister Gertrude's intentions may have been at the time of dispensation in 1831, the same cannot be said with any confidence at the time of her death in 1867.

Moreover, seven months after Wightt's funeral, Sabina Iturbide wrote to her brother asking, "Did Miss Wightt die a Catholic?"[2] The fact that Sabina raises this question reveals that the issue of Wightt's religious affiliation at the time of her death remained somewhat ambiguous, at least in the mind of one of her oldest friends. There is also the possibility that Sabina was hoping that Wightt had reconciled to the Church of Rome by the time of her death. Whatever the concerns of her Catholic friend about Wightt's church affiliation at her death, the reality is that Wightt left her imprint in such areas as female education, anti-Catholicism and public scandals, capital parlor politics, Catholic religious life, the process of religious conversion, and the history of Catholicism in nineteenth-century America.

GROWTH OF VISITATION ACADEMIES IN THE NINETEENTH CENTURY

The curriculum highlighted in the 1827 prospectus, issued when Sister Gertrude was directress of the academy, remained basically unchanged over the next three decades in both Georgetown and the other Visitation academies established before the Civil War. There is some irony in the fact that when Mother Madeleine founded Georgetown's first daughter house in Mobile, Alabama, in December 31, 1832, she reported, "The good reputation which our Monastery of Georgetown enjoyed for its success in the education of youth, was a great advantage to us, and we saw at once that we might expect a happy issue to our enterprise."[3] Likewise, when planning a Visitation colony in his diocese of Wheeling, [West] Virginia, in 1848, Bishop Richard Whelan took out an advertisement in local newspapers announcing that the school would be modeled on Georgetown Visitation Academy: "They who are the least acquainted with the female institutions of the East cannot be ignorant of the high repute and eminent success attained by Academies at Georgetown and Baltimore."[4]

It was not until 1858 that Georgetown Academy produced a new prospectus. Even then, changes in the curriculum were minor, with the addition of courses in bookkeeping and German language.[5] At that time ten Visitation convents and academies dotted the national landscape; by the time of the Georgetown centennial in 1899, those totals reached twenty-five. Sister Josephine Barber underscored Wightt's seminal role in this process in writing, "When an extension plan & higher range of studies for the Academy were called for." The Georgetown annalist acknowledged, "Sr. W's superior qualifications pointed her out as the one best fitted for the undertaking. She devoted her whole soul to literature, & all the energies of her powerful mind to the task of raising the Academy to the highest standard of modern times."[6]

THE ESCAPED NUN PHENOMENON

Ann Gertrude Wightt's legacy as the first runaway nun in the United States is a mixed one. Ironically, several of the real and alleged escaped nuns that trailed in her wake over the next century are far better remembered.[7] At the same time, other than Rebecca Reed and Maria Monk, there is surprisingly little biographical information on most of the other such women in pre–Civil War America.[8] And even much of that history is questionable because of the biased viewpoint expressed in many of the primary sources.

In his 1856 petition to the Maryland legislature demanding inspection of convents in the state, the Reverend Andrew B. Cross, an Old School Presbyterian, provided his list of the best-known runaway nuns to appear over the last quarter century: "Miss [Elizabeth] Harrison and [Rebecca] Reed, in Charlestown, MA; Maria Monk in Montreal; Milly McPherson, in Kentucky;

Louise Wortman, at St. Louis; Ann Fallon, at Providence, R.I.; Olevia Neal [*sic*], in Baltimore; Miss [Josephine] Bunkley, from Emmitsburg, *and also other cases*."[9] Elizabeth Harrison (Sister Mary John) was a "cradle Catholic" and a professed nun who did briefly "flee" the Ursuline Convent in Charlestown, near Boston. She returned soon after, of her own will, and remained a member of the order for the rest of her life.[10] Milly McPherson was also baptized Catholic as an infant, but there is no evidence that she ever actually entered a convent.[11] Olivia Neale (Sister Isabella of the Angels) hailed from a prominent southern Maryland Catholic family. Suffering from mental illness, she fled the Carmelite Convent in Baltimore in 1839. Her actions triggered three nights of mobs gathering outside the convent, until physicians certified her insanity and placed her in an institution under the care of the Sisters of Charity.[12] Josephine Bunkley was a convert to the faith who actually spent some months as a novice with the Daughters of Charity in Emmitsburg, Maryland, before she left and wrote a sensational bestseller about her alleged experiences.[13] No additional information about either Louise Wortman or Ann Fallon was found.

Andrew Cross was one of the most obsessed opponents of convents and probably knew as much about escaped nuns—real and alleged—as anyone in antebellum America. That being the case, it begs the question as to why he failed to include Sister Gertrude on his select list. As a young minister Cross helped found the *Baltimore Literary and Religious Magazine* with senior editor the Reverend Robert J. Breckinridge in 1835. Despite its anodyne title, the journal published some of the most controversial anti-Catholic material in the country over the course of its nine-years in print. In the 1850s, with the passage of convent inspection legislation in Great Britain and the rise of the Know Nothing movement in the United States, Cross resurfaced to lead an extensive petition campaign in the state of Maryland. It stretches credulity to think that someone as steeped in anti-convent rhetoric as Cross would have been unaware of Sister Gertrude Wightt, considering that her reputation as a runaway nun was commonly known in the social circles of nearby Washington, DC. One can only surmise that Cross left Sister Gertrude off his list because her story did not stand to advance the agenda of anti-popery. Wightt had made no effort to disparage the Catholic Church in public or private. Perhaps Cross found it easier to ignore Wightt as one of the "other cases" to which he alluded but failed to identify. Better for him to focus attention on those women whose narrative promoted the cause of convent inspection that he had championed for over two decades.

In any case, tales of runway nuns revived after the Civil War and remained grist for the anti-popery mill during periodic revivals of anti-Catholic nativism well into the twentieth century. Less than three months after Wightt's death, an Irish immigrant named Edith O'Gorman (Sister Teresa de Chantal) "escaped" from her convent after almost six years as a member of the Sisters of Charity of New Jersey. Church authorities covered up her allegations of sexual assault against a priest, Father William Walsh. Also Ireland-born, Walsh had arrived in America after first being stationed in Australia. After apparently admitting to "some impropriety," he was transferred back to the Land Down Under. O'Gorman, for her part, later married, converted to the Baptist Church, and wrote an exposé of her ordeal, which went through numerous editions and was translated into several languages. O'Gorman made a long career of her story, touring in Britain, Australia, and the United States delivering anti-Catholic lectures.[14]

Unlike those of Maria Monk, O'Gorman's charges of clerical sexual abuse have a ring of truth, especially in light of recent revelations of the widespread abuse documented from Church records in the late twentieth and early twenty-first centuries. Two groundbreaking articles by historian Catherine O'Donnell have discovered cases of clerical sexual misconduct that occurred in St. Peter's parish in New York City during the first decade of the nineteenth century which Church authorities, including John Carroll, addressed only "awkwardly and hesitantly."[15] Such incidents suggest that though some ministers and editors may have been primarily motivated by anti-Catholic nativism, it does not mean the charges they publicized were always without merit.

Edith O'Gorman had turned out to be the kind of asset to the anti-popery cause in the 1870s and 1880s that George Bourne, editor of *The Protestant,* had hoped Wightt might become in the 1830s. Wightt had other ideas, however, and anti-Catholic agitators like Bourne, Breckinridge, and Cross either forgot, or chose to ignore, her story, while those of Rebecca Reed, Maria Monk, Milly McPherson, Olivia Neale, and Josephine Bunkley proved more amenable to their purposes. As a result, Wightt's status as the first runaway nun in the United States was gradually forgotten by nativist propagandists and Catholic apologists alike. Only two groups remembered her example: the members of Georgetown Visitation Convent, for whom Wightt's story served as a cautionary tale, and local Washington journalists and historians, who remained fascinated by the mystery behind her flight from the convent and her transition into capital society.

CAPITAL SOCIETY AND PARLOR POLITICS

In 1814 Margaret Bayard Smith described the unusual social situation for elite women in the young capital city:

> The women here are taking a station in society which is not known elsewhere. On every public occasion . . . in the representative hall, as well the drawing room, they are treated with a mark'd distinction. . . . I think the manners here are different from those in other places. At the drawing room, at our parties, few ladies ever sit. . . . [T]he consequence is, the ladies and gentlemen stand and walk about . . . in mingled groups, which certainly produces more ease, freedom and equality, than in those rooms where the ladies sit and wait for gentlemen to approach and converse.[16]

Mentored by the likes of Smith and Dolley Madison, Wightt belonged to the second generation of political women who set the tone of capital society. From these role models of the revolutionary generation, Wightt learned how "to live a secular life as Ladies in the world live," as Archbishop Whitfield once feared might happen. The Washington City in which Wightt entertained dinner guests still provided opportunities to an elite woman who could hold her own in the company of male politicians, diplomats, and military officers and their wives. Wightt demonstrated the skill and talent to take advantage of these opportunities and begin to establish a reputation of her own beyond that of the runaway nun.

Historian Amy Greenberg has argued the following about First Lady Sarah Childress Polk, one of Wightt's contemporaries in capital circles: "Polk had no need for women's rights. Her political power stemmed not from the ability to vote but from her connections, her class position, and the willingness of men around her to recognize as a façade her public embrace of the idea of separate spheres for men and women."[17] Much of what Greenberg identifies as Polk's source of power likewise applies to Ann Gertrude Wightt. Both women were educated and accomplished daughters of the Upper South who learned how to survive in Washington politics and society successfully and to exercise influence, even a degree of power, within those circles.

THE QUESTION OF SOLEMN VOWS

Gertrude Wightt was not only the first runaway nun in the United States. By obtaining a dispensation from living within cloister, she also set a precedent within the American Catholic Church in general and the Visitation Order in particular. Although Wightt never asked to be dispensed from all of her vows, her case did begin a process that after three decades resulted in Rome issuing a decision on the solemnity of the vows of Visitation nuns. The name Sister

Ann Gertrude Wightt appeared in Vatican records in the 1857 case of Mary Loughborough, known in religion as Sister Mary Emmanuel.

Mary Loughborough was the daughter of the wealthy Georgetown lawyer Hamilton Loughborough and his wife, Maria Louisa Ricaud Loughborough, originally of Chester, Kent County, Maryland. Mary received the habit in Georgetown Visitation in January 1852, taking the name Sister Mary Emmanuel. She professed solemn vows two years later. After being loaned out to the fledgling Visitation colony in Wheeling, [West] Virginia, Loughborough returned to Georgetown in 1855. Struggling with her vocation and harboring romantic feelings for a young man she had known before entering religious life, Loughborough left the convent, apparently without permission. When she later sought to return, she was denied entrance by both Georgetown and Wheeling.[18] In spring 1856 Loughborough took a page from Wightt's book by writing directly to the pope to plead her case. Echoing Wightt's case twenty-five years before, Loughborough's petition resurrected questions among the American hierarchy and the Vatican about the nature of solemn vows in Visitation convents.

After waiting eight months without receiving an answer from the Holy Father, she suspected that her letter had been waylaid by the bureaucracy of the Propaganda Fide. Loughborough took the unique step of writing to US Secretary of State William L. Marcy. From the tone of her letter, Marcy appears to have been a family friend. She petitioned Marcy to instruct the US minister to Rome to intercede with Pope Pius IX on her behalf.[19]

There is evidence that Loughborough's gambit did open diplomatic channels over her case. Moreover, both of her parents soon got involved in the process. Her mother wrote directly to the pope in February 1857. Her father, a leading Georgetown attorney, followed up in April with a message to Francis Kenrick, archbishop of Baltimore. Maria Loughborough's missive is most interesting because, in arguing in favor of her daughter's desire to receive a dispensation from her vows, she brought up two earlier cases, one of which was Sister Gertrude's. "With all due respect," the worried mother erroneously informs the Holy Father, "permit me to call your attention to the fact that Miss Wightt was released from her vows about 25 years ago."[20] She contends that Wightt's vows "were solemn, and I am told my daughter's are simple." In a postscript the mother notes that "Miss Wightt was called Sister Gertrude. She was of the Visitation Georgetown." A resident of the District of Columbia, Maria recalled that Wightt's flight had occurred only a few months before her own wedding. Almost three months after his wife's plea to the pope, Hamilton Loughborough appealed to Archbishop Kenrick. The lawyer-father noted that his daughter was about to marry in violation of her vow of chastity. Even worse, her fiancé was a Protestant, a case of double jeopardy for her soul.[21]

FIGURE 10.1. Francis Patrick Kenrick, Sixth Archbishop of Baltimore (1851–63). Courtesy Archives of the Archdiocese of Baltimore, Associated Archives at St. Mary's Seminary & University, Baltimore.

Less than three weeks later, Kenrick reacted to these concerned parents by contacting his fellow prelates for their advice on the thorny issue of the vows taken by Mary Loughborough. Kenrick asked his brother bishops for their understanding of the binding of solemn vows, citing the earlier cases of two Georgetown nuns—"Gertrude Wyght [*sic*]" (Sister Ann Gertrude Wightt) in 1831 and "Adelaidem [*sic*] O'Sullivan" (Sister Mary John) in 1840.[22] "In the middle of the year 1831, Gertrude Wyght fled from the monastery," Kenrick writes. "In time this notorious fugitive sought from Archbishop Whitfield to be freed from her vows, but it was never granted [*nupsit*], due to the supposition that one could not be freed of the vow of chastity." Here the archbishop got wrong some minor details of Wightt's case—starting with the spelling of her surname and erring regarding the time of year of Wightt's exit from the convent. Of more consequence was Kenrick's false contention that Wightt had petitioned to be released from her vows of poverty, obedience, and chastity. Kenrick thereby not only repeated the error made by Father Deluol a quarter century before but compounded the Deluol's mistake by adding chastity to the mix.[23] In truth, Wightt had never asked the archbishop or the pope for release from all of her vows. Perhaps in his rush to settle the case of Mary Loughborough, who had recently married a non-Catholic, Kenrick did not review Wightt's case with his usual care.

Kenrick also reports to the bishops, "On November 22, 1840, [Pope] Gregory XVI responded to my petition on behalf of Adelaide O'Sullivan, dispensed her from poverty and obedience, but not from chastity." Using the earlier cases of both Wightt and O'Sullivan for guidance, the scholarly archbishop issued his decision in the Mary Loughborough case: "On this basis," Kenrick acknowledges, "I have exercised the power given me to free Maria [*sic*] Loughborough from her vows of poverty and obedience; the vow of chastity alone remains." He then confided the need for haste on his part. "Yesterday, her mother saw me and told me she had married [*nupsisse?*] a man who until very recently was non-Catholic, indeed was an open heretic. On that account, I moved to attend to the case as promptly as I could."

Ultimately, in light of the occasion of her marriage endangering her immortal soul, Kenrick decided to release Mary Loughborough from her vows of poverty and obedience, as well as chastity. His decision may have been influenced more than a little by the recent creation of "nunnery committees" in the state legislatures of both Massachusetts (1855) and Maryland (1856), whose Know Nothing majorities entertained petitions to investigate Roman Catholic convents. In one passage Kenrick alludes to this concern, if only abstractly: "As for the pertinent civil power, nothing in these matters [threatens?] the preservation of freedom of conscience; in so far as it recognizes the power of vows in courts, or to prevent someone from being detained against their will." The legislatures in Massachusetts and Maryland responded to calls to inspect convents in those states by establishing committees to investigate charges that women were being held against their will.

The idea the convents were nothing more than "priests' prisons for women" is a message put forth by anti-Catholic ministers in Baltimore and elsewhere, who had been preaching on the subject for the previous twenty years. Only recently, publication of *The Escaped Nun; or, Disclosures of Convent Life* (1855) by Josephine Bunkley, a young convert and former novice in the motherhouse of the Daughters of Charity in Emmitsburg, Maryland, had triggered angry demonstrations outside of convents in the archdiocese and fueled a grassroots petition campaign to subject convents to state inspection.[24] Kenrick acknowledges that "crowds are easily aroused if they suspect some injustice" and in consequence, he announces, "I have thus reported . . . to dispense Maria [*sic*] Loughborough completely and freely from the vows, which have so long weighed down her soul."[25] Just as Whitfield faced the challenge presented by Sister Gertrude a quarter century before, Kenrick faced the challenge of his own "notorious fugitive" in the person of Mary Loughborough and he, too, moved to defuse the threat a former nun posed to the Church he led.

Seven years later, on September 30,1864, the Vatican finally addressed the question about whether the vows of the members of Visitation convents were simple or solemn. Pope Pius IX recognized as solemn the vows of the members of the Visitation convents in Georgetown, Mobile, Kaskaskia, St. Louis, and Baltimore, "by virtue of the Rescripts already obtained from the Holy See."[26] As for other Visitation convents already established—Frederick, Maryland (1846); Mount de Chantal, Wheeling, West Virginia (1848); Washington, DC (1850); Mount de Sales, Catonsville, Maryland (1852); Wilmington, Delaware (1853); Brooklyn, New York (1855); Evanston, Illinois (1864); Parkersburg, West Virginia (1864); and Riverdale, New York (1864)—the vows were simple "except when they have obtained an Apostolical Rescript for taking solemn vows." For all Visitation convents subsequently founded in the United States, "the vows to be made by Nuns are simple." Although no case of an individual nun is mentioned in this papal statement, Wightt had first broached the question of the solemnity of the vows of Visitation sisters in her letter to Gregory XVI in April 1831. Vatican records show that the case of Adelaide O'Sullivan (Sister Mary John) followed in 1840 and Mary Loughborough (Sister Mary Emmanuel) in 1855. By issuing the rescript of 1864, the Vatican set a policy for resolving a vexing question that had popped up periodically since Wightt broke enclosure "irregularly" more than three decades before.

In clarifying the question of vows for the members of some Visitation convents like Georgetown and Baltimore, the papal rescript simply muddied the waters for others. Richard Whelan, bishop of Wheeling, immediately voiced his fear to the new archbishop of Baltimore, Martin Spalding, that the papal rescript left in limbo the status of the vows for nuns in some Visitation convents: "I see by the Rescript from Rome respecting the Vows of the Visitation that Mt de Sales & Wheeling are not included among the houses where the Vows are recognized as solemn," Whelan writes. "From the late Rescript," he concludes, "it would appear that Rome does not wish the Solemn vows multiplied."[27] Whelan points out the fly in the Vatican ointment: "May it not then become necessary to have some rule prescribed for Sisters who have taken the Solemn vows" and may transfer to "houses not approved?" "What is all important," the bishop argues, "is to secure for the houses not mentioned the privileges, indulgences etc attached to the order."

Two weeks later Whelan followed up with another message to Spalding. "As a general thing the 5 year probation seemed to me sufficient."[28] However, he worried not only about the solemnity of the vows of the nuns in his diocese but also about the authority of the shepherd of that diocese. "I would say with you that the propriety of admitting individuals to the solemn vow after that period should *always* rest with the Bishop," he assures the Baltimore prelate, "so that it may no where be claimed as a right of the individual or the Convent demand it." To avoid confusion and tension among members of monasteries, Whelan argues "that the indulgences & privileges granted to the order should be equally extended to *all* the houses, to insure contentment among the inmates."

Demonstrating that the question of solemn vows was not simply the parochial concern of a single bishop, when church leaders met at the Second Plenary Council in Baltimore two years later they put the issue on their agenda. The prelates sought a uniform policy that would apply in all dioceses and provide bishops with necessary guidelines to handle such questions. Among the fourteen titles found in the decrees issued from the meeting and signed by seven archbishops, thirty-nine bishops, and two abbots is "Title VIII, Of Regulars and Nuns." Chapter 2 of Title VIII ruled the following on the matter of vows: "Nuns are not to make solemn *vows* until ten years after the taking of simple *vows*."[29]

This statement by the council discusses "nuns" in the formal rather than the popular sense. While in popular usage any woman religious, whether active or contemplative, is referred to as a nun, a strict definition of nun is a member of an order with solemn vows whose chief purpose and work is to worship in a cloistered setting. Said another way, although all nuns are sisters, not all sisters are nuns. Moreover, a vow is a promise deliberately made to God. Solemn vows are taken publicly, are perpetual, and are found only in certain ancient orders carrying very strict obligations. Simple vows are for stated time periods or for life.[30]

Gertrude Wightt kept her vow of chastity throughout her life, but she gradually abandoned her vows of poverty and obedience as she engaged more fully in the temporal world. Archbishop Whitfield had hoped she would remain economically dependent on those with whom she lived.[31] She maintained a vow of poverty, at least technically, until the early 1850s, when she collected the $10,000 left her by Isis Iturbide. She then successfully invested that stake in stocks and businesses in the 1850s. When holding Wightt to her vow of obedience, Whitfield had enjoined her to see her confessor regularly. Undoubtedly, Wightt did so during the two years she lived with the Iturbide family in Georgetown and for a short time in Philadelphia (April 1831 to May 1833). After leaving the Iturbide home, however, she assumed the hostess duties at the Van Ness Mansion. Wightt's journey to the Episcopalian Church may have begun in the decade or more that she dwelt with that family.

A PRACTICAL EPISCOPALIAN

Understandably, students of American Catholic history have demonstrated great interest in documenting the lives of converts to the Roman faith but have given much less attention to cradle Catholics who converted to a different faith. It seems clear that for at least the last dozen years of her life, and probably more, Wightt was "a practical Episcopalian." At the same time, conclusive (as opposed to circumstantial) evidence that she was ever formally received into the Episcopal Church has not been found. Questions, therefore, remain about the process of her change, if not conversion: At what point in time did Wightt begin the journey from the Church of Rome to the Church of England, or at least its American offshoot? Exactly when did she begin to attend its services? And when, if ever, did she identify as a member of that church? Was Wightt ever formally received into the Episcopal Church? The answer to the first two questions is that Wightt likely began attending Episcopal services sometime after moving into the Van Ness Mansion in the 1830s. The answers to the last two are less clear. John Peter and Marcia Burnes Van Ness had been founding members of St. John's Episcopal, Lafayette Square, 1816.[32] Moreover, the general's nephews and nieces, the adult children of his deceased brother, William, who resided at the mansion, were also of the Episcopalian persuasion. The family rented a pew in the church. A natural, if not official part of Wightt's duties as social hostess in the Van Ness Mansion would have involved attending religious services with the patriarch and his family. After all, Wightt stood in for her deceased first cousin as the lady of the house, and her responsibilities could well have included accompanying the family to Sunday worship.

It must be noted that despite the claims of Archbishop Whitfield, General Van Ness personally exhibited no overt prejudice against Roman Catholicism. Indeed, Van Ness was an actual benefactor of the Catholic Church, as indicated by his donation of the land on which St. Mary Mother of God Church in Washington, DC, was erected in October 1846. His gift came with the following strings attached: that Catholic worship should begin there within one year of the donation, that worship be regularly continued there, and that if worship were ever to cease there, the land would return to the Van Ness family.[33] It is unlikely that General Van Ness would have been so generous to a religious denomination for which he harbored hostility.

In addition to the Van Ness family with whom she resided, Wightt's closest friends in Washington City were all members of the Episcopalian Church. These included her primary mentor at the time, Dolley Madison, herself a convert who was baptized into the Episcopal Church in 1845. The John Young Mason family also professed the Episcopal faith, as did the Peter/Kennon family of Tudor Place, attending both St. John's Church and Christ Church in Georgetown. The latter parish was the local favorite of most families of politicians from the Southern states, and during the war it became known as the "secesh Church." Moreover, there are the claims in Wightt's letter of December 11, 1867, where she acknowledges having attended Emmanuel Episcopal Church when visiting her relative Anna Van Ness Loney in Baltimore.

Two other documents offer convincing evidence that Wightt must have been attending Episcopal churches no later than 1855. The first is her letter from that time, explaining that she needed to travel to Baltimore to stand as godmother to her namesake, Ann Gertrude Wightt Van Ness, the then-newborn daughter of Eugene and Julia Van Ness.[34] No bishop of the Episcopal Church in 1855, a year when revived anti-Catholicism was peaking in the United States as shown by the electoral strength of the Know Nothing Party, would have sanctioned a practicing member of the Roman Catholic Church to act as godparent at an Episcopal baptismal ceremony. Likewise, no Roman Catholic prelate would have approved a practicing Catholic to stand as godparent at an Episcopalian baptism. Nonetheless, Ann Gertrude Wightt did stand as godmother to the Van Ness baby. This action alone suggests that Wightt had been accepted as an Episcopalian.

Further complicating this issue, however, is the fact that in her will Wightt also mentions her godson Pearson (or Preston) Farley. Based on his surname, Farley was likely of Irish ethnicity. He may have been Catholic as well. Wightt left Farley "my Raphaels Madonnas & my Mexican buckle silver mounted & given me by Salvador de Yturbide."[35] The Catholic nature of the paintings and the buckle from one of the Iturbide sons suggest a link between the Farley family and the Iturbide family. Other bequests in her will also testify to Wightt's desire to match her beneficiaries to gifts of personal value for them. It is possible that Wightt stood as godmother to Pearson Farley sometime in the late 1840s, when she was in Philadelphia nursing Isis Iturbide.

If uncertainty remains about the denomination into which her godson was baptized, it is possible to verify that in her final decades Wightt worshipped

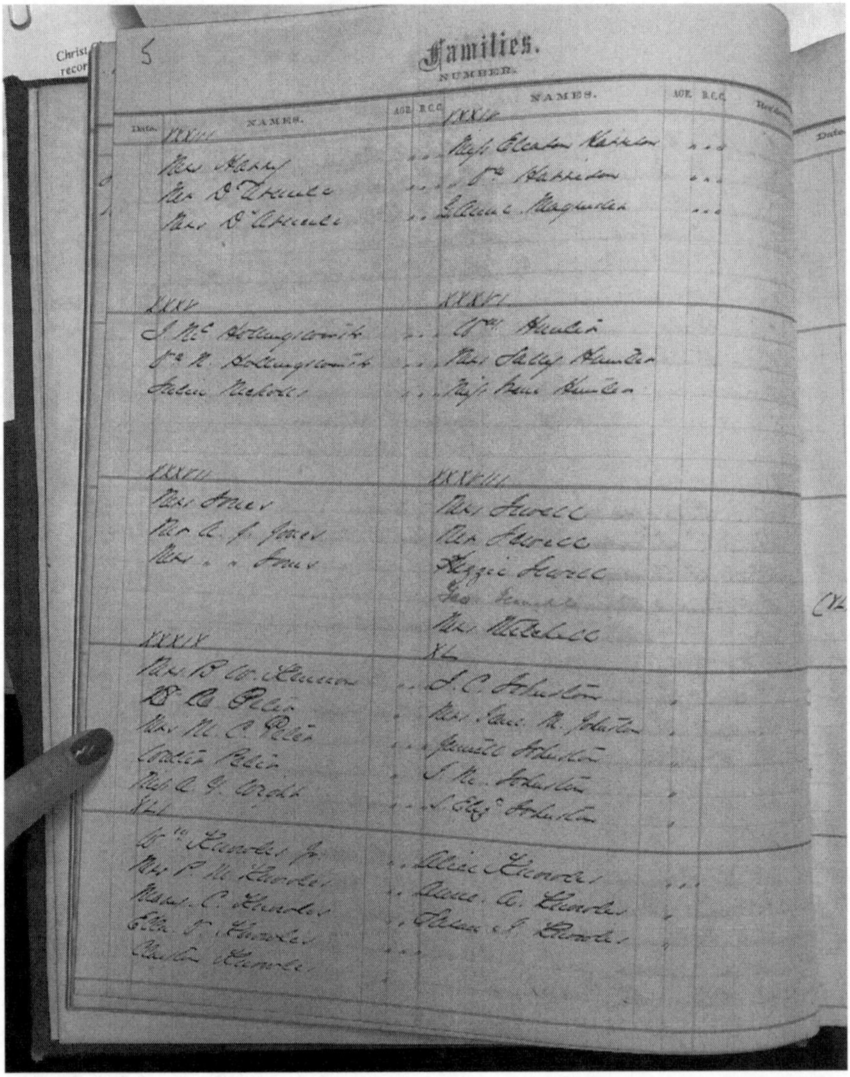

FIGURE 10.2. Christ Church (Georgetown) attendance register, 1866. Courtesy Christ Church, Georgetown, Washington, DC.

regularly in the Episcopal Church. The attendance ledger for the year 1866 at Christ Church in Georgetown lists the name "Ann Gertrude Wight" [*sic*] along with that of other members of the Peter/Kennon family.[36] Further, after composing her will in 1865, Wightt appointed Britannia Kennon to make her funeral arrangements. Never once did Wightt mention that she wished to be laid out in a Catholic ceremony or buried in a Catholic cemetery. Rather, by leaving the details to Kennon, a non-Catholic, Wightt was by default expecting not to be buried as a Roman Catholic.[37] Indeed, Kennon honored her dear teacher and friend by having Wightt interred in the family plot in Oak Hill Cemetery, a nondenominational graveyard within walking distance of Tudor Place and, ironically, just a short carriage ride from Georgetown Visitation Convent.[38]

WIGHTT AND THE CATHOLIC CONUNDRUM

Just as there is an instructive contrast connected to issues of class and gender in how Washington society reacted to the scandals associated with Ann Gertrude Wightt and with Margaret Eaton, so too there is an instructive comparison to be made between the responses of capital elites to the entrance of Wilhelmina Jones into Georgetown Convent in 1825 and the reaction of Visitation nuns to the entrance of Ann Gertrude Wightt into Washington society.[39]

Wilhelmina Jones (Sister Mary Stanislaus) and Ann Gertrude Wightt followed opposite spiritual life cycles. Jones was baptized into the Episcopal Church then converted to Catholicism as an adult and in her twenties entered Georgetown Convent, thus renouncing the temporal world for a cloistered life. "Sister Stanny" died a revered and honored member of the Visitation Order. In contrast, Wightt was a cradle Catholic who entered Georgetown Convent at age fifteen, renounced the cloistered world and reentered the temporal world in her early thirties, died a much-lamented former member of the Visitation Order, and was buried in an Episcopalian service.[40]

The spontaneous public response to the entrance of Wilhelmina Jones into Georgetown Convent provides an example of what the late historian Jon Gjerde styled the nineteenth-century "Protestant conundrum."[41] According to Gjerde's formulation, the Protestant conundrum "was the puzzle of how to integrate non-Protestants into a nation that," if not founded on Protestant doctrine, was believed to have been established on Protestant principles. "It was how this puzzle was solved or at least addressed," contends Gjerde, "that led the American nation toward a pluralist vision." Gjerde further argues, "It was Roman Catholicism, as the first major challenge of a religious minority to the nation, that was pivotal in allowing it to attend to these questions." Protestant Americans in the nineteenth century confronted this problem as the number of Catholics grew exponentially from a tiny minority of approximately 35,000 at the nation's first census in 1790 to a flock estimated at

1.6 million sixty years later. By midcentury, although still a minority faith among America's Christians, Roman Catholics had grown into the largest single denomination in the country. As many Protestant Americans saw the situation, it was bad enough that rising waves of Catholic immigrants were abusing freedoms and liberties derived from Protestant principles to practice their popish idolatry. It became even more disturbing, as in the case of Wilhelmina Jones, when one of their own did so. Incomprehensibly, the handsome and accomplished daughter of one of America's military heroes exercised those same rights and liberties to join a papist convent, thus embracing a faith that many of their forebears had come to the New World to escape. To some Protestant Americans, Jones, by this act, was rejecting the family, church, and community that had nurtured her. And doubts lingered among some others as to whether she did so willingly.

Rather than showing the bemused reaction in capital circles to Jones's choice to give up society and enter the cloister, Washington's social and political elites readily accepted, even welcomed Wightt's choice to flee the convent and reenter society. Indeed, the public scandal associated with Wightt may have been an embarrassment to the American Catholic Church, but her actions did not brand her as a scandalous woman in the eyes of a great many Americans at the time. Rather, she was viewed as the mirror image of Jones. Wightt had acted in a way that most non-Catholics might not necessarily applaud but could at least sympathize with. This is partly why she was readily accepted into the highest circles of capital society. Also, Wightt's reputation was not tainted by public scandal. Rather, she emerged in the press as a heroic figure escaping the despotic rule in convents and by extension the Catholic Church.

In contrast to the public response to Wilhelmina Jones's conversion, the Catholic response to Ann Gertrude Wightt's departure from the convent and her eventual association with the Episcopal Church provides an example of what Gjerde's styles the "Catholic conundrum." The quandary facing Catholic Church leaders was how to be "pluralistic and liberal, on the one hand" and yet maintain exclusive claims to salvation on the other.[42] Said another way: How could Catholics participate in American life, from electoral politics to economic enterprises and yet remain simultaneously distinct from others not of their persuasion?[43] The evidence from the second half of her life shows that Wightt did engage successfully in both business ventures and capital politics, not as a voter or candidate but as a recognized player with influence. At the same time, Wightt personally found it no longer possible, desirable, or necessary to "remain simultaneously distinct" from her non-Catholic friends and relatives on her religious path.

FAREWELL ENCOUNTER WITH VISITATION NUNS

Only about five weeks before her death, Wightt met with nuns in Baltimore Visitation Convent whom she had known when all were members of Georgetown Visitation Convent. This encounter in October 1867 was either the result of amazing coincidence or—as the Visitandines might have said—all-knowing Providence. We know of this event because, after learning of Wightt's death in Richmond, Mother Paulina Millard, superior of Baltimore Visitation Convent, commissioned one of the nuns ("Sister X") to describe the meeting in a letter sent to Georgetown Visitation Monastery for their archives. Mother Paulina had known Sister Gertrude when both were members of Georgetown almost four decades before.

The letter was composed on December 11, 1867, and an excerpt was later copied into the Georgetown annals by Sister Josephine Barber. It is the only known firsthand account of the last meeting between Sister Gertrude, as she was still known to them, and some of her former companions in religious life. In addition, Sister X adds a brief postscript recounting what she termed the "unhappy death" of "poor Sr. W."[44]

When introducing the letter into Georgetown's annals, Sister Josephine writes, "I am not informed whether Sr. W. ___ remained with Madam I[turbide] until the death of the latter. Most probably she did."[45] As both a witness to events surrounding Sister Gertrude's flight and a recorder of those events decades later, Sister Josephine offers a unique perspective on how Wightt was remembered among the members of Georgetown Convent. This entry implies that they did not have any further contact or communication with Wightt in the years following her departure. Indeed, as Sister Josephine claims, "The following letter received from our Sisters in Baltimore is all we know of the last years of our poor Sr. W. ___."

According to Sister X's telling, Wightt arrived in Baltimore near the end of September and spent two weeks at the home of her friend "Ellen." Although her host's surname is not mentioned, it is clear from the context that Ellen is the biological sister of Sister X. Wightt and Ellen visited Baltimore Visitation Convent, which had been founded by nuns from Georgetown in 1837. This was the first encounter between Wightt and Mother Paulina Millard, the convent superior, since that fateful afternoon in March thirty-six years earlier. The account of that reunion, as recorded by an eyewitness, is therefore especially valuable and telling. What stands out is their mutual love and concern for each other despite the passage of time and the divergence of their respective life paths. Uppermost in Mother Paulina's mind is the question of

Wightt's salvation, a point also stressed by various Georgetown nuns at the time of her flight and by Sister Mary Austin Barber in the letter to her daughter in the mid-1830s.

"Mother Paulina said to her, 'Sister W. ___ you must come to us: I have a place for you here.' She replied: 'No, no!' Mother insisted: 'Oh yes, you must come; you must die with us.' She was very much agitated & still said no, but not proudly." Likewise, Sister X said to Wightt that "I would be so happy to have her come & die with me. She then said, 'I must come & die with her.'" In this way Wightt parried each thrust from the Visitandines.

Although the primary concern of both nuns remained ensuring Wightt's eternal salvation, Wightt herself was more interested in using the opportunity to catch up and reminisce "about several of the old Sisters." She was especially interested in learning about the recent passing of Mother Juliana Matthews at the Richmond Visitation Monastery, a foundation that she had helped establish only the previous year. "Then Mother Paulina detached from her beads a medal of the Holy Family which M. Juliana had had about her when dying, & gave it to poor Sr. W." Surely Wightt was deeply moved to receive this token of her former superior to whom she remained much devoted.

Then Mother Paulina tried a new tack to get Wightt to remain with them, warning that Wightt's planned trip to Richmond would be dangerous. Wightt responded that she had no qualms about making the trip, that "she was not afraid of any thing; she loved to travel." Recognizing that she was not about to persuade Wightt either to enter Baltimore Visitation or to return to the Georgetown Convent, Millard "told her she put her daily in the wounds of Jesus. She answered: 'I hope I am in the wounds of Jesus.'" Upon Wightt making this statement, the nuns found her to be "very much agitated, struggling against something; & persons who saw her said the same." References to "being in the wounds of Jesus" is language very evocative of, if not exclusive to, Roman Catholic devotional practice. Meditation by the sinner on "the wounds of Jesus" is a reminder of one's own woundedness and points to the means to salvation. Wightt's use of this language suggests that she had not so much consciously broken with her Roman Catholic faith as gradually drifted away from it. She found that the Episcopalian version of Christianity was spiritually satisfying to her soul and socially compatible with the families and friends she had come to know since leaving the Iturbide home in 1833.

This notion, that Wightt's religious observances were as much about politeness as piety combined with a demonstration of good manners and respect for those with whom she associated, is reinforced by the fact that when staying with Ellen, Wightt attended Catholic services at least two times, and possibly more. Ellen notes that Wightt "made no genuflection, but bowed most reverently, & knelt at the elevation, as if in deep prayer. Yet she was never seen saying any prayers at all, morning, noon or night: made no pretentions whatever to any kind of religion."[46] Assuming this testimony is accurate, though perhaps biased, Wightt's religious practice appears to have been pragmatic, adapting to the company she kept. This impression is reinforced by the following passage from the letter: "Mrs. L[oney] called one Sunday & said to her: 'Aunty, did you go to Church today?' 'Yes my dear: I went with my Cousins to their Church.' Passing by the Emmanuel (Episcopal) Church afterwards with Ellen, she said: 'Ah! there's the Church.' Ellen did not answer." The implications of this passage seem clear: Ellen was silent for three reasons. First, as a devout practicing Catholic, she may have been shocked into silence by Wightt's unabashed admission of attending a non-Catholic church. Second, she was likely taken aback by Wightt's casual commitment to churchgoing, as more a social rather than devotional exercise. Wightt attended the denominational services of the family whose guest she happened to be at the moment. Third, she was distressed by Wightt's apparent disregard for the impact her choice of churches had on her own salvation. Ellen had difficulty understanding the spiritual indifference of a person whom she found otherwise likable. This idea is further reinforced by subsequent sections of the letter, where Sister X laments, "Ellen talked with her during her stay, as if she thought her a Catholic; but, dear Mother, I fear she was far from it. She never spoke of any religious topics whatever: from morning to night was fixing her little articles of dress, though in deep mourning. Ellen was by no means, anxious for a repetition of the visit."[47]

Following the practice of seeing the finger of God in such events, Sister X finds in Wightt's "unhappy death" a reminder of the need for penitence. Barely a month after her visit to Baltimore, Wightt was struck down, apparently without the chance to repent. "While at Mrs. M[ason]'s [*sic*] in Richmond she had an attack of pneumonia, but was convalescent & able to walk across the room, when the family, one day, heard a heavy fall in the bedroom overhead. Hastening up they found poor Sr. W. __ lying on the floor with her hand raised to her head. On seeing them she exclaimed: 'Oh! Am I crazy?' & in fifteen minutes was no more."

Any nun reading this passage would get the message of how the unexpected demise of the body may imperil the unprepared soul: Do not put yourself in the danger that Sister Gertrude ignored to her detriment. At the same time, all should pity the poor sinner but find in her life a lesson and avoid her fate. As Sister X commiserates, "Poor Sr. W. __! I felt her death very, very much: __ never had such uneasy moments about any deceased relative." Wightt's passing, however sad, provided the Visitandines with an instructive example of misplaced priorities, putting the material before the spiritual. According to Sister X, Wightt had boasted to Ellen that "she had a handsome support; several times spoke of her investments &c; kept a will &c." For the Visitandines, who were enjoined to renounce the world, nothing could be so foolish as to count up treasures on earth as opposed to storing riches in heaven. Talk of investments and wills is a reminder of exactly the concerns of the temporal world that Catholics in general, but nuns in particular, are supposed to subordinate to those of heaven. That Wightt would speak approvingly of such matters suggested to the nuns just how warped her values had become since leaving the convent. The letter's addition of another item makes this same point in what, at first, seems a trivial way. Sister X points out, "One of her [Wightt's] requests was that her hair might be cut off after death & distributed among her friends." This request smacks of the futile attachment to the things of this world, especially to nuns for whom the cutting of one's hair is a sign of renunciation of the impermanent beauty of the body for higher concerns. Wightt suggests cutting her hair to offer as a permanent memento to her loved ones of her life on earth. From the point of view of the nuns, this reversal of values could not be more evident, nor more tragic.

The point about the loss of salvation is made a final time when discussing the burial of Wightt's remains following her death in Richmond. "Her body was conveyed to Georgetown & buried in the protestant cemetery. The Episcopalians boasted she had died a true Christian & member of the Church." The "protestant cemetery" in question is Oak Hill Cemetery in Georgetown, where she was interred in the Peter/Kennon family plot.[48] The reference to Episcopalians claiming Wightt "as a true Christian and member of the Church" drips with bitter irony. The Visitandines were certain that just the reverse was the case, since in their view the "true" Christian church was the one Wightt had left. Just in case any sister missed this point, the final lines from the letter copied into the Georgetown annals draws the contrast between the "unhappy death" of Sister Ann Gertrude Wightt and the "happy death" of her blood sister, Sister Mary Margaret Wightt more than four decades earlier. This "saintly sister reposes in the vaults of the Visitation Cemetery. She died July 18, 1821, aged twenty years, five months & five days: professed four years & five months."[49] From the Visitandines' perspective Sister Mary Margaret had the good fortune to die young within the cloistered confines of Georgetown, far from the temptations of the world to which her older sister later succumbed.

In the eyes of the temporal world, the life of Ann Gertrude Wightt was a success and Sister Mary Margaret's was tragic. The Visitandines begged to differ with this popular notion, however. When Wightt sought to reassure the Baltimore sisters that she was fine by pointing to her sound investments and profitable business ventures, it had the opposite effect. However accurate as to her

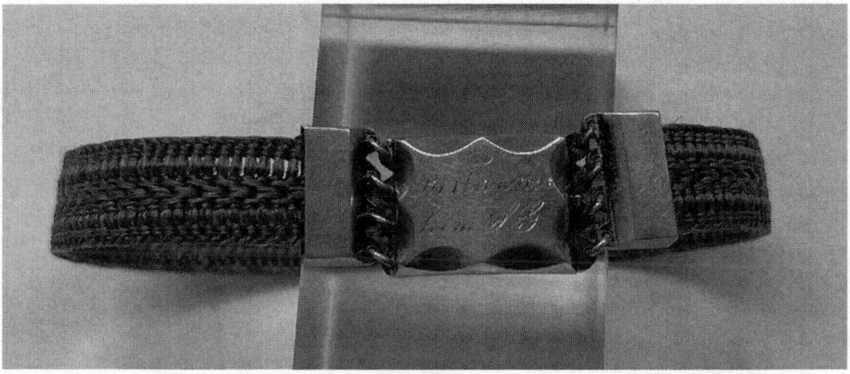

FIGURE 10.3. Hair bracelet of Ann Gertrude Wightt, given to Britannia Kennon. Courtesy Tudor Place Historic House & Garden Archives, Washington, DC.

financial affairs, Gertrude's focus on her material well-being did not assuage the concerns of the Visitation nuns preoccupied with her spiritual well-being. Perhaps no incident better exemplifies the dichotomy between the two worlds of Ann Gertrude Wightt than her bittersweet farewell to her former sisters in faith.

It is worth recalling Wightt's own advice to another about death and the afterlife, this world and the next, given when she was a twenty-four-year-old nun in Georgetown: "*Think frequently of death which thought will be of great service to you,*" she told the teen-aged Eliza Neale. "It *will show you the emptiness of all sublunary* things + make you set just value on time which if well managed will at the end of your mortal pilgrimage put you in possession of eternal Bliss."[50] *Merriam-Webster's Dictionary* defines "sublunary things" as those of the temporal world. The counsel offered by the young Sister Gertrude to her even younger friend in 1823 matches closely that offered by her former Visitation colleagues to herself more than four decades later.

IN THE WORLD, BUT NOT OF THE WORLD

When dispensing Sister Gertrude from living in a cloistered convent in 1831, Archbishop Whitfield had also cautioned her against embracing the world. "Though you live in the world," he urged, "be not of the world—love not its pleasures and amusements—as much as possible lead a pious and retired life." He also told Father Dzierzynski that Wightt did not "wish to live a secular life as Ladies in the world live."[51] Only a few years later, however, we find two of her former colleagues in Georgetown—Sister Agnes Brent and Sister Mary

Austin Barber—praying for Wightt's "conversion" in reaction to reports that "she lives entirely according to the world."[52] This charge of Wightt's "worldliness" appears with some frequency in the writings of several women (all but one Roman Catholic) who had personal contact with Wightt during the last two decades of her life: Sabina Iturbide, Marian Campbell Gouverneur, Maria Green Devereux, and Sister X and her biological sister, Ellen. Each of these women used the term "worldly," or an equivalent, in the pejorative sense, as "of, relating to, or devoted to this world and its pursuits, rather than to religion or spiritual affairs." But there is also a more positive meaning of worldly, that is, "sophisticated," as in possessing or displaying significant experience and knowledge about life and the world. The antonym for worldly in this sense of the word is not "spiritual" and "religious" but "naïve" and "unsophisticated." The fact that Wightt may have been sophisticated does not therefore mean that she was lacking in all spirituality or consumed by material concerns only.

Despite the failure of Wightt's friends and former sister colleagues to recognize it, the truth is that for her entire adult life, Wightt had always been worldly in the sophisticated sense of the word. Even as a member of Georgetown Convent, her precocious mind fueled her rapid rise within the convent hierarchy, and her engaging personality cemented Sister Getty's popularity with students, parents, and her fellow nuns. Her natural intellect, her love of literature, and her command of foreign languages all made Wightt a brilliant instructor and led to her elevation to important offices within the convent and academy. In her post-convent life, her social connections, her powers of conversation, her love of travel, her knowledge of domestic politics and world affairs, and her financial acumen led to establishing lasting friendships with men and women of power and influence in capital society. It is this latter meaning of worldly that earned "Miss Wightt" the kudos and respect from such Washington figures as Dolley Madison, Daniel Webster, Franklin Pierce, and James Buchanan, among others.

Well before she received the dispensation from Whitfield in November 1831, Wightt's name had already disappeared from the front pages of newspapers across the country. Journalists soon pursued other stories and covered other personalities in an effort to feed the public's seemingly insatiable appetite for scandal and controversy. No longer just a runaway nun, Wightt in her post-convent years earned a more positive reputation as a Washington socialite and political broker of sorts. Following her death, a few local reporters and capital observers recalled her moment of notoriety and remained intrigued by its unsolved mysteries. Into the twentieth century, some local historians, memoirists, and family genealogists repeated reports of her prowess as a graceful capital hostess, a charming dinner guest, and a sparkling conversationalist much in demand in capital circles. After more than a century of scholarly neglect, however, the name Ann Gertrude Wightt remains all but unknown today. Nevertheless, this enigmatic woman played a sometimes remarkable, sometimes commonplace role in the history of Georgetown Visitation Monastery, in the early American Catholic Church, and in antebellum Washington society.

A final ironic coincidence is that Oak Hill Cemetery is the final resting place of Ann Gertrude Wightt but also of her notorious capital contemporary, Margaret Eaton. The cemetery's website highlights eight "women of interest" interred on its grounds. Representatives from the Early Republic dominate the list and include not only the scandalous Eaton but also philanthropist Marcia Burnes Van Ness, sentimental novelist E.D.E.N. Southworth, and three female Confederate spies.[53] Nowhere on the list, however, does one find the name "Ann Gertrude Wightt." One might wonder, would she care?

GLOSSARY

Based on *Marvels of Charity: History of American Sisters and Nuns* by George C. Stewart, Jr. (Huntington, IN: Our Sunday Visitor, 1994).

active order: Religious group organized for Christian activity as the chief means of growing in spirituality, as opposed to a cloistered order.

annals (chronicles): Chronological records kept by a religious community.

aspirant: One who aspires (has ambition) to become a sister or nun.

autonomous house: Self-governing religious community not under the jurisdiction of a motherhouse.

branch house: Group of women religious living apart from the motherhouse of a community but under its jurisdiction and general supervision.

canon: Can refer to Church law, a portion of the Mass, or a member of the clergy.

Canon Law: The body of Catholic Church law contained in the Code of Canon Law.

canonical status: Official recognized status in relation to the Vatican (pontifical), with accountability to the pope, or to the local diocese (diocesan) with accountability to the bishop.

Carmel: Autonomous community of Carmelites. It is often used in preference to terms such as "monastery."

cloister: Enclosed building, set of buildings, or part of a building into which only members of the religious community may enter.

cloistered order: An enclosed religious community governed by a rule.

chapter: Official meeting of a community for the purpose of elections or the subject of governance. (Distinguished from "chapter of fault" wherein members declare their faults to the community as acts of mortification.)

community: Body of religious women or men who live voluntarily under a common rule.

congregation: Community of women religious with simple vows.

constitution: Official document establishing the legal existence of a community and its internal procedures, statutes, rule, charism ministries, and external relationships. Must be approved by the Vatican for pontifical status or the local bishop for diocesan status.

contemplative life: Religious way of living organized for prayer and missionary presence. Sometimes exists without "enclosure."

convent: Place of residence where a group of religious live a communal life.

council: Governing group acting as advisors to a superior.

daughter house: Autonomous community established out of an older and previously established community.

evangelical counsels: The three general tenets of poverty, chastity, and obedience as recorded in the New Testament. They are not mandatory for Christian life in the same way as the Ten Commandments, although after religious profession they become mandatory.

extern: Member of a contemplative or cloistered community who performs duties outside the monastery.

habit: Distinctive dress worn by a religious person as a sign of membership in an established community.

Holy See: The pope or the Vatican.

indult: Grant of a special faculty by the Holy See to bishops or others in authority to do something not otherwise permitted by the general laws of the Church.

miracle: Phenomenon clearly seen and outside the ordinary laws of nature, thus brought about by some power beyond nature.

mission: (1) Small house of temporary accommodation for those living away from the motherhouse; (2) particular assignment of work; (3) small or dependent community.

monastery: Autonomous religious house of a community, usually contemplative.

motherhouse: Headquarters of a community.

mother superior: Title used for the head of an order, congregation, or community, both official and ordinary.

novice: Person received into a novitiate as a candidate for full membership in the community (clothed with the habit or specially signed).

novitiate: Place or period of training that precedes the taking of vows and becoming a professed member.

nun: Used popularly for any woman religious, but strictly, a member who has taken solemn vows of an order and whose chief work is worship in a cloistered setting.

order: Used popularly to denote any religious community but, strictly, a community professing the religious life in accordance with a Rule approved by the Church and recognized as having the obligation of solemn vows.

ordinary: Bishop of a diocese.

postulant: Candidate received for membership in a religious community prior to taking the habit of a novice.

professed: Sister or nun who has taken either temporary vows or final vows and entered into full membership of a community.

province: Administrative subdivision of a large congregation with a generalate as its headquarters.

religious: Person who has vowed to live according to the three evangelical vows of chastity, poverty, and obedience through a rule of life in a community, that exists for the purpose of carrying out these counsels. All sisters and nuns are religious, as well as priests and brothers who are members of a religious congregation or order.

religious life: Living as a member of a religious community.

rescript: Official written response by the pope or Vatican official to a request, petition, question, or report.

rule: Guide for life formulated by a religious community or its founder to aid members in living an order's evangelical counsels. Only four are Church-recognized:, those of Saint Basil, Saint Augustine, Saint Benedict, and Saint Francis. Used interchangeably with "constitution."

sacrament: Visible sign of grace imparted by someone authorized by the Church. The Catholic Church celebrates seven sacraments: Baptism, Eucharist (Holy Communion), Reconciliation (Confession and Penance), Matrimony, Anointing of the Sick, Confirmation, and Holy Orders (Ordination).

see: Official seat or jurisdiction of a bishop.

semi-monastic order: Order or subdivision of an order with a rule that engages in a limited ministry (usually within the confines of the convent). Such as the Sisters of the Visitation.

simple vows: Private or public vows that operate for a stated time period or for life.

sister: Member of a congregation of women religious.

sisterhood: All-encompassing term used to designate women religious.

solemn & simple vows: Solemn vows are taken publicly, are perpetual, and are found only in certain ancient orders carrying very strict obligations.

Other vows, private and public, are called simple, and are for stated time periods or for life.

temporary vows: Vows taken for a specified time period.

Vatican: Vatican State in Rome and residence of the pope. Also, a descriptive term for the official office of the Church and its government.

vicar apostolic: Representative of the Vatican, normally assigned to a territory not ready for diocesan status.

vicar general: Priest within a diocese empowered with the authority of the bishop

Visitation: The Virgin Mary's visit to her cousin Elizabeth (Lk 1:39–45).

vow: Promise voluntarily and deliberately made to God. Religious vows are of two kinds: private (both solemn and simple) and public.

NOTES

INTRODUCTION

1. Diary entry, March 22, 1831, Louis R. Deluol Diary, LRDP.
2. Kathryn Kish Sklar, *Catharine Beecher: A Study in American Domesticity* (New Haven, CT: Yale University Press, 1973); Barbara A. White, *The Beecher Sisters* (New Haven, CT: Yale University Press, 2003); Elizabeth Alden Green, *Mary Lyon and Mount Holyoke: Opening the Gates* (Hanover, NH: University Press of New England, 1979); Amanda Porterfield, *Mary Lyon and the Mount Holyoke Missionaries* (New York: Oxford University Press, 1997).
3. Britannia Kennon, May 11, 1900, in *A Georgetown Life. The Reminiscences of Britannia Wellington Peter Kennon of Tudor Place,* ed. Grant S. Quertermous (Washington, DC: Georgetown University Press, 2020), 112; "Whyte (Wightt), Mary Gertrude (Anna)," Membership (permanent and temporary), box 2, folder 65, GVM.
4. On Georgetown Academy enrollments in the antebellum era, see Eleanore C. Sullivan, *Georgetown Visitation Since 1799* (Baltimore: Privately published, 1975), 93–95.
5. Cassandra L. Yacovazzi, *Escaped Nuns: True Womanhood and the Campaign Against Convents in Antebellum America* (New York: Oxford University Press, 2018).
6. Gerald Shaughnessy places the US Catholic population in 1830 at 318,000, much less than the 500,000 estimate given by the bishops at the First Provincial Council meeting in Baltimore in 1829. See Shaughnessy, *Has the Immigrant Kept the Faith? A Study of Immigration and Catholic Growth in the United States, 1790–1920* (New York: Macmillan, 1925), 117–19. Michael DeStefano points out that estimates of the size of the Catholic population in antebellum America ranged widely, but all agreed that the Church was growing. See DeStefano, "'We shall be a Catholic country': Counting Catholics in the Antebellum United States," *U.S. Catholic Historian* 39, no. 4 (Fall 2021): 49–75.
7. On women's practice of parlor politics in the capital of the early republic, see Catherine Allgor, *Parlor Politics: In Which the Ladies of Washington Help Build a City and a Government* (Charlottesville: University of Virginia Press, 2002).
8. Louis P. Masur, *1831: Year of Eclipse* (New York: Hill and Wang, 2001); Yacovazzi, *Escaped Nuns.*
9. Ray Allen Billington, *The Protestant Crusade, 1800–1860: A Study in the Origins of American Nativism* (Chicago: Quadrangle, 1964 [1938]).

10. See Matthew Leo Panczyk, "James Whitfield, Fourth Archbishop of Baltimore, the Episcopal Years: 1828–1834," *Records of the American Catholic Historical Society of Philadelphia* 75, no. 4 (1964): 242n71; and Marie Anne Pagliarini, "'Glorify and Bear God in Your Body': Rituals of Discipline and Resistance in the Lives of Nineteenth-Century Georgetown Visitation Nuns" (PhD diss., University of California, Santa Barbara, 2003), 95–97.
11. George Alfred Townsend, *Washington, Outside and Inside: A Picture and a Narrative of the Origin, Growth, Excellences, Abuses, Beauties, and Personages of Our Governing City* (Hartford, CT: James Betts, 1874), 610–11.
12. Sister Josephine Barber, quoted in George Parsons Lathrop and Rose Hawthorne Lathrop, *A Story of Courage: Annals of the Georgetown Convent of the Visitation of the Blessed Virgin Mary, From the Manuscript Records* (Cambridge, MA: Riverside, 1894), 319. This chapter in the Lathrops' book is based on "Attempt to Change the Order," in "History of the Establishment of the Order of the Visitation in the United States—1799," 179–86, SLVA.
13. Townsend, *Washington, Outside and Inside,* 611.
14. J. F. Riley, "Riley's Memorial of Washington: Local History of the Capital from 1790 to 1880," *Washington Evening Star,* April 2, 1887, 2.
15. Allen C. Clark, "General John Peter Van Ness, a Mayor of the City of Washington, His Wife, Marcia, and Her Father, David Burnes," *Records of the Columbia Historical Society, Washington, D.C.* 22 (1919): 183.
16. Townsend, *Washington, Outside and Inside,* 611.
17. Benjamin Perley Poore, *Perley's Reminiscences of Sixty Years in the National Metropolis,* 2 vols. (Philadelphia: Hubbard, 1886), 1:161.
18. Riley, "Riley's Memorial of Washington," 2.
19. John F. Coyle, "She Left a Convent," *Washington Evening Star,* March 26, 1892, 8.
20. Marian Campbell Gouverneur, *As I Remember: Recollection of American Society during the Nineteenth Century* (New York: D. Appleton, 1911), 224.
21. Lathrop and Lathrop, *A Story of Courage,* 309–22.
22. Rose Hawthorne Lathrop's biographer contends that the book was primarily the work of Rose, with George providing only some editorial assistance. See Patricia Dunlay Valenti, *To Myself a Stranger: A Biography of Rose Hawthorne Lathrop* (Baton Rouge: Louisiana State University Press, 1991), 120. See also Farrell O'Gorman, "'Daughter of the Puritans'?: Rose Hawthorne Lathrop and American Identity," *American Catholic Studies* 135, no. 4 (Winter 2024): 9.
23. See "History of the Establishment of the Order" (abridged), 1–2, MDCM. Sister Josephine Barber, the main chronicler (and daughter of Sister Mary Augustine Barber), along with other nuns compiled the information in the annals relying on the recollections of Mother Agnes Brent and Mother Genevieve King, from manuscript sources from both the Georgetown Visitation and Baltimore Visitation Convents, and from a "small notebook" kept by Sister Mary Augustine for the years 1816 to 1833. The annals were begun in 1866 for the fiftieth anniversary of the papal indult recognizing Georgetown as a house of the Visitation Order. Their chronicling was resumed in 1880. This manuscript is a 193-page abridgement of "History of the Establishment of the Order of the Visitation in the United States—1799," the original Georgetown Visitation annals.
24. Sullivan, *Georgetown Visitation Since 1799,* 79. A new edition of this book, revised and expanded by Susan Hannan, offers no additional information on "Sister Gertrude

Whyte." See Eleanore C. Sullivan, *Georgetown Visitation Since 1799*, 2nd ed., revised and expanded by Susan Hannan (Washington, DC: Georgetown Visitation Convent, 2004), 93.

25. Canden Schwantes, *Wicked Georgetown: Scoundrels, Sinners, and Spies* (Charleston, SC: History Press, 2013), 69–78.
26. Margaret Bayard Smith to Mrs. Kirkpatrick, November 7, 1831, in *The First Forty Years of Washington Society Portrayed by the Family Letters of Mrs. Samuel Harrison Smith*, ed. Gaillard Hunt (New York: Charles Scribner's Sons, 1906), 322n1.
27. John Clagett Proctor, "Scandal in Early Washington," *Washington Sunday Star*, July 14, 1950, C2.
28. Poore, *Perley's Reminiscences*, 1:161.
29. Clark, "General John Peter Van Ness," 182.
30. A copy of this missive is found in the Archives of the Archdiocese of Baltimore, among the correspondence sent to the Propaganda Fide, the Sacred Congregation for the Propagation of the Faith in Rome.
31. In particular, I uncovered few primary sources related to Ann Gertrude Wightt for the years 1834–37 and during the Civil War years, 1861–65.
32. Daniel Webster to Mariano Arista, May 1, 1851, Papers of Daniel Webster Digital Edition (Charlottesville: University of Virginia Press, 2018), accessed May 27, 2021, https://rotunda.upress.virginia.edu/founders/WBST-03-02-02-0006-0005-0023 (hereafter cited as *DWDE*).
33. Following the death of her husband in 1898, Rose Hawthorne Lathrop founded the Servants of Relief for Incurable Cancer in 1899, later renamed the Dominican Sisters of Hawthorne. See Valenti, *To Myself a Stranger*, 158.

CHAPTER 1

1. Joseph G. Mannard, "'Our Dear Houses Are Here, There + Everywhere': The Convent Revolution in Antebellum America," *American Catholic Studies* 128 (Summer 2017): 1–27.
2. Margaret McGuinness, *Called to Serve: A History of Nuns in America* (New York: New York University Press, 2013), 8.
3. Reverend Ignatius Mathews to Mother Bernadina Mathews, n.d., Carmelite Death Book (unpaginated), Archives of the Carmelite Monastery, Baltimore; also quoted in Charles W. Currier, *Carmel in America: A Centennial History of the Discalced Carmelites in the United States* (Baltimore: John Murphey, 1890), 86.
4. Peter Guilday, *The Life and Times of John Carroll, Archbishop of Baltimore (1785–1815)* 2 vols. (New York: Encyclopedia Press, 1922); Thomas T. McAvoy, CSC, "The Catholic Minority in the United States, 1789–1821," *Historical Records and Studies* 39–40 (1952): 33–34.
5. Currier, *Carmel in America*, 60–69.
6. John Carroll to Vitaliano Borromeo, November 10, 1783, JCP, 1:80–88.
7. John Carroll to Leonardo Antonelli, August 5, 1789, JCP, 1:376.
8. John Carroll to Leonardo Antonelli, March 1, 1785, JCP, 1:179–82.
9. Thomas O'Brien Hanley, SJ, *The American Revolution and Religion: Maryland 1770–1800* (Washington, DC: Catholic University of America Press, 1971), 174; Jay P. Dolan, *The*

American Catholic Experience: A History from Colonial Times to the Present (Garden City, NY: Doubleday, 1985), 86–87.

10. Tricia Pyne, "Ritual and Practice in the Maryland Catholic Community, 1634–1776," *U.S. Catholic Historian* 26, no. 2 (Spring 2008): 17–46; Beatriz Betancourt Hardy, "Papists in a Protestant Age: The Catholic Gentry and Community in Colonial Maryland, 1689–1776" (PhD diss., University of Maryland, College Park, 1993); Dolan, *The American Catholic Experience*, 89–94.
11. The "contagion of liberty" is examined in Bernard Bailyn, *The Ideological Origins of the American Revolution* (Cambridge, MA: Belknap, 1967), chap. 6; see also Sister M. Augustina Ray, *American Opinion of Roman Catholicism in the Eighteenth Century* (New York: Octagon, 1974 [1936]), 396.
12. "Letter from Pacificus" to Mr. Fenno (publisher), *Gazette of the United States* (New York City), June 10, 1789, 65, quoted in Guilday, *Life and Times of John Carroll*, 368.
13. McAvoy, "Catholic Minority in the United States, 1789–1821," 33–50; Dolan, *American Catholic Experience*, 97–102.
14. On the general concept, see James Hennesey, SJ, "Roman Catholicism: The Maryland Tradition," *Thought* 51, no. 201 (September 1976): 282–95. On the Maryland tradition among the Jesuits, see Robert Emmet Curran, SJ, ed., *American Jesuit Spirituality: The Maryland Tradition, 1634–1900* (New York: Paulist, 1988), especially chap. 6, "Benedict Joseph Fenwick and the Maryland Tradition," 171–90. On the continuation of the Maryland tradition into the nineteenth century, see Thomas W. Spalding, *The Premier See: A History of the Archdiocese of Baltimore, 1789–1994* (Baltimore: Johns Hopkins University Press, 1995), 1–2, 17–20, 59–56, 131.
15. Paul A. Gilje, "corporatism," in *Encyclopedia of American History: Revolution and New Nation, 1761 to 1812*, rev. ed., ed. Paul A Gilje and Gary B. Nash (vol. 3) (New York: Facts on File, 2010). See also Gordon S. Wood, *The Radicalism of the American Revolution* (New York: Alfred A. Knopf, 1992).
16. Spalding, *Premier See*, 59–65, 131. See also the chapters by Richard Duncan, "Catholics and the Church in the Antebellum Upper South," and Jon L. Wakelyn, "Catholic Elites in the Slaveholding South," in *Catholics in the Old South: Essays on Church and Culture*, 2nd ed., ed. Randall M. Miller and Jon L. Wakelyn (Macon, GA: Mercer University Press, 1999), 77–98, 211–40, respectively. Andrew Stern argues that cooperation and religious pluralism generally prevailed in Catholic-Protestant encounters throughout the Old South. See Stern, "Southern Harmony: Catholic-Protestant Relations in the Antebellum South," *Religion and American Culture* 17 (Summer 2007): 165–90.
17. On the generally harmonious relations between Catholics and their non-Catholic neighbors in the Federal District in the early republic, see William W. Warner, *At Peace with All Their Neighbors: Catholics and Catholicism in the National Capital, 1787–1860* (Washington, DC: Georgetown University Press, 1994), quotation on p. x.
18. Carroll to Antonelli, August 5, 1789.
19. James Hennesey, SJ, *American Catholics: A History of the Roman Catholic Community in the United States* (New York: Oxford University Press, 1981), 85–86; Dolan, *American Catholic Experience*, 107; Edmund J. Goebel, *A Study of Catholic Secondary Education During the Colonial Period Up to the First Plenary Council of Baltimore, 1852* (Washington, DC: Catholic University of America Press, 1936), 109. On the founding and first century of Georgetown University by the Jesuits, see R. Emmett Curran, *The Bicentennial History of Georgetown University: From Academy to University, 1789–1889*, vol. 1 (Washington,

DC: Georgetown University Press, 1993). On the founding of St. Mary's Seminary and College by the Sulpicians, see Christopher J. Kauffman, *Tradition and Transformation in Catholic Culture: The Priests of Saint Sulpice in the United States from 1791 to the Present* (New York: Macmillan, 1988).

20. "Nunnery Projected in Philadelphia, June 22, 1786," *American Catholic Historical Researches* 7 (1891): 178.
21. Currier, *Carmel in America*, 54–69; Lois Green Carr, "Ann Teresa Mathews," in *Notable American Women: A Biographical Dictionary*, 3 vols., ed. Edward T. James, Janet W. James, and Paul S. Boyer (Cambridge, MA: Belknap, 1971), 2:509–10.
22. John Carroll to Charles Plowden, May 26, 1788, JCP, 1:312.
23. Currier, *Carmel in America*, 36–39; R. Emmett Curran, *Papist Devils: Catholics in British America, 1574–1783* (Washington, DC: Catholic University of America Press, 2014); and R. Emmett Curran, ed., *Intestine Enemies: Catholics in Protestant America, 1605–1791: A Documentary History* (Washington, DC: Catholic University of America Press, 2017).
24. John Tracy Ellis, *Catholics in Colonial America* (Baltimore: Helicon, 1965), 349; Hanley, *American Revolution and Religion*, 173–74; Hennesey, *American Catholics*, 45.
25. Hennesey, *American Catholics*, 124, 144–46.
26. The information on colonial Maryland nuns living in European convents is taken from tables compiled by Thomas Spalding, CFX, in *The Jesuit Missions of St. Mary's County, Maryland*, 2nd ed., ed. Edwin W. Beitzell (n.p., 1976).
27. Currier, *Carmel in America*, 69, 80–82; Carr, "Ann Teresa Mathews," *Notable American Women*, 2:509–10.
28. Catherine O'Donnell, "John Carroll and the Origins of an American Catholic Church, 1783–1815," *William and Mary Quarterly* 68 (January 2011): 101–26; Thomas P. McCarthy, CSV, ed., *The Guide to Catholic Sisterhoods in the United States* (Washington, DC: Catholic University of America Press, 1964), 6–7; Joan M. Lexau, ed., *Convent Life: Roman Catholic Religious for Women in North America* (New York: Dial, 1964), 228.
29. Currier, *Carmel in America*, 18–19, 69–70.
30. Currier, *Carmel in America*, 82–83, 100–102.
31. John Carroll to Leonardo Antonelli, April 22, 1792, JCP, 2:32.
32. John Carroll to Mother Bernadina Mathews, March 1, 1793, JCP, 2:84–85.
33. Currier, *Carmel in America*, 82, 99–100.
34. No surname is given for Sister Saint Luc. See Gabriel J. Naughten, OFM, "The Poor Clares in Georgetown: Second Convent of Women in the United States," *Franciscan Studies* (1943): 63–72.
35. Naughten, "Poor Clares in Georgetown," 64–65.
36. Lexau, *Convent Life*, 359.
37. Naughten, "Poor Clares in Georgetown," 66.
38. Naughten, "Poor Clares in Georgetown," 67.
39. Naughten, "Poor Clares in Georgetown," 68.
40. "History of the Establishment of the Order of the Visitation in the United States—1799" (abridged), 20, MDCM. Eleanore Sullivan disputes the story of the shipboard meeting of the three women, calling it a "pretty legend" that "seems not to have been true" (*Georgetown Visitation: Since 1799* [Baltimore: n.p., 1975], 72).
41. "History of the Establishment of the Order" (abr.), 22.
42. "History of the Establishment of the Order" (abr.), 23.
43. "History of the Establishment of the Order" (abr.), 25–26.

44. "History of the Establishment of the Order" (abr.), 27–29.
45. McCarthy, *Guide to Catholic Sisterhoods*, 28–29; Lexau, *Convent Life*, 384.
46. "History of the Establishment of the Order" (abr.), 24, 29.
47. Naughten, "Poor Clares in Georgetown," 68–70.
48. Naughten, "Poor Clares in Georgetown," 71; "History of the Establishment of the Order" (abr.), 18–21, 25.
49. In 1807 Father Stephen Badin tried to found a community of women religious in Kentucky, which was then part of the Diocese of Baltimore. Had the convent house not been destroyed by fire while in the building stage, it would have preceded Mother Seton's Sisters of Charity as the first indigenous American order. Thanks to the late Father Felix Donahue of the Trappist Abbey of Gethsemani in Kentucky for calling my attention to this attempted founding. See also Benedict J. Webb, *Centenary of Catholicism in Kentucky* (Louisville: Charles A. Rogers, 1884).
50. Hennesey, *American Catholics*, 110; Spalding, *Premier See*, 114–78.
51. John Gilmary Shea, *The Hierarchy of the Catholic Church in the United States* (New York: Office of Catholic Publications, 1886), 64–65; Dolan, *American Catholic Experience*, 123–24.
52. Shea, *Hierarchy of the Catholic Church*, 65–68; Archbishop Ambrose E. Maréchal to Lorenzo Cardinal Litta, October 16, 1818, here translated from Latin by Reverend Urban J. Stang, *Catholic Historical Review* 1 (January 1916): 439–53, reprinted in John Tracy Ellis, ed., *Documents of American Catholic History* (Milwaukee: Bruce, 1956), 207–10. In his report Maréchal also estimated that only 800 Catholics lived in Baltimore town in 1792. Determining the accuracy of the population figures reported by bishops regarding their dioceses is problematic. According to the most reliable study of Catholic demographics in the nineteenth century, Maréchal believed the American Catholic population in 1820 was 244,000, an exaggeration of approximately 49,000. Maréchal's mistake, however, came as a result of his overestimation of the Catholic population in the Louisiana and Florida Territories by at least 50,000. Therefore, his total for the rest of the nation was fairly accurate and lends credence to his figures for his own diocese. See Gerald Shaughnessy, *Has the Immigrant Kept the Faith? A Study of Immigration and Catholic Growth in the United States 1790–1920* (New York: Macmillan, 1925), 72–73; and Michael De Stefano, "'We shall be a Catholic country': Counting Catholics in the Antebellum United States," *U.S. Catholic Historian* 39, no. 4 (Fall 2021): 49–75.
53. "Archbishop Maréchal's Report to Propaganda," October 16, 1818, in Ellis, *Documents of American Catholic History*, 212. An unsuccessful attempt to establish a community of French Trappistine nuns in the Archdiocese of Baltimore occurred sometime between 1811 and 1814, when the convent was moved to Manhattan, New York, but four members stayed in Maryland. Those four eventually joined the Sisters of Charity in Emmitsburg. My thanks to the late Father Felix Donahue for supplying this information.
54. "Maréchal's 1818 Report," 211.
55. "Book of the Foundations of the Monasteries of the Visitation in the United States, with a Little Account from Each, as a Souvenir of Our Tercentenary, 1610–June 6, 1910," 10, manuscript copy in MDCM.
56. Leonard Neale to Annecy motherhouse, quoted in "Book of the Foundations of the Monasteries," 11.
57. "Maréchal's 1818 Report," 211.

58. "Maréchal's 1818 Report," 211.
59. "Maréchal's 1818 Report," 212.
60. On the convent revolution, see Mannard, "'Our Dear Houses,'" 1–27
61. Anne M. Boylan, *The Origins of Women's Activism: New York and Boston, 1797–1840* (Chapel Hill: University of North Carolina Press, 2002), 18.
62. Ellin M. Kelly, ed., *Numerous Choirs: A Chronicle of Elizabeth Bayley Seton and Her Spiritual Daughters: Volume 1, The Seton Years, 1774–1821* (Evansville, IN: Mater Dei Provincialate, 1981), 44–45. The most recent biography of Elizabeth Seton is Catherine O'Donnell, *Elizabeth Seton: American Saint* (Ithaca, NY: Cornell University Press, 2018). See also Annabelle M. Melville, *Elizabeth Bayley Seton, 1774–1821* (New York: Scribner, 1951).
63. The Upper South is distinguished from the Deep South or Lower South. In the antebellum era, the Upper South included the District of Columbia and the eight slave states of Arkansas, Delaware, Kentucky, Maryland, Missouri, North Carolina, Tennessee, and Virginia.
64. On the key leadership roles held by widows in all-female voluntary societies, see Boylan, *Origins of Women's Activism*, 57–63. On the leadership roles of widows in three early convents in the United States, see Joseph G. Mannard, "Widows in Convents of the Early Republic: The Archdiocese of Baltimore, 1790–1860," *U.S. Catholic Historian* 26, no. 2 (2008): 111–32.
65. Quoted in Barbara Berg, *The Remembered Gate: Origins of American Feminism* (New York: Oxford University Press, 1978), 155.

CHAPTER 2

1. "Attempt to Change the Order," chapter in "History of the Establishment of the Order of the Visitation in the United States—1799," 179–86, SLVA.
2. William Ward Wight, *The Wights: A Record of Thomas Wight of Dedham and Medfield and of His Descendants, 1635–1890* (Milwaukee: Swain & Tate, 1890), 312. Some families added the second "t" to the name. See also J. W. S. Clements, *Origins of Clements-Spalding and Allied Families of Maryland and Kentucky* (Louisville, KY: Standard, 1928), 38–39.
3. US Census Bureau, 1800 Second Census, Prince George's County, Maryland, series 32 (microfilm, Family History Library Film roll 11), 292. This census lists Benjamin Wightt as head of a farm household of sixteen people in Prince George's County, which included his wife, Mary; three young white females, one of whom was his daughter Mary Ann; and eleven enslaved people. Susanna, his younger daughter, often referred to as "Susan" in later sources, was not born until 1801, so she must not be counted. The identity of the other two young white females is not known.
4. Executed will of John Wightt, September 13, 1806, BQFP, 017.
5. Allen C. Clark, "General John Peter Van Ness, a Mayor of the City of Washington, His Wife, Marcia, and Her Father, David Burnes," *Records of the Columbian Historical Society* 22 (1919): 193.
6. Will of John Wightt.
7. Benjamin Wightt, November 23, 1802, Bonds of Prince George's, Maryland, 1799–1807 and 1824–47, 130; State of Maryland Wills and Probate Record, 1604–1998; "History of the Establishment of the Order," 180.

8. Wightt later testified that her teachers serving as role models was one of the reasons she had been attracted to religious life. See Ann Gertrude Wightt to Propaganda Fide, April 30, 1831, #286, vol. 77, folios 179–85, PFUNDA.
9. "Sr. M. Margaret Wight" [*sic*], "Book of All Deceased Sisters," vol. 2, 2, GVM.
10. Being "clothed as a novice" refers to wearing of "the little habit" by a student who aspired to religious life but was not yet of age. Constitution 38 defines the duties of the sacristan as having "charge and keep[ing] a list of everything belonging to the Church and Chapel of the community." See *Rules of Saint Augustine and Constitutions of the Visitation After the Original Manuscripts,* trans. from the French (London: Manresa, 1930), 190–91.
11. Frances Carpenter Huntington, "The Heiress of Washington City: Marcia Burnes Van Ness, 1782–1832," *Records of the Columbia Historical Society* 69–70 (1969–70): 80–101.
12. George Parson Lathrop and Rose Hawthorne Lathrop, *A Story of Courage: Annals of the Georgetown Convent of the Visitation of the Blessed Virgin Mary, From the Manuscript Records* (Cambridge, MA: Riverside, 1894), 215–16.
13. "History of the Establishment of the Order" (abridged), 33–37, MDCM; Lathrop and Lathrop, *A Story of Courage,* 215–16. In convent records the surname of Sister Mary Clare is spelled as both "Cummins" and "Cummings."
14. "List of the Nuns of G[eorge] T[own]," 1819, Archbishop Ambrose Maréchal Papers, 22I12, AAB; "History of the Establishment of the Order" (abr.), 163. Mary Margaret Wightt's obituary is included in Georgetown Visitation Monastery to European Houses of the Order, January 9, 1822, Circular Letter (typed copy of the handwritten original), here translated by Brigid Taylor, 20–21, GVM.
15. Eleanore C. Sullivan, *Georgetown Visitation Since 1799* (Baltimore: Privately published, 1975), 64.
16. Joseph G. Mannard, "Widows in Convents of the Early Republic: The Archdiocese of Baltimore, 1790–1860," *U.S. Catholic Historian* 26 (Spring 2008): 111–32.
17. Joseph G. Mannard, "Converts in Convents: Protestant Women and the Social Appeal of Catholic Religious Life in Antebellum America," *Records of the American Catholic Historical Society of Philadelphia* 104 (Spring–Winter 1993): 79–90.
18. Constitution 1, *Rules of Saint Augustine and Constitutions,* 92.
19. Susan Nalezyty, "The History of Enslaved People at Georgetown Visitation," *U.S. Catholic Historian* 37, no. 2 (Spring 2019): 39; Joseph G. Mannard, "'We Are Determined to Be White Ladies': Race, Identity, and the Maryland Tradition in Antebellum Visitation Convents," *Maryland Historical Magazine* 109 (Summer 2014): 132–57. On institutional slavery such as existed in Georgetown Visitation, see Jennifer Oast, *Institutional Slavery: Slaveholding Churches, Colleges, and Businesses in Virginia, 1680–1860* (New York: Cambridge University Press, 2016).
20. Mother Teresa Lalor to Archbishop Ambrose Maréchal, October 27, 1818, Archbishop Ambrose Maréchal Papers, 18B22, AAB.
21. Mother Teresa Lalor to Archbishop Ambrose Maréchal, November 10, 1818, Archbishop Ambrose Maréchal Papers, 18B23, AAB.
22. In making this argument I do not mean to suggest that the residents of the Old South were monolithic and static in their thinking or that that there were no cultural alternatives to the planter class. The late historian Johanna Nicol Shields offers a convincing argument to the contrary in her case study of urban middle-class writers, describing what she calls "the rising South" of the Old Southwest. See Shields, *Freedom in a Slave Society: Stories from the Antebellum South* (New York: Cambridge University Press, 2012). My point rather is that the Maryland tradition as inherited, practiced, and extended by the

Visitation Order found itself highly compatible with key elements of the culturally dominant planter ethos of the antebellum period.

23. All statistics in this section are taken from tables found in Joseph G. Mannard, "'Wild Girls Make the Better Nuns': Class and Ethnicity in Visitation Convents of the Upper South, 1799–1860," paper delivered at Southern Historical Association 65th Annual Meeting, Fort Worth, Texas, November 3–6, 1999.
24. Thomas T. McAvoy, CSC, "The Formation of the Catholic Minority in the United States, 1820–1860," *Review of Politics* 10 (January 1948): 13–34.
25. "List of the Nuns of G[eorge] T[own]"; "Georgetown Community of the Visitation, [1828]," box 103, folder 4, MPA.
26. See Mannard, "Wild Girls Make the Better Nuns," tables C1, C2, C3.
27. See, for example, Stephanie McCurry, *Masters of Small Worlds: Yeoman Households, Gender Relations, and the Political Culture of the Antebellum South Carolina Low Country* (New York: Oxford University Press, 1997); Elizabeth Fox-Genovese, *Within the Plantation Household: Black and White Women in the Old South* (Chapel Hill: University of North Carolina Press, 1988); and the historiographical chapters by Charles C. Bolton, "Planters, Plain Folk, and Poor Whites in the Old South" and Michelle Gillespie "Women in the Old South," in *A Companion to the Civil War and Reconstruction,* ed. Lacy K. Ford (Malden, MA: Blackwell, 2005): 75–93 and 128–51.
28. Constitution 1, *Rules of Saint Augustine and Constitutions*, 88.
29. Constitution 1, *Rules of Saint Augustine and Constitutions*, 88–89.
30. Constitution 1, *Rules of Saint Augustine and Constitutions*, 90–91; Constitution 41, *Rules of Saint Augustine and Constitutions,* 199–200.
31. Constitution 1, *Rules of Saint Augustine and Constitutions*, 92.
32. Constitution 42, *Rules of Saint Augustine and Constitutions,* 201–5.
33. Both women are discussed in Mother Teresa Lalor to Archbishop Ambrose Maréchal, January 12, 1818, 18A11, AAB.
34. "Sr. M. Margaret Wight," 2:2.
35. Constitution 33, *Rules of Saint Augustine and Constitutions,* 170–71.
36. Monastery of the Visitation of Georgetown (Mother Juliana Matthews) to the European Houses of the Order (Annecy), September 8, 1828, Circular Letters 1–5, here translated by Brigid Taylor, GVM.
37. The "inspired teacher" quote is found in "Whyte (Wightt), Mary (Anna) Gertrude," Membership (permanent and temporary), box 2, folder 65, GVM. The "Sister Getty" reference is found in the memoirs of Britannia Peter Kennon, one of her former students, see Britannia Kennon, May 11, 1900, *A Georgetown Life: The Reminiscences of Britannia Wellington Peter Kennon of Tudor Place,* ed. Grant S. Quertermous (Washington, DC: Georgetown University Press, 2020), 112.
38. Sister Jane Scholastica Neale to Eliza Neale, addendum by Sister Ann Gertrude Wightt, October 6, 1822, box 103, folder 4, MPA.
39. Jane Neale to Eliza Neale, October 6, 1822.
40. Sister Jane Scholastica Neale to Miss Eliza Neale, October 5, 1823, box 103, folder 4, MPA.
41. Sullivan, *Georgetown Visitation,* 68–73; Suzanne Krebsbach, "From the Assassin Limolean to Father Clorivière: Political and Religious Conflict in Early Republican Charleston," *South Carolina Historical Magazine* 120, no. 2 (2019): 102–30.
42. Sullivan, *Georgetown Visitation,* 64–65
43. Sullivan, *Georgetown Visitation,* 73.

44. Sullivan, *Georgetown Visitation*, 73–75.
45. Nalezyty, "The History of Enslaved People," 33–37.
46. Constitution 31, *Rules of Saint Augustine and Constitutions*, 164.
47. Constitution 30, *Rules of Saint Augustine and Constitutions*, 161.
48. Constitution 47, *Rules of Saint Augustine and Constitutions*, 223–24.
49. Counsellors of the Visitation to Archbishop Maréchal, November 5, 1823, Archbishop Ambrose Maréchal Papers, 22U3, AAB.

CHAPTER 3

1. Mother Harriet Agnes Brent to Archbishop Ambrose Maréchal, October 30, 1823, Archbishop Ambrose Maréchal Papers, 13N7, AAB.
2. Pagliarini thoroughly documents the anxieties that Visitation nuns felt throughout the nineteenth century regarding whether they were following the Visitation Rule and practicing an authentic religious life based on the European model. See Pagliarini, "'Glorify and Bear God in Your Body': Rituals of Discipline and Resistance in the Lives of Nineteenth-Century Georgetown Visitation Nuns" (PhD diss., University of California, Santa Barbara, 2003), 25.
3. Pagliarini, "'Glorify and Bear God in Your Body,'" 161–62. Times are approximate and based on the 1834 constitutions and spiritual directory as well as the written records of the sisters. The sisters were given permission to have three meals a day, thus an additional meal was most likely scheduled before dinner. On Thursday and Sunday evenings the sisters attended Mass and confessions were heard, most likely sometime after Vespers.
4. Pagliarini, "'Glorify and Bear God in Your Body,'" 25–102.
5. Pagliarini, "'Glorify and Bear God in Your Body,'" 37–39; Mother Harriet Agnes Brent to Archbishop Ambrose Maréchal, December 7, 1822, Archbishop Ambrose Maréchal Papers, 13N3, AAB.
6. Mary Ewens, OP, *The Role of the Nun in the Nineteenth Century: Variations on an International Theme* (New York: Arno), 107–8.
7. Barbara Misner, SCSC, *"Highly Respectable and Accomplished Ladies": Catholic Women Religious in America, 1790–1850* (New York: Garland, 1988), 53–55; Pagliarini, "'Glorify and Bear God in Your Body,'" 39–40.
8. "History of the Establishment of the Order of the Visitation in the United States—1799" (abridged), 79–83, MDCM; George Parsons Lathrop and Rose Hawthorne Lathrop, *A Story of Courage: Annals of the Georgetown Convent of the Visitation of the Blessed Virgin Mary, From the Manuscript Records* (Cambridge, MA: Riverside, 1894); Eleanore C. Sullivan, *Georgetown Visitation Since 1799* (Baltimore: Privately published, 1975).
9. Thompson borrows the concept of "mythistory" from historian William R. McNeill's "Mythistory, or Truth, Myth, History, and Historians," *American Historical Review* 91, no. 1 (February 1986): 1–10. See Margaret Susan Thompson, "Difficult Women and Dangerous Memories: Silenced, Suppressed, and Misrepresented Founders in the History of American Religious Life," *American Catholic Studies* 134, no. 4 (Winter 2023): 26–27. The Misner quote appears in Barbara Misner, "Historiography of Women Religious Communities in the 19th Century," paper presented at the Conference about Perspectives on American Catholicism, University of Notre Dame, 1982, 2.

10. Mother Teresa Lalor to Archbishop Ambrose Maréchal, June 10, 1818, Archbishop Ambrose Maréchal Papers, 18B18, AAB.
11. "Diary of Archbishop Maréchal, 1818–1825," *Records of the American Catholic Historical Society of Philadelphia* 11, no. 4 (December 1900): 418.
12. Mother Teresa Lalor to Archbishop Ambrose Maréchal, July 19, 1818, Archbishop Ambrose Maréchal Papers, 18B19, AAB.
13. Mother Teresa Lalor to Archbishop Ambrose Maréchal, October 20, 1818, December 24, 1818, and February 15, 1819, all in Archbishop Ambrose Maréchal Papers, 18B21, 18B24, and 18B25, respectively, AAB.
14. Sister M. Frances McDermott to Archbishop Ambrose Maréchal, June 6, 1819, Archbishop Ambrose Maréchal Papers, 19D3, AAB.
15. "History of the Establishment of the Order" (abr.), 79–83; Lathrop and Lathrop, *A Story of Courage*, 377.
16. "Rigden, M. Catherine (Ann)," Membership (permanent and temporary), box 1.1, folder 52, GVM; "History of the Establishment of the Order" (abr.), 69–79.
17. "History of the Establishment of the Order" (abr.), 79.
18. Sister Eleanor de Sales Miles to Archbishop Ambrose Maréchal, March 16, 1820, Archbishop Ambrose Maréchal Papers, 19J6, AAB.
19. Sister Mary Magdalen Neale to Archbishop Ambrose Maréchal, April 19, 1820, Archbishop Ambrose Maréchal Papers, 18M1, AAB.
20. Sister Eleanor de Sales Miles to Archbishop Ambrose Maréchal, May 15, 1820, Archbishop Ambrose Maréchal Papers, 19J7, AAB.
21. Miles to Maréchal, May 15, 1820.
22. See "Mary de Sales Neale (Mary Fenwick)," Membership (permanent and temporary), box 1.1, folder 43, GVM.
23. Mother Mary de Sales Neale to Archbishop Ambrose Maréchal, January 5, 1821, Archbishop Ambrose Maréchal Papers, 19Q1, AAB.
24. "History of the Establishment of the Order" (abr.), 79.
25. Lathrop and Lathrop, A *Story of Courage*, 214–17.
26. Circular letter of Georgetown Convent to Our Monasteries of the Visitation, January 9, 1822, quoted in "History of the Establishment of the Order" (abr.), 67–68.
27. "History of the Establishment of the Order" (abr.), 68–69.
28. Mother Agnes Brent to Archbishop Ambrose Maréchal, December 7, 1822, Archbishop Ambrose Maréchal Papers, 13N3, AAB.
29. Mother Agnes Brent to Archbishop Ambrose Maréchal, January 6, 1823, Archbishop Ambrose Maréchal Papers, 13N4, AAB.
30. Mother Agnes Brent to Archbishop Ambrose Maréchal, March 15 and April 23, 1823, both in Archbishop Ambrose Maréchal Papers, 13N5 and 13N6, respectively, AAB.
31. Mother Agnes Brent to Archbishop Ambrose Maréchal, October 30, 1823, Archbishop Ambrose Maréchal Papers, 13N7, AAB.
32. Georgetown Counsellors to Archbishop Ambrose Maréchal, November 5, 1823, Archbishop Ambrose Maréchal Papers, 22U3, AAB.
33. Archbishop Ambrose Maréchal to Archbishop Joseph-Octave Plessis, November 6, 1823, "Correspondence between the Sees of Quebec and Baltimore," *Records of the American Catholic Historical Society of Philadelphia* 18 (December 1907): 451–52.
34. Archbishop Joseph-Octave Plessis to Archbishop Ambrose Maréchal, November 18, 1823, in "Correspondence between the Sees," 453.

35. Mother Agnes Brent to Archbishop Ambrose Maréchal, November 23, 1823, Archbishop Ambrose Maréchal Papers, 13N8, AAB.
36. Archbishop Joseph-Octave Plessis to Archbishop Ambrose Maréchal, December 16, 1823, "Correspondence between the Sees," 454.
37. Archbishop Ambrose Maréchal to Archbishop Joseph-Octave Plessis, January 8, 1824, "Correspondence between the Sees," 448.
38. Sister St. Francis de Sales Bowling to Archbishop Ambrose Maréchal, March 3, 1824, Archbishop Ambrose Maréchal Papers, 13M5, AAB.
39. Archbishop Ambrose Maréchal to Archbishop Joseph-Octave Plessis, May 16, 1824, "Correspondence between the Sees," 455–56.
40. Archbishop Ambrose Maréchal to Archbishop Joseph-Octave Plessis, November 6, 1824, "Correspondence between the Sees," 456–57.
41. Joseph G. Mannard, "'Wilhelmina Jones, Come Out': Public Reaction to the Reception of Sister M. Stanislaus Jones into Georgetown Visitation Monastery, 1825–26," *U.S. Catholic Historian* 39, no. 4 (Fall 2021): 32–36.
42. Sisters of the Visitation to Archbishop Ambrose Maréchal, September 1, 1825, Archbishop Ambrose Maréchal Papers, 13N9, AAB.
43. Mother Teresa Lalor and Counsellors to Archbishop Ambrose Maréchal, September 15, 1825, Archbishop Ambrose Maréchal Papers, 22U4, AAB; Constitution 47, *Rules and Constitutions*, 215–22, 244–45. Sister Gertrude either failed to sign this letter or she was no longer a counsellor.
44. Lalor and Counsellors to Maréchal, September 15, 1825.
45. Reverend William Matthews to Reverend Francis Dzierozynski, October 8, 1825, box 4, folder 19, MPA (author's translation).
46. Reverend Charles Neale, SJ, to Reverend Francis Dzierozynski, October 4, 1825, box 4, folder 19, MPA.
47. Sister Eleanor de Sales Miles to Archbishop Ambrose Maréchal, November 14, 1825, and November 21, 1825, both in Archbishop Ambrose Maréchal Papers, 19J7a and 19J8, respectively, AAB. Apparently restless, Miles asked permission to leave the Georgetown convent and enter an Ursuline convent as a lay sister. She explained that she never felt called to be a Visitation nun and had wanted to be a Carmelite, but her health did not permit it. Her request must have been denied, for in 1832 Miles, by then called Sister Mary Ignatia, was identified as the assistant at the Mobile convent, the second Visitation location. The following year Miles accompanied Mother Madeleine to her monastery in Fribourg, France. After stints in monasteries in Paris and Reims, Miles returned to the United States in 1845. She left religious life and thereafter lived in Baltimore. See "A Sketch of the Life of Sister Madeleine-Augustine d'Arregger," typescript, RG 3, series 6, 15, 19, GVM.
48. Mother Juliana Matthews to Archbishop Ambrose Maréchal, October 29, 1825, Archbishop Ambrose Maréchal Papers, 19A3, AAB.
49. Mother Juliana Matthews to Archbishop Ambrose Maréchal, May 12, 1826, Archbishop Ambrose Maréchal Papers, 19A4, AAB.
50. Mother Juliana Matthews to Archbishop Ambrose Maréchal, September 20, 1826, Archbishop Ambrose Maréchal Papers, 19A5, AAB.
51. "Prospectus of the Ladies' Academy of the Visitation, in Georgetown D.C," *National Gazette* (Philadelphia), September 4, 1827, 1. To reassure parents, the prospectus mentions that the directress would read all the correspondence of their daughters.
52. "The Iturbide Family," in "History of the Establishment of the Order" (abr.), 139–40.

53. "History of the Establishment of the Order" (abr.), 141, 144. The birth order of the four Iturbide daughters was Sabina (1809), Juana de Dios (1811), Josefa (1814), and Maria de Jesus (1818).

CHAPTER 4

1. Monastery of the Visitation of Georgetown (Mother Juliana Matthews) to the European Houses of the Order (Annecy), September 8, 1828, Circular Letters 1–5, here translated by Brigid Taylor, GVM.
2. Circular Letters, September 8, 1828, 4.
3. On the tendency of education historians to overlook Catholic female education efforts in the antebellum era, see Carol Mattingly, *Secret Habits: Catholic Literacy Education in the Early Nineteenth Century* (Carbondale: Southern Illinois University Press, 2016).
4. Assistant Superior and Counsellors to Archbishop Ambrose Maréchal, November 5, 1823, Archbishop Ambrose Maréchal Papers, 18B26, AAB; Eleanore C. Sullivan, *Georgetown Visitation Since 1799* (Baltimore: Privately printed, 1975), 73.
5. "History of the Establishment of the Order of the Visitation in the United States—1799" (abridged), 163–64, MDCM; Sullivan, *Georgetown Visitation*, 74–75.
6. Excerpts of the 1827 prospectus are found in articles titled "Female Education," *Baltimore Gazette and Daily Advertiser*, September 1, 1827, 2, and "Prospectus of the Ladies' Academy of the Visitation, in Georgetown D.C," *National Gazette* (Philadelphia), September 4, 1827, 1; and Sullivan, *Georgetown Visitation*, 74. The Odeum, sometimes spelled Odeon, was initially planned by Father Clorivière as a music hall. Father Wheeler also used it to house apparatus used by instructors to perform scientific experiments and demonstrate scientific theories. The Geocyclic of Delamarche, for example, was a machine that illustrated the rotation of the earth. It was produced by the Maison Delamarche, a map publisher founded by Charles Francois Delamarche in the eighteenth century and continued by his son, Felix, into the nineteenth century.
7. Mary Kelley, *Learning to Stand and Speak: Women, Education, and Public Life in America's Republic* (Chapel Hill: University of North Carolina Press, 2006).
8. "Prospectus of the Ladies' Academy," *National Gazette* (Philadelphia), September 4, 1827, 1.
9. *The Georgetown Directory for the Year 1830* (Georgetown, DC: Benjamin Homans, 1830), 22.
10. "Prospectus of the Ladies' Academy," 1. Catharine Beecher, the founder of Hartford Female Seminary in 1823, came to be identified as the chief advocate of the new field of "domestic economy." The 1827 prospectus preceded by more than a decade Beecher's most famous work on the subject, *Treatise on Domestic Economy for the Use of Young Ladies at Home and at School* (1843). See Kathryn Kish Sklar, *Catharine Beecher: A Study in American Domesticity* (New Haven, CT: Yale University Press, 1973), 151–67.
11. Rebecca Rogers, *From the Salon to the Schoolroom: Educating Bourgeois Girls in Nineteenth-Century France* (University Park, PA: Pennsylvania State University Press, 2005), 245. Curiously, French is not among the languages listed in the 1827 prospectus. But this omission is clearly erroneous: Father Clorivière had given French lessons to several nuns, including Sister Gertrude, before his death in 1826. The nuns also wrote in French all letters addressed to the motherhouse in Annecy.
12. "Prospectus of the Ladies' Academy," 1; Sullivan, *Georgetown Visitation*, 73–75.

13. Sullivan, *Georgetown Visitation*, 102.
14. "Prospectus of the Ladies' Academy," 1.
15. "An Act to incorporate the Sisters of Saint Joseph and the Sisters of the Visitation of Georgetown in the District of Columbia," in Sullivan, *Georgetown Visitation*, 166–67.
16. Anne M. Boylan, *The Origins of Women's Activism: New York and Boston, 1797–1840* (Chapel Hill: University of North Carolina Press, 2002), 21, 43.
17. Lori Ginzberg, *Women in Antebellum Reform* (Wheeling, IL: Harlan Davidson, 2000), 26.
18. "History of the Establishment of the Order of the Visitation in the United States—1799," 180, SLVA.
19. Diary entry for July 30, 1828, in *Memoirs of John Quincy Adams: Comprising Portions of His Diary from 1795 to 1848*, 12 vols., ed. Charles Francis Adams (Philadelphia: J. B. Lippincott, 1876), 8:71.
20. "Scene at Washington," *Richmond Enquirer*, June 23, 1829, 2, describes "a beautiful pageantry," as the girls "with their matrons" marched to the White House of Andrew Jackson "and there made him a return of respect" for a visit the president had made to their school.
21. "Letter to the Editor," *Baltimore Gazette and Daily Advertiser*, August 10, 1830, 3.
22. Sullivan, *Georgetown Visitation*, 77–80, 100–101.
23. Allen C. Clark, "General John Peter Van Ness, a Mayor of the City of Washington, His Wife, Marcia, and Her Father, David Burnes," *Records of the Columbia Historical Society* 22 (1919): 182–83.
24. Lingon Street was renamed 36th Street in Georgetown in 1895. See *A Georgetown Life: The Reminiscences of Britannia Wellington Peter Kennon of Tudor Place*, edited by Grant S. Quertermous (Washington, DC: Georgetown University Press, 2020), 193.
25. General William Joseph Hickey to Sister Gertrude Wightt, March 26, 1830, GVM; "In the Senate [March 2]," *Pensacola (FL) Gazette*, March 27, 1830, 3. Senator Kane is the "Mr. Kane" who is "much pleased with his good daughter," whom Father Wheeler referenced in a letter to Georgetown Convent. See Father Michael Wheeler to Mother Juliana Matthews et al., Rome, January 30, 1829, typescript, Rev. Michael Wheeler, PSS, Papers, box 1, AASUS. See also the mention of Kane's daughter in the annual report of the Alumnae Association of the Georgetown Academy of the Visitation (Washington, DC, 1913), 21, GVM.
26. Sullivan, *Georgetown Visitation*, 98–99.
27. Boylan, *Origins of Women's Activism*, 136.
28. *National Gazette* (Philadelphia), November 6, 1830, 2.
29. "Commencement Young Ladies Academy, Georgetown," *Baltimore Republican*, reprinted in the *Baltimore Gazette and Daily Advertiser*, August 7, 1829, 2. See a similar *Baltimore American* story that was reprinted in *Cape Fear Recorder* (Wilmington, NC), July 1, 1829, 2.
30. "Nunnery in the United States," *Richmond Family Visitor*, March 13, 1829, reprinted in *Hillsborough (NC) Recorder*, June 17, 1829, 2.
31. Sullivan, *Georgetown Visitation*, 76.
32. "Scene at Washington," *Richmond (VA) Enquirer*, June 23, 1829, 2.
33. *Georgetown Directory 1830*, 22–23.
34. Patricia Byrne, CSJ, "Sisters of St. Joseph: The Americanization of a French Tradition," *U.S. Catholic Historian* 5, no. 3–4 (Summer–Fall 1986): 263.
35. "Letter to the Editor," *Baltimore Gazette*, August 10, 1830, 3.
36. Sullivan, *Georgetown Visitation*, 76–80.
37. Robert Emmett Curran, *A History of Georgetown University, Vol. 1, From Academy to University, 1789–1889* (Washington, DC: Georgetown University Press, 2010), 219–22.

38. George Parson Lathrop and Rose Hawthorne Lathrop, *A Story of Courage: Annals of the Georgetown Convent of the Visitation of the Blessed Virgin Mary, From the Manuscript Records* (Cambridge, MA: Riverside, 1894), 315–16.
39. Mother Juliana Matthews to Archbishop James Whitfield, September 22, 1828, Archbishop James Whitfield Papers, 23V1, AAB. As the assistant superior Sister Gertrude also signed this letter, as did the four sister counsellors. The letter notes that Father Wheeler "will visit many of our monasteries and obtain the knowledge of many useful things which appertain to our Institute" but does not say that Wheeler plans to bring European Visitandines with him when he returns.
40. Nuns of Georgetown Visitation to Father Eccleston, October 1, 1827, Archbishop Samual Eccleston Papers, 27K2, AAB.
41. The Georgetown annals do not give a precise date for when Sister Gertrude submitted the proposal. But it must have been sometime in late October or early November 1828.
42. "History of the Establishment of the Order," 179–86. The fullest published account of Wightt's time in the Georgetown Visitation Convent, although strongly biased against her, is chapter 16, "Attempt to Change the Order: Secession of Sister Gertrude," in Lathrop and Lathrop, *A Story of Courage,* 309–22.
43. "History of the Establishment of the Order" (abr.), 164–65.
44. Lathrop and Lathrop, *A Story of Courage,* 315.
45. Mother Juliana Matthews to Archbishop James Whitfield, January 23, 1829, Archbishop James Whitfield Papers, 23M13, AAB.
46. Reverend Michael Wheeler to Mother Juliana Matthews, Rome, February 18, 1829, typescript, Rev. Michael Wheeler, PSS Papers, box 1, AASUS. Sister Gertrude suffered a similar breakdown of mental and physical health following her flight from the convent two years later.
47. Quoted in "Book of Foundations of the Monasteries of the Visitation in the United States," 15. This unpublished work was compiled in 1910 and 1911 in celebration of the tercentenary of the Visitation Order, 1610–1910, MDCM.
48. Father Wheeler to Archbishop Whitfield, Annecy, May 30, 1829, Archbishop James Whitfield Papers, 23T8, AAB.
49. Reverend Michael Wheeler to Mother Juliana Matthews, New York, August 19, 1829, Reverend Michael Wheeler, Papers, box 1, AASUS.
50. "A Sketch of the Life and Virtues of Sister Madeleine Augustine d'Arregger," typescript, RG 3, series 6, 8, GVM.
51. Quoted in "History of the Establishment of the Order" (abr.), 137.
52. "Continuation of the Foundation of Our Monastery of Baltimore (1845–1861)," 60–63, MDCM. Paulina Millard served four terms as Baltimore's superior (twice between 1851 and 1857 and twice between 1863 and 1869). Tertiaries are "lay persons living in the world who are striving after Christian perfection as their station in life allow, according to the spirit of a religious order to which they are affiliated." See John A. Hardon, SJ, *Pocket Catholic Dictionary* (Garden City, NY: Image, 1985), 430.
53. Fribourg Monastery Circular Letter, March 1, 1870, excerpted in "History of the Establishment of the Order" (abr.), 137.
54. "Sketch of the Life and Virtues of Sister Madeleine-Augustine d'Arregger," 1. In the Lathrops' chronology the date of her election is given as Ascension Day, 1830 (May 12). However, in the list of the convent's superiors on the next page, her election date is given as September 11, 1830. See Lathrop and Lathrop, *A Story of Courage,* 376–77.

55. Sister Ann Agatha Combs to Father Samuel Eccleston, President of St. Mary's College, April 8, 1831, Archbishop Samuel Eccleston Papers, 27AB2, AAB. About two weeks after Sister Gertrude's flight, Sister Agatha alleged to Father Eccleston that she (Combs) had been punished by Father Wheeler for having complained to Archbishop Whitfield about Wheeler's favoring Sister Agatha Langlois over Sister Madeleine in the election for superior the previous summer.
56. Louis P. Masur, *1831: Year of Eclipse* (New York: Hill and Wang, 2001), 3–8.
57. Archbishop James Whitfield to Reverend Stephen Dubuisson, January 26, 1831, box 103, folder 6, MPA. In 1823 Mattingly had undergone a much-publicized miraculous cure following an extended bout of breast cancer. Her story brought positive attention to the Catholic Church locally, while Sister Gertrude's actions later brought negative. Mattingly left Georgetown Convent without ever taking vows, but she remained close to the nuns there. On reactions to her "miraculous cures," see Nancy Lusignan Schultz, *Mrs. Mattingly's Miracle: The Prince, the Widow, and the Cure That Shocked Washington City* (New Haven, CT: Yale University Press, 2011), 133–42; and Robert Emmett Curran, "'The Finger of God Is Here': The Advent of the Miraculous in the Nineteenth-Century American Catholic Community," in *Shaping American Catholicism: Maryland and New York, 1805–1915*, ed. Robert Emmett Curran (Washington, DC: Catholic University of America Press, 2012), 69–91.
58. James Myers, *Narrative of Two Wonderful Cures Wrought in the Monastery of the Visitation at Georgetown, in the District of Columbia in the Month of January, 1831* (Baltimore: William A. Francis, 1831).
59. Fribourg Monastery Circular Letter, March 1, 1870. See also "Sketch of the Life and Virtues of Sister Madeleine d'Arregger," 8.
60. Diary entries of Very Reverend Louis R. Deluol, March 22 and 23, 1831, LRDP.
61. Matthews to Whitfield, January 23, 1829; Sullivan, *Georgetown Visitation*, 74. The "relative worth" of $1,618.5025 "spent on a purchase" in 1828 would be $55,312.46 in 2024, accessed June 24, 2024, https://www.measuringworth.com/dollarvaluetoday/?amount=1618.5025&from=1828.
62. Curran, *History of Georgetown University*, 1:150–56.
63. Matthews to Whitfield, January 23, 1829.
64. As Wightt's academic expertise was in literature and Barber was a gifted instructor of natural science, chemistry, and physics, the observatory may have been the latter's idea. Similarly, Wheeler's field being mathematics and physics, he may have been the progenitor. Whatever the case, Wightt's support for its construction is a measure of her commitment to improving female education generally. See Sullivan, *Georgetown Visitation*, 64. On the importance of science instruction in girl's schools of the Early Republic, see Kim Tolley, "Science for Ladies, Classics for Gentlemen: A Comparative Analysis of Scientific Subjects in the Curricula of Boys' and Girls' Secondary Schools in the United States, 1794–1850," *History of Education Quarterly* 36, no. 2 (Summer 1996): 129–53.
65. Reverend Michael Wheeler to Mother Juliana Matthews et al., January 30, 1829.
66. Wheeler to Mother Juliana et al., January 30, 1829.
67. For more on Georgetown Convent's lean times in the early 1820s, see chapter 3.
68. "Female Education," September 1, 1827, and "Prospectus of the Ladies' Academy," September 4, 1827, 1.
69. "History of the Establishment of the Order" (abr.), 163–65; Lathrop and Lathrop, *A Story of Courage*, 309–22.

70. Marie Pagliarini, "'Glorify and Bear God in Your Body': Rituals of Discipline and Resistance in the Lives of Nineteenth-Century Georgetown Visitation Nuns" (PhD diss., University of California, Santa Barbara, 2003), especially chapter 1.
71. "Semi-monastic order" is defined as "an order . . . with a monastic rule that engages in some limited ministry—usually within the confines of the convent" in George Stewart Jr., *Marvels of Charity: History of American Sisters and Nuns* (Huntington, IN: Our Sunday Visitor, 1994), 577. The "limited ministry" of the Visitation Order in the United States was female education in the academy and benevolent school on convent grounds.
72. Lathrop and Lathrop, *A Story of Courage*, 313.
73. "History of the Establishment of the Order" (abr.), 164.
74. Lathrop and Lathrop, *A Story of Courage*, 312, 316.

CHAPTER 5

1. Journal entry, March 29, 1831, Reverend Stephen Dubuisson, SJ, Journal, box 176, folder 2, MPA.
2. Sister Ann Gertrude Wightt to Archbishop James Whitfield, March 22, 1831, Archbishop James Whitfield Papers, 23A2, AAB. Except where noted, in this chapter all quotations attributed to Wightt are taken from this letter.
3. I have retained original spellings for certain words like "tranquillity" and "parlours."
4. Marie Anne Pagliarini, "'Glorify and Bear God in Your Body': Rituals of Discipline and Resistance in the Lives of Nineteenth-Century Georgetown Visitation Nuns" (PhD diss., University of California, Santa Barbara, 2003), 96, n163. Pagliarini cites the Wightt to Whitfield letter, which I had shared with her when she was researching her dissertation.
5. Diary entry, March 22, 1831, Louis R. Deluol Diary, LRDP; Diary entry, March 22, 1831, Jean-Marie Tessier Diary, JMTP. Father Jean-Marie Tessier (1758–1840) was born in France and belonged to the group of priests that founded the Society of Saint Sulpice in the United States. Tessier served as the community's superior (1800–1829) and as vicar general to John Carroll, Leonard Neale, and Ambrose Maréchal, as well as James Whitfield during Whitfield's first year in office. Father Louis Regis Deluol (1787–1858) was born in France and came to America in 1817, living in Baltimore until 1849, when he returned to France. In addition to serving as Whitfield's vicar general and the superior of the Sulpicians (1829–49), Deluol was superior of St. Mary's Seminary in Baltimore (1829–49) and twice was superior general of the Sisters of Charity of Saint Joseph in Emmitsburg, Maryland (1826–29 and 1841–49). See the website of the Sulpicians, accessed December 7, 2021, http://sulpicians.org/project/deluol-father-louis-regis/.
6. The known sources fail to identify the catalyst for Archbishop Whitfield calling the March 9 meeting of his clerical advisors. But it may have been a letter written on February 8 that Mother Madeleine secretly entrusted to Father Dubuisson for personal delivery to the prelate. Mother Madeleine's writing style is frustratingly vague, and she herself admits that it is a "very enigmatic letter." But she does offer some tantalizing clues when speaking of "a problem of this magnitude which can have serious consequences" and "that I want what is for the particular good of the house." Mother Madeleine Augustine d'Arregger to Archbishop James Whitfield, February 8, 1831, here translated from the French by Dr. Vivien Linkhauer with assistance from Dr. Michelle Chossat, Archbishop James Whitfield Papers, 23L7, AAB.

7. Diary entry, March 9, 1831, Louis R. Deluol Diary, LRDP.
8. Diary entry, March 18, 1831, Louis R. Deluol Diary, LRDP.
9. Deluol diary entry, March 22, 1831; Tessier diary entry, March 22, 1831.
10. Deluol diary entry, March 22, 1831.
11. Diary entry, March 23, 1831, Louis R. Deluol Diary, LRDP.
12. "Extract of a Letter from Washington D.C.," included in "Papal Education," *Episcopal Recorder* 9, no. 1 (April 2, 1831): 3.
13. On the subject of escaped nuns in the pre–Civil War United States, see Cassandra L. Yacovazzi, *Escaped Nuns: True Womanhood and the Campaign Against Convents in Antebellum America* (New York: Oxford University Press, 2018); Jenny Franchot, *Roads to Rome: The Antebellum Protestant Encounter with Catholicism* (Berkeley: University of California Press, 1994); and Joseph G. Mannard, "'What Has Become of Olevia Neal?': The Escaped Nun Phenomenon in Antebellum America," *Maryland Historical Magazine* 115, no. 4 (Winter 2010): 348–67.
14. Andrew B. Cross, *Priests' Prisons for Women: . . . in Twelve Letters to T. Parkin Scott* (Baltimore: Sherwood, 1854).
15. Ray Allen Billington, *The Protestant Crusade, 1800–1860: A Study in the Origins of Nativism* (Chicago: Quadrangle, 1964 [1938]).
16. Maria Monk claimed to have been a nun in a convent in Montreal, Canada. However, her notoriety was most prominent in New York City, where Harper & Brothers published her book. See Billington, *Protestant Crusade,* 101–2.
17. Martha Hartnet (or Hartwell) is also a contender for the dubious honor of being the first escaped nun in American history. A resident of Philadelphia, Hartnet had entered the motherhouse of the Sisters of Charity in Emmitsburg, Maryland, as a candidate for membership on April 3, 1815. After living there for only a few weeks, and before taking any vows, Hartnet secretly left the convent in the dead of night by means of the cellar door. Her case, however, appears to have remained an internal affair known only among members of the Sisters of Charity. Wightt differed from Hartnet in that she had taken vows and also because her flight occurred in the middle of the day and created a public scandal for the Catholic Church. On the Hartnet story, see Regina Bechtle, SC, and Judith Metz, SC, eds., *Elizabeth Bayley Seton Collected Writings*, vol. 3b (New York: New City, 2006), 121–24.
18. Allen C. Clark, then president of the Columbia Historical Society, contended, "An unfounded report that the Catholics intended to recover her [Sister Gertrude] by force nearly caused a mob." I have been unable to uncover any contemporary evidence to corroborate this claim. See Clark, "General John Peter Van Ness, a Mayor of the City of Washington, His Wife, Marcia, and Her Father David Burnes," *Records of the Columbia Historical Society* 22 (1919): 182.
19. *Episcopal Recorder*, April 2, 1831.
20. The sample was drawn from a keyword search in these databases: America's Historical Newspapers, the Newspapers Room, the Library of Congress, and newspapers.com. Reprints of the original article appeared in newspapers published in the District of Columbia and fourteen of the then-twenty-four states in the Union. While forty-three periodicals were from northern states, only nine were from the South. Of the northern newspapers, twenty-nine were from New England and eight from New York State. This disproportionate representation draws on the greater level of literacy in New England, the stronger hold of the Puritan legacy of religious adherence, and the existence of actual

towns with publications. The Northeast also exhibited a higher level of intolerance for Catholicism. In contrast, the South was lower on three of those counts: literacy rates, level of urbanization, and degree and intensity of organized anti-Catholicism. Regarding anti-Catholic sentiment, see Andrew Stern, "Southern Harmony: Catholic-Protestant Relations in the Antebellum South," *Religion & American Culture* 17, no. 2 (Summer 2007): 165–90.

21. *Columbian Centinel* (Boston), April 6, 1831, 1.
22. *Newburyport (MA) Herald,* April 7, 1831, 1.
23. *Philadelphia Gazette,* April 9, 1831, reprinted in *Spirit of the Times* (Bridgeport, CT), April 13, 1831, 3.
24. *I Won't Be a Nun,* notated sheet music, retrieved April 7, 2018, Library of Congress, https://www.loc.gov/item/2015562063/.
25. *Rhode Island American* (Providence), April 12 and 29, 1831, 4, 4; *Microcosm and Weekly American* (Providence, RI), April 30, 1831, 1. David Brion Davis was the first scholar to identify the common themes in the literature of the otherwise diverse anti-Mason, anti-Catholic, and anti-Mormon movements. See his classic article, "Some Themes of Counter-Subversion: Anti-Masonic, Anti-Catholic, and Anti-Mormon Literature," *Mississippi Valley Historical Review* 47 (September 1960): 205–24.
26. "Catholic Schemes Exposed!!" *Boston Recorder,* June 8, 1831, 89.
27. Monk's book was published under various similar titles. The full title is *Awful Disclosures of Maria Monk, as Exhibited in a Narrative of Her Sufferings During a Residence of Five Years as a Novice, and Two Years as a Black Nun, in the Hotel Dieu Nunnery at Montreal* (1836). Reverend George Bourne, founding editor of *The Protestant,* was rumored to be one of the clergyman ghostwriters of Maria Monk's *Awful Disclosures.* See Billington, *Protestant Crusade,* 108, 116n139.
28. The other Catholic newspapers publishing in 1831 were Bishop John England's *U.S. Catholic Miscellany* in Charleston, South Carolina, (est. 1822), and the *Jesuit and Catholic Sentinel* in Boston (est. 1829). See Paul J. Foik, "Pioneer Efforts in Catholic Journalism in the United States (1809–40)," *Catholic Historical Review* 1, no. 3 (1915): 265–66.
29. *Catholic Press* (Hartford, CT), June 11, 1831, 2.
30. *Catholic Press,* June 11, 1831, reprinted in the *Georgian* (Savannah), June 28, 1831, 1.
31. Results are based on a keyword search of the holdings of America's Historical Newspapers Collection, Library of Congress, Washington, DC, and newspapers.com.
32. On the continuation of the Maryland tradition in the Archdiocese of Baltimore, see Thomas W. Spalding, *The Premier See: A History of the Archdiocese of Baltimore, 1789–1989* (Baltimore: Johns Hopkins University Press, 1995 [1989]), 1–2, 17–20, 59–65.
33. *The Protestant,* March 27, 1830, 104, quoted in Mary St. Patrick McConville, *Political Nativism in the State of Maryland* (Washington, DC: Catholic University of America Press, 1928), 96.
34. On *The Metropolitan,* see Ralph Frasca, "The Ministry of the Press: Baltimore's Provincial Council and the First American Catholic Magazine," *Maryland Historical Magazine* 111, no. 2 (Fall–Winter 2016): 174–78.
35. Archbishop James Whitfield to Cardinal Prefect of Propaganda Fide, August 27, 1830, Archbishop James Whitfield Papers, 23A-Q1, AAB.
36. Mannard, 'What Has Become of Olevia Neal,' 354–63; "The Protestant Association," *Baltimore Literary and Religious Magazine* 1, no. 5 (May 1835): 153–55. On the worsening sectarian relations within the Irish community in Baltimore during the 1830s, see Tracy

Matthew Melton, "'We Are United as a Band of Brothers': The Hibernian Society and Sectarian Relations in Baltimore, 1803–1854," *Maryland Historical Magazine* 111, no. 1 (Spring–Summer 2016): 41–85.

CHAPTER 6

1. Archbishop James Whitfield to Propaganda Fide, June 6, 1831, here translated by Alun Walpole, Letterbook for 1828–32, 19–23, Archbishop James Whitfield Papers, AAB. See also a microfilm copy of the original letter, James Whitfield to Propaganda Fide, June 6, 1831, #1355, folios 542–43, PFUNDA. In 1831 the Archdiocese of Baltimore's boundaries and jurisdiction comprised the entire state of Maryland and the District of Columbia.
2. "Attempt to Change the Order," in "History of the Establishment of the Order of the Visitation in the United States—1799," 179–80, SLVA.
3. George Parsons Lathrop and Rose Hawthorne Lathrop, *A Story of Courage: Annals of the Georgetown Convent of the Visitation* (Boston: Houghton Mifflin, 1894), 318–19. See also "History of the Establishment of the Order of the Visitation in the United States—1799" (abridged), 163, MDCM.
4. Sister Ann Agatha Combs to Father Samuel Eccleston, April 8, 1831, Archbishop Samuel Eccleston Papers, 27A–B2, AAB. Between 1838 and 1847 Combs served three terms as superior of Georgetown Visitation. See Lathrop and Lathrop, *A Story of Courage*, 377.
5. Lathrop and Lathrop, *A Story of Courage*, 319.
6. Nancy Lusignan Schultz, *Fire and Roses: The Burning of the Charlestown Convent, 1834* (New York: Free Press, 2004).
7. Diary entry, April 10, 1831, Louis R. Deluol Diary, LRDP.
8. Diary entry, April 11, 1831, Louis R. Deluol Diary, LRDP.
9. Diary entry, April 12, 1831, Louis R. Deluol Diary, LRDP.
10. Ann Mattingly to Reverend Stephen L. Dubuisson, April 16, 1831, box 103, folder 6, MPA.
11. Diary entry, May 16, 1831, Louis R. Deluol Diary, LRDP. Mother Madeleine was first elected the previous year following the resignation of Mother Juliana Matthews after serving less than two years of her second three-year term. Under normal circumstances, Mother Madeleine's presidency would not have come up for reelection until the fall of 1831.
12. The day after Mother Madeleine left for Mobile, Alabama, to found a new Visitation Convent there, Sister Stanislaus Jones, Wightt's successor as headmistress, wrote to Whitfield, complaining of the superior's constant meddling in her duties as directress of the academy. See Sister Stanislaus Jones to Archbishop James Whitfield, December 1, 1832, Archbishop James Whitfield Papers, 23M10, AAB.
13. Sister Cecilia Brooks to Archbishop James Whitfield, June 8, 1831, Archbishop James Whitfield Papers, 23V1, AAB. Brooks later succeeded Sister Ann Agatha Combs as superior of Georgetown Convent, serving two terms from 1847 to 1852. See Lathrop and Lathrop, *A Story of Courage*, 377.
14. "History of the Establishment of the Order" (abr.), 82–87; Lathrop and Lathrop, *A Story of Courage*, 221–22.
15. "Prospectus of the Ladies' Academy of the Visitation of Georgetown, District of Columbia," *National Gazette* (Philadelphia), August 17, 1831, 1.
16. The Lathrops contend the visitors were the rector of Georgetown (Thomas Mulledy) and another Jesuit priest, but they fail to identify either by name. See Lathrop and Lathrop, *A Story of Courage*, 317–18.

17. Diary entry, March 26, 1831, Louis R. Deluol Diary, LRDP.
18. Diary entry, March 31, 1831, Louis R. Deluol Diary, LRDP.
19. Deluol diary entry, April 10, 1831.
20. Diary entry, March 23, 1831, Louis R. Deluol Diary, LRDP.
21. Chapter 22, *Rules of Saint Augustine and Constitutions of the Sisters of the Visitation, after the Original Manuscripts,* revised according with the Code of the Canon Law, translated from the French (London: Manresa, 1930), 71: "There ought not to be among you any sensual love, but spiritual."
22. Diary entry, March 25, 1831, Louis R. Deluol Diary, LRDP.
23. Just before Wightt was granted a formal dispensation on November 22, 1831, Deluol commanded Wheeler to cease further correspondence with her. See diary entry, November 17, 1831, Louis R. Deluol Diary, LRDP.
24. Deluol diary entry, April 10, 1831.
25. Ray A. Billington, *The Protestant Crusade, 1800–1860: A Study in the Origins of Nativism* (Chicago: Quadrangle, 1964 [1938]).
26. Diary entry, March 24, 1831, Louis R. Deluol Diary, LRDP.
27. Sister Ann Gertrude Wightt to Archbishop James Whitfield, March 22, 1831, Archbishop James Whitfield Papers, 23A2, AAB.
28. Deluol diary entry, March 25, 1831.
29. Samuel L. Young, "An Agent of Anarchy and Tyranny: Martin Luther and American Democracy in Antebellum Catholic Apologetics," *U.S. Catholic Historian* 39, no. 4 (Fall 2021): 1–24.
30. The most famous European work exposing the alleged immorality taking place within religious convents is the novel *La Religieuse,* known in English as *The Nun,* or *Memoirs of a Nun* (1792), published posthumously by the French philosophe Denis Diderot. See also the chapter on celibacy and nunneries in *Practical and Internal Evidence Against Catholicism* (1825) by the Spanish ex-priest José María Blanco White, and the memoirs of Scipio de Ricci, late bishop of Pistoia, translated from the Italian as *Female Convents: Secrets of Nunneries Disclosed* (1829) See Billington, *The Protestant Crusade,* 45–46.
31. Point #12 in "Pastoral Letter to the Laity" (1829), quoted in Hugh J. Nolan, ed., *Pastoral Letters of the United States Catholic Bishops: Volume 1, 1792–1940* (Washington, DC: United States Catholic Conference, 1984), 41.
32. Billington, *The Protestant Crusade,* 53–55.
33. Point #16 in "Pastoral Letter to the Clergy" (1829), quoted in Nolan, *Pastoral Letters,* 59.
34. Diary entry, April 3, 1831, Louis R. Deluol Diary, LRDP.
35. On the reaction of the American press to Sister Gertrude's flight, see chapter 5.
36. "Escape of a Nun," *The Protestant* (New York), vol. 2, April 9, 1831, 118–19.
37. Kara M. French, "Prejudice for Profit: Escaped Nun Stories and American Catholic Print Culture," *Journal of the Early Republic* 39, no. 3 (Fall 2019): 503–35.
38. "Escape of a Nun," April 9, 1831. See also, "The Devil Is Come to You," *The Protestant* (New York), vol. 2, September 24, 1831, 305.
39. Deluol diary entry, April 11, 1831.
40. Ann Gertrude Wightt to Propaganda Fide, April 30, 1831, #286, vol. 77, folios 179–85, PFUNDA.
41. Because this document is a letterbook copy of her original letter, we do not know how Wightt signed herself when petitioning the pope. As a supplicant she likely signed herself "Sister Ann Gertrude," just as she had signed her March missive to Archbishop Whitfield.

42. Saint Augustine, *The City of God,* trans. Marcus Dodds (New York: Modern Library, 2000), 842–43.
43. Deluol diary entry, May 16, 1831.
44. Whitfield to Propaganda Fide, June 6, 1831.
45. Whitfield to Propaganda Fide, June 6, 1831.
46. Whitfield to Propaganda Fide, June 6, 1831.
47. Whitfield and Chance left for Georgetown on April 7 and returned to Baltimore on April 11. Whitfield's meeting with Sister Gertrude must have occurred on Friday, April 8, or Saturday, April 9. See Deluol diary entries for April 7, 10, 11, and 12, 1831, Louis R. Deluol Diary, LRDP.
48. Whitfield to Propaganda Fide, June 6, 1831. This section of Whitfield's letter, describing his meeting with Wightt, is corroborated in Deluol's diary entry of May 16.
49. Cardinal Pedicini, Prefect of the Sacred Congregation of Propaganda Fide, to Archbishop James Whitfield, August 20, 1831, here translated by R. Emmett Curran, in Archbishop James Whitfield Papers, 23R19, AAB.
50. See the copy of the dispensation given to Sr. Gertrude Wightt by Archbishop of Baltimore James Whitfield, November 22, 1831, box 103, folder 4, MPA.
51. Copy of dispensation, November 22, 1831. Whitfield's call for Wightt to "rethink often on your death" ironically echoes the advice to "think frequently of death" offered almost a decade before by a then–very young Sister Gertrude in a letter to Miss Eliza Neale, blood sister of Sister Jane Scholastica Neale. See Sister Jane Scholastica Neale to Eliza Neale, addendum by Sister Ann Gertrude Wightt, October 5, 1823, box 103, folder 4, MPA.
52. Margaret Bayard Smith to Mrs. Kirkpatrick, November 7, 1831, in *The First Forty Years of Washington Society Portrayed by the Family Letters of Mrs. Samuel Harrison Smith,* ed. Gaillard Hunt (New York: Charles Scribner's Sons, 1906), 322.
53. The fullest treatment of the Eaton scandal appears in John F. Marszalek, *The Petticoat Affair: Manners, Mutiny, and Sex in Andrew Jackson's White House* (New York: Free Press, 1997), vii. Marszalek contends that neither Margaret nor her family ever referred to her as "Peggy" and deliberately refrains from using the name so as not to reinforce popular preconceptions about Margaret Eaton. I have chosen to do likewise.
54. Margaret Bayard Smith to Mrs. Kirkpatrick, January 1, 1829, in Hunt, *The First Forty Years,* 252. In light of her collaborations with John Eaton when she was still living in Georgetown Convent, Wightt must have known about the controversy surrounding Margaret Eaton and Eaton about her. It is intriguing to ponder whether these two women, both momentarily the center of overlapping scandals in the nation's capital, ever met or knew each other.
55. William W. Warner, *At Peace with All Their Neighbors: Catholics and Catholicism in the National Capital, 1787–1860* (Washington, DC: Georgetown University Press, 1994), xi.

CHAPTER 7

1. Diary entry, April 26, 1833, Louis R. Deluol Diary, LRDP.
2. Diary entry, November 5, 1832, Louis R. Deluol Diary, LRDP. Sabina Iturbide was too ill to travel with the family to Philadelphia in November, but joined them after she recovered from what may have been an attack of cholera.

3. Allen C. Clark, "General John Peter Van Ness, a Mayor of the City of Washington, His Wife, Marcia, and Her Father David Burnes," *Records of the Columbia Historical Society* 22 (1919): 175–78.
4. Constance McLaughlin Green, *Washington: Village and Capital, 1800–1878* (Princeton, NJ: Princeton University Press, 1962), 105–6.
5. Archbishop James Whitfield to Propaganda Fide, June 6, 1831, here translated by Alun Walpole, Letterbook for 1828–32, 19–23, Archbishop James Whitfield Papers, AAB.
6. Copy of the dispensation given to Sr. Gertrude Wightt by Archbishop of Baltimore James Whitfield, November 22, 1831, box 103, folder 4, MPA.
7. Margaret Bayard Smith to Mrs. Kirkpatrick, November 7, 1831, *The First Forty Years of Washington Society Portrayed by the Family Letters of Mrs. Samuel Harrison Smith*, ed. Gaillard Hunt (New York: Charles Scribner's Sons, 1906), 322.
8. Ben Perley Poore, *Perley's Reminiscences of Sixty Years in the National Metropolis*, 2 vols. (Philadelphia: Hubbard Brothers, 1886), 1:161. Poore claims that some years after leaving the convent, Wightt "accompanied the family of the American Minister to Spain, and resided for some time at Madrid, where she was a great favorite in Court circles." But this single report is not confirmed by any other writers. What makes the claim seem plausible is that Cornelius P. Van Ness did serve as US minister to Spain from 1829 to 1836. And Cornelius's first wife, Rhoda Savage Van Ness, passed away in Spain in 1834 while her husband was stationed there. But the minister remarried within the year to Madalena Allus, a much younger woman of Hungarian descent. It is not likely that Cornelius would have needed Wightt in Madrid, as by then his children were adults and his second wife would have been able to assume any hostess duties during their remaining year in Madrid. What is more likely is that Poore confused Cornelius Van Ness with John Young Mason, the US minister to France (1854–59). Wightt did accompany Mason's family on the voyage to France in 1854 and stayed with them in Paris (discussed in chap. 8).
9. Green, *Washington*, 105–6.
10. Michael W. Fazio and Patrick A. Snadon, *The Domestic Architecture of Benjamin Henry Latrobe* (Baltimore: John Hopkins University Press, 2006), 452.
11. Fazio and Snadon, *Domestic Architecture*, 453.
12. Green, *Washington*, 154–55.
13. US Census Bureau, Sixth Census of Washington, District of Columbia, 1840, Family History Library Film, microfilm roll 35, 23.
14. Copy of dispensation, November 22, 1831, box 103, folder 4, MPA.
15. Lee Virginia Chambers-Schiller, *Liberty, A Better Husband: Single Women in America, The Generations of 1780–1840* (New Haven, CT: Yale University Press, 1984), 24–26.
16. Joseph G. Mannard, "'Maternity . . . of the Spirit': Nuns and Domesticity in Antebellum America," *U.S. Catholic Historian* 5 (Summer-Fall 1986): 313–22.
17. Kara French analyzes different identities exhibiting sexual restraint in antebellum America, including the Shakers, Catholic nuns and priests, and followers of Sylvester Graham's health reforms. See French's *Against Sex: Identities of Sexual Restraint in Early America* (Chapel Hill: University of North Carolina Press, 2021).
18. See Chambers-Schiller, *Liberty*.
19. See Louisa May Alcott's journal entry dated February 14, 1868, in *Louisa May Alcott: Her Life, Letters, and Journals*, ed. Ednah D. Cheney (Boston: Little, Brown, 1898), 197.

20. Marie S. Molloy, *Single, White, Slaveholding Women in the Nineteenth-Century American South* (Columbia: University of South Carolina Press, 2018), 5, 72.
21. Sister Mary Augustine Barber to Sister Mary Josephine Barber, January 19, 1836, in Sister Files: Barber, Mary Augustine (1 of 3), 1835–1856, box 1OVZ, SLVA records #200.
22. William Gore Ouseley to John Peter Van Ness, Paris, February 16, 1843, box 15, folder 10, Van Ness–Philip Family Papers, NYHS.
23. John Peter Van Ness to Dolley Payne Madison, February 22, 1838, *The Dolley Madison Digital Edition*, edited by Holly C. Shulman (Charlottesville: University of Virginia Press, 2004), http://rotunda.upress.viriginia.edu/dmde/DPM2049 (hereafter cited as DMDE).
24. Dolley Payne Madison to Miss Van Ness, June 10, 1839, DMDE. The recipient appears to be Matilda E. Van Ness, the daughter of John Peter Van Ness's deceased brother William.
25. Clark, "General John Peter Van Ness," 182.
26. Kate Kearney Henry, quoted in Allen C. Clark, ed., *Life and Letters of Dolly Madison* (Washington, DC: W. F. Roberts, 1914), 382.
27. "Attempt to Change the Order," in "History of the Establishment of the Order of the Visitation in the United States—1799," 180, SLVA.
28. The following are the original titles of the French and Spanish editions of the books in the personal library of Ann Gertrude Wightt: *Discourse de Saint Bernard a Sa Soeur La Religieuse* (Paris: Libraire Greoque-Latine-Allemande, 1820); letters of Saint Basil, Saint Gregory Nazianzen, Saint John Chrysostom, Saint Augustine, and Saint Nilus in *Lettres Choisies des Peres*, vol. 1 (Paris: Libraire Classique-Elementaire, 1824); letters of Saint Jerome and verse of Saint Cyprien, in *Lettres Choisies des Peres*, vol. 2 (Paris: Libraire Classique-Elementaire, 1824); *L'Office de la Saint Vierge, suivant La Reformation du S. Councils de Trente et du Pape Urbain VIII, Dispose a l'usage des Religieuses de la Visistation de Sainte-Marie, Revu, Corrige et Augmente* (Lyon: Chez M. P. Rusand, 1824); Juan Gabriel De Contreras, *Despertador Eucaristico Y Dulce Convite* (Mexico City: Reimpreso en Casa de Benavente, 1815); *Lecciones Elementales de Logica: Dispuestaa con Method Sencillo Y Facil* (Paris: Bossange Hermonos Calle de Seine1826). These volumes are part of the Virginia San Peter Collection of Books from the library of Britannia Peter Kennon, gifted to Tudor Place Historic House & Garden, December 2002.
29. Samuel Parkes, *The Chemical Catechism, with Notes, Illustrations, and Experiments*, 9th London ed. (New York: Collins, 1821).
30. Parkes, *The Chemical Catechism*, 58.
31. Germaine de Staël, *Corinne, or Italy*, vol. 2, new revised and corrected ed. (Paris: Treuttel and Wurtz, 1836).
32. Dolley Madison to Ann Gertrude Wightt, March 18, 1842, DMDE.
33. Dolley Madison Visits Received, November 27 [and November 29], 1841, DMDE; Dolley Madison Visits Returned, 1841, DMDE.
34. C. Dallett Hemphill, *Bowing to Necessities: A History of Manners in America, 1620–1860* (New York: Oxford University Press, 1999), 151.
35. Hemphill, *Bowing to Necessities*, 152.
36. Amy S. Greenberg, *Lady First: The World of First Lady Sarah Polk* (New York: Alfred A. Knopf, 2019), 127–29.
37. Catherine Allgor, *Parlor Politics: In Which the Ladies of Washington Help Build a City and a Government* (Charlottesville: University Press of Virginia, 2000), 138–39.
38. Allgor, *Parlor Politics*, 2.

39. Ann Gertrude Wightt to Dolley Madison, May 20, 1846, DMDE.
40. Dolley Madison to Mary Anne Fort Mason, May 4, 1844, DMDE; Dolley Madison to John Young Mason, March 15, 1847, DMDE; Dolley Madison to John Young Mason, September 7, 1847, DMDE.
41. Ann G. Wightt to Mary Fort Mason, June 6, 1846, Mason Family Papers, 1805–1886, section 35, VMHC. Annie Payne Causten and Mary Cutts were both Dolley's nieces. In her correspondence with Madison, Cutts frequently mentions Ann Gertrude Wightt. See these examples: Mary Cutts to Dolley Madison [June–September 1845], DMDE; Mary Cutts to Dolley Madison, August 20, 1847, DMDE. See also Mary Cutts to Anna Coles Payne Causten, October 6, 1846, DMDE.
42. "Viva La Baatelle," *Richmond Enquirer*, September 14, 1847, 1. On the social and cultural significance of the summer spas to the planter class, see Charlene M. Boyer Lewis, *Ladies and Gentlemen on Display: Planter Society at the Virginia Springs, 1790–1860* (Cambridge: Cambridge University Press, 2001); and Thomas S. Chambers, *Taking the Waters: Creating an American Leisure Class at Nineteenth-Century Mineral Spring* (Washington, DC: Smithsonian Institution Press, 2002).
43. Ben Marsh, "The Republic's New Clothes: Making Silk in the Antebellum United States," *Agricultural History* 86, no. 4 (Fall 2012): 213–16, 222–23 (table 1), 226.
44. Marsh, "Republic's New Clothes," 221.
45. Journal entry, May 29, 1840, Ann G. Wightt Journal, l, Tudor Place Historic House & Garden Archives, Papers of Britannia Peter Kennon, manuscript 7, box 8, TPA.
46. On Chapter and Corrections of Faults, see Constitutions 24, 25, and 26 in *Rules of Saint Augustine and Constitutions of the Sisters of the Visitation, After the Original Manuscripts*, translated from the French (London: Manresa, 1930), 142–49.
47. Journal entry, June 20, 1840, Ann G. Wightt Journal, 6, TPA.
48. Journal entry, June 22, 1840, Ann G. Wightt Journal, 6 7, TPA.
49. Journal entry, June 26, 1840, Ann G. Wightt Journal, 8, TPA.
50. Journal entry, June 27, 1840, Ann G. Wightt Journal, 8, TPA.
51. Marsh, "Republic's New Clothes," 227.
52. Journal entry, August 30, 1840, Ann G. Wightt Journal, 14, TPA.
53. Wightt journal entry, August 30, 1840, 14–15.
54. Journal entry, June 19, 1840, Ann G. Wightt Journal, 3, TPA.
55. Journal entry, June 29, 1840, Ann G. Wightt Journal, 6, TPA.
56. Green, *Washington*, 226.
57. Fazio and Snadon, *Domestic Architecture*, 452. The authors claim John. P. Van Ness was "land rich but often cash poor, [yet] he still died the wealthiest man in the District, and one of its most influential."
58. Britannia Kennon, May 11, 1900, quoted in *A Georgetown Life: The Reminiscences of Britannia Wellington Peter Kennon of Tudor Place*, ed. Grant S. Quertermous (Washington, DC: Georgetown University Press, 2020), 115.
59. Richard Smith to Cornelius P. Van Ness, January 29, 1847, box 3, folder 11, Van Ness–Philip Family Papers, 1743–1951, NYHS. The relative worth of $600.00 in 1847 is $23,614.21 today (accessed June 24, 2024, https://www.measuringworth.com/dollarvaluetoday/?amount=600&from=1847).
60. Richard Smith to Cornelius Van Ness, June 24, 1847, and Cornelius Van Ness to Richard Smith, June 24, 1847, box 3, folder 11, Van Ness–Philip Family Papers, NYHS. Smith and Van Ness exchanged at least four different letters (two from each man) on this day.

61. Cornelius Van Ness to John Young Mason, June 18, 1847, box 15, folder 9, Van Ness–Philip Family Papers, NYHS. The relative worth of $15,000 in 1847 is $576,590.33 today (accessed June 24, 2024, https://www.measuringworth.com/dollarvaluetoday/?amount=15000&from=1847).
62. Van Ness to Mason, June 18, 1847.
63. Richard Smith, trustee, Account of Receipts and Payments, October 5, 1847, box 3, folder 12, Van Ness–Philip Family Papers, NYHS.
64. Kennon, May 11, 1900, 115. Thomas Green, an attorney from Virginia, purchased the Van Ness Mansion about four years after the death of John Peter Van Ness.
65. Robert P. Letcher to Manuel Larrainzar, Communication to the Mexican Government, September 10, 1850, Letterbook 0186, 71–72, RG 84.
66. Diary entry, February 17, 1848, James K. Polk Diary, 3:342, quoted in "Historical Notes," *Records of the American Catholic Historical Society* 27 (1916): 174.
67. Diary entry, February 24, 1848, James K. Polk Diary, 7:505, quoted in "Historical Notes," *Records of the American Catholic Historical Society* 27 (1916): 174.
68. Polk diary, February 17, 1848.
69. William G. Shade, *Democratizing the Old Dominion: Virginia and the Second Party System, 1824–1861* (Charlottesville: University of Virginia Press, 1996), 252; Daniel W. Crofts, *Old Southampton: Politics and Society in Virginia County, 1834–1869* (Charlottesville: University of Virginia Press, 2015).
70. "Copy of the Will of Jesus de Yturbide sent me her Executor [trix] Sabina de Yturbide, July 5, 1849," enclosure with Robert P. Letcher to Manuel Larrainzar, September 10, 1850. It is not clear exactly how long Wightt acted as Isis's nurse. But Letcher wrote: "[Isis] lay ill for years, Miss Wight was her friend her comforter and her nurse, and as fondly attached to her as a sister could be."

CHAPTER 8

1. Daniel Webster to Mariano Arista, May 1, 1851, in *Daniel Webster's Diplomatic Papers, Vol. 2, 1850–1852,* ed. Kenneth Shewmaker and Kenneth R. Stevens (Hanover, NH: University Press of New England, 1987), 556–59.
2. Mariano Arista to Daniel Webster, June 2, 1851, *Daniel Webster's Diplomatic Papers, Vol. 2, 1850–1852,* 560–62.
3. The relative worth of $10,000 in 1852 is $419,317.76 today (accessed June 24, 2024, https://www.measuringworth.com/dollarvaluetoday/?amount=10000&from=1852).
4. "In the Senate [March 2]," *Pensacola (FL) Gazette,* March 27, 1830, 3; Eleanore C. Sullivan, *Georgetown Visitation Since 1799* (Baltimore: Privately printed, 1975), 98–99; Ann Gertrude Wightt to Propaganda Fide, April 30, 1831, #286, vol. 77, folios 179–85, PFUNDA.
5. Ann Gertrude Wightt to John M. Clayton, December 21, 1849, Claims Papers 1828–1938, box 1, RG 84. "Yturbide" is the Spanish spelling of the family name. Maria de Jesús de Iturbide was called "Isis" by her family.
6. John M. Clayton to Robert P. Letcher, December 24, 1849, Claims Papers 1828–1938, box 1, RG 84.
7. Robert P. Letcher to Manuel Larrainzar, September 10, 1850, Communication to the Mexican Government, Letterbook, vol. 186, 71–72, RG 84.

8. Letcher concluded his letter cryptically by saying, "This hasty note is not intended by any means as an official one."
9. Robert P. Letcher to Daniel Webster, October 22, 1850, Communications to the Government at Home, Letterbook vol. 7, 140–44, RG 84.
10. Ultimately Jackson received only half of the $5,000 allotment, and the Iturbides received $28,500, barely half the amount for which they hoped.
11. Allen C. Clark, "General John Peter Van Ness, a Mayor of the City of Washington, His Wife, Marcia, and Her Father, David Burnes," *Records of the Columbia Historical Society* 22 (1919): 183.
12. Ann Gertrude Wightt to Daniel Webster, June 3, 1851 (received June 22), Claims Papers 1828–1938, box 1, RG 84.
13. Louis S. Hargous was a wealthy New Jersey merchant and land speculator serving in the American consulate in Vera Cruz. See "Editorial Note," DWDE, 583.
14. Webster and Letcher envisioned a land route across the isthmus, either by road or rail, to provide Americans with easier access to the goldfields of California and commerce across the Pacific.
15. The Garay grant was a concession made by the government of Mexico in 1842 that gave to private businessman Jose de Garay the right to construct a "line of communication" (road, canal, or railroad) across the Isthmus of Tehuantepec. At the end of the Mexican-American War, Garay sold these rights to a British company. In 1849 that British company transferred the rights to the American brothers Peter and Louis Hargous. The Hargous brothers retained a one-third interest in the enterprise and sold shares for the other two-thirds to a group of American speculators under the name New Orleans Tehuantepec Company. For a detailed account of the role played by the Garay grant in the contentious diplomacy around the proposed treaty, see J. Fred Rippy, "Diplomacy of the United States and Mexico Regarding the Isthmus of Tehuantepec, 1848–1860," *Mississippi Valley Historical Review* 6, no. 4 (March 1920): 503–31. See also "Editorial Note," DWDE.
16. Wightt to Webster, June 3, 1851.
17. See chapter 9, "The Gunpowder Minister," in David Brown, *Palmerston: A Biography* (New Haven: Yale University Press, 2011), 279–333.
18. On Ouseley, see James J. Barnes, *Private and Confidential: Letters from British Ministers in Washington to the Foreign Secretaries in London, 1844–1867* (Selinsgrove, PA: Susquehanna University Press, 1993), 182.
19. Wightt to Webster, June 3, 1851.
20. See Marian Campbell Gouverneur, *As I Remember: Recollection of American Society during the Nineteenth Century* (New York: D. Appleton, 1911), 224.
21. Gouverneur, *As I Remember*, 224–25.
22. Sabina Iturbide to Angel Iturbide, August 18, 1850, folder 5, AIP (microfilm box 17, reel 13).
23. Sabina Iturbide to Angel Iturbide, July 16,1851, folder 6, AIP (microfilm box 17, reel 13). The first page and a half is written in Spanish; the second page and half is in English. Sabina's sending "My love to . . . Miss Wightt" makes it appear that both Angel and Gertrude were both in Mexico at this time. Likely they made the voyage to Vera Cruz together.
24. [Robert Perkins] Letcher to dear Sir [Angel Iturbide?], January 5 and 9, 1852, folder 6, AIP (microfilm box 17, reel 13).

25. Lionel Davidson to Mr. [William Wilson] Corcoran and [George Washington] Riggs, April 16, 1852, box 239, folder 6, RFP. The letter, dated April 19, 1852, is signed by four of the Iturbide brothers, Agustín, Angel, Salvador, and Agustín C. The letter is also signed Robert P. Letcher, attesting to the authenticity of the signatures of the Iturbide brothers.
26. "Copy of the Will of Jesus de Yturbide sent me her Executor [trix] Sabina de Yturbide, July 5, 1849," enclosure with Letcher to Larrainzar, September 10, 1850.
27. Sabina Iturbide to Angel Iturbide, February 28, 1852, folder 5, AIP (microfilm box 17, reel 13).
28. Sabina Iturbide to Angel Iturbide, February 28, 1852: "In a day or two, I will write to Miss Wightt + yourself I have only time to say that I have the will but not the power to say that I am perfectly satisfied with your decision as regards the division you have made of, the $50,000 – But you all know that neither I nor any of your house [have] the right to give [blank space] the larger share." See also the sentiments of younger daughter Josephine in Josephine Iturbide to Angel Iturbide, February 26,1852, folder 6, AIP (microfilm box 17, reel 13).
29. Sabina Iturbide to Angel Iturbide, May 22, 1852, folder 5, AIP (microfilm box 17, reel 13). See also, Lionel Davidson to [William Wilson] Corcoran and [George Washington] Riggs, May 11, 1852, Papers of George Washington Riggs, 1836–71, box 240, folder 7, RFP.
30. AMH de Iturbide to Hon R.M [*sic*] Letcher, May 24, 1852, AIP (microfilm box 17, reel 14).
31. Sabina Iturbide to Angel Iturbide, May 27, 1852, folder 5, AIP (microfilm box 17, reel 13).
32. Iturbide Petition, July 3, 1852, folder 5, AIP (microfilm box 17, reel 13).
33. Sabina Iturbide to Angel Iturbide, October 19, 1852, folder 5, AIP (microfilm box 17, reel 13). See also Papers of George Washington Riggs for May 1852, RFP.
34. Appointed secretary of the Mexican Legation in Washington in 1854, Angel Iturbide married an American woman, Alice Forrest Green, at her home, Rosedale estate, in Washington, DC, the following year.
35. Extract of letter from Mrs. [Alice] Iturbide to Mrs. [Maria] Devereux, June 4, 1859, folder 5, AIP (microfilm box 17, reel 13). At nearly forty years old, Maria Devereux was much older than her sister Alice. She may have also been a widow.
36. Frances Leigh Williams, "The Heritage and Preparation of a Statesman, John Young Mason, 1799–1859," *Virginia Magazine of History and Biography* (1967): 305–30.
37. Franklin Pierce to John Young Mason, May 8, 1854, Mason Family Papers, 1805–1886, sec. 24, VMHC.
38. David Potter, *The Impending Crisis, 1848–1861* (New York: Harper & Row, 1976); Robert E. May, *The Southern Dream of a Caribbean Empire, 1854–1861* (Baton Rouge: Louisiana State University Press, 1973); Matthew Karp, *This Vast Southern Empire: Slaveholders at the Helm of American Foreign Policy* (Cambridge: Harvard University Press, 2016).
39. Ann G. Wightt to Mary Fort Mason, June 6, 1846, Mason Family Papers, 1805–1886, sec. 35, VMHC.
40. "Miss Sallie Archer Anderson, of Richmond (a daughter of the late Colonel Archer Anderson), vividly recalls the death of Miss Wight—'Sister Jettie'—as she was affectionately called by the children of the Anderson connection who were devoted to her and she to them." Augusta Blanche Berard to Mary Berard, April 18, 1856, quoted in "Arlington and Mount Vernon 1856: As Described in a Letter of Augusta Blanche Berard," in ed.

Clayton Torrance, *Virginia Magazine of History and Biography* 57, no. 2 (April 1949): 153n25. The different spellings suggest a simple difference in pronunciation.

41. Ann Gertrude Wightt to Bettie Mason, January 25, 1855, Mason Family Papers, 1825–1902, sec. 32, VMHC. This letter was begun and completed on January 25, 1855, but appears to have been added to on January 27, 1855.
42. Ann Gertrude Wightt to Bettie Mason, January 27, 1855, Mason Family Papers, 1825–1902, sec. 32, VMHC. This letter appears to be an addendum to the letter dated January 25. Mollie was the nickname for the Masons' daughter Mary Ann, who later married Colonel Archer Anderson, CSA.
43. Wightt to Bettie Mason, January 25 and 27, 1855.
44. Wightt to Bettie Mason, January 27, 1855.
45. Wightt to Bettie Mason, January 27, 1855.
46. Ann Gertrude Wightt to Bettie Mason, March 22, 1855, Mason Family Papers, 1825–1902, sec. 32, VMHC.
47. In her 1865 will, Wightt mentions that McAllister owed her $8,000, presumably from a loan or an investment she advanced to him. See Last Will and Testament of Ann Gertrude Wightt, July 12, 1865, PFP.
48. Ann Gertrude Wightt to Judge Mason, March 28, 1852, Mason Family Papers, 1825–1902, sec. 6, VMHC.
49. Ann G. Wightt to Judge Mason, [1854], Mason Family Papers, 1825–1902, sec. 8, VMHC.
50. Ann Gertrude Wightt to Judge Mason, March 22, 1855, Mason Family Papers, 1825–1902, sec. 6, VMHC.
51. Wightt to Judge Mason, March 22, 1855.
52. Ann Gertrude Wightt to Judge Mason May 21, 1855, Mason Family Papers, 1805–1886, sec. 6, VMHC.
53. On the views of the war generally held by Americans, see William Frederick Liebler, "The United States and the Crimean War, 1853–1856" (PhD diss., University of Massachusetts, 1972). On the South, specifically, see Horace Perry Jones, "Southern Opinion on the Crimean War," *Journal of Mississippi History* 29 (May 1967): 95–117.
54. Wightt to Judge Mason, May 21, 1855.
55. James Buchanan to Ann Gertrude Wightt, December 11, 1856, copied in Ann Gertrude Wightt to Judge Mason, December 13, 1856, Mason Family Papers, 1805–1886, sec. 24, VMHC.
56. Buchanan to Wightt, December 13, 1856.
57. Wightt to Judge Mason, December 13, 1856.

CHAPTER 9

1. Augusta Blanche Berard to Mary Berard, April 18, 1856, in "Arlington and Mount Vernon 1856: As Described in a Letter of Augusta Blanche Berard," ed. Clayton Torrance, *Virginia Magazine of History and Biography* 57, no. 2 (April 1949): 153, 157. Wightt also conversed with Markie Williams during this visit. See Markie Williams diary entry for May 1, 1856, in *The Arlington Journals of Martha Custis Williams*, ed. Douglas Breton, 181, AHLM, (hereafter AJMCW), accessed January 12, 2024, https://home.nps.gov/arho/learn/historyculture/upload/Diary-of-Martha-Custis-Williams.pdf.

2. Britannia Kennon, May 11, 1900, in *A Georgetown Life: The Reminiscences of Britannia Wellington Peter Kennon of Tudor Place*, ed. Grant S. Quertermous (Washington, DC: Georgetown University Press, 2020), 117.
3. "Britannia Wellington Peter Kennon: A Biographical Sketch," in Quertermous, *A Georgetown Life*, 30–33.
4. Quertermous, *A Georgetown Life*, 38.
5. Diary entry, November 10, 1854, Anna Maria Thornton Diary, vol. 7: 1850–61, AMTP.
6. The reference to "Aunt Wightt" is found in Martha Custis Kennon to Britannia W. Kennon, December 18, 1858, Papers of Britannia W. Kennon, MS 7, box 1, TPA. See also Quertermous, *A Georgetown Life*, 38.
7. Richard F. Grimmett, *St. John's Church, Lafayette Square: The History and Heritage of the Church of Presidents, Washington, DC* (Maitland, FL: Mill City Press, 2009), 4–8; Alexander B. Hagner, "History and Reminiscences of St. John's Church, Washington, D.C.," *Records of the Columbia Historical Society* 12 (1909): 90–91.
8. Clayton Colman Hall, *Baltimore: Its History and Its People, Vol. 2, Biography* (New York: Lewis, 1912), 533–34.
9. Unlike St, John's Church in Washington City, Emmanuel Episcopal Church in Baltimore was decidedly low church in its worship. Email correspondence with Mary Klein, archivist, Episcopal Diocese of Maryland, May 22 and 23, 2023.
10. On this question the historian of Catholicism R. Emmett Curran writes, "For Catholics, even attending a Protestant service was considered '*communicatio in sacris*,' i.e., participating in a worship service which Church law did not recognize. Even more so would they be prohibited from serving as a Godparent in an Episcopal baptism. So I think it is safe to regard A[nn] G[ertrude] W[ightt] as a practical Episcopalian as early as 1855" (email message to author, March 29, 2023). Mary Klein concurs with Curran: "I do agree that in 1855, it would not have been possible for a practicing Roman Catholic to be listed as a 'sponsor' at an Episcopal Church baptism. The anti-Roman prejudice was strong in the Church at that time, and, if I am not mistaken, attendance at any 'protestant' church service would have been strictly forbidden by the Roman Catholic church" (Mary Klein, archivist, Episcopal Diocese of Maryland, email message to author, November 27, 2023).
11. Mary Mitchell, *Divided Town: A Study of Georgetown, D.C.* (Barre, MA: Barre, 1968), 19.
12. Richard F. Grimmett, historian of St. John's Episcopal Church, Lafayette Square, email message to author, March 20, 2023; and Klein email, May 23, 2023.
13. Markie Williams diary entry, March 28, 1858, in AJMCW, 164–65.
14. Markie Williams diary entry, April [4], 1858, in AJMCW, 165.
15. On the varieties of religious conversion found in America, see Lincoln Austin Mullen, *The Chance of Salvation: A History of Conversion in America* (Cambridge, MA: Harvard University Press, 2017).
16. Grimmett email message, March 20, 2023; Klein email message, May 23, 2023.
17. "Attempt to Change the Order," in "History of the Establishment of the Order of the Visitation in the United States—1799," 184–85, SLVA.
18. Markie Williams diary entry for August 9, 1856, AJMCW, 109.
19. Maria Devereux to Alice Green Iturbide, July 5, 1859, folder 5, AIP (microfilm box 17, reel 13); Quertermous, *A Georgetown Life*, 41.
20. Kennon, May 11, 1900, 116–17.
21. Kennon, May 11, 1900, 116.

22. Elizabeth Lindsay Lomax, ed., *Leaves from an Old Washington Diary, 1854–1862* (New York: Dutton, 1943), 71.
23. Lomax, *Leaves from an Old Washington Diary*, 91.
24. Sabina Iturbide to Angel Iturbide, June 18, 1855, folder 5, AIP (microfilm box 17, reel 13).
25. Sabina Iturbide to Angel Iturbide, June 18, 1855.
26. Sabina Iturbide to Angel Iturbide, March 19, 1856, folder 5, AIP (microfilm box 17, reel 13).
27. E. W. F. Sloan to Madame de Iturbide, June 4, 1858, folder 6, AIP (microfilm box 17, reel 13).
28. Alice Green Iturbide to Maria Devereux, April 18, 1859, folder 5, AIP (microfilm box 17, reel 13).
29. Maria Devereux to Alice Green Iturbide, May 10, 1859, folder 5, AIP (microfilm box 17, reel 13).
30. Mrs. [Alice] Iturbide to Mrs. [Maria] Devereux, June 4, 1859, folder 5, AIP (microfilm box 17, reel 13).
31. Alice Iturbide to Maria Devereux, June 11 or 17, 1859 (reply to May 15, 1859), folder 5, AIP (microfilm box 17, reel 13).
32. Maria Devereux to Alice Green Iturbide, July 5, 1859, folder 5, AIP (microfilm box 17, reel 13).
33. Maria Devereux to Alice Green Iturbide, August 15, 1859, folder 5, AIP (microfilm box 17, reel 13).
34. Alice Iturbide to Maria Devereux, October 1, 1859 (reply to August 15 letter), folder 5, AIP (microfilm box 17, reel 13).
35. Maria Devereux to Alice Green Iturbide, October 13, 1859 (received November 27; answered December 4, 1859), folder 5, AIP (microfilm box 17, reel 13).
36. Angel Iturbide to Madame Iturbide, November 18, 1859, folder 5, AIP (microfilm box 17, reel 13).
37. Alice Iturbide to Maria Devereux, December 4, 1859 (reply to November 5 letter), folder 5, AIP (microfilm box 17, reel 13).
38. Alice Iturbide to Maria Devereux, Mexico, May 3, 1861, folder 5, AIP (microfilm box 17, reel 13). See also Statements by Angel de Iturbide to American Ministers Thomas Corwin and John B. Weller, Mexico, February 23, 1861, folder 5, AIP (microfilm box 17, reel 13); Statement of the Children of Agustin de Iturbide that "the children" ["family" scratched out] of Don Agustin de Yturbide have received only about sixty-five or sixty-six thousand dollars, Iturbide Statement No. 2 (1861), folder 5, AIP (microfilm box 17, reel 13): "From $1,000,000 deduct $100,00; the remainder is $900,000; from deduct one fifth or $180,000. This latter remainder or $720,000, being divided by 9, gives for a quotient, $80,000. From it deduct $12,500; because $10,000 have been paid to Miss Wightt, and $2,5000 to Dr. Jackson; and you have $67,500 for a remainder, leading to the following proportion, $67,500: $22,222 to be pd in lands to Miss Isis de Yturbide will."
39. The fascinating story of Agustín de Iturbide y Green, the only child of Angel Iturbide and Alice Green, is captured by C. M. Mayo in the historical novel *The Last Prince of the Mexican Empire* (Denver, CO: Unbridled, 2009).
40. Mitchell, *Divided Town*, 119; Quertermous, *A Georgetown Life*, 41–42.
41. Lomax, *Leaves from an Old Washington Diary*, 219.
42. Britannia Kennon, February 26, 1897, 83–84.

43. Constance McLaughlin Green, *Washington: Village and Capital, 1800–1878* (Princeton, NJ: Princeton University Press, 1962), 236, 285.
44. Mitchell, *Divided Town,* 136–37.
45. Mitchell, *Divided Town,* 135–36.
46. Mitchell, *Divided Town,* 137–38.
47. Britannia Kennon, February 12, 1897, 87–88.
48. Hall, *Baltimore,* 533–34.
49. Last will and testament, Ann Gertrude Wightt, July 12, 1865, box 10, folder 7, PFP.
50. J. W S. Clements, *Origins of Clements-Spalding and Allied Families of Maryland and Kentucky* (Louisville, KY: Standard, 1928), 39.
51. Quertermous, *A Georgetown Life,* 44–45: Mitchell, *Divided Town,* 113.
52. Ann Gertrude Wightt to Britannia W. Peter Kennon, July 13, 1865, box 10, folder 7, RM-1186, PFP.
53. Kennon diary entry May 11, 1900, 116–17n229.
54. "History of the Establishment of the Order," 184–85.
55. Colonel Archer Anderson, CSA, was the son of Brigadier General Joseph R. Anderson, CSA, owner of the famous Tredegar Iron Works in Richmond.
56. Kennon, May 11, 1900, 117–18.
57. *New York Evening Post,* November 21, 1867.
58. Wightt Last Will and Testament.
59. "Death of Hall M'Allister," *New York Times,* December 2, 1888.
60. Wightt Last Will and Testament.
61. For more on Taylor, see Buffalo Trace Distillery website, accessed January 14, 2024, https://www.buffalotracedistillery.com/legendary-people/taylor.html.
62. On William Queen, see Robert Emmett Curran, *American Catholics and the Quest for Equality in the Civil War Era* (Baton Rouge: Louisiana State University Press, 2023), 267–68, 427n10.

EPILOGUE

1. Archbishop James Whitfield to Reverend Francis Dzierzynski, SJ, October 27, 1831, box 103, folder 6, MPA.
2. Sabina Iturbide to Angel Iturbide, June 19, 1868, folder 6, AIP (microfilm box, 17, reel 13).
3. "A Sketch of the Life and Virtues of Sister Madeleine Augustine d'Arregger ," typescript, 15, RG 3, series 6, GVM.
4. "Academy of the Visitation," *Wheeling Times Advertiser,* March 27, 1848, 2.
5. Eleanore C. Sullivan, *Georgetown Visitation Since 1799* (Baltimore: Privately printed, 1975), 102.
6. "Attempt to Change the Order," in "History of the Establishment of the Order of the Visitation in the United States—1799," 180, SLVA.
7. Cassandra Yacovazzi, *Escaped Nuns: True Womanhood and the Campaign Against Convents in Antebellum America* (New York: Oxford University Press, 2018).
8. On Rebecca Reed, see Daniel A. Cohen, "The Respectability of Rebecca Reed: Genteel Womanhood and Sectarian Conflict in Antebellum America," *Journal of the Early Republic* 16, no. 3 (Fall 1996): 419–61; and Nancy Lusignan Schultz, *Fire and Roses:*

The Burning of the Charlestown Convent, 1834 (New York: Free Press, 2004), 120–21. On Maria Monk, see Maureen McCarthy, "The Rescue of True Womanhood: Convents and Anti-Catholicism in 1830s America" (PhD diss., Rutgers University, 1996); and Ray Allen Billington, *The Protestant Crusade, 1800–1860: A Study in the Origins of Nativism* (Chicago: Quadrangle, 1964 [1938]), 99–108.

9. Andrew B. Cross, "To the Citizens, to the Honorable, the General Assembly, and Governor of Maryland," January 31, 1856, reprinted as "The Cry from the Priests' Prisons," *Baltimore Clipper*, February 8, 1856, 1.
10. On Elizabeth Harrison, see Schultz, *Fire and Roses*, 153–58; and Billington, *The Protestant Crusade*, 71–74.
11. On Milly McPherson, see C. Walker Gollar, "The Alleged Abduction of Milly McPherson and Catholic Recruitment of Presbyterian Girls," *Church History* 65, no. 4 (December 1996): 596–608.
12. On Olivia Neale, see Joseph G. Mannard, "'What Has Become of Olevia Neal?': The Escaped Nun Phenomenon in Antebellum America," *Maryland Historical Magazine* 105, no. 4 (Winter 2010): 348–67.
13. On Josephine Bunkley, see Billington, *The Protestant Crusade*, 310–31; and Yacovazzi, *Escaped Nuns*, 129–32.
14. Edith O'Gorman, *Convent Life Unveiled: Trials and Persecution of Miss Edith O'Gorman, Otherwise Sister Teresa de Chantal, Written by Herself* (1871). Numerous editions of this work have been published and translated; see Augustine J. Curley, OSB, "The Identity of Edith O'Gorman, the 'Escaped Nun'" (Newark Abbey, NJ: Unpublished paper, n.d), 1, 7–8. Regarding O'Gorman's lecture tours, see Rene Kollar, OSB, "An American 'Escaped Nun' on Tour in England: Edith O'Gorman's Critique of Convent Life," *Feminist Theology* 14, no. 2 (2006): 205–20.
15. Catherine O'Donnell, "'A Dreadful Wolf Loose in the Fold of Christ': St. Peter's Parish, Manhattan, 1806," *American Catholic Studies* 134, no. 3 (Fall 2023): 1–26; and Catherine O'Donnell, "'Ten Thousand Pardons': Accusations of Clerical Misconduct in St. Peter's Parish, 1806–1809," *American Catholic Studies* 134, no. 4 (Winter 2023): 1–24. On the broader pattern of clerical abuse from a transnational perspective, see Luca Condignola, "The Catholic Clergy in the North Atlantic Area, 1763–1830: Patterns of Deviancy," *Almanack* 26 (2020): 1–34, ed00719.
16. Margaret Bayard Smith to Mrs. Fitzpatrick, March 14, 1814, *The First Forty Years of Washington Society Portrayed by the Family Letters of Mrs. Samuel Harrison Smith*, ed. Gaillard Hunt (New York: Charles Scribner's Sons, 1906), 97.
17. Amy S. Greenberg, *Lady First: The World of First Lady Sarah Polk* (New York: Alfred A. Knopf, 2019), xv.
18. "Loughborough, M. Emmanuel (Mary)," Membership list (permanent and temporary), box 1.1, folder 1.1, GVM.
19. Mary Loughborough to William L. Marcy, December 18, 1856, vol. 77, folios 838–39, PFUNDA.
20. Maria Louisa Loughborough to Holy Father, February 5, 1857, Archbishop Francis Kenrick Papers, 30K5, AAB.
21. Hamilton Loughborough to Archbishop Francis P. Kenrick, April 23, 1857, Archbishop Francis Kenrick Papers, 30K6, AAB.
22. Francis Patrick Kenrick to [Propaganda Fide], May 11, 1857, here translated by R. Emmett Curran, 1434, vol. 126, folios 1321–22, PFUNDA.

23. Diary entry, April 11, 1831, Louis R. Deluol Diary, LRDP.
24. Mannard, "'What Has Become of Olevia Neal,'" 357–62; Yacovazzi, *Escaped Nuns*, 130. In true nineteenth-century fashion, the full title of Bunkley's treatise is much longer: Josephine M. Bunkley, *The Escaped Nun; or, Disclosures of Convent Life and Confessions of a Sister of Charity: Giving a More Minute Detail of Their Inner Life and Bolder Revelation of the Mysteries and Secrets of Nunneries Than Have Ever Before Been Submitted to the American Public* (New York: De Witt & Davenport, 1855).
25. Archbishop Francis P. Kenrick to Propaganda Fide, May 11, 1857, PFUNDA.
26. Cardinal Quaglia, Prefect of the Sacred Congregation of the Bishops and Regulars, to the Most Reverend Archbishop of Baltimore [Martin Spalding], September 30, 1864, here translated by R. Emmett Curran, GVM.
27. Bishop Richard Whelan to Archbishop Martin Spalding, December 8, 1864, Archbishop Martin Spalding Papers, 36N5, AAB.
28. Bishop Richard Whelan to Archbishop Martin Spalding, December 20, 1864, Archbishop Martin Spalding Papers, 36N6, AAB.
29. See "Of Regulars and Nuns," in The Second Plenary Council of Baltimore, accessed January 15, 2024, https://www.newadvent.org/cathen/02235a.htm.
30. See the glossary for definitions of terms related to the Catholic religious life.
31. Archbishop James Whitfield to Propaganda Fide, June 6, 1831, here translated by Alun Walpole, Letterbook for 1828–32, 19–23, Archbishop James Whitfield Papers, AAB.
32. Richard F. Grimmett, *St. John's Church, Lafayette Square: The History and Heritage of the Church of Presidents, Washington, DC* (Maitland, FL: Mill City Press, 2009), 4–8.
33. Thomas W. Spalding, *The Premier See: A History of the Archdiocese of Baltimore, 1789–1994* (Baltimore: Johns Hopkins University Press, 1995), 138.
34. Ann Gertrude Wightt to Bettie Mason, March 22, 1855, Mason Family Papers, 1825–1902, section 32, VMHC.
35. Last Will and Testament, Ann Gertrude Wightt, July 12, 1865, box 10, folder 7, PFP.
36. The attendance ledger, titled *A New Parish Register by Rev. Charles Wells Hayes, 5th Edition Revised, 1866–1875,* is found in Christ Church Georgetown Archives, Washington, D.C.
37. Ann Gertrude Wightt to Britannia W. Peter Kennon, July 13, 1865, box 10, folder 7, RM-1186, PFP.
38. Brittania Kennon, May 11, 1900, quoted in Grant S. Quertermous, ed., *A Georgetown Life: The Reminiscences of Britannia Wellington Peter Kennon of Tudor Place* (Washington, DC: Georgetown University Press, 2020), 118.
39. Joseph G. Mannard, "'Wilhelmina Jones, Come Out!': Public Reaction to the Reception of Sister M. Stanislaus Jones into Georgetown Visitation Monastery, 1825–26," *U.S. Catholic Historian* 39, no. 4 (Fall 2021): 25–47.
40. For where the faith journeys of Wilhelmina Jones and Ann Gertrude Wightt fit into the larger framework of nineteenth-century religious conversions, see Lincoln Mullen, *The Chance of Salvation: A History of Conversion in America* (Cambridge, MA: Harvard University Press, 2017).
41. Jon Gjerde and S. Deborah Kang, eds., *Catholicism and the Shaping of Nineteenth-Century America* (New York: Cambridge University Press, 2012), 13. Gjerde died before completion of this work, and Kang edited the final published version.
42. Gjerde and Kang, *Catholicism Shaping Nineteenth-Century America*, 91.
43. Gjerde and Kang, *Catholicism Shaping Nineteenth-Century America*, 15.

44. For purposes of clarity, the unidentified author of the original letter is referred to here as "Sister X." From a review of membership lists for Baltimore Visitation Monastery, I have been unable to confirm the identity of the unnamed nun.
45. Baltimore Visitation to Georgetown Visitation, December 11, 1867, in "Attempt to Change the Order," in "History of the Establishment of the Order," 184–86.
46. Baltimore Visitation to Georgetown Visitation, December 11, 1867, in "History of the Establishment of the Order," 185.
47. Wightt's "deep mourning" dress may have been for Colonel Eugene Van Ness, USA, or for Colonel William Orton Williams, CSA, and Lieutenant Walter Gibson Peter, CSA—the nephew and first cousin, respectively, of Britannia Kennon. Or perhaps her dress was for all three casualties of the war.
48. Although the Visitandines called Oak Hill a "Protestant cemetery," the banker William W. Corcoran designed it in 1849 to be a nondenominational burial ground (accessed January 13, 2024, https://oakhillcemeterydc.org/explore/notable-figures/).
49. Baltimore Visitation to Georgetown Visitation, December 11, 1867, in "History of the Establishment of the Order," 186.
50. Sister Jane Scholastica Neale to Miss Eliza Neale, addendum by Sister Ann Gertrude Wightt, October 6, 1822, box 103, folder 4, MPA.
51. Archbishop James Whitfield to Propaganda Fide, June 6, 1831, Letterbook of Archbishop James Whitfield, 1828–32, and Archbishop James Whitfield to Reverend Francis Dzierzynski, October 27, 1831, both in Archbishop James Whitfield Papers, box 103, folder 6, AAB.
52. Sister Mary Augustine Barber to Sister Mary Josephine Barber, January 19, 1836, in Sister Files: Barber, Mary Augustine (1 of 3), 1835–1856, box 1OVZ, SLVA records #200.
53. Oak Hill Cemetery website, accessed June 5, 2024, https://oakhillcemeterydc.org/explore/notable-figures/.

INDEX

ABOUT THE AUTHOR

Joseph Mannard received his master's degree in US history from the University of South Florida, Tampa, and his PhD in US history from the University of Maryland, College Park. Since 1989 he has been a member of the Department of History at Indiana University of Pennsylvania. He regularly teaches the courses Thought and Culture in Early America, The Early Republic, Women in America, and Fear of Conspiracy in US History. Most of Mannard's research has focused on American Catholics prior to the US Civil War, especially women religious. He has twice been recognized by the Catholic Press Association for publishing the best scholarly article in American Catholic history. This is his first book.